D0812603

Clinical
Neuropsychology
Interface with Neurologic
and Psychiatric
Disorders

Clinical Neuropsychology
Interface with Neurologic and Psychiatric Disorders

Charles J. Golden, Ph.D.
Associate Professor of Medical Psychology
University of Nebraska Medical Center
Omaha, Nebraska

James A. Moses, Jr., Ph.D.
Coordinator, Psychological Assessment Unit
Psychology Service, Veterans Administration Medical Center
Palo Alto, California
Clinical Assistant Professor of Psychiatry and Behavioral Sciences
Stanford University School of Medicine
Stanford, California

Jeffrey A. Coffman, M.D.
Research Fellow in Psychiatric Genetics
Department of Psychiatry
University of Iowa
Iowa City, Iowa

William R. Miller, Ph.D.
Associate Professor of Psychology
University of New Mexico
Albuquerque, New Mexico

Fred D. Strider, Ph.D.
Professor of Medical Psychology
University of Nebraska Medical Center
Omaha, Nebraska

Grune & Stratton
A Subsidiary of Harcourt Brace Jovanovich, Publishers
New York   London
Paris   San Diego   San Francisco   São Paulo
Sydney   Tokyo   Toronto

Library of Congress Cataloging in Publication Data
Main entry under title:

Clinical neuropsychology.

    Bibliography.
    Includes index.
    1. Neuropsychiatry. 2. Neuropsychology. I. Golden,
Charles J., 1949-   [DNLM: 1. Nervous system
diseases—Complications. 2. Mental disorders—Complica-
tions. WL 100 C6437]
RC341.C694 1983   616.8   82-21043
ISBN 0-8089-1541-X

Grune & Stratton, Inc.
111 Fifth Avenue
New York, New York 10003

Distributed in the United Kingdom by
Academic Press Inc. (London) Ltd.
24/28 Oval Road, London NW 1

Library of Congress Catalog Number 82-21043
International Standard Book Number 0-8089-1541-X

Printed in the United States of America

Contents

Preface

Within the past five years there has been an obvious and continuing increased interest in clinical neuropsychology and in publications on the subject. In general, books in this field have concentrated on behavioral localization in the brain and individual psychological tests or test batteries, with only passing or brief references to such topics as the effects of differing disease etiologies on neuropsychological results. Even less often have attempts been made to explore such issues as tumor caused impaired brain function or the way in which the mechanics of head trauma lead to the symptoms seen in trauma patients. Little has been written in neuropsychological testing on behavioral effects other than cognitive symptoms. There has been little summary work on the potential role of brain damage in emotional disorders such as schizophrenia.

These deficits have generally been caused not by a lack of interest but by a focus on introductory books. Although these books are clearly valuable and play an important role in training both graduate students and practitioners, this orientation limits greatly the depth with which topics such as those described above can be covered.

The present volume attempts to provide a start toward remediation of these deficits in the literature. The emphasis is on information that the authors consider crucial for anyone who wishes to practice in the field of clinical neuropsychology, but that has not generally been found in books aimed at the psychologist. Many current practitioners have picked up this information through contact with physicians or, in the worst case, have never clearly understood the role of the variable discussed in this volume.

The book is divided into two parts. Part I deals with the effects of the most common neurologic disorders likely to cause brain damage: tumors, head trauma, cerebrovascular disorders, metabolic disorders, multiple sclerosis, aging degenerative disorders, and so on. It is not our intent to create neurologists or physicians out of psychologists, but rather to give the psychologist a greater understanding of and feeling for the way these conditions produce behavioral impairment. In addition, we are attempting to extend further the awareness of the psychologist regarding the types of psychiatric impairment that accompany some of these conditions.

Since it is not our intention to reteach the behavioral role of specific areas of the brain, we have assumed that the reader is familiar with general introductory comments on the roles of the right and left hemisphere. If not, the reader is strongly urged to read such material (e.g., Golden, 1981; Luria, 1973). Nor is it our intention to advocate particular tests or test batteries. Thus, references to specific tests are minimal, except when a test offers a specific example to further the discussion. Each chapter concludes with a section on neuropsychological implications, which attempts to examine the importance of the information in conducting or interpreting a neuropsychological examination.

Part II updates the literature in several important areas of clinical neuropsychology. These chapters—on alcoholism, schizophrenia, and the affective disorders—represent reviews in areas in which the size and complexity of the literature demand an integrative review to understand fully its implications, or areas in which recent findings contradict certain traditional beliefs in clinical psychology and clinical neuropsychology. Compared to the areas covered in Part I, the topics discussed and the positions taken in Part II are generally more controversial. These chapters are intended to update the reader's information and to provide alternative theoretical explanations of the findings in order to generate other possible approaches in these areas for both diagnosis and treatment.

We invite comments from readers on topics that might be covered in future volumes.

Authors

Bruce N. Carpenter, Ph.D.
Assistant Professor of Psychology
Department of Psychology
University of Tulsa
Tulsa, Oklahoma

Jeffrey A. Coffman, M.D.
Research Fellow in Psychiatric Genetics
Department of Psychiatry
University of Iowa
Iowa City, Iowa

Charles J. Golden, Ph.D.
Associate Professor of Medical Psychology
Nebraska Psychiatric Institute
University of Nebraska Medical Center
Omaha, Nebraska

Benjamin Graber, M.D.
Assistant Professor of Psychiatry
Clinical Director, Adult Inpatients
Nebraska Psychiatric Institute
University of Nebraska Medical Center
Omaha, Nebraska

William MacInnes, Ph.D.
Postdoctoral Intern
University of Nebraska Medical Center
Omaha, Nebraska

James A. Moses, Jr., Ph.D.
Coordinator, Psychological Assessment Unit
Psychology Service, Veterans Administration Medical Center
Palo Alto, California
Clinical Assistant Professor of Psychiatry and Behavioral Sciences
Stanford University School of Medicine
Stanford, California

William R. Miller, Ph.D.
Associate Professor of Psychology
The University of New Mexico
Albuquerque, New Mexico

David B. Newlin, Ph.D.
Assistant Professor
Department of Psychological Sciences
Purdue University
West Lafayette, Indiana

Carlos F. Saucedo, Ph.D.
Assistant Clinical Professor of Psychiatry
   and the Behavioral Sciences
University of Southern California School of Medicine
Los Angeles, California

Fred D. Strider, Ph.D.
Professor of Medical Psychology
Nebraska Psychiatric Institute
University of Nebraska Medical Center
Omaha, Nebraska

Clinical
Neuropsychology
Interface with Neurologic and Psychiatric Disorders

PART I

Neurologic and Psychiatric Disorders

Chapter 1

Cerebral Tumors

Cerebral tumors are common causes of severe neuropsychological deficits in humans. In many cases, these individuals are not seen by neuropsychologists because they present with strong signs of intracranial increases in pressure, strong focal neurologic signs, or epileptic seizures which lead rapidly to medical care and treatment. Other tumors, however, present very subtle signs which can be missed or ignored when the patient is evaluated. Indeed, the symptoms may superficially present as an apparently clear-cut psychiatric disorder. Although this is a rare occurrence in behaviorally disturbed populations, the presence of psychiatric or cognitive symptoms with such tumors is frequent; the exact symptoms depend upon such factors as the location of the tumor, the rate of growth, the stage of development, and the effects on brain organization and metabolism as a whole (Lishman, 1978).

IMPAIRMENT OF CONSCIOUSNESS

The most common psychological change due to a tumor is disturbed level of consciousness. When minor, it appears as diminished attention and concentration, faulty memory, decreased responsiveness, and easy mental fatigue. In the early stages this impairment varies in degree, with lucid intervals common. Subtle changes of this nature may be the first and for long periods the only indicator of a lesion. Later, drowsiness and somnolence appear, followed by further decline and coma if the condition remains untreated.

Disorganization

Intellectural disorganization is commonly seen with cerebral tumors even in the absence of impaired consciousness. These difficulties can be diffuse, as in a mild dementia, with slowed thinking, faulty abstractions, poor judgment, impoverished associations, and impaired recent memory. Perseveration and mental fatigue may be marked. Speech, even in the absence of dysphasia, may be slowed and incoherent. All these changes tend to fluctuate over time.

Focal cognitive changes, however, generally occur as one would expect with a given lesion site. Or at least, a focal emphasis may be part of a more generalized disturbance. Cognitive dysfunction of a focal nature due to tumors in specific locations will be discussed below.

Affective Changes

Affective disturbances rarely occur alone, but often are found with other mental disorders. With damage to the intellect, there is often emotional dullness, apathy, and lack of spontaneity; alternatively, euphoria discordant with the patient's degree of illness may be present. Depression and anxiety also occur commonly and may be appropriate to the situation or pathologic in nature. Querulousness and irritability may be marked, or emotional lability may predominate.

Henry (1932), in an attempt to outline the common sequence of mood changes during the progress of cerebral tumors, found that irritability and peevishness in the early stages tended to give way to increasing anxiety and depression followed by indifference, apathy, euphoria, or emotional lability.

Hallucinations

Hallucinations in cerebral tumor patients commonly occur as part of an epileptic disturbance but also may present in the absence of any paroxysmal activity. The nature of these hallucinations will generally depend on the location of the tumor. Visual hallucinations are usually associated with occipital tumors; complex visual, auditory, gustatory, and olfactory hallucinations with temporal lobe tumors; and tactile hallucinations with parietal lobe tumors. Circumscribed frontal lobe tumors may at times produce visual, auditory, or even gustatory hallucinations, possibly through irritation of the adjacent temporal lobe (Strauss & Keschner, 1935).

CHARACTERISTICS OF MENTAL SYMPTOMS

Any aspect of psychological function may be affected by a cerebral tumor, which frustrates the search for a specific mental picture with these disorders. On occasion, certain areas are affected in isolation—for example, the level of consciousness and aspects of cognition or affect—although typically several areas are disturbed. This interaction may produce a personality change. Complex symptoms such as delusions and hallucinations may also appear, as well as paroxysmal disorders due to an epileptic focus. Frank psychosis may develop or neurotic disturbances may be exacerbated. Generally, slowly growing tumors tend to produce changes in personality; more rapidly growing tumors cause cognitive defects; and the most destructive tumors evoke acute organic reactions with obvious impairment of consciousness (Minski, 1933).

ETIOLOGIC FACTORS IN THE PRODUCTION OF SYMPTOMS

Raised Intracranial Pressure
Elevations in intracranial pressure are often responsible for many mental symptoms due to tumor. The lowering of pressure by surgical or medical means can produce dramatic improvement in the mental state, resolving confusion, drowsiness, apathy, and even coma.

Variations in the level of consciousness may result from fluctuations in cerebrospinal fluid dynamics. Other diffuse symptoms stemming from impairment of consciousness—difficulties with perception and memory, emotional dullness, and apathy—may also be due to raised intracranial pressure. The pathophysiology of these changes is found in a disturbance of the brain stem reticular formation and its cortical projections, but increased pressure also causes dysfunction by direct compression of brain tissue and impeded circulation of blood and cerebrospinal fluid (Lishman, 1978). If the elevation of pressure is allowed to persist for a sufficient length of time, permanent irreversible damage will result from compression, ischemia, and metabolic derangement. However, raised intracranial pressure is not the only cause of impaired consciousness, which can be severe even when the intracranial pressure is normal.

Type of Tumors
Tumors can be classified into two major groups: infiltrative tumors, which take over and destroy brain tissue, and noninfiltrative tumors, which cause deficits by compressing tissue. These groups can be further subdivided into specific types. The most common infiltrative tumor is glioblastoma multiforme, a disorder of the glial cells, which are responsible for supporting brain tissue. Glioblastoma generally arises in middle age and is usually found in the cerebral hemispheres. Because of its location and its rapid rate of growth, the psychological symptoms are pronounced and arise in a short time.

Astrocytomas are infiltrative tumors of astrocytes, a type of glial cell. They are generally slower growing than glioblastoma, but may approach glioblastomas in terms of destructiveness and symptomatology. However, since astrocytomas are slower growing they allow greater compensation; this is discussed in this chapter in the section entitled "Compensation for Deficits."

An alternative method of classifying these tumors is by grade. Tumors may be graded 1 to 4, with 1 representing a relatively mild, benign tumor and 4 a severely destructive tumor such as glioblastoma. The grade of the tumor represents its malignancy. Tumors can change grades, causing a sudden change in symptoms if they shift to a higher grade.

Extrinsic noninfiltrative tumors arising in the membranes surrounding the brain are much less serious than infiltrative tumors, although they can still cause severe psychological symptoms and even death. The most common extrinsic tumor is the meningioma, which represents about 15% of all tumors (Robbins, 1974). These tumors arise in the arachnoid layers of the meninges, creating an irregular growth that presses upon the brain tissue. Since their effect is produced by pressure rather than tissue destruction, the effects of meningioma and other noninfiltrative tumors are generally less precise than those of infiltrative tumors. Indeed, it is possible for meningioma to displace brain tissue so that loci far from the tumor are compressed, causing psychological symptoms which have nothing to do with the location of the tumor (although related to the pressure effects). Meningiomas may show no deficits at all if they fail to compress the brain to a sufficient extent.

Another group of infiltrative tumors are the metastatic tumors. They generally arise secondary to cancer elsewhere in the body, especially the lungs, breasts, adrenal system, and lymphatic system. These tumors may represent up to 40% of all tumors seen in the elderly (Earle, 1955). They are generally fast growing and multiple, causing lesion foci throughout the brain. As a result, the presentation of these tumors can be similar to that of any other tumor in terms of specific symptoms, although in general, since they are multiple, the overall effects of these tumors are more severe.

The greater incidence of mental symptoms with malignant as opposed to benign tumors may be due in part to the higher incidence of elevated intracranial pressure in the malignant group. Wider invasion of the brain also occurs with malignant tumors, and this wider involvement of brain tissue is probably an important factor. This may also be the reason that cases of multiple cerebral metastases show more mental disturbance than those with single primary tumors (Keschner, Bender, & Strauss, 1938).

Compensation for Deficits

Another major factor in the effect of a tumor is the ability of the brain to compensate for the deficits that have occurred. With the slow-growing tumor, the brain is able to withstand and adjust for the small changes in pressure which develop over time. Even when minor brain tissue is destroyed, the individual often is able to complete the behavior by using alternative functional systems (Luria, 1973). In such cases, temporary deficits may occur while the substitute system is developed or implemented. However, these symptoms are transient and, if noticed by the patient or others, may be dismissed as meaningless. In reviewing the patient's history, it may not be unusual to find evidence of the growing tumor in transient symptoms and changes in the individual's behavior which went unnoticed.

With faster-growing tumors, the process is not benign. Whether or not actual tissue damage occurs, the speed of tumor growth precludes a switchover to other skills. Since the brain is continuously losing its effectiveness due to tumor growth, it has no time to fully compensate for deficits caused by the tumor. The brain can partially reorganize, however, which can also modify the patient's behavior. In the early stages especially, these deficits can be directly related to precise areas of the brain. For example, one patient seen by the senior author showed highly specific temporal lobe symptoms but no other problems, and also was judged to be normal on a computed tomography (CT) scan. However, 6 weeks later a follow-up CT scan identified a rapidly growing tumor in the temporal lobe which had been missed initially because of its small size.

Although slow-growing tumors may produce few if any deficits on psychological testing, fast-growing tumors invariably cause poor performance on all such tests, especially in the middle stages of growth. In an extremely fast-growing tumor, this stage can be reached as early as 6-8 weeks after the onset of the tumor. In other cases, the tumor may impair function progressively, taking 3-5 years to produce symptoms, if indeed any appear. On the Halstead-Reitan Neuropsychological Battery, for example, fast-growing tumors may show Impairment Indexes of 1.0, indicating disruption on all major tests, whereas some static tumors may have indexes of 0.0, showing no evident impairment.

Premorbid Functioning Level of the Patient

The course of psychological symptoms resulting from a tumor is also affected by the premorbid functioning level of the patient. In general, individuals with a higher intelligence level are better able to find alternative means of doing a given task because of a greater reserve of skills and greater flexibility and ability to adjust. In these cases, the tumor may appear—by psychological symptoms—to be less severe than it actually is. On the other hand, individuals with low to normal intelligence will show definitive symptoms fairly early in the course of a tumor because of an inability to compensate. In such cases, then, identification of symptoms is often easy. With the more intelligent patient, in contrast, symptoms may be elicited only under very specific conditions. For example, we saw one patient who could read or write sentences and paragraphs without difficulty but, when asked to write a nonsense syllable, wrote backward. She could determine what normal words and sentences should look like, but not an unfamiliar, unlearned nonsense syllable. Because of this ability to compensate, brain tumors in the intelligent person may be missed by standard testing techniques.

Location of the Tumor

The relationship of tumor location to the frequency of mental disturbance remains a matter of controversy. Claims for specific regional effects are often countered by negative findings. The difficulties in studying tumors and inconsistencies in methods and definitions across studies make setting the debate even more difficult. The majority of tumors are progressive and produce variable symptoms during their growth. In addition, factors such as increased intracranial pressure may complicate the picture. Distant effects due to the tumor, which may result from distortions of the brain within the rigid skull, displacement of portions of the brain through bony and dural openings, or pressure effects on the blood supply, may occur even in the absence of elevated intracranial pressure. The patient's response to the illness also plays a role in the development of symptoms. All of these factors contribute to the difficulty of determining the effect of tumor location.

Special associations between tumor location and certain types of psychiatric disturbance have emerged in the literature. Focal cognitive deficits have been noted to appear with parietal lobe tumors, and focal amnesic symptoms have been associated with diencephalic tumors. Difficulty arises when an attempt is made to link more subtle symptoms with specific lesions. Disturbances of affect and personality are difficult to link convincingly to tumors in specific locations of the brain, and functional psychoses, when they appear, seem to be largely determined by other factors. There have been attempts to relate frontal lobe tumors to personality changes and schizophreniform psychoses to temporal lobe tumors, but the evidence supporting these associations remains inconclusive.

With regard to the overall frequency of mental symptoms with tumors in specific locations, Lishman (1978) examined the results of two earlier large studies which had sought to evaluate symptoms against constant criteria. Supratentorial tumors, compared with infratentorial tumors, were found to have a greatly increased incidence of mental disturbances, especially when attention was restricted to symptoms appearing early in the course of illness. Patients with frontal and temporal lobe tumors had a somewhat higher incidence of mental disturbance than did those with parietal or occipital lobe lesions. Parry (1968), in reviewing the same two studies, reported that many of the groups with temporal and parietal lobe tumors suffered from paroxysmal disturbances. By eliminating these groups and concentrating on those with enduring symptoms, a preponderance of frontal lobe involvement emerged.

Individual Patient Response

The patient's response also influences the outcome of a cerebral tumor in a number of ways. The development of a tumor may serve as a precipitating event in those individuals who are genetically predisposed to mental illness, especially in the case of neurotic disorders or functional psychoses. Emotional and personality disruption will often be present in response to physical disabilities such as paralysis, seizures, or visual changes, or to headaches or the prognostic implications of the illness. In all of these conditions, the patient's response will be colored by his or her premorbid personality and habits.

SYNDROMES ASSOCIATED WITH SPECIFIC TUMOR LOCATIONS

Frontal Lobe Tumors

Frontal lobe tumors are widely noted for their tendency to suggest a primary dementing illness. The lack of striking neurologic signs and the general frequency of mental disturbances with these tumors are probably responsible for mistaken diagnoses of primary dementia. Tumors of the left and right frontal lobes may both be associated with cognitive disorders. However, the incidence of such disturbances is greatly increased when both lobes are involved, as with midline lesions (Strauss & Keschner, 1935). Luria (1973) has suggested that dominant lesions are more likely to disrupt brain processes as a whole through impairment of "executive" functions.

Although dementia is the most frequent result of frontal lobe tumors, isolated memory disturbances have been seen. In 10 of 80 cases, Hecaen and Ajuriaguerra (1956) found that *amnesie de fixation* was prominent. Difficulty in interpretation arises because the apparent failure of memory often occurs in a background of profound apathy and indifference, making it difficult to decide whether the patient is even attempting to give the answer, let alone remember it.

General cognitive disturbance found in these patients usually includes a loss of spontaneity, inertia, and slowing. Mental and physical activities may be greatly decreased. Speech may be slow and labored, even in the absence of dysphasia or dominant frontal lobe involvement. Akinetic states, in which the patient is mute and immobile, yet when roused shows normal orientation, have been reported.

Affective disorders characteristic of frontal lobe tumors are irritability, depression, euphoria, and apathy. Irritability is often stressed and may be a presenting symptom. Direkze, Bayliss, and Cutting (1971) reported several such patients who had been admitted initially to psychiatric units for treatment of depression, but were found to be unresponsive to electroconvulsive therapy and reevaluated. Apathy and euphoria generally accompany intellectual deficits or other organically caused changes in temperament or personality.

Tumors of the frontal lobe may first be suspected because of changes in behavior even in the absence of neurologic signs or intellectual deficits, particularly in the case of slow-growing meningiomas. Strauss and Keschner

(1935) found personality change to be one of the very early changes in about a fourth of their patients. Irresponsibility, childishness, and lack of reserve are said to occur frequently, even before intellectual changes take place. A tendency to facetiousness and indifference to those around them adds to the general picture. Disinhibition may be the first sign of change, leading to major social lapses or minor indiscretions.

Lack of insight is often marked and may represent impaired feedback from environmental stimuli. The patient is frequently indifferent to his or her situation even when the intellect is undisturbed. Denial of illness may coexist with compliance and placid acceptance of therapy.

Specific cognitive disturbances occur in frontal lobe disorders, but only in the absence of massive or acute damage. In diffuse cases, the ability to coordinate behavior of any kind is lost (especially when the dominant frontal lobe is impaired), resulting in massive cognitive disturbances (Luria, 1966). In the absence of this widespread behavioral disturbance, the most likely deficits are seen in complex tasks in which the patient must follow a set of internalized instructions. Luria (1973) suggests that such patients are likely to perseverate in such tasks, causing severely impaired performance. A good example of this behavior can often be seen on the Halstead Category Test (Halstead, 1947) or the Wisconsin Card Sorting Test (Milner, 1963).

Specific frontal lobe deficits can be seen in such tests as the Stroop Color and Word Test (Perrett, 1974). On this test, for example, the patient must substitute color naming for the automatic response of word reading when presented with the word RED written in green ink. This change from a well-learned automatism to a new response requires inhibition and shifting of cognitive set that is extremely difficult for the patient with a frontal lobe tumor. Patients may also show impairment in word-generating ability, as well as in speech and motor symptoms, if the lesion extends to the posterior frontal lobe.

Right frontal lobe deficits are generally less well defined than those of the left frontal lobe. As a consequence, they are more likely to go unnoticed when the patient is examined. Deficits may be seen on the skills discussed above, except generally for speech-related skills. However, more subtle deficits may also be present, such as disruption of expressive musical skills (Botez and Wertheim, 1959) and disturbance of sequencing skills and general complex spatial abilities (Corkin, 1965; Milner, 1971; Teuber, 1964).

Corpus Callosum Tumors

Corpus callosum tumors produce a high incidence of mental disturbances. The largest series in the literature was reported by Schlesinger (1950), who found mental changes in 92% of the patients with rostral turmors, 57 percent with midcallosal tumors, and 89% with tumors of the splenium. The frequency of mental symptoms due to anterior and posterior callosal tumors when compared with those of the middle portion was confirmed by Selecki (1964). Anterior callosal tumors especially tend to produce rapid mental deterioration before any other signs. Typically, there is rapid, progressive cognitive impairment beginning with severe memory difficulties. Personality change may also appear early on, similar to that seen with frontal lobe tumors. In addition, florid psychosis may occur. These marked mental changes probably result from involvement of the corpus callosum tumor with adjacent structures. Anterior callosal tumors rapidly invade both frontal lobes, whereas those of the genu invade the thalamus and midbrain posteriorly. Almost all corpus callosum tumors involve the third ventricle and diencephalon at some point, resulting in somnolence, akinesia, and stupor (Selecki, 1964). By itself, however a lesion of the corpus callosum is likely to be important for the disturbance of interhemispheric coordination and the disruption of important associated areas adjacent to the neighboring cingulate gyrus (Schlesinger, 1950). These lesions may lead to mental changes even before elevation of intracranial pressure develops.

Temporal Lobe Tumors

Of all the cerebral tumors, those of the anterior temporal lobes may produce the highest frequency of mental disorder. This predominance may be partly due to the phenomena associated with temporal lobe epilepsy, although it persists when epilepsy-related disturbances are not considered (Keschner, Bender, & Strauss, 1936). Aside from syndromes associated with temporal lobe epilepsy, no specific form of mental disturbance allowing localization to the anterior temporal lobe seems to exist. Some investigators believe that the early onset and rapid progression of dementia in these cases are characteristic, but this assessment may be the result of the severe dysphasia which often follows tumors in the middle to posterior portion of the dominant temporal lobe. In contrast, tumors of the nondominant hemisphere can be clinically silent until they reach great size.

Other effects of tumors of the dominant and nondominant temporal lobes are difficult to evaluate. In a report of one of the largest series of temporal lobe tumors, Bingley (1958) concluded that tumors on the dominant side produced greater impairment of intellect, both in verbal and nonverbal functions. This effect was even more pronounced when patients with papilledema, and presumably elevated intracranial pressure, were excluded.

Slowing and aspontaneity of speech, often seen with frontal lobe tumors, have been reported frequently with temporal lobe tumors. No substantial difference between these two types of tumors was found (Keschner et al., 1936). Of the group with temporal lobe tumors, 63% showed dullness, apathy, and lack of spontaneous speech. When roused, they spoke deliberately but without dysphasic features. Indifference to the environment, as well as impaired memory, may be seen in temporal lobe cases.

Affective alterations are fairly common. Euphoria may be as frequent with temporal as with frontal lobe tumors (Schlesinger, 1950) and also occurs mainly with intellectual deficits. Outbursts of anger or anxiety have been reported. Depression, irritability, and anxiety commonly are present. Bingley (1958) found that dominant temporal lobe tumors generally brought more emotional changes, especially flattening of affect, than nondominant temporal lobe tumors. Depression may be more common with nondominant lesions. All in all, frontal, frontotemporal, and temporal tumors, when grouped, have shown twice the frequency of affective changes of tumors in other locations (Hecaen & Ajuriaguerra, 1956).

No specific form of personality change emerges with temporal lobe tumors. Facetiousness and childish behavior similar to those seen with frontal lobe tumors may appear. Most frequently, changes such as psychopathic and paranoid trends, irritability, and hypochondriasis occur, often reflecting a reaction to the disease itself or aspects of the premorbid personality.

Occasionally, schizophreniform psychoses may develop in patients with temporal lobe tumors and can be the initial manifestation of the disorder. Davison and Bagley (1969) reviewed a group of 77 reported cases of this rare disturbance. A significantly higher proportion of temporal lobe and pituitary tumors was found in the schizophrenic group when compared with two large unselected tumor patient populations. It was not possible to ascertain the effect of genetic predisposition or to determine whether the symptoms were directly due to the temporal lobe disease.

In addition, complex hallucinations due to temporal lobe tumors may lead to diagnostic difficulty. Keschner et al. (1936) reported that 15 of 110 patients had hallucinations in the absence of epileptic phenomena. Auditory and visual hallucinations may be either simple or complex; the latter especially can lead to a diagnosis of functional psychosis. Visual hallucinations isolated to a hemianopic visual field are nearly always diagnostic of a disturbance in the temporal lobe. Olfactory and gustatory hallucinations may arise in the region of the uncinate gyrus. Usually the patient, after accepting the hallucinations as real, gains insight regarding their abnormality, unlike the usual psychotic (Lishman, 1978).

Epilepsy is seen in about 50% of individuals with temporal lobe tumors (Strobos, 1953). The epileptic auras may contain, in addition to frank hallucinations, such abnormal subjective experiences as unreality, deja vu, dreamy states, forced thoughts, and overwhelming fears. Complex psychomotor seizures and automatisms may occur, but less frequently than with other causes of temporal lobe epilepsy (Bingley, 1958). Injuries to the middle and posterior temporal lobe may produce the psychiatric symptoms seen with anterior injuries, but are accompanied most prominently by severe problems in receptive language. These deficits are most commonly called *Wernicke's aphasia* or *receptive aphasia*.

Injuries involving the nondominant middle to the posterior temporal lobe cause much more subtle symptoms than those in the dominant lobe. As a result, these lesions are frequently misdiagnosed. Loss of function in this area may cause a disturbance of visual or auditory pattern analysis, but only when the stimuli are unfamiliar (Kimura, 1963; Meier & French, 1965). A second loss may occur in the area of receptive musical skills (Kimura, 1963). Such losses, however, may also be seen in dominant temporal lobe lesions, especially in tests such as the Seashore Rhythm Test (Golden, 1977). Since these deficits rarely interfere with day-to-day behavior, the patient may not even be aware that a problem exists.

Parietal Lobe Tumors

Psychiatric changes seem to be less likely with parietal lobe tumors than with frontal or temporal lobe tumors. In addition, these tumors are likely to produce early sensory and motor abnormalities, making an erroneous diagnosis of primary psychiatric illness less probable.

Affective changes have been noted, with depression in particular occurring frequently (Hecaen & Ajuriaguerra, 1956). Personality changes, on the other hand, are unusual. Hallucinatory disturbances, when present, consist of kinesthetic or tactile sensations limited to the contralateral side of the body, and tactile perseveration with perception of a stimulus continuing long after its removal.

Complex and unusual cognitive disturbances may emerge. In the face of these disorders, mistaken labels of dementia or hysteria may be applied. Dysphasia or, more rarely, ideational dyspraxia may result from dominant parietal lobe tumors. Symptoms of the Gerstmann syndrome (finger agnosia, dyscalculia, dysgraphia, right—left disorientation) may be found in isolation or as part of a more generalized disturbance of cognition. Nondominant parietal lobe tumors are associated with visuospatial orientation disturbances, dressing difficulty, and topographic disorientation. Any of these symptoms, if present with social withdrawal or indifference, may lead to an incorrect diagnosis of dementia.·

Nondominant parietal lobe tumors have also been associated with complex and unusual disorders of body image. These include the well-known phenomena of unilateral inattention and anosognosia, in which the patient seems to be unaware of a left hemiplegia and/or denies the disability when it is pointed out. The degree of disturbance may range from denial of ownership of the affected limbs to attribution of the limbs to another person. Although these disturbances are less common with tumors than with other parietal lobe lesions, they may suggest hysteria. Neurologic examination, even of a cursory nature, generally obviates such an error. Other similarities to hysterical illness have been noted by Critchley (1964), who stated that difficulties in communication may produce a seeming lack of cooperation, whereas performance inconsistencies suggest functional rather than organic disease.

Epileptic signs of parietal lobe tumors may consist of transient disturbances of body image and may occur prior to the appearance of neurologic signs. They may be rather bizarre; the following have been reported: the feeling of someone standing close by, displacement or absence of part of the body, transformation of a limb into an inanimate object, and phantom appearance of an extra limb.

Parietal lobe tumors are almost invariably marked by signs of tactile, kinesthetic, and proprioceptive disorders. These can include basic losses of sensation or the inability to analyze sensation, to locate body parts, to recognize objects by touch, or to recognize site of touch (Chusid, 1973; Golden, 1981a; Roland, 1976). Large lesions of either parietal lobe may cause bilateral losses, which are common in fast-growing tumors. This effect is especially serious in the dominant hemisphere (Corkin, Milner, & Taylor, 1973). Disruption of motor activities is also seen, since adequate somatosensory feedback is necessary for most motor activities.

The dominant parietal lobe is associated with deficits in most verbally mediated skills, whereas the nondominant parietal lobe mediates basic nonverbal functions such as direction, angle, and pattern (Luria, 1973). Because of these symptoms, which can influence almost all major neuropsychological tests, tumors in this area are without question the easiest to diagnose using such tests.

Occipital Tumors

In the early literature, a high incidence of mental disturbance was reported in association with occipital tumors (Allen, 1930). However, detailed comparisons of tumors in different parts of the brain have failed to identify an increased frequency of mental disorders with occipital tumors (Lishman, 1978).

The predominant symptom with occipital lobe tumor is the loss of the visual field in one-half of each eye in the field contralateral to the tumor. Smaller tumors may result in scotomas, or partial loss of the visual field in the appropriate half of each eye. In addition, occipital tumors may cause visual agnosia. In this disorder, the individual is unable to combine inputs to form visual patterns. An alternative disorder may be simultaneous agnosia, in which the patient is unable to see two objects at the same time. Lesions of the dominant lobe may also result in loss of verbal−visual skills.

Diencephalic Tumors

Tumors originating in the diencephalon (thalamus, hypothalamus, etc.) are not common causes of psychiatric illness. When such disturbances do occur, however, they can be striking and may be useful in localization.

Severe amnesic difficulties are now recognized as typical results of tumors emerging near the third ventricle (Delay, Brion, & Derouesne, 1964). These difficulties include impairment of new learning, and faulty recollection of the recent past. Remote memory and other cognitive functions seem to remain intact (Lishman, 1978). Confabulation, similar to that seen in Korsakoff's psychosis, may be present. This disorder may be related to interference with the function of the hippocampus (Scoville & Milner, 1957).

Steadily progressive dementia secondary to diencephalic tumors usually results from cortical atrophy following chronic obstruction of the cerebrospinal fluid circulation. This may occur even with simple cysts of the third ventricle. Craniopharyngiomas, when discovered in middle or old age, may present with clinical syndromes dominated by failure of intellect and memory in the absence of obvious neurologic signs, simulating presenile or senile dementia (Russell & Pennybacker, 1961). Visual symptoms (bitemporal hemianopia), although common, are not universal, as visual field defects (secondary to compression of the optic chiasma), even when demonstrated, may not be apparent to the patient. Symptoms of hypothalamic disturbance such as marked somnolence, when present, may provide the distinguishing clue.

Tumors of the thalamus have been said to show early and severe dementia with a rapid course. In two of six such cases reported by Smyth and Stern (1938), severe dementia existed in the absence of raised intracranial pressure or ventricular dilatation, and the tumor itself was found at autopsy not to have widely invaded the surrounding white matter. This suggested that the focal lesion may have caused the disorder, perhaps by disrupting thalamocortical tracts. In these cases, sensory and motor signs were often absent or of late onset.

Diencephalic tumors are often associated with somnolence, which is an important localizing symptom. True hypersomnia must be distinguished from the impairment of consciousness due to elevated intracranial pressure. Hypersomnia is essentially an excess of normal sleep; after awakening, the patient is fully alert. In contrast, patients suffering from torpor due to elevated intracranial pressure remain confused upon awakening.

This disorder of sleep results from lesions which impinge on the hypothalamus posteriorly and on the adjacent areas of the rostral midbrain. Third ventricle tumors, craniopharyngiomas, and pituitary tumors may all be at fault. The sleep disturbance is often accompanied by other hypothalamic symptoms, such as amenorrhea, impotence, diabetes insipidus with polyuria and polydipsia, voracious appetite, or anorexia nervosa. These disturbances can occur in the absence of hypersomnia as well.

Pituitary Tumors

Tumors of the pituitary gland often present with visual failure, raised intracranial pressure, or pituitary dysfunction. Other tumors in the region around the sella turcica, such as craniopharyngiomas and suprasellar meningiomas, may cause similar symptoms. All may produce early mental changes.

Some of the mental changes due to pituitary tumors may be caused by endocrine abnormalities, as the hormone-producing cells themselves may be involved. Therefore, it is often difficult to distinguish hormonal effects from the effects of the neuronal lesion itself. Extension of the tumor into neighboring tissue seems to be responsible for a large amount of the psychiatric disturbance in these cases. Upward extension in the direction of the third ventricle causes symptoms typical of diencephalic tumors. Forward extension may involve the frontal or temporal lobes. Pituitary tumors are also well located to cause disturbance of cerebrospinal fluid circulation. Not surprisingly, then, pituitary tumors are reported to cause a high incidence of mental disorders.

Infratentorial Tumors

Tumors of the cerebellum, cerebellopontine angle, and brain stem are included here. As previously stated, tumors originating below the tentorium produce mental symptoms much less frequently than those above it, even though elevation of intracranial pressure occurs earlier and more often in the former. Cognitive, affective, and personality disorders are all less common with infratentorial tumors. In addition, Keschner et al. (1937) found that those symptoms which did emerge were milder, rarely persistent, and later in onset.

Cognitive disturbance appears to be closely related to increased intracranial pressure. The impairment is usually diffuse, develops insidiously, and parallels the development of internal hydrocephalus. Slow-growing infratentorial tumors may produce profound ventricular enlargement before becoming apparent with an accompanying severe dementia.

Disturbances of affect include emotional lability and euphoria, with cognitive impairment, depression, apprehension, or irritability. The emotional symptoms may be a result of the threat of the disease and associated neurologic deficits. Personality change may be part of a general dementing process or may result from the effects of internal hydrocephalus on the frontal lobes.

IMPLICATIONS FOR NEUROPSYCHOLOGICAL TESTING

As the foregoing discussion indicates, it is not easy to predict the effects of a tumor on neuropsychological test results. In general, any rules are likely to be wrong in a large number of cases. Some tumors are obvious with even relatively insensitive screening tests, whereas others—especially those which grow slowly and do not affect the general functioning of the brain—may show deficits only on the most sensitive and comprehensive test batteries, if at all. In the absence of neuropsychological findings (assuming a comprehensive battery), one can usually conclude only that the likelihood of an acute, fast-growing tumor is low. Indeed, any comprehensive neuropsychological practice includes individuals whose tumor is found only after existing for years without causing apparent impairment of functioning. In these cases, the presence of the tumor may be signaled only by an epileptic seizure, or it may occasionally show up on an autopsy of a patient who has died for a totally unrelated reason. In one case handled by the senior author, the tumor was found on the CT scan of a person who was being tested as a normal control for a research project.

These facts suggest several important rules for neuropsychological evaluation of patients with known or suspected tumors. First, since tumors may occur anywhere and cause deficits through changes in pressure, blood flow, and other related factors, such patients must have comprehensive examinations. Such examinations are also required because localized tumors may produce very specific neuropsychological deficits. Skills which may be highly related statistically in many more diffuse disorders may relate differently to the tumor depending on its exact effects. Consequently, assumptions that given skills are related are dangerous and may lead to incorrect conclusions. Only with comprehensive testing of the major neuropsychological skills can one be relatively certain that a serious deficit does not exist. For example, the senior author saw one patient with a limited frontal lobe tumor who did extremely well on traditional tests of frontal lobe function (such as the Wisconsin Card Sorting Test and the Category Test from the Halstead-Reitan Battery), but did very poorly on the Stroop Color and Word Test because of an inability to give an unusual response to a well-learned stimulus (naming the color of a printed word rather than reading the word). The patient's inflexibility surfaced only when he was faced with a strong competing alternative rather than in decision making in general.

Assessment of tumors after surgery is beset by similar problems. Tumors may leave residual deficits, as may the surgery itself. However, tumors that affect the brain mainly by producing pressure (extrinsic tumors which do not destroy brain tissue) may leave relatively small residual deficits even if symptoms are severe. On the other hand, tumors which destroy brain tissue generally do cause permanent and often severe deficits which can be highly localized after the tumor itself has been removed and the acute recovery period is over. Surgery itself may cause unavoidable localized deficits. These deficits may be acute and disappear within weeks or months, but, they may also be permanent injuries. It is generally expected that because of the acute effects of surgery, a patient will often perform as poorly or even worse soon after surgery, although later testing will show significant improvement in many symptoms.

In general, the neuropsychologist will rarely localize the effects of a tumor for a physician since most tumors can be localized through neuroradiologic techniques. The neuropsychologist is usually responsible for describing the deficits due to tumors, either for vocational evaluation or to study the effects of given treatment. In the latter case, serial testing beginning before treatment, using a battery with relatively mild test-retest effects, is necessary. Such evaluations are frequently used in determining the functional impairment of the patient for legal purposes or for rehabilitation planning. Because of the highly variable nature of the tumor, such examinations must, as discussed above, be more comprehensive than an intelligence test or a short screening test such as the Bender—Gestalt.

The single exception occurs with the extremely small tumor. In some cases, such tumors may be missed on neuroradiologic examination, although their number is being decreased dramatically by improvements in technology. In patients who show deficits on neuropsychological examination, the tumor is usually fairly new but relatively fast growing, since small, slow-growing tumors may have little or no cognitive effect. The small, slow-growing tumor, then, may be missed by neuropsychological examination, although the conclusion that the patient does not have impairment of cognitive skills may be quite accurate. With the small, fast-growing tumor, a comprehensive neuropsychological examination will reveal a specific, highly focal area of damage with many acute (severe) impairments that are inconsistent with the patient's history and are often pathognomonic of a brain injury. Such results should alert the clinician to the need to follow such a patient over time if the patient's physician is unable to find any condition which can be treated.

These results cannot be used reliably to diagnose a tumor, but only to identify patients for whom relatively close coverage over time is strongly suggested. Since a good number of these patients are seen with an initial complaint of headache, which is suspected of being psychogenic because of the absence of clear medical findings, it is often possible to follow them closely for relaxation training, biofeedback, or other treatments while monitoring the extent and severity of their cognitive symptoms and reporting these on a regular basis to the physician. Increase in the severity of the symptoms generally justifies repeat neuroradiologic examination. Such cases demand close cooperation with the patient's physician. In all cases, pathognomonic signs—behaviors almost never seen in normals—should be attended to closely regardless of other findings.

Because of the localized nature of tumors, these patients are ideal candidates for rehabilitation after the tumor has been removed or controlled. Often when the tumor is completely removed or becomes static, the patient will show significant spontaneous improvement. In such cases, rehabilitation training probably speeds the patient's recovery and can be done easily. In contrast, where permanent deficits exist, rehabilitation training may focus on the use of alternative functional systems, using the patient's strengths to do the tasks in different ways. This helps to promote recovery, which can be relatively complete except when the tumor seriously affects large areas of the brain or interferes with basic planning and evaluation skills through impairment of the frontal lobes. Affective disturbances can also be difficult to treat but will often respond to medication. A more thorough description of rehabilitation approaches can be found in Golden (1981a).

The assessment of affective disorders in tumors, as well as the other disorders we will discuss, is probably the most complex task faced by the neuropsychologist. Traditional tests of personality functioning may be administered to the patient, but evaluation of the test results must be extremely cautious. All such tests reflect cognitive as well as personality functioning, and traditional interpretation generally carries the implicit assumption that the patient is cognitively capable of doing the tasks requested. For example, we assume on the Minnesota Multiphasic Personality Inventory (MMPI) that the patient is capable of reading at an adequate level of understanding, understanding items with complex grammar and syntax, reading and answering the questions in a considered rather than an implusive manner, and being aware of the nature of personal problems.

This analysis is further complicated by the fact that many of the symptoms we associate with emotional disorders may be caused by brain dysfunction without the presence of an accompanying emotional problem. The Rorschach, Draw a Person, and Thematic Apperception Test (TAT) may be affected by visual–spatial difficulties or perceptual problems which suggest emotional problems that may not be present. The Draw a Person Test, as well as other similar drawing tests of personality function, may also be seriously affected by motor problems that may suggest immaturity or perceptual fragmentation.

As a consequence, such tests must be interpreted together with the neuropsychological results of the personality test. In this manner, one can begin to separate the results related to the patient's cognitive deficits from those which reflect other causes. However, even if the interpretation is correct, there still remain problems in determining the etiology of the personality traits. The problems may have existed premorbidly. It is not unusual for a brain injury to bring to light problems that existed previously but were either missed, ignored, or thought to be unimportant. Thus, an extensive history, including collateral sources, is mandatory. In other cases, the emotional problems may be the result of a reaction to the brain injury. A serious tumor may lead to depression or a high level of anxiety which may leave the patient unable to return to work or to perform self-care, even in the absence of any real functional impairment. In such cases, neuropsychological test results may be impaired due to the excessive anxiety or a sense of anxiety. This problem is likely to show up on tests which are relatively complex and which demand speed, attention, and concentration. Such patients may tire unusually rapidly, not because of the brain injury but because of the excessive psychic energy which must be invested even in the simplest testing situations. In such cases, neuropsychological test results may be impaired due to the excessive anxiety or a sense of anxiety. This problem is likely to show up on tests which are relatively complex and which demand speed, attention, and concentration. Such patients may tire unusually rapidly, not because of the brain injury but because of the excessive psychic energy which must be invested even in the simplest testing situations. In such cases, testing is best attempted when frequent breaks are allowed and when tests for measuring a given cognitive function are kept as brief as possible. The examiner should be extremely sensitive to the patient's mood and act to create a testing situation in which the patient can feel maximally relaxed. Patients should not be pushed beyond their limits or over their objections; poor performance may simply reflect the patient's fatigue and desire to finish the battery. Even when the patient is cooperative, the extreme effort required can result in impaired performance despite an intact cognitive structure.

Another serious problem is an emotional disorder which is intermittent in nature. Often the emotional problem is associated with a temporal lobe disorder which may be initiated by an epileptic seizure on a clinical or subclinical level. This will be discussed in the chapter on epileptic disorders.

Overall, the assessment of the tumor patient must be comprehensive and based on an appreciation of the numerous factors which may affect the expression of the disorder. Simple attempts to reach conclusions on the basis of rigid rules regarding the presence or absence of tumors will usually result in many significant errors in mild cases, which are those most likely to be missed by physicians or mistaken for nonneurologic disorders. Simple screening examinations are rarely justified in these cases, since they are not reliable for diagnosis of borderline cases and do not provide information for assessment of status that is necessary for rehabilitation or legal evaluation of the patient.

Chapter 2
Cerebrovascular Disorders

The primary cerebrovascular disorders are defects in the blood vessels which supply the brain. These syndromes result in either a reduced or an absent blood supply to certain parts of the brain. In addition, hemorrhages can cause blood to spill into the brain, killing brain tissue, by pressure and ischemia and destroying functional systems as a result.

The exact defects seen in a given individual in the diseases discussed below depend upon the degree of collateral circulation available to the lesioned area. Collateral circulation enables a given area of the brain to be supplied with blood from a different source, which substitutes for the one that has been blocked. If collateral circulation is adequate, occlusion (blockage) of a vessel may produce no psychological symptoms whatsoever.

The amount of collateral circulation depends upon several factors. First, the adequacy of the circle of Willis must be considered. The circle of Willis is formed by communications (linkages) between branches of the internal carotid and basilar arteries. The anterior communicating artery connects the two anterior cerebral arteries which branch off from the two internal carotid arteries. The two posterior cerebral arteries (branches of the basilar artery) are connected to the internal carotid artery on the same side of the brain by the posterior communicating arteries. However, in some individuals one or more of the communicating branches are missing, which can enhance the effects of vascular disorders. Collateral circulation will also be impaired if the collateral arteries are unable to supply blood in greater volume. Finally, additional collateral circulation can be generated by the brain when the disorder is localized and slow to develop. Thus, if one carotid artery is slowly occluded, by the time occlusion is complete there may be no symptoms of a disorder. In contrast, a quickly developing lesion in the same place will have disastrous effects.

Arteriosclerosis

Arteriosclerosis is common in the United States and is usually accelerated by such factors as aging, hypertension, smoking, diabetes, and hyperlipoproteinemia (Duncan, Lees, Ojemann, & David, 1977).

Atheromas tend to occur more frequently at certain sites in the cerebral vasculature: the internal carotids at their origin in the neck, the horizontal stem of each middle cerebral artery, the vertebral arteries, and the basilar artery. With time, the atheromatous plaque grows, progressively reducing the cross-sectional size of the artery. The plaque can become ulcerated, exposing subendothelial collagen to the blood. Platelets in the blood tend to accumulate with fibrin on the ulcerated plaque. As the diameter of the artery decreases, the chance of complete blockage increases.

Arteriosclerosis can occur as early as ages 30−40. Symptoms may include headache, dizziness, tinnitus, and insomnia (Chusid, 1973). Personality changes of all kinds may take place, and any cognitive deficit may appear, especially in later stages of the disease. In these stages, neuropsychological test batteries generally show diffuse impairment of varying degrees.

Restriction of flow in one or more arteries will not necessarily lead to neuropsychologic deficits. Arteries may be restricted up to 90−100%, with no neuropsychological impairment being present. In the case of full restriction, it is likely that collateral circulation, discussed above, is responsible for the lack of deficits, which presupposes that the blockage developed slowly over time. When the blockage develops quickly, as is discussed below, massive deficits can occur. In the case of partial restriction, deficits may be absent simply because overall blood flow has not been changed. Massive changes in the diameter of a vessel such as an artery may be compensated for by an increase in the flow rate of the liquid involved. This will generally result in increased pressure as well, which itself can predispose the patient to the more serious disorders discussed below.

In general, then, one cannot assume that there will be neuropsychological deficits simply because there are restrictions (even massive ones) in arterial width. A much better technique for assessing the likelihood of such disorders is to measure regional cerebral blood flow. Such techniques measure the flow of blood to specific regions in the brain by monitoring radioactive elements placed in the bloodstream through inhalation or injection. Since these techniques measure actual blood flow, they presumably reflect the status of any given area of the brain much more effectively than assessment of arterial size or blockages—which, as noted above, may be entirely unrelated to apparent flow.

Transient Ischemic Attacks

Transient ischemic attacks, or TIAs as they are commonly called, result from temporary blockages of cerebral arteries. The symptoms include any of those which can be caused by brain dysfunction: partial or complete paralysis, aphasic signs, confusion, personality change, or any of the various other cognitive symptoms. These deficits are transient because the arterial blockage that caused them is transient and disappears spontaneously. In general, symptoms should dissipate within 24 hours for the disorder to be labeled a TIA. Patients with arteriosclerosis are at a much greater risk for TIAs because the reduced width of their vessels makes them much easier to occlude. This usually involves the processes discussed below in the sections on thrombotic and embolic occlusions. A TIA should, by definition, leave no residual neuropsychological symptoms. If permanent symptoms are found, then the disorder is usually not classified as a TIA but rather as one of the conditions discussed later in this chapter. A TIA may be the first indication that significant arterial narrowing has occurred. This suspicion is usually confirmed by arteriography, a technique for investigating the status of the vascular system through the injection of an x-ray opaque dye.

When a TIA has occurred, the patient is generally considered to be a prime candate for the development of a major, permanent vascular disorder. For this reason, such patients are frequently considered for carotid endarterectomy (an operation which uses surgical techniques to "clean out" the artery affected by arteriosclerosis). These operations generally have good success rates in patients under 60 who are otherwise healthy. Such operations appear to reduce the risk of serious stroke in patients with significant arteriosclerotic progression (usually defined as reduction of the width of the vessel by 50% or more).

Thrombotic Occlusion

Thrombotic occlusion of an artery usually occurs in the presence of a preexisting disease. The most common preexisting disorder is arteriosclerosis, but thrombosis can also occur with such conditions as arteritis (inflammation of a vessel), migraine, meningitis, syphilis, fibromuscular dysplasia, or other similar disorders. In all of these diseases, progressive narrowing of the artery occurs. This is followed by the development of blood clots, which can be classified in a number of ways depending on their origin and makeup. The blood clots complete the blockage of the artery and result in the occlusion.

Thrombotic occlusion may also arise from the breaking off of chunks of plaque in arteries. This material is then carried to smaller arteries, where it causes an occlusion. Since the plaque material is fragile, this can happen easily. For this same reason, however, the occlusion itself may be only temporary since the plaque may become further fragmented. It is this mechanism which has been hypothesized as the cause of TIAs (Duncan, Pessin, Mohr, & Adams, 1976).

Embolic Occlusion

Cerebral arteries which are free of occlusive disease may be blocked by the arrival of an embolus of sufficient size. Emboli are usually clot fragments from another part of the circulation, that is, the wall of the heart, or an atheromatous plaque on the wall of a vessel between the heart and the occluded point. The emboli may also be composed of air, fat, or tumor cells. Emboli from the heart are probably the most common, and are formed secondary to cardiac disease such as congenital or rheumatic valve disease, arrhythmias (particularly of the left atrium), endocarditis, or myocardial infarction. Depending on their size and their tendency to break apart, emboli may cause either TIAs or major strokes.

Arterial Rupture

The rupture of small arteries within brain tissue results in intracerebral hemmorrhage. Usually this condition occurs in individuals with long-standing hypertension. In these cases, hypertensive lipohyalinosis occurs, implying structural weakness in the arterial wall, which then dilates to aneurysmal proportions, to be followed by rupture. Arteries can also be weakened by trauma, septic emboli, arteritis, arteriovenous malformations, collagen diseases, and neoplasms.

DISEASES DUE TO CEREBROVASCULAR DISORDERS

Ischemia and Infarction

The neuronal tissue of the brain is extremely sensitive to oxygen deprivation. Interruption of blood flow (and oxygen delivery) for only 30 seconds disrupts cerebral metabolism and function. If anoxia lasts for more than 5 minutes, irreversible ischemic infarction (tissue death) occurs. The term *stroke* implies limited infarction of an area of the brain caused by deprivation of oxygenated blood. Generalized ischemia or markedly diminished blood flow such as that caused by hypotension or cardiac arrhythmias produces diffuse cerebral dysfunction but rarely causes infarction.

Following occlusion of an artery, the size of the resultant infarct depends upon the adequacy of the collateral blood supply. This is highly variable from patient to patient and is responsible for the variation in the size of infarcts following blockage of arteries in similar locations.

Intracerebral Hematoma

After rupture of a small intracerebral artery, blood leaks into the brain, disrupting surrounding tissue. The force of blood leaking under pressure may tear other vessels, enlarging the hematoma (Fisher, 1971). The function of brain tissue is disrupted by destruction and distortion of normal structures. The extravasations vary in size from tiny hemorrhages to large hematomas several centimeters in diameter. The blood may leak into the ventricular system. Common sites of bleeding are the basal ganglia (putamen and caudate nucleus), cerebral white matter, thalamus, pons, and cerebellar hemispheres.

STROKE SYNDROMES

The hallmark of a stroke is its rapid onset. Regardless of the nature of the resultant symptoms, the neurologic deficit usually appears over a period of minutes or hours. The rate of onset depends upon the nature of the underlying vascular lesion. In cerebral embolism, the onset is usually abrupt, occurring a few seconds to a few minutes, and the deficit is greatest at the outset. The onset of thrombosis is more variable. It often occurs during sleep, and the victim awakens with symptoms of a stroke. The stroke will often then progress in a stuttering or steady fashion, with the maximal neurologic deficit occurring in 48−72 hours. Frequently, thrombotic strokes are preceded by cerebral TIAs, which are shorter versions of the coming stroke. Cerebral hemorrhages usually develop over a period of minutes to hours of smooth progression, accompanied by nausea, vomiting, and headache.

All patients who survive strokes improve, beginning the first week or so, as in thrombosis. In some cases, there is temporary worsening due to edema surrounding the lesion.

Symptoms of a stroke depend on the cerebral vessel involved and the area of the brain it supplies. The more common neurovascular syndromes, which primarily affect motor function, will be discussed only briefly, nonparalytic stroke syndromes will be the focus of the discussion.

PARALYTIC STROKE SYNDROMES

Occlusion of the internal carotid artery can be asymptomatic, provided collateral circulation is adequate. However, it can cause symptoms of ipsilateral monocular blindness, contralateral hemiparesis and hemianesthesia, aphasia (if the dominant hemisphere is involved), and, less often, homonymous hemianopsia (blindness in the same half of each visual field bilaterally). Occlusion of the anterior cerebral artery can be recognized by the predominance of motor and sensory symptoms in the contralateral leg and foot. Middle cerebral artery occlusion has effects similar to those of internal carotid artery occlusion, except that although the eye itself is spared, homonymous hemianopsia is more common and the hemiparesis is often more pronounced. Occlusion in the vertebrobasilar system produces unilateral or bilateral sensory and motor deficits involving the extremities, with obvious brain stem dysfunction (diplopia, ataxia, crossed motor and sensory signs, dysarthria, dysphagia, or cranial nerve dysfunction).

The middle cerebral artery syndrome is by far the most common. Along with the typical hemiparesis, individuals with such symptoms show dramatic cognitive symptoms, the exact nature of which depends on the branches of the middle cerebral artery involved (see Gardner, 1975, or Golden, 1981a, for a description of the areas served by the middle cerebral artery). This common disorder predominates in most of the neuropsychological works on cerebral vascular disorders. For this reason, one may conclude wrongly that striking motor symptoms are consistent with all cerebral vascular occlusions.

NONPARALYTIC STROKE SYNDROMES

Carotid Arterial System Syndromes

Ophthalmic Artery

The ophthalmic artery is the first major branch of the internal carotid artery. The central retinal artery, a branch of the ophthalmic artery, supplies the optic nerve and retina. Two major syndromes are related to the occlusion of this artery.

Amaurosis fugax is a transient monocular blindness which is brief in duration (1−15 minutes). It begins with a black shade that smoothly descends or ascends within 1 or 2 seconds to obscure part or all of monocular vision. Vision then returns completely. As the episodes of blindness are so brief, the symptomatic patient is rarely seen during an attack. Fisher (1959) had this rare opportunity and noted white plugs, thought to be platelet−fibrin masses, moving through the retinal arteries. The diagnosis is made by the history. Some 50−60% of such cases are associated with internal carotid occlusive disease. Other causes include cranial arteritis, migraine, papilledema, global retinal ischemia, and contraceptive pill-induced vascular disease.

Permanent monocular blindness usually occurs suddenly, generally due to occlusion of the ophthalmic or central retinal artery. Extracranial vascular disease and aortic valvular disease are unusual causes of embolism.

Anterior Cerebral Artery

Specific syndromes following occlusion of the anterior cerebral artery have been imperfectly studied. The diagnosis is made only when sensorimotor symptoms involve primarily the foot and leg. Proximal branches of the anterior cerebral artery pierce the substance and supply the white matter beneath the frontal lobe cortex. With occlusion of these branches, infarction of the white matter beneath Broca's speech area in the frontal lobe may produce an isolated Broca's aphasia. Also possible is infarction of the frontal poles, which results in an isolated frontal lobe syndrome. Neither event is a likely sequela to anterior cerebral artery occlusion.

Middle Cerebral Artery

Isolated aphasic syndromes are often caused by occlusion of cortical branches of the middle cerebral artery, with resulting limited infarctions of the dominant cerebral hemisphere. In most of these cases, there is sudden onset of fluent paraphrasic speech and impaired auditory comprehension typical of Wernicke's aphasia. Conduction aphasia, Broca's aphasia, and Gerstmann's syndrome are seen less frequently. With acute onset, these syndromes should be attributed to a stroke, probably due to embolism of the smaller branches of the middle cerebral artery.

Isolated nondominant hemisphere syndromes, which occur with occlusions of the branches of the middle cerebral artery in the nondominant hemisphere, are less frequently diagnosed than isolated aphasic syndromes. Symptoms, although quite variable, often consist of clumsiness of the contralateral hand, dressing or constructional apraxia, and inattention to and denial of the contralateral side of the body.

Posterior Cerebral Artery

Syndromes of posterior cerebral artery strokes can be divided into two groups, proximal and distal, depending on which of the areas supplied by the artery are involved. The distal portion of the posterior cerebral artery supplies the occipital and medial temporal lobes. The thalamus, hypothalamus, and subthalamus are supplied by penetrating branches of the proximal segment of this artery.

The major proximal artery syndrome is the pure sensory stroke (Fisher, 1965). This is the result of a small (lacunar) infarct in the central sensory relay nuclei of the thalamus. This lesion results in complaints of subjective sensory symptoms which split the midline. On examination, decreased sensation to multiple sensory modalities in the symptomatic area is found. This unusual pattern of sensory loss may sometimes be difficult to distinguish from conversion symptoms. With the syndrome of pure sensory stroke, patients rarely complain of other symptoms, such as visual disturbance, pain, or weakness. Fisher (1965) noted that although total loss of sensation seldom occurs, the sensory symptoms often so overshadow the physical findings that the syndrome could be termed the *pure paresthetic stroke*. In a conversion reaction with hemisensory loss, it has been found useful to test the vibratory sense over the forehead and nose. Since these bony structures are essentially fused, the vibratory sense should not change abruptly near the midline, as does the ability to appreciate pain or touch.

A small infarct in the subthalamic nucleus causes hemiballismus, a wild, flinging, uncontrollable movement in the contralateral limbs. Choreiform and athetoid movements on one side of the body are also possible with infarcts in this area.

Most distal artery lesions produce the symptom of contralateral homonymous hemianopsia because the calcarine cortex, the primary visual area, is supplied by the distal end of the artery. This may be the only finding in most of the cases. Other signs and symptoms of distal artery origin accompany the homonymous hemianopsia depending on the extent and location of the damage.

Infarction involving the left medial occipital lobe and the splenium of the corpus callosum produces a right hemianopsia and the syndrome of alexia without agraphia (Geschwind, 1965). These individuals can speak and write fluently without errors but are unable to read aloud what they have written. Color dysnomia and disturbances of recent memory may also be present (Mohr, Leicester, Stoddard, & Sidman, 1971). Another possible variation is the syndrome of agitated delirium with visual impairment (Medina, Chokroverty, & Rubin, 1977). This syndrome can occur in the presence of either hemianopsia or bilateral cortical blindness. Individuals typically experience onset of visual impairment, followed within hours or a few days by delirium. The patient may not realize the visual deficit. After the delirium ends, the visual impairment and a short-term memory deficit often persist even though no other deficits are present. Computed tomography often shows a lesion at one or both sites in the medial temporal and occipital lobes (Wells & Duncan, 1980).

Patients with posterior cerebral artery occlusion often have memory disturbances. This problem is thought to result from ischemic damage to the inferior medial temporal lobe, including the hippocampus. Bilateral temporal lobe lesions have generally been thought necessary to disrupt memory, but instances of amnesia have been reported after unilateral (usually dominant) temporal infarcts (Mohr et al, 1971). Amnesia due to unilateral damage may improve in time, unlike bilateral amnesia. Amnesia does not occur in isolation, but accompanies other disturbances in the posterior cerebral artery distribution. Cerebrovascular disease is often associated with the syndrome of transient global amnesia. However, in the absence of other neurologic signs and symptoms and without good pathologic evidence, such a theory is tenuous at best.

Vertebrobasilar Artery

The Wallenberg or lateral medullary syndrome is the major syndrome of vertebral artery occlusion (Fisher et al., 1961). The occlusion occurs at the origin of the posterior-inferior cerebellar artery and blocks both the vertebral and posterior inferior cerebellar arteries. Less often, the syndrome results from occlusion of the posterior-inferior cerebellar artery alone. The area of infarction lies in the posterolateral portion of the medulla, sparing the more anterior corticospinal tracts and thus producing no paralysis. Symptoms and signs include impairment of pain and the sense of heat or cold over the contralateral arm and leg and occasionally over the face ipsilaterally, hoarseness, dysphagia, dysarthria, vertigo, nausea, diminished gag reflex on the same side, and ipsilateral ataxia.

A catastrophic stroke with coma or at least bilateral paralysis results after basilar artery occlusion. Often, the smaller branches of the basilar artery which penetrate into the pons may become occluded, producing limited syndromes, with combinations of various brain stem deficits.

The cerebellum is supplied by three major arteries, and occlusion of any of them may cause infarction. Cerebellar hemorrhage may also occur. Both conditions are important because of the potentially disastrous results if swelling takes place and causes significant brain stem compression. Cerebellar hemorrhage develops over several hours. There is sudden onset of dizziness with headache and severe imbalance that prevents the individual from standing. Downward pressure on the pons may cause ipsilateral sixth or seventh cranial nerve palsies or a conjugate lateral gaze palsy. Weakness of the extremities usually does not occur until late in the course, when coma sets in.

Cerebellar infarction can go completely unnoticed unless postinfarction edema causes a massive effect, compressing the vital centers of the brain stem. Early symptoms of compression include sudden onset of rotatory dizziness, nausea, vomiting, horizontal nystagmus, and imbalance, closely resembling a nonspecific labyrinthine disorder.

Hemorrhage

Hemorrhage into the brain or meninges results from the rupturing of one or more cerebral vessels, usually secondary to weakness caused by arteriosclerosis. However, hemorrhage can also result from trauma, aneurysm, congenital malformation of an artery, acute infection, or toxic agents. The latter two factors may result in numerous hemorrhages due to weakening of many vessels. Hypertension may also play a role in these disorders. A common hemorrhage secondary to trauma is subarachnoid hemorrhage, in which bleeding occurs between the dura and arachnoid layers of the meninges. This disorder is briefly discussed in the chapter on trauma.

When blood is released into the brain matter, the resultant blood clot destroys the brain tissue. Small hemorrhages cause localized signs (depending on the location), whereas large hemorrhages may destroy an entire hemisphere as well as subcortical areas, preventing precise localization. In cases of eventual recovery, the blood is removed by the brain metabolism and new connective tissue, glial cells, and blood vessels occupy the space, creating a smaller, fluid-filled area.

Since the hemorrhage and clot destroy brain tissue, the deficits are generally as severe as those seen in fast-growing tumors. However, since the disorder is not progressive, the prognosis is better than that of a tumor, especially if the area of hemorrhage is limited. In larger hemorrhages, such as those of the main trunk of the middle cerebral artery, however, the prognois is much more guarded because of the widespread tissue destruction and the generalized loss of skills which might substitute for the lost functions. This problem is especially serious when the dominant hemisphere is involved.

Aneurysms

An aneurysm is an enlargement (dilatation) of a blood vessel at a specific site secondary to arteriosclerosis, a congenital abnormality, or an embolism. The aneurysm can vary from the size of a pea to that of an apple. In a given patient, the size of the aneurysm can also vary over time. Larger aneurysms can compress nearby tissues, causing many of the symptoms produced by a slow-growing tumor of the same size and location. Thus, psychological symptoms are usually mild but highly focal when present. Chronic aneurysms such as those which result from a congenital malformation of an artery may show no deficits whatsoever. More focal and acute signs, however, will be present if the aneurysm suddenly increases in size or if bleeding (hemorrhage) occurs. In young people not seen for head trauma but for symptoms suggesting a vascular disorder, an aneurysm is most likely the underlying cause.

Aneurysms may change in size because of such factors as increased blood pressure. Thus, the individual may develop headaches or nausea under stress or on exertion. In some cases, especially in younger people, these symptoms are mistaken for psychological rather than neurologic problems, even by excellent physicians. In all such cases, the possibility of a neurologic disorder must be carefully evaluated.

Most aneurysms are associated with the internal carotid or middle cerebral artery. They also occur commonly at the bifurcation of the vessel. Once an aneurysm has been located or identified, the treatment must be seriously considered because of the chance of eventual rupture. Modern treatment techniques may include "clipping" the aneurysm or spraying it with plastics in order to increase the strength of the vessel walls.

IMPLICATIONS FOR NEUROPSYCHOLOGICAL TESTING

Cerebrovascular disorders, like tumors (see Chapter 1) and head trauma (see Chapter 3), can result in a variety of problems ranging from essentially none with small, static aneurysms to complete disruption of brain processes with massive hemorrhages. Thus, there can be no specific guidelines regarding the likely symptons of cerebrovascular disorders, and many of the comments made in the last chapter are applicable here.

However, certain specific findings should be considered. First, cerebrovascular disorders can generally be distinguished from tumors in that they usually have a much more sudden onset or, alternatively, a slow development of deficits that abruptly quickens. In tumors, the course of development is generally more even, although this feature may occasionally be missed because of the lack of a reliable or accurate historian. When these disorders are considered, a detailed history is mandatory. The clinician may have to ask questions regarding the development of specific symptoms rather than rely on open-ended questions to yield all the necessary information.

Second, cerebrovascular disorders are more often associated with loss of motor and sensory skills on one side of the body than on the other. In fact, the few studies which have attempted to distinguish these disorders have generally found motor and sensory signs to be the most useful discriminators. The major reason for this is the relatively high frequency of middle cerebral or internal carotid artery disorders in patients with cerebrovascular disorders. Since the middle cerebral artery is the primary source of blood for the major motor and sensory areas of the brain, and the internal carotid artery is the primary source of blood for the middle cerebral artery, it is not surprising that these disorders lead to severe and characteristic impairment of one side of the body compared to the other. Indeed, this pattern is so often associated with cerebrovascular disorders that one can achieve a high rate of diagnostic accuracy by assuming that a disorder is likely to be cerebrovascular when such symptoms are present.

In addition, many of the classic aphasic syndromes are most often seen in cerebrovascular disorder. Included are such disorders as Wernicke's aphasia (receptive aphasia), Broca's aphasia (expressive aphasia), conduction apahsia, and other similar syndromes. The sudden appearance of classic cases of these disorders in the absence of head trauma is most often associated with a cerebrovascular disorder. It should be emphasized that neither these disorders nor the motor or sensory disorders described in the previous paragraph are due to cerebrovascular disorders alone; statistically, however, their appearance should alert the clinician to the likelihood of such disturbances. For example, in a patient recently seen by the authors, the question was whether the symptoms were due to a slowly progressive disease or cerebrovascular problems. The appearance of Wernicke's aphasia suggested that the problem was probably cerebrovascular in origin, a finding which was later confirmed by angiography.

Cerebrovascular disorders must also be considered highly likely when transient, highly focal symptoms occur. In these cases, transient ischemic attacks (TIA's) must be considered, as well as aneurysms which may have increased in size or bled for short periods, causing the acute symptoms. Aneurysms are especially likely in younger individuals (in the absence of head trauma or infection), in whom the probability of most tumors is relatively low.

Another major stroke pattern is the unilateral neglect or inattention syndrome. This syndrome results in the inability of the patient to show awareness of the deficits. As described earlier, these patients may be unaware of their deficits and deny their existence. In addition, they will characteristically ignore the left side of stimulus objects. The sentence "I went to the store" may be read as "to the store." Only the right side of a figure may be copied—so that a circle is copied as a half circle, a triangle copied with only two sides, and a square copied with only three sides. These patients are often unable to dress themselves, since they are ignoring the left side of their own body. They are also characteristically paralyzed on the left side of the body. This syndrome is most often associated with right hemisphere disorders involving the middle cerebral artery, although other disorders can also cause the syndrome. In rare cases in which the left hemisphere is the nondominant side of the brain, unilateral neglect of the right side may develop. However, very few of these cases have been described.

Cerebrovascular disorders, like tumors, may produce other symptoms. Occlusion of the anterior cerebral artery, as noted earlier, may result in a characteristic loss of motor abilities in the lower extremities alone. Other characteristic patterns of symptoms have also been described. However, the effects of cerebrovascular disorders are not limited to these symptoms; any combination of problems is possible. Therefore, such disorders cannot be ruled out on the basis of symptoms alone, although their probability lessens as the patient's problems deviate from the patterns discussed in this chapter.

In evaluating cerebrovascular disorders, one must be careful not to overestimate the degree of deficit. Because of the effects of motor and speech problems seen in these patients and their inability to understand orally presented instructions, the psychologist may assume deficits in other areas, when in fact the only problem is the failure to understand what is requested rather than an inability to do the task. In these cases, instructions must be modified to maximize the patient's understanding. A written presentation of instructions, simplification and repetition of oral instructions, the use of pantomime, or other techniques may be required. In other cases, the patient may be unable to communicate answers verbally, and the answers may have to be written (assuming dysgraphia is not also present) or much more time allowed for answering. For example, on the Luria—Nebraska Neuropsychological Battery, many items that require a verbal response are scored according to the moment the response is begun rather than when it is finished so as not to penalize such individuals.

Motor and sensory problems of the hands may cause one to overestimate the deficit. For example, sensory problems may cause defects in many motor tasks (most of which require sensory feedback). Motor skills are also used in some sensory tests, such as those for sensory recognition of objects placed in the hands. As a consequence, one may overstate the degree of sensory loss. In both cases, there is a need for very simple items to test both motor and sensory modalities in order to help separate them. For example, a motor skill as simple as opening and closing the hand may be employed, since this is relatively independent of sensory skills. Simple sensory items such as recognition of the site or strength of touch are also useful. In no case should evaluation depend only on such complex tests as the Purdue Pegboard Test or the Tactual Performance Test.

Cerebrovascular disorders may also be accompanied by a large number of behavioral or affective problems. Some deficits, such as the denial associated with unilateral neglect, appear to be clearly related to the impairment in brain function. In others, the relationship between the brain injury and the affective symptoms is far less clear. In addition to the effects of the brain injury itself, the sudden loss of skills in individuals who are often functioning at a high level, the inability to do basic tasks such as motor movements and speech, and the patient's premorbid personality may also be considered.

Denial is common in many patients, although not the extreme form of denial seen with unilateral neglect. These patients simply insist that the symptoms, which they acknowledge, do not interfere with their lives. This attitude may be reflected in high Hysteria and Hypomania scale scores on the Minnesota Multiphasic Personality Inventory (MMPI). This reaction seems to be primarily a function of the premorbid personality rather than an indication of the location or extent of the injury.

Depression is also seen frequently in cerebrovascular patients. Although we would expect some such reaction in any individual with a sudden serious injury, Post (1975) has reported more depression in stroke patients than in other brain-injured persons, and Folstern, Maiberger, and McHugh (1977) found more depression in stroke patients than in equally disabled orthopedic patients. They also found that depression was more common in individuals with lesions of the right (nondominant) hemisphere, suggesting some relationship between such injuries and affective disorders. This is considered more fully in the chapter on affective disorders.

Other psychological reactions to stroke may also occur. Anxiety is common, often because of fear of the present and future strokes. Extreme anxiety and depressive syndromes may both interfere with neuropsychological test performance. These patients may be easily frustrated, rejecting tasks as "too simple" or "a waste of time" or refusing to continue with testing. Intense anxiety may become disabling even when the patient is cooperative. Younger patients who have suffered severe strokes may be particularly susceptible to anxiety and depression since their problems are usually unexpected and are considered unfair. Severe psychological regression can occur but is relatively rare. One must be careful not to foster excessive dependency in these patients by treating them as severely disabled and not allowing them to perform to their maximum capacity.

In conclusion, whereas cerebrovascular disorders, like tumors, can produce a wide variety of disorders, common strokes will result in much more predictable patterns which are highly suggestive of cerebrovascular disorders. However, one must always realize that these patterns can be caused by other injuries as well. In addition, the cerebrovascular disorder itself may be secondary to other conditions. In separating cerebrovascular disorders from other problems, the history is an important tool. In evaluating these disorders, it is important not to allow motor, sensory, or speech problems to make one overestimate the extent of the patient's deficits. Alternative testing methods and properly chosen batteries will allow the clinician to evaluate better the specific deficits present and to estimate better the patient's capacity for adaptive behavior. In making long-term prognoses, it is also important to note the role of affective disturbances (both primary and secondary), as well as typical patterns of recovery over time.

Chapter 3

Head Injury

PATHOPHYSIOLOGY OF HEAD INJURY

Trauma to the skull resulting in brain injury is one of the more common neurologic disorders. It is also the cause of most referrals of individuals under 40 years of age to a neuropsychologist. Most head injuries which occur in nonmilitary circumstances are blunt or closed injuries with no damage to the skull itself. Serious trauma usually results in loss of consciousness. When complete recovery occurs in the absence of neurologic deficits, the condition is usually labeled *cerebral concussion*. The basis for the loss of consciousness in concussion remains in doubt. Cerebral ischemia was originally believed to be responsible, but little supportive evidence for this idea has been discovered. Rotational shear stresses are now believed to be at fault, with swirling motions of the brain within the rigid skull causing diffuse injury with breakdown of myelin and interruption of nerve fibers. Brain stem involvement may also be present. Respiratory arrest, generalized vasoconstriction, and losses of corneal blink and pharyngeal reflexes often accompany unconsciousness, suggesting injury of brainstem centers.

More severe blows to the skull, resulting in neurologic abnormalities or intellectual deficits, are usually called *cerebral contusions*, and those producing definite focal defects are called *cerebral lacerations*. These injuries tend to be present most often at the site of impact (coup), at a point opposite to the impact (contrecoup), and at the hemispheric poles. Lesions tend to be maximal at the point of impact when the head is at rest on impact. When the head is in motion during impact, contrecoup injuries tend to predominate.

Temporal and orbital (frontal) regions of the brain are especially susceptible to contrecoup effects, with such lesions leading to local neuronal loss and subsequent subcortical demyelination.

Vascular lesions following head injury range from scattered tiny hemorrhages to infarcts of variable amounts of tissue that can produce necrosis of the territory of a major cerebral artery. Such lesions may be the result of several factors, including vascular spasm due to mechanical strain, embolism, occlusion by preexisting atheroma, arterial occlusion secondary to increased intracranial pressure, and systemic hypotension (Strich, 1969). Laceration of vessels may lead to extensive blood collection in the subarachnoid space surrounding the brain. Venous blood may accumulate in the subdural space and become organized over the cerebral hemispheres, producing pressure effects. Organized collections of blood may lead to adhesions which can obstruct the flow of cerebrospinal fluid, producing hydrocephalus. An intracerebral hematoma is the result of bleeding within the brain tissue itself.

A further complication which may appear during the acute period is cerebral edema, or leakage of fluid into the spaces surrounding brain cells. Edema is more likely to appear near contusions, lacerations, hematomas, and infarcts than in other locations. The additional fluid accumulation in the fixed cavity of the skull produces elevated intracranial pressure, which can cause brain herniation through the constricted spaces marginated by the tentorium and falx cerebri, as well as openings in the skull itself such as the foramen magnum. Such herniations can cause death by producing brain stem compression. Milder cases, which produce local vascular compromise, can lead to focal necrosis and hemorrhage, especially in the structures of the medial temporal lobe and brain stem.

As mentioned previously, respiratory arrest may occur in cases of head injury. If respiration fails to resume within a very brief period, anoxic damage to the brain results. Respiratory arrest and other causes of widespread cerebral anoxia, such as impaired cerebral circulation, lead especially to cortical necrosis, lesions in the hippocampus and basal ganglia, and disappearance of Purkinje cells from the cerebellar cortex, as these areas are particularly sensitive to hypoxia.

As healing occurs and the acute changes produced by head injury resolve, differing degrees of gliosis (scarring) and cerebral atrophy result. This is often accompanied by considerable distortion of brain tissue, ventricular enlargement, or cyst formation. When injury is followed by prolonged coma, pathologic findings in the central portion of the upper brain stem may be expected.

THE PHYSICS OF CLOSED HEAD INJURY

As noted above, the effects of a head injury depend on the relative movement and size of the object causing the trauma and the head. Several possibilities can occur with a head trauma. First, the object can hit the skull, causing it to accelerate away from the striking object. When acceleration is not transmitted to the brain, however, it causes the skull to pull away from the brain at a point opposite the original impact point. This effect, if severe enough, can cause the tearing of brain tissue and the cerebrovascular system at this opposite point. Alternatively, if the head is in motion, it can be stopped by the object (as in a car accident), causing the brain to slam into the skull on the side hit (coup mechanism) and producing injury, and pulling away from the skull on the opposite side, producing the contrecoup effect (injury on the opposite side). In some cases, the skull can be crushed inward without breaking, causing injury by compression. Injury may also occur when the brain is thrust forward by a blow to the skull which is directly transmitted to the brain, causing it to move in the direction of the blow against the skull. This is especially serious when the brain is thrust against the frontal-orbital area of the skull, which is irregularly rather than smoothly shaped. The thrust of the frontal lobes against the internal bony irregularities can result in bruising and bleeding as well as compression (Courville, 1942). This same mechanism can cause the brain at the site of the injury to pull away from the skull, again applying stress to the cerebral tissue and the vascular system, which results in tearing and bleeding.

These mechanisms differ with small and large objects. Whereas the results desribed above may be produced by large objects, small objects may cause bruising and bleeding only at the point of contact because of an inability to move the brain or skull. In addition, the relative speeds of the objects must be taken into consideration, as well as the angle at which the head is moving, the angle of the object, the angle of the neck, and the freedom it has to move in the direction of the object or out of its path. Another major consideration is the strength of the skull at different points and the strength of the various vessels of the brain. For example, a vessel already weakened by a congenital malformation may rupture before a more intact vessel, even though it is not at the focus of the trauma. As a consequence, it is often impossible to predict from an accident what localization, if any, a head trauma will assume.

OPEN HEAD TRAUMA

Although open head traumas share many of the characteristics of the closed head traumas discussed, there are important differences both in mechanisms and in effects. In open head traumas the skull is actually broken, either as the result of penetration (such as a bullet wound) or from the effects of the force used. If the skull is fractured rather than penetrated, unusual results can be produced. In these cases, the force of the blow is stopped by the skull. The energy transmitted to the brain itself, therefore, is much less than the energy used when the skull transmits the entire force. Fractures can result in little or no continuing cognitive or personality deficit after the acute effects have disappeared, despite what one might expect when hearing a description of the injury.

However, when the skull is actually penetrated, there is usually damage to the underlying meninges and brain tissue. Laceration is caused by penetration rather than stress forces, as it is with closed head traumas. Injury is usually limited to the site of penetration and its extent, with contrecoup injuries being rare. Penetration can involve the hitting object or fragments of the broken skull itself, which are forced into the brain tissue by the power of a blow. The disrupted, necrotic tissue thus created provides an excellent base for bacterial growth and the development of meningitis or an abscess. Secondary inflammation flowing injury or infection can lead to a connective tissue reaction, causing a scar which can adhere to the dural covering of the brain, eventually distorting the shape of the brain. These scars may also cause epileptic foci.

The cognitive effects of open head injuries obviously depend upon the area injured. In the absence of secondary complications such as infection, these lesions can create some of the more focal deficits seen in neuropsychology, with little impairment of any tissue except that damaged in the trauma. As a consequence, such patients (common after wars) serve as excellent research subjects and have been used in many studies on cerebral localization.

ACUTE EFFECTS OF HEAD INJURY

Impairment of consciousness, however brief, follows most closed head injuries, except those that are very mild, especially when the head is in motion at impact. Although it is seen in cases of open head injury, it is less common. On occasion, there may be no outward sign of impaired consciousness. Only transient dizziness, blurred vision, or faulty recollection of the injury may occur, suggesting at least partial interruption of brain function. Typically, however, complete loss of consciousness occurs with complete loss of responsiveness; these functions are regained in an interval that varies with the severity of the injury. Once consciousness returns, a period of drowsiness, headache, and confusion follows.

Unconsciousness lasting for several hours is not incompatible with complete recovery. The longer the period of unconsciousness resulting from an injury, however, the more likely it is that permanent brain damage has occurred, with concomitant increases in the period of post-traumatic confusion and physical and mental sequelae. Lewin (1959) assessed the recovery in 102 patients who had remained unconscious for more than a month. Of these, 39 died, 15 became severely disabled, 29 recovered partially, and 19 improved enough to return to their former employment. Some improvement was apparent and was usually seen within the first month following injury.

Prolonged post-traumatic coma may be profound from the onset or may worsen rapidly, due to intracerebral or subarachnoid bleeding in the early stages. Decerebrate rigidity is common, with tonic convulsions and disturbances of heart rate, breathing, and temperature regulation. Ominous signs suggesting brain stem compression and impending demise include fixed, dilated pupils, falling blood pressure, irregular respiration, and muscular flaccidity.

As recovery ensues and unconsciousness recedes, the patient experiences disorientation and cognitive impairment. This stage varies with the degree of injury, the premorbid personality, and the environment. The length of the period of disorientation generally corresponds closely to the severity of the injury. The form of the cognitive disturbance also varies, ranging from apathetic withdrawal to irritability to florid delirium. Outward behavior is often little disturbed, except for obvious lethargy and cognitive dysfunction with some initial restlessness. Progress thereafter follows a slow return to full consciousness. Some patients, on the other hand, pass through an excitable phase with florid behavioral disturbances which can be persistent, posing serious management problems. These changes are sometimes the result of delusional misinterpretations during post-traumatic delirium, or they may foreshadow permanent changes of behavior resulting from the injury. In this recovery stage, impairment of consciousness is accompanied by some degree of failure to retain new information. Accordingly, the period of acute traumatic psychosis merges with the post-traumatic amnesic gap.

Whether or not an acute post-traumatic psychosis has followed recovery of consciousness, there is a period of memory gap. This period is referred to as a *post-traumatic amnesic gap*. It may last for a few moments to a few months but usually ends abruptly, with the return of normal continuous memory. Behavior during the post-traumatic amnesic period may range from apparent normality to obvious difficulty with memory and confusion. Some degree of time disorientation is almost always found, however, if it is tested for with care. Usually the patient is unaware of the faultiness of his or her memory functions and may confabulate in an attempt to weave together the defective threads of memory.

Memory for events preceding the injury may also be impaired and is termed a *retrograde amnesic gap*. Retrograde amnesia is often quite dense, involving details of the accident itself. Generally, it is rather uniform in extent, lasting for a few seconds to a minute. Longer gaps sometimes occur with more severe injuries and may persist for days to weeks, although some mild injuries produce no retrograde amnesia at all. Many instances of long retrograde gaps following mild injury have proved to be psychogenic in origin.

Russell (1932) was probably the first to show the importance of the duration of amnesia as a guide to the degree of injury and the expectations for recovery. In this regard, post-traumatic amnesia has proved to be more valid and useful than retrograde amnesia. The duration of post-traumatic amnesia in closed head injuries is related to the time which may elapse before the patient returns to work (Steadman & Graham, 1970). More specifically, objective evidence of damage to brain tissue, reflected in deficits such as motor impairment, dysphasia, amnesia, or defects of memory and calculation, is closely correlated with the duration of post-traumatic amnesia (Russell & Smith, 1961; Smith, 1961).

Psychiatric disability, represented by intellectual impairment, euphoria, disinhibition, or the frontal lobe syndrome, also appears to be closely related to the duration of post-traumatic amnesia. Steadman and Graham (1970) showed that the mean duration of post-traumatic amnesia was significantly increased in patients who showed post-traumatic personality changes. The relationship between the length of post-traumatic amnesia and the amount of psychiatric disability holds for open head as well as closed head injuries, although the incidence of such amnesic episodes is much lower for open head injuries, (Lishman, 1968).

CHRONIC SEQUELAE OF HEAD INJURY

Following recovery from the acute problems associated with head injury, patients with mild injury can be expected to return to their previous level of performance, both physically and mentally. A fair amount of long-term disability, however, can result from head injury. Physical defects include cranial nerve lesions, amnesia, paralysis of the eye musculature and visual field defects, motor disorders resulting from various lesions of the cerebral cortex, midbrain and brain stem, and sensory deficits. Although these deficits are more common after penetrating injuries and as complications following intracranial bleeding, they may be seen in all types of head trauma.

The range of cognitive and psychiatric sequelae of head trauma is broad. At one end of the spectrum lie enduring deficits in cognitive ability which can easily and with some assurance be attributed to localized or diffuse brain damage. At the opposite end are groups of symptoms—anxiety states, phobias, and depression—which can follow the slightest injury and are often interwoven with environmental and historic factors which are both related and unrelated to the circumstances of the injury. In reality, a wide variety of etiologic factors bear upon the long-term psychiatric outcome of any injury to the brain. These factors, as outlined by Lishman (1978), are mental constitution, premorbid personality, emotional impact of the injury, environmental factors, compensation and litigation, response to intellectual impairment, development of epilepsy, and the amount and location of brain damage. Each of these factors will be explored briefly.

Mental Constitution

Several studies have attempted to evaluate the importance of constitutional factors by comparing patients with head injuries to noninjured neurotics. Lewis (1942) studied two groups of soldiers and found sufficient similarity between them to conclude that an intractable post-concussional syndrome will occur in individuals predisposed to develop emotional symptoms. Head-injured patients who lacked obvious signs of brain damage were found by Ruesch and Bowman (1945) to resemble non-head-injured neurotics very closely, both in their subjective complaints and in their MMPI profiles.

Comparison of head-injured twins with noninjured controls (Dencker 1958, 1960) showed that the head-injured twins were inferior to their controls on several tests of intellectual function, although the defects were usually subtle. Monozygotic twin pairs were more concordant than dizygotic pairs for certain symptoms (headache, dizziness, memory impairment, sensitivity to noise), suggesting that at least some symptoms can be attributed to heritable influences rather than to a specific trauma.

Many aspects of post-traumatic disability, especially intellectual impairment, increase with age at injury. This may be due to the decreased plasticity of the nervous system with age, as well as the degenerative processes which may accompany aging. Associated mortality also rises with age. Even fear and anxiety in the aging head-injured patient tend to be more frequent, which may reflect increased difficulty in occupational and financial adjustment in this population.

Premorbid Personality

Head injury tends to make personality weaknesses more apparent as the resources of a given personality are drawn upon during recovery. It has been noted that more psychiatric disability appears after head injury in those with unstable or inadequate personalities (Adler, 1945). Although specific personality weaknesses have been identified, it is not established which traits are important, although high scores on the hysteria, depression, and hypochondriasis scales of the MMPI have been associated with long-standing neurotic complaints (Walker & Eroulei, 1969). Personality features, however, may influence the type of post-traumatic disability which emerges.

Emotional Impact of the Injury

Neurotic symptoms and the post-traumatic syndrome seem to be closely associated with emotional shock. These problems appear more commonly when the injury occurs in an emotionally loaded setting (Guttmann, 1946) and may be most frequent after minor injuries. Neurotic disabilities may be particularly common in situations where no post-traumatic amnesia has been present to obscure the memory of the accident and its consequences.

Environmental Factors

Environmental problems are often present in the head injury patient. At times, these difficulties antedate the injury and may increase or even create some of the long-term disability. Careful management of the recovery and a healthy home situation have been given great prognostic significance, especially with less severe injuries (Aita, 1948).

Compensation and Litigation

Impending, unresolved litigation can provide strong motivation for exaggeration and prolongation of disability. Sometimes, avarice will prompt a fraudulent illness. In most cases, the picture is muddled. Complex legal dealings, frustration caused by delay, conflicting advice, and cross-examination by lawyers and physicians all complicate the situation, raising anxiety and calling attention to symptoms. Disability may improve after the compensation issue is resolved.

Response to Intellectual Impairment

Direct loss of neurons produces certain symptoms attributable to brain injury, whereas compensatory activities of the remaining neurons produce other symptoms. Goldstein (1942, 1952) explored the interrelationships of these groups of symptoms and concluded the larger group of symptoms including anxiety, restlessness, and social withdrawal were secondary, falling in the latter category. The fundamental disabilities, according to Goldstein, are primarily intellectual, with disturbances in conceptual thinking foremost. The twin studies of Dencker (1958, 1960), among others, found that these features distinguished the injured from the noninjured twin. Denial of intellectual impairment may lead to a neurotic responses after head injury. Therefore, when psychiatric explanations are sought for behavior after injury, minor intellectual deficits must not be overlooked. Deficits in intellectual cognitive skills should be consistent with the focus of the brain injury, as in other lesions, although multiple or scattered foci are possible in traumas.

Development of Epilepsy

Epilepsy frequently follows head injury. In those injuries which involve penetration of the dura, it occurs in about 30% of patients, whereas in closed head injuries the rate is about 5%. As a cause of occupational difficulty, it is second only to frank intellectual deficits (Jennett, 1962). Epilepsy itself represents evidence of physiologic disruption, if not structural damage, to the brain. After closed head injury, temporal lobe epilepsy is the most common variety, as well as the form of epilepsy most often blamed for psychological disorders. Lishman (1968) found a significant relationship between the development of epilepsy and the amount of overall psychiatric disability, especially when the epilepsy was of early onset. Finally, the socially disruptive qualities of epilepsy interfere with rehabilitation, increasing self-concern and limiting self-confidence, creating fertile soil for development of further psychopathology.

Amount and Location of Brain Damage

The amount of brain damage in a living patient is difficult to assess. The techniques presently available have been unable to consistently detect small changes in brain structure and function. Findings in more severely damaged individuals have led physicians to attribute growing intellectual impairment to increasing amounts of damage, but the connections between emotional and behavioral disorders and brain damage have been tenuous. New techniques of study, such as computed tomography and noninvasive assessment of regional cerebral blood flow, combined with more modern neuropsychological evaluation, are beginning to shed new light in this area, but the results are controversial and open to many alternative interpretations.

The search for evidence of damage contributing to the psychiatric disability of patients with head injury has produced conflicting results, although the weight of evidence favors a connection. Cortical atrophy determined by pneumoencephalography has been found in head injury patients whose symptoms had been thought to be psychogenic in origin (Falk & Silfverskiold, 1954; Friedman, 1932; Haug, 1962). In contrast, changes on electroencephalography have correlated poorly with the incidence of psychological symptoms.

Alternative methods of study compared symptoms with clinical indices suggesting brain damage, such as the length of coma or the duration of post-traumatic amnesia. Using such methods, personality change and overall psychiatric disability were found to be more common in more seriously damaged head injury patients (Aita, 1948; Kremer, 1943; Steadman & Graham, 1970). Norrman and Savahn (1961), however, found only intellectual impairment to be clearly correlated with the severity of injury; other psychiatric symptoms were poorly correlated. In all these studies, there is some question as to whether the definition and characterization of brain injury or psychiatric dysfunction are adequate.

The localization of traumatic brain injuries has been studied extensively in at least a few regions of the brain in an attempt to link regional disorders and functional problems. At the outset, it is useful to remember that focal trauma may have generalized effects and the damage to particular regions may remain unnoticed.

In a study of frontal lobe injuries, Phelps (1898) concluded that there was a relationship between injury and higher cortical phenomena. Feuchtwanger (1923) compared 200 patients with frontal lobe gunshot wounds to 200 persons with head wounds in other areas. Clear-cut differences in the frontal lobe group included euphoria, facetiousness, irritability, apathy, and attention deficits. Where defects of intellect occurred, disorders of volition and emotion seemed to be at fault. These findings have been well supported by the results of iatrogenic injury in the form of frontal leukotomy. Later studies noted differences between wounds of the convex lateral surface and the orbital portions of the lobe. The former were found to affect intellectual and motor function, and the latter were associated with personality changes.

After studying the effects of injury to the basal parts of the brain (midbrain, hypothalamus, orbital frontal cortex), Kretschmer (1949, 1956) described a "basal syndrome" which has been supported in the German literature. It consists of marked sluggishness and apathy coupled with a disturbance of fundamental drives such as appetite, thirst, sleep patterns, and sexual behavior.

Little has been written of the distinctive psychiatric symptoms following injury to parts of the brain other than those noted above. Left temporoparietal damage has been associated with intellectual deficits. Temporal lobe injuries, with or without epilepsy, seem to be associated with disorders of personality. In addition, Hillbom (1960) noted a preponderance of atypical psychoses after temporal lobe injury. In the same study, parietal, occipital, and cerebellar lesions were more or less free of gross psychiatric disturbance.

In all, psychiatric disability is likely to vary with the amount and location of brain injury. The literature tends to support varying regional susceptibility producing symptoms that range from emotional and behavioral to cognitive disturbances. Previous studies were unable to localize easily the structural and functional disturbances. New techniques are now available which may enhance the understanding of the problem.

POST-TRAUMATIC PSYCHIATRIC DISORDERS

Cognitive Impairment after Head Injury

Dominant hemisphere damage will affect intellectual function more than nondominant hemisphere injury. Following closed head injury, impairment of intellect is usually global. Severe post-traumatic dementia is usually accompanied by striking neurologic findings of a paretic nature. In the most severe cases, the patient is mute and immobile for a long period on recovery from coma. In these cases, the focus of damage is likely to be in the brain stem. Somewhat less severe damage leaves the patient apathetic and slow to respond, often with gross dysarthria and incontinence. Intellectual processes are severely affected. Further recovery may bring with it emotional lability. When faced with a seemingly impossible task, the patient may exhibit sudden flushing, restlessness, and explosive anger or weeping—the so-called catastrophic reaction.

In most cases, slow improvement over time may be expected. The final level of dysfunction is often marked by mental slowing, impairment of memory, and blunting of affect. Apathy, loss of libido, and paranoid ideation may be seen. Of the cognitive functions, logical and abstract thinking will be the most severely impaired, as in other forms of dementia.

Slight degrees of impairment, however, are the most difficult to assess clinically. Complaints of forgetfulness and difficulty with concentration are difficult to evaluate, as they may be part of either deficits caused by actual damage to the brain or syndromes of psychogenic orgin. Careful and comprehensive psychometric testing can resolve the question, but follow-up and further evaluation may be necessary.

Some forms of brain injury, particularly penetrating injuries, produce focal damage; however, this is not always so. A search for focal disturbances needs to be made, not only for rehabilitative purposes, so that strengths may be identified and emphasized, but also because dementia can be suspected where there is only dysphasia or amnesia.

Selective impairment of memory may remain after all other intellectual functions have returned to normal. Presumably, this depends on damage to diencephalic or medial temporal lobe structures. Dominant hemisphere damage usually causes language impairments which can include difficulty with comprehension, reading, writing, spelling, speech production, and arithmetic. Subtle linguistic impairments such as deficits in verbal fluency, verbal learning, or verbal retention may be revealed only by special testing. Nondominant hemisphere damage tends to produce deficits in spatial functions, including visuospatial agnosia and topographic disorientation.

The finding that many traumatically brain-injured patients tend to improve significantly over time (Miller and Stern, 1965) is encouraging, and sheds doubt on the idea that the degree of brain dysfunction is due solely to the amount of tissue damaged. The improvement is certainly not the result of restoration of such tissue. It may be that the slow course of recovery reflects the time required to retrain the remaining intact portions of the brain to assume the lost functional capabilities. In addition, early dysfunction after injury may be due to affective and motivational problems, making the appearance of brain damage greater than the reality.

Personality Change after Head Injury

The term *personality change* implies a change in the patient's habits, attitudes, and behavior. This sort of change may occur following head injury and is often most disturbing for the patient's family. The alterations may be gross or subtle and may be apparent even to the patient, although he or she is uaually unaware of a change.

Personality change can be just one facet of a global dementia following head injury, with associated cognitive deficits in evidence. Or the change may be understood as part of the patient's response to a perceived deficit. In still other cases, localized damage to brain structures upon which personality attributes depend may produce changes in personality without accompanying intellectual deficits.

Intellectual impairment may bring with it simply a lessened vitality of behavior which passes transiently but which while it exists, may create problems in marriage or work. Anxiety and depression may result especially if feelings of personal inadquacy were present before injury. More severe dementia may produce slowing, withdrawal, loss of motivation, and decreased libido. Emotional blunting or instability, apathy, or euphoria may result. Childish dependency may develop, with petulance and egocentricity as features. In severe cases, the patient may lose individuality.

In terms of regional damage, frontal lobe lesions are perhaps the best known for their effect on personality. As previously described, frontal lobe lesions interfere with abstracting abilities, particularly those involving foresight, planning, and judging the results of actions. Disinhibition is often marked, particularly in regard to sexual behavior. All these qualities lead to problems in social conduct. Because of the sensitivity of frontal lobe areas to injuries due to irregularities of the skull in the orbital area, this pattern is not unusual.

Psychoses after Head Injury

In addition to the psychoses which may develop in the acute period after head injury previously described, psychotic episodes may develop following the acute event. An organic basis can be identified when these episodes occur in association with post-traumatic epilepsy, but a causal relationship is sometimes uncertain when schizophreniform, paranoid, or affective psychoses emerge, especially when a fair amount of time has passed since the trauma.

A number of explanations can be offered. Injury of brain tissue may contribute directly to psychosis, or it may precipitate the illness in a predisposed individual. Cerebral injury, by altering the patient's pattern of response to stress, may create a tendency toward a psychotic reaction. These issues are discussed more fully in later chapters on schizophrenia and affective illness. Organic factors alone, on the other hand, may have little to do with the emergence of psychosis. The injury or its repercussions may act as nonspecific stressors to precipitate psychosis, or changes in the patient's mileu produced by the injury may provide a psychogenic etiology. Coincidence alone is, of course, possible. The most plausible possibility is that all of these factors play a role, with some being more important than others in individual cases. The question is not likely to be easily resolved, since cases vary so widely as to make comparative study difficult.

Neurotic Disability after Head Injury

Of all the psychiatric sequelae of head injury, post-traumatic neuroses are the most common. In some studies, they have been reported to outnumber all the others put together (Ota, 1969). These neuroses include anxiety, mild depression, tension, conversion hysteria, obsessional neurosis, and a wide variety of somatic complaints, such as headache and dizziness. These disorders can be present in any combination and may occur in differing combinations in the same individual over time. They may be mild and transient or become severe and persistent, providing difficult diagnostic and therapeutic problems.

Psychogenic factors are clearly operative in most of these cases, often exclusively. The question which arises is whether subtle varieties of brain damage may be operating in addition to these functional syndromes. Slater's (1943) study of soldiers who were subject to breakdown in war appeared to indicate that organic factors played a role, at least in the acute situation. In chronic conditions, the contribution of organic factors seems to be minimal. For example, there seems to be little relationship between the severity of the injury and the severity of the enduring neurotic disability (Lishman, 1978). Ruesch and Bowman (1945) may have been correct when they concluded that the longer neurotic symptoms persist, the less likely they are to be the result of brain damage.

The post-traumatic syndrome is an indistinct clinical entity whose boundaries merge with those of the post-traumatic neuroses. Major symptoms include headache, dizziness, irritability, emotional lability, sensitivity to noise, anxiety, complaints of poor memory, and impaired concentration. These symptoms appear in many patients just after the trauma. In most, there are no neurologic deficits, and the acute symptoms are believed to result from nonspecific effects of the trauma. For most patients, the symptoms quickly recede and disappear. In some, however, they persist and worsen, and occasionally are joined by others such as depression, insomnia, nightmares, phobias, obsessions, fatigue, anhedonia, and impotence or frigidity. The clinical picture fits no pattern that is generally recognized as organic brain disease or a specific type of psychiatric disorder; for this reason, it is designated a syndrome. Mental status examination and psychologic testing usually reveal poor performance on formal tests, with incongruity and inconsistency on tests requiring the use of similar faculties. For example, complaints of poor memory and poor performance on tests of memory often contrast to the ability to recall symptoms, diagnostic procedures, and treatment failures in accurate detail.

Little evidence has emerged to support a neural origin for the syndrome. Symptoms do not correlate with even a generous estimate of neuronal damage. However, a psychogenic origin is not clearly supported either. Patients who develop the syndrome have not been found to have been significantly more neurotic before injury than others. No clear evidence of malingering or of secondary gain in consistently apparent (Wells & Duncan, 1980). Psychiatric treatment is rarely effective even with the cooperation of the patient.

HEMATOMAS: SUBDURAL AND EPIDURAL

Bleeding into the subdural space of the meninges, which lies between the dura mater and the arachnoid layers of the membranes surrounding the brain, may occur frequently even with relatively small head injuries. In general, the chances of such a disorder increase with the age of the patient. Subdural hematoma may occur in the presence or absence of the symptoms already discussed, often complicating the differential diagnosis. Although acute sub-dural hematomas may be handled by mechanisms within the brain, they may also be life-threatening and demand immediate surgical intervention. If they are handled successfully, there may be little residual deficit, as the effects of subdural hematoma are caused by pressure on brain tissue rather than tissue destruction. The exception occurs when the hematoma ruptures, causing symptoms similar to those of any hemorrhage depending on the exact location of the bleeding. (See Chapter 2 for more details of these syndromes.)

In more chronic cases, the blood will continue to build up in the subdural space, causing the hematoma to increase gradually in size. This process will cause the gradual development of symptoms due to increased intracranial pressure and its effects on the brain area on which the hematoma impinges. This growth may be so slow that after the accident the patient seems perfectly well, even after an extensive diagnostic workup. Thus, the patient may be seen 3–6 months later with vague psychiatric or cognitive deficits that appear to have no cause. In such cases, this disorder must be considered. This diagnosis is highly dependent on getting a good history, as the client may well forget to mention a head trauma which was considered minor at the time. This problem is especially serious in elderly patients, in whom a minor injury may produce the rupture necessary for the development of a subdural hematoma.

The cognitive effects of subdural hematomas are similar to those of slow-growing meningiomas (see Chapter 1). Typically, there is a weak area of localization surrounded by an area of more diffuse symptoms. This pattern contrasts to that of the brain laceration, for example, which produces highly focal results that are much more serious than those of the milder injuries associated with the hematoma. However, the hematoma is not benign. If allowed to grow, it can eventually result in death. Alternatively, it may spontaneously stop growing and produce a static disorder of the brain which largely resolves with time, despite the continued presence of the hematoma. As a result, patients may be seen who are found to have significant hemato-mas but little or no neuropsychological deficit. In addition, hematomas treated promptly by surgical drainage may leave only minor deficits, although more serious chronic deficits are possible. This result is not due to defects in the tests used but is characteristic of these disorders. Similar findings are also present, as noted, in many chronic head injuries.

Epidural hematomas differ from subdural hematomas in that they lie outside the dura and are usually due to a rupture of the middle meningeal artery. Chusid (1973) indicates that such disorders are difficult to diagnose; an initial brief period of impairment will be followed by a return to normal functioning. This period may last for a day or more, during which time the size of the hematoma increases and symptoms of intracranial pressure appear. The symptoms are similar to those described above.

IMPLICATIONS FOR NEUROPSYCHOLOGICAL TESTING

Like tumors and cerebrovascular disorders, head injuries produce a wide range of deficits which may potentially affect any area of the brain, either in isolation or in almost any combination. Indeed, unlike the disorders discussed in the previous chapters, head injury can cause deficits in parts of the brain remote from the locus of the most obvious deficit. Thus, one cannot search only for certain syndromes or deficits in head-injured patients, as obvious deficits may conceal still other deficits whose presence affects the patient's potential for recovery as well as his or her subjective complaints. It is important to emphasize, however, that patients or their families may be unaware of these deficits (as may other observers) and may not complain of problems. As a result, test batteries chosen only to evaluate the areas in which the patient complains of deficits are often likely to miss important aspects of the patient's performance, and the clinician may be unaware of the problems. Moreover, in comparison to tumors and cerebrovascular disorders, effects of head injuries are much more difficult to localize to specific areas of the brain by using neuroradiologic or other neurodiagnostic techniques. These measures are often normal in the case of many closed head traumas, or they may reflect only some of the areas of injury. As a consequence, medical referral sources may be unaware of the actual extent and effects of the patient's injury insofar as neuropsychological testing is concerned.

Nevertheless, one area of deficit is common to many head injuries and should be considered here. In many head traumas, as reported earlier, there is a high likelihood of injury to the frontal lobes of the brain because of the tendency of these areas to absorb many blows that may occur at the back or front of the head. Such injuries are extremely common in automobile accidents. Frontal lobe deficits are important because their effects may be so substantial as to make one think that there is diffuse, widespread damage or, alternatively, damage so subtle as to be missed completely or mistaken for another deficit. In all of these cases, the neuropsychologist has a good chance of reaching wrong conclusions about the patient.

With more severe injuries, frontal lobe damage may cause a complete loss of ability to inhibit and control behavior. Such patients, upon clearing of coma or initial disorientation, may be very emotionally labile. They may be unable to take standardized tests because of an inability to follow instructions or to deal with any level of complexity. When such patients are given standardized or other tests their performance may indicate widespread problems well beyond the frontal lobes, based on their inability to control behavior voluntarily and to inhibit subcortical impulses. The clinician should view such situations as evidence that retraining in other areas, such as perceptual skills, is not necessary or useful in these patients since there is no real deficit in elementary cortical functions.

In many cases, this type of frontal lobe disorder is time limited and related to the acute effects of the brain injury. In general, the disorder is permanent only when there is extensive and permanent damage to both frontal lobes and to many of the underlying cortical areas, particularly in the orbital frontal zone, and in connections to the limbic or reticular activitating systems. Luria (1966) describes such deficits with injuries limited to the dominant frontal lobe. In the experience of the authors, however, such patients can usually be shown to have bilateral involvement when more sophisticated measures of brain function (such as regional cerebral blood flow or positron emission tomography) are employed that were not available to Luria. When the damage is permanent and limited to the frontal lobes, the behavior of the severely injured patient usually stabilizes eventually at a level characteristic of an 8- to 10-year old child. However, this is complicated by the presence of possibly strong sexual drives, as well as the larger physical size and greater strength of the adult patient. In such cases, the patient may engage in significantly dyssocial acts not seen in the child. Such acts cannot be inhibited despite the patient's promises to avoid such behavior. These promises cannot be trusted even when the patient is judged to be sincere. As one might imagine, patients with such disorders may prove to be extremely serious management problems since this disinhibitory propensity, if present, requires constant supervision. Although such serious problems do not occur in all patients with frontal lobe injuries, the possibility must be considered when permanent destruction of tissue in the frontal lobes is known or suspected.

This syndrome can also occur when frontal lobe damage is combined with other serious injuries, including, most commonly, partial or complete paralysis resulting from involvement of the posterior frontal lobe (the primary motor areas of the brain). In such cases, the patient is prevented from expressing his or her impulses by motor or other impairments. This problem, although less dangerous to society, still represents a problem for rehabilitation training and nursing care, and consequently needs to be recognized. Such problems can become even more difficult to identify when they are combined with severe aphasic problems. The examiner must be sensitive to the presence of signs of impulsive or emotional behavior that are inconsistent with the patient's other deficits rather than dismissing occurrences of unusual behavior without considering their basis.

At the other end of the spectrum, frontal lobe deficits may be so subtle as to be missed completely or mistaken for other problems. One common deficit is a problem in simultaneous processing. Here, the role of the frontal lobes may be substantially impaired in the simultaneous processing of information from multiple sources. This processing is necessary for the ability to evaluate the behavior of others as an individual needs to react to subtle as well as obvious aspects of a given situation. This is especially important in social or other situations in which the patient must choose from a large number of options. It has relatively little effect on behaviors which are well known or overlearned, since little integration is then required. As a result, such individuals may do just as well on intelligence tests after the injury as they would have done premorbidly. Drawing tasks may be quite simple for them (unless the injury extends to other areas of the brain responsible for motor or spatial skills), as may memory tasks. With the latter, the type of memory task makes a significant difference. The frontal lobe patient will have difficulty in processing complex stimuli. As a result, he or she may have problems with initial performance but may improve over time. Here, the problem does not involve memory but rather a limited ability to process the characteristics of the stimulus and difficulty in forming plans for doing the task. In some of these cases, repetition will not improve the performance because the patient will not recognize that significant features are being missed. Performances can improve if the patient's mistakes are pointed out and attention is drawn to the missing characteristics. However, this can result in the loss of initially remembered material due to information overload.

This differential response can lead clinicians to unfortunate conclusions about the patient. For example, one patient seen by the senior author had been given a test of nonverbal memory which involved remembering a very complex figure. The patient reproduced only a few of the stimulus characteristics, leading another examiner to conclude that the patient had a nonverbal memory deficit. This was further reinforced by the patient's final normal performance on a task which required the memorization of 15 words with repeated trials. Although the initial performance was impaired, the final performance was not. This led to the conclusion that although verbal memory was intact, nonverbal memory appeared to be impaired. As a result, a great deal of money was invested in memory retraining, which eventually proved useless since the patient did not have a nonverbal memory deficit.

Frontal lobe patients may also show subtle disorders in planning skills. Such patients do well in situations which are well learned but show difficulty with new situations or with old ones which demand new approaches. Thus, the patient may perform well on intelligence tests and other similar well-learned material, but poorly on items which require new analysis or planning. This is closely related to a tendency to perseverate and to show little change in behavior even when tasks change dramatically. This inflexibility may be missed in patients whose jobs or responsibilities demand few of these skills, but it may be disastrous in those who must devise creative or new solutions. In these cases, what appears to be at most a mild deficit on neuropsychological testing may be of ultimate importance in predicting the continued employability of the patient. This dramatic effect of mild frontal lobe disorders must be considered when evaluating individuals who functioned at a high level prior to the head injury and who subsequently still function well, but at a lower level. In many of these cases, it should be noted, patients seek help not because of their own awareness of the problems but rather at the insistence of supervisors or co-workers who see a diminution in the quality of their work.

Another important deficit, but one that is often difficult to recognize, is the inability of some frontal lobe patients to evaluate the accuracy of their own responses. These patients do not notice errors, including those which are within their intellectual capacity. In other cases, such errors generally cause the patient to show concern or to attempt to correct the answers. Frontal lobe patients with a self-evaluation deficit see no errors and blithely accept their own answers even when they are severely impaired. The problem is much more difficult to identify in patients in whom other errors are minimal or nonexistent because of their otherwise high level of functioning. These patients generally are not helped by corrections from the examiner since they recognize no deficit which needs to be corrected. This deficit can be an obvious and serious problem in patients whose vocational or personal responsibilities demand constant self-evaluation. It should be noted that this deficit is often interpreted psychiatrically as "denial" when a better description would be "lack of awareness."

Another type of deficit that is commonly seen in head injuries is memory disorder. These disorders can range from anterograde amnesia, in which events after the accident are forgotten, to retrograde amnesia, in which events prior to the accident, are forgotten. Amnesia may include all material or only certain types; it may involve one of the basic sensory modalities or all of them; it may or may not be lessened through cueing or rehearsal; or it may show a temporal gradient, with the memory of earlier events being more or less impaired. The form of the memory disorder will depend on the nature, extent, and development of the injury and will vary widely across patients. These memory disorders may be seen in isolation, in various patterns of memory problems, or in conjunction with cognitive or sensorimotor deficits. A detailed memory examination is often warranted because of the localizing value of such problems (Butters & Cermak, 1980) and their important disruptive effects in the personal life of the patient.

All of these deficits can occur in patients with tumors, cerebrovascular disorders, or other neurologic diseases discussed in previous and subsequent chapters. Thus, they are in no way diagnostic of head trauma but rather are sets of deficits that are seen commonly with this condition because of the vulnerability of the frontal lobes to head trauma and the increased likelihood of bilateral frontal injuries in these cases as opposed to tumors or cerebrovascular problems.

Several other common findings in head trauma should be noted. First, in head trauma without vascular complication, motor deficits are much rarer than in middle cerebral artery stroke. The classic middle cerebral artery pattern described in the last chapter is rarely seen in head trauma unless a cerebrovascular accident is caused by the tearing of cerebral blood vessels or the effects of head penetration. In general, head trauma patients will show faster recovery in motor and sensory areas than in the higher cognitive skills represented by the frontal lobes and other areas. Early disorientation and confusion will eventually clear in many cases, so that early testing of these patients may overestimate the degree of long-term pathology. In general, most neuropsychological recovery will take place in 6 months to 2 years after the patient recovers from coma or other acute effects such as hydrocephalus. The existence of hydrocephalus will generally cause serious motor and sensory problems, although these are not likely to be bilateral.

Another problem in evaluation of the head trauma patient is the effect of noncortical injuries, including impairment to the subcortical centers of the brain, impairment in the functioning of the spinal cord, and impairment outside the central nervous system in the peripheral nervous system or the musculoskeletal system. Obviously, a patient with an uncomplicated serious neck injury may have trouble speaking, and a patient with a cervical spinal injury may do poorly on many sensorimotor tests without necessarily showing evidence of brain damage. Such injuries may also have a more indirect effect: severe pain due to an injury may make concentration and attention variable, at best, and cause unexplained deficits. Injuries to the liver or kidneys may cause a buildup of toxins in the bloodstream which can cause acute impairment of brain function. These and other injuries may simply weaken the patient physically and cause impairment on tests that require long sessions because of the buildup of fatigue or the lessening of motivation. The clinician should avoid testing a patient over several hours on a single day even if the patient appears to be cooperating. In our experience, patterns of deficits showing increasing impairment over a session may often be due to these effects.

There is no rule that can be used to decide which deficits are related to cortical or subcortical functioning and which are related to spinal or peripheral injuries since there are many possible combinations. When working with these patients, however, one must be aware of the patient's other problems and their possible effects before reaching conclusions about the state of brain function. Without this information, the clinician is liable to make errors about brain function as well as the patient's potential for recovery or various vocational opportunities. These errors are difficult to detect at the time they are made. It is consequently very easy to make these errors repeatedly, if the clinician is not sensitive to these possibilities and does not conduct long-term follow-up of cases.

Chapter 4

Intracranial Infections

With Benjamin Graber

Intracranial infectons are usually unimportant in the differential diagnosis of neuropsychological disorders, and except for enduring mental sequelae, the assistance of the psychologist is rarely requested for their diagnosis and treatment. Therefore, this chapter will deal in detail only with those major problems which produce lasting sequelae that may result in later referrals. Neurosyphilis and encephalitis fall into this category.

SYPHILIS OF THE CENTRAL NERVOUS SYSTEM

Despite the rapid decline in the number of syphilitic infections of the nervous system since the introduction of penicillin, the disease continues to be perhaps the most important intracranial infection in psychiatric practice. The phenomenal success of treatment brings risks, since the growing rarity of the disease increases the chance of overlooking it. The classic presentation of general paresis is rare at present, and syphilis of the central nervous system can present with nearly any type of psychiatric complaint.

Traditionally, the effects of syphilis are categorized into four stages: the primary stage, with the appearance of the local lesion at the site of inoculation; the secondary stage, with early generalized lesions, chiefly manifested as a variety of skin rashes which appear 4–8 weeks after infection; the tertiary stage, with the appearance of late destructive lesions such as gummatous ulcers, glossitis, and bone changes; and the quaternary stage, parenchymatous changes in the central nervous system leading to tabes dorsalis and general paresis. Other central nervous system disorders can be produced by meningo-vascular syphilis, which can occur in the secondary or tertiary stages.

Subacute and Chronic Meningovascular Syphilis

The clinical syndromes grouped under the heading of subacute and chronic meningovascular syphilis are often best understood in terms of their underlying pathology. These disorders usually appear within 1–5 years of the first infection, although they may occur from a few months to 30 years after inoculation.

Pathology

Changes occur in the meninges and the cerebral vasculature. In the men-inges, there is a diffuse inflammatory exudative process. This process is most noticeable at the base of the brain, producing cranial nerve lesions or obstructive hydrocephalus. Less frequently, the changes localize over the convex surface of the brain. Similar processes may occur within the brain by spreading along perivascular channels.

Vascular involvement is part of the meningeal pathology and may be separate. The vessels at the base of the brain are most severely affected, first the small and then the larger branches of the circle of Willis. This disorder may lead to a vascular thrombosis, which in turn can cause the stroke symptoms noted earlier.

Clinical Picture

Subacute forms of meningitis may progress rapidly once begun, although the chronic forms are frequently insidious in development and intermittent in progression. Early generalized symptoms consist of intermittent headache, lethargy, and malaise. The patient is often slow and forgetful, with poor concentration and faulty judgment. Emotional instability is common. Cogni-tive impairment may progress to dementia, sometimes with fleeting delusions or episodes of overactivity. In other cases, there may be periods of clouded consciousness interrupted by intervals of relative normalcy. The patient may retain enough insight into his impairments so that his anxiety leads to a misdiagnosis of neurosis. Vague complaints and fleeting disabilities may damp-en the suspicion of an organic disorder for some time.

Focal evidence of basal meningitis consists mainly of cranial nerve dysfunction. Papilledema, optic nerve atrophy, and visual field defects caused by chiasmatic lesions also occur. Hypothalamic involvement may produce polyuria, obesity, and somnolence. "Pseudobulbar palsy" may emerge with bilateral spasticity and marked emotional lability.

Tabes Dorsalis

Tabes dorsalis is seen in about 20% of cases of general paresis (which will be discussed subsequently), although it can occur alone. Its characteristic signs and symptoms may alert the clinician to the latter disorder. The onset typically occurs 8–12 years after the primary infection, with a range of 3–20 years. Men are affected much more frequently than women. The pathology of the disorder involves degeneration of the ascending fibers from the dorsal root ganglia, resulting in atrophy of the dorsal roots and shrinkage and demyelination in the posterior columns of the spinal cord.

Characteristic symptoms are pain, paresthesias, and marked disturbance in gait. All of these symptoms tend to develop insidiously. The shooting pains of tabes are extraordinarily severe and localized to the legs although cases of visceral pain can also occur. Attacks last for only a few seconds. Paresthesias are usually confined to the legs and feet; the skin may be hyperesthetic to touch, or the patient may feel as if he or she is walking on wool. The ataxia is sensory in origin, due to a loss in proprioceptive input. The patient walks with a wide-based, high-stepping gait and has greater difficulty in the dark when visual cues are reduced (Lishman, 1978). Without treatment, the disease is slowly progressive. General paresis may appear after many years, or psychotic illnesses of a different nature may develop.

General Paresis

General paresis became the first psychiatric disorder for which a clear-cut etiology could be determined. Prior to the demonstration of *Treponema pallidum* within the brain, a syphilitic source for the illness remained in dispute, and hereditary taint, alcohol consumption, mental strain, and sexual excess were championed by some as the source of insanity.

Pathology

General paresis is the only syphilitic disease in which spirochetes can be seen in the tissues of the brain; the lesions of this disorder are thought to be the direct result of their presence and the body's response to it. Macroscopically, the dural membrane is thickened, and the pia is firmly adherent to the underlying cortex. The brain itself is atrophied, with widened sulci and enlarged ventricles.

Microscopically, there are inflammatory lesions throughout the cortex made up of dense collections of lymphocytes and plasma cells due to spirochetal irritation. Equally notable are degenerative changes, with cortical thinning and loss of neurons especially in the frontal and parietal regions. Typically, disorganization is so severe that the normal cytoarchitecture is completely unrecognizable. The spinal cord may show secondary pyramidal tract degeneration, or a combination of paretic and tabetic pathology may be seen with deterioration of the posterior columns.

Clinical Features

The disorder appears in men about three times as often as in women. The age of onset usually falls between 30 and 50, with a wide range on either side. The time from infection is difficult to establish, but it is uaually stated as 5–25 years, with an average of 10–15 years.

Presentation

Retrospectively, minor symptoms such as headache, insomnia, and lethargy are often found to have been present several months before more definite signs appear. Often the patient's relatives report a gradual change of temperament such as moodiness, apathy, temper outbursts, or emotional lability. Frontal lobe involvement may be suggested by coarsening of behavior and egocentricity.

The first cognitive change is usually episodic forgetfulness followed by defective concentration, reduction of interests, and mental and physical slowing typical of dementia. Difficulties with calculation, speech, and writing may occur early. Insight is also impaired from an early stage.

In nearly 50% of cases the presentation is abrupt, with some striking incident bringing the patient to medical attention (Dewhurst, 1969). Then it is found that the dementing process had been present but unsuspected for some time. It may be a lapse of social conduct which reveals the problem or some foolish, eccentric, or reckless behavior. Alternatively, amnesia, an epileptic seizure, or an acute delirium may provoke a medical investigation.

In recent years, patients have begun to seek medical help on their own initiative and at an earlier stage of illness than in the past (Froshaug & Ytrehus, 1956). Therefore, in these cases there may be little in the patient's outward behavior to suggest a dementing illness, which makes careful evaluation of cognitive functioning even more important.

The course of the disease is readily typified by several terms which group symptoms into categories. The *grandiose* form of the disease, which had been the most commonly described type of general paresis, was very impressive, possibly leading to its major role in the literature. It now comprises 18% of cases (Dewhurst, 1969). The hallmark of this type is the patient's bombastic and expansive demeanor, with delusions of power, wealth, and social position. The patient's mood is euphoric, good-humored, and often condescending. However, the underlying dementia usually adds a certain shallowness and naiveté to the whole display.

A form of *simple dementia* now seems to be the more common type (20% in Dewhurst's series). It consists of a generalized dementia with memory impairment, slowed and difficult thinking, and early loss of insight. The affect is shallow, with a mild and benign euphoria commonly seen.

The *depressive* form also seems to have increased in incidence over the years, with Dewhurst (1969) finding a frequency of 27%. In this type, the patient presents with classic depressive symptoms. If dementia has become advanced, the affect may be shallow, but on occasion no such distinction is present and differentiation may be difficult.

In about 20% of patients, general paresis and tabes dorsalis are combined. Dementia then occurs along with tabetic symptoms (Dewhurst, 1969). Mental symptoms may be rather mild.

Untreated Course

Without treatment, the dementia increases steadily, along with severe physical deterioration. Incontinence of urine often appears early, at first due to inattention. Delusions and other florid features gradually fade away and the patient typically becomes quiet, apathetic, and incoherent (Storm-Mathiesen, 1969). Spastic paralysis and ataxia increase until the patient becomes feeble and bedridden. Epileptic attacks occur in about half the cases. Before the advent of effective therapy, death usually occurred within 4–5 years of presentation, with many patients dying as a result of their prolonged confinement to bed with intercurrent infection or status epilepticus.

Outcome with Treatment

The outcome of treatment has been described in a study by Han and colleagues (1959). Eighty percent of patients with early or mild disease obtained a clinical remission and were able to return to work. In this group, paresis led to very few deaths. The prognosis regarding a return to work and the community was found to be directly related to the duration of the illness at the time of treatment.

The quality of recovery extended to a wide range of organic mental symptoms. Five years after treatment, more than half of the patients who had had disorientation, convulsions, tremors, incontinence, euphoria, and depression had experienced a resolution of symptoms. The overall death rate, at 31% remained about four times higher than that of nonsyphilitics of the same age, with a 9% rate directly attributable to general paresis.

ENCEPHALITIS

Encephalitis is the term applied to inflammatory disease of the brain itself. Although general paresis involves active inflammation of cerebral tissue, and although an encephalitic process occasionally results from septicemia or direct extension of an abscess or bacterial meningitis, encephalitis in the strict sense refers to a viral or presumed viral infection of the brain.

In some instances of viral infection, it is unkown whether the virus itself enters the central nervous system or whether the central nervous system manifestations represent a hypersensitivity or autoimmune reaction to a viral infection at another site in the body. The latter may be the most likely mechanism in postinfectious encephalitides of childhood.

Recently, viruses and viruslike agents have been implicated in a variety of subacute and chronic degenerative brain diseases. Two of these disorders, subacute sclerosing panencephalitis and Creutzfeldt-Jakob disease, will be discussed below.

Acute Encephalitis

The clinical picture in most types of acute encephalitis is that of a rapidly developing illness with headache, prostration, and indications of central nervous system involvement. The dominant feature of cerebral involvement is disturbance of consciousness which can range from slight somnolence to coma. Delirium is sometimes a prominent feature. Epileptic seizures are common, particularly in children, and may be the presenting feature of the disease. Focal neurologic signs vary greatly with the site of major inflammatory involvement and may be slight or absent.

The course can vary widely from one patient to another and from bout to bout in a single patient, without regard to the causative organism. Profound coma may end abruptly after days or weeks, or relapse may interfere with what had been steady improvement. After the acute phase, there is usually a long period of physical and mental recuperation which may take months. On occasion, the acute phase is followed by a prolonged phase of disturbed behavior that outlasts all evidence of active infection and resembles a psychogenic reaction (Lishman, 1978).

Residua may range from none at all, through trivial neurologic signs, to profound brain damage. Organically mediated personality change may result. Young children are at high risk. Greenbaum and Lurie (1948) described 78 children referred for personality difficulties or behavior disorders related to previous encephalitis. The psychiatric sequelae were worsened with decreasing age at the onset of illness. There was characteristically a lack of inhibition, restlessness, impulsiveness, and distractability. Although the intellect was usually well preserved, the prognosis for social adjustment remained poor. This may reflect disorder of the frontal lobes, which is not easily recognized in children.

The subacute and chronic encephalitides tend to create more psychiatric findings and sequelae than do the majority of the acute varieties of encephalitis. Therefore, the remainder of this chapter will concern these entities.

Subacute Sclerosing Panencephalitis

For many years certain rare diseases have been suspected, on the basis of pathologic findings, to result from subacute infection of the brain. Recently, the measles virus has been incriminated as a major cause of these disorders (Connolly, Allew, Hurwitz, & Miller, 1967). These diseases often present with features of dementia, but some may initially suggest the possibility of functional psychiatric illness. Until just a few years ago, such disorders were believed to be uniformly fatal, with a progressive course lasting for weeks or months, but occasional reports of arrest or even improvement over time have emerged.

Pathology

Greenfield (1963) has described the usual pathologic findings. The brain may be grossly normal or firm and shrunken with focal necrosis. Microscopically, there is evidence of subacute inflammation, usually in both white and gray matter. There is perivascular infiltration with lymphocytes and plasma cells, and proliferation of astrocytes and microglia. In the gray matter, neuronal degeneration with intranuclear inclusions is seen; in the white matter, areas of demyelination with fibrous gliosis appear. Much variation is seen from case to case. However, rapidly progressive cases are more likely to show intranuclear inclusions, whereas chronic cases show greater demyelination. The changes may be focal, affecting primarily the parieto-occipital and temporal lobes or the hippocampus and subcortical nuclei.

Clinical Features

Most patients are children or adolescents, although a few are middle-aged. Classically, the affected child shows insidious intellectual deterioration and begins to fail at school, becoming forgetful and inattentive. Other early symptoms include nocturnal delirium, lethargy, and uncontrollable behavior. These manifestations may occur alone for several months, but generally neurologic signs develop early. The patient frequently develops marked involuntary movements including myoclonic jerks of the face, fingers, and limbs, athetosis, or rapid torsion spasms of the trunk which lead to sudden stumbling. The limbs develop bilateral extrapyramidal rigidity or spasticity. Epileptic seizures are common and aphasia, apraxia, or akinetic mutism may appear (Lishman, 1978).

The first descriptions of the disorder seemed to indicate a hopeless prognosis, with rapidly progressive dementia over 6 weeks to 6 months and death following a period of coma. The prognosis may be somewhat better as cases of arrest and partial remission have begun to appear. Kennedy (1968) reported that 2 of 5 children he studied with the disease achieved a remission and that one improved sufficiently to return to school.

Differential Diagnosis

Difficulties with diagnosis are particularly likely in the prodromal period. In children a behavior disorder or autism may be suggested. In adults functional psychiatric illness may be simulated. Careful attention must be given to minor neurologic abnormalities, sudden jerks, and evidence of nocturnal delirium. These disorders may also be confused with presenile dementia in adults, multiple sclerosis, and other types of encephalitis.

Creutzfeld-Jakob Disease

Creutzfeldt-Jakob disease, a rare disorder, consists of a dementing illness which runs a very rapid course, that is usually accompanied by a number of marked neurologic symptoms and signs. In addition to the cerebral cortex, the neuropathology tends to involve structures such as the subcortical nuclei, cerebellum, brain stem, and spinal cord.

Etiology

One of the greatest stimuli to interest in this disease has come from the finding that a transmissible agent may be involved, at least in certain cases (Gibbs, Gajdusek, Asher, Alpers, Beck, Daniels, & Matthews, 1968). A homogenate of biopsy tissue from a patient was inoculated intracerebrally and intravenously into a chimpanzee, and the animal developed a fatal neurologic disease 13 months later. The clinical and neuropathologic pictures were similar in both man and animal, seemingly representing the same disease (Beck, Daniel, Gajdusek, & Gibbs), 1969a; Beck, Daniel, Matthews, Stevens, Alpers, Asher, Gajdusek, & Gibbs, 1969b).

Clinical Features

Men and women seem to be affected with equal frequency. The onset typically occurs in the fourth or fifth decade, although varied adult ages have been reported. The clinical features, although variable, have been reviewed by May (1968).

A prodromal stage, lasting for weeks or months, is often described. Complaints of fatigue, insomnia, anxiety, and depression are noted during this period, along with the gradual emergence of mental slowness and increased unpredictability of behavior. The mood may be somewhat elevated, with loquacity and inappropriate laughter. Even at this early stage, there may be signs of impaired memory and concentration, weakness of the limbs, and unsteady gait. Often there is a paucity of objective findings and a functional psychiatric disorder is blamed, especially when the early symptoms wax and wane.

Soon afterward, intellectual deficits or neurologic findings begin to emerge. The latter may involve motor function, speech, or vision. Depending on the regions of the brain affected, there may be cerebellar ataxia, spasticity of limbs with progressive paralysis, extrapyramidal rigidity, tremor, or choreoathetosis. Anterior horn cell involvement may lead to muscular fibrillation and atrophy. Speech disturbances frequently occur, with dysphasia and dysarthria as well as parietal lobe symptoms such as finger agnosia, dyscalculia, and right–left disorientation. Vision may be severely affected, with rapidly progressive cortical blindness. Apart from this, sensory deficits are rare. Myoclonic jerks are frequent, and seizures may occur.

Intellectual deterioration follows or accompanies the neurologic defects and evolves quickly. An acute organic brain syndrome may be initially present, with clouding of consciousness or frank delirium. Auditory hallucinations and delusions may be severe. Ultimately, a profound dementia appears accompanied by marked spastic paralysis and frequently by a decorticate or decerebrate posture. Death often occurs with the patient in a badly emaciated condition.

Course of the Disease

The course tends to be much more rapid than that of the majority of primary dementias. The majority of patients are dead within 9 months and all but a few within 2 years. A period of deepening coma lasting for several weeks usually precedes death.

Pathologic Findings

The brain frequently does not appear clearly abnormal on gross inspection, although it may be slightly atrophied. Microscopic examination reveals much variability but essentially shows neuronal degeneration, astrocytic proliferation, and usually a spongy appearance of the gray matter. In some cases, the sponginess may be seen by the unaided eye.

The areas of major involvement vary, explaining the wide range of clinical presentations. The cortex is almost always involved, frequently with relative sparing of the parietal and occipital lobes. The hippocampus may also escape. In different cases there may be marked involvement of the corpus striatum, thalamus, cerebellum, substantia nigra, brain stem, and spinal cord. The corticospinal tracts and extrapyramidal pathways have often greatly deteriorated.

There are usually no senile plaques or neurofibrillary tangles as in Alzheimer's disease, no circumscribed severe atrophy as in Pick's disease, and no signs of inflammation. The cerebral vessels are usually healthy in appearance (Lishman, 1978).

Abscess Formation

Intracranial abscesses may arise from a large number of sources. These may include extradural abscesses which begin as infections of the skull itself and which may not spread beyond the dura mater (the outer layer of the meninges). In subdural abscess, the infection penetrates the dura and the pus of the abscess lies between the brain and the dura layer in the subarachnoid space. Intracerebral abscesses involve infection within the brain itself, and may be single or multiple. These may represent a spread from an abscess outside the brain, as described above, or they may be the result of infections carried from the bloodstream or other sources into the brain.

Intracerebral abscesses go through three stages. In the first stage, there is an acute inflammation of the brain (encephalitis), with no pus formation present. In the second stage, pus begins to form but the abscess is not well defined. In the third stage, a wall is formed which delineates the size of the abscess as well as its location. However, in a patient who is not able to resist the infection successfully, the wall may never form and the infection will spread throughout the brain, leading to death.

The most common etiologies of the abscess are infections of the ear, followed by infections in other areas of the body which enter the bloodstream. Infections of the heart can lead to abscesses, as can simple boils or even skin infections. Lung infections can also lead to abscess in the brain. Infections may arise secondary to open head injury as well. In these cases, the individual may begin with relatively slight or no neuropsychological symptoms and later progress to fairly severe impairment.

Abscesses affect brain functions in several ways. They can cause general symptoms of infection, including headache, lethargy, concentration problems, and general physical fatigue, all of which can affect the individual's psychological performance. The abscess may cause increased intracranial pressure, which will have a diffuse effect similar to that described in the chapter on tumors. Finally, focal symptoms may arise at the location of the abscess. These will differ depending on their exact location.

Headache and fever are common symptoms associated with cerebral abscess. Symptoms may progress as far as stupor or coma, and epilepsy may be seen. Symptoms associated with the mass effects of tumors are generally less significant in abscesses. Thrombosis of cerebral arteries may occur with the development of appropriate symptoms. (See Chapter 2). Cerebellar signs may develop when the abscess is located in the cerebellum. These symptoms can include nystagmus, hypotonia, impairment of bilateral coordination, and cranial nerve symptoms.

IMPLICATIONS FOR NEUROPSYCHOLOGICAL TESTING

Like the disorders described in previous chapters, intracranial infections may cause a wide range of neuropsychological deficits. In general, however, higher cortical functions that are mediated by the tertiary areas of the brain are most impaired, primarily the frontal lobes, as discussed in the last chapter, and the tertiary parietal areas, which are primarily responsible for integrative academic, language, and spatial skills (see Golden, 1981a, for a further discussion of these areas). The deficits generally involve those skills which are not overlearned. Although a patient may not show deficits in the overlearned skills represented by achievement or intelligence tests, he or she may still have many of the subtle deficits that are characteristic of the frontal lobe patient or deficits in such intellectual areas as interpretation of complex grammar and syntax. As with head trauma, memory disorders are also highly likely, as are neurologic symptoms suggestive of subcortical dysfunction. Since many tests do not identify these functions, it is easy to mistake the lack of findings for the presence of no deficit.

It is appropriate to discuss this important point in detail at this level. In these disorders, in which patients in the acute phase may be very severely impaired and even in coma, they will frequently show impressive improvements as the acute disorder is brought under control. In light of this improvement, which may be seen in other diseases with acute phases that do not necessarily destroy brain tissue but may only temporarily impair function, it is natural for the physician, the family, and the neuropsychologist to want to believe that the patient is completely well, especially if computed tomography scans, electroencephalograms, and other similar neurologic devices reveal normal findings. The problem with these normal findings, as well as those on the neuropsychological measures, is that they do not rule out the presence of a disorder, only that of a detectable disorder on the tests given. As a result, especially in disorders which may be subtle, one must be cautious about interpreting test data and about making statements to the patient and the family until the patient has readjusted to normal life without difficulty. In the experience of the authors, very subtle deficits in patients with these diseases have later led to significant problems. As expected, these problems are most pronounced in patients with a high level of functioning before the onset of the disease. This is not a problem when deficits are obvious or extensive.

Another problem is that skills, which are originally carefully practiced products of these higher brain centers, over time become learned and automatic. In these cases, the behaviour may remain relatively intact even when tertiary zone injuries have occurred. Intact areas of cognitive function must therefore be carefully probed to discriminate between intact skills and overlearned responses. For example, in the case of reading, reading of common words is not sufficient. The patient should also demonstrate intact basic reading skills by reading nonsense syllables or rare words which are not likely to be overlearned.

A final common set of deficits seen in these disorders, and indeed in most of the disorders discussed in this book, are memory problems. These involve the same possibilities outlined in the previous chapter. It can be difficult to identify a specific disorder by the memory pattern, since the same pattern can be seen in a wide variety of injuries which affect similar areas of the brain. However, memory problems can be used to rule out certain disorders. For example, patients with frontal lobe disorders due to encephalitis will show little current memory impairment but may demonstrate extensive retrograde amnesia, usually forgetting events in the remote past and those which occurred more recently before the onset of the disease. Amnesic patterns of other common diseases which have been identified clinically will be reviewed in the appropriate chapters.

In severe cases, intracranial infections may cause diffuse brain damage anywhere in the cortex or the subcortical areas. The deficits may also be due to bilateral impairment of frontal lobe function, which Luria (1966) suggests can mimic a diffuse brain disorder. Fortunately, these cases are generally easy to recognize. The referral question is not whether the patient is impaired but rather what the patient can do. Often, very simple basic tests, as well as great patience in eliciting the individual's best performance, are necessary. In some cases, the impairment is so severe that standardized test procedures are impossible and the clinician must rely on observation.

With the result of the impairment is very much like that of fast-growing tumors; indeed, it can be difficult to discriminate between the two on the basis of neuropsychological test results. The patient with brain abscess generally has a history of an infectious disorder, however, and often is younger than the typical tumor patient, although abscesses are possible at all ages. In these cases, the test results suggest an area of highly focal impairment surrounded by an area of lesser impairment, although secondary disruption of brain processes such as by hydrocephalus can cause more diffuse effects similar to those seen in fast-growing tumors. Since abscesses frequently destroy areas of brain tissue as well, they are likely to leave significant long-term brain injuries. The deficits depend on the brain localization. Abscesses may also cause more generalized symptoms of increased brain pressure or may push against the brain itself, similar to the actions of extrinsic tumors. (The comments in Chapter 1 on tumors are appropriate here as well.)

Another important area to consider is the effect of these diseases on the brain functioning of children. Infectious disorders and head trauma are the major causes of acquired brain injury in children, and these cases must be considered separately from those of adults. Since the area of child neuropsychology is not within the scope of this book, the reader is referred to Golden (1981) for an introduction and further references. For the purpose of this discussion, the important aspect of child neuropsychology is the observation that the child's brain has not fully developed until middle or late adolescence. As a result, injuries to certain areas may show little or no effect on the child at the time of the injury or disease, but may become evident many years after the onset of the initial lesion. The basic stages of this development and their implications will be discussed.

The initial development of the brain, involving the basic primary projection areas of the cerebral cortex (those areas responsible for the reception of basic sensory information or the transmission of motor impulses) and the secondary areas (those areas responsible for organization of perceptual information within a given modality, as well as the organization and smoothness of motor movements), takes place during the first 5 years or so of a child's life. In general, most learning that takes place during this time involves the secondary areas, as well as their influence on subcortical areas of the brain. Children who receive injuries to these areas will generally show deficits similar to those seen in adults with comparable injuries. The effects of these injuries, however, become much more dramatic over time, since the child has not developed a full overlearned repertoire of behavior, as has the adult. In some cases, however, the effects of the injury will be somewhat lessened by the ability of the child's brain to transfer functions to other brain areas. The mechanism involved in this process is not clear. It appears to take place more effectively in younger children and in children with unilateral cortical injuries. However, there is wide variation within children, and predictions of such occurences are tenuous at best. Such children will show initial deficits as a rule, although the impairment may be expressed only as a cessation of new learning. In these cases, the child will show a developmental lag over time as other children develop and the age-appropriate expectations for the child are raised. Clearly, serial testing is necessary for children with suspected injuries to these cerebral areas, at least through age 8. If no secondary deficits have appeared by that time (most appear by age 5), it is unlikely that secondary or primary deficits will later emerge.

Injuries to the tertiary areas of the brain offer additional problems. The tertiary parietal area, which is responsible for most academic skills and advanced linguistic and spatial abilities, generally develops after age 5, although its earlier development is possible. Thus, a tertiary injury which does not involve the secondary or primary areas may not show up clearly until ages 8–10, and may become serious only in the fourth or fifth grades. For example, one tertiary zone-injured child who was seen by the senior author had received a confirmed injury at age 3 (due to a rare tumor) but did not show problems relative to other children until age 7; by age 11, the child was performing at a significantly impaired level, showing severe learning disabilities. Evaluation of the child at age 3 as normal because no deficits were seen would have been inaccurate as well as misleading to the parents and school officials. Such errors can be especially costly when legal suits are involved, as often happens in cases of head injury. As a consequence, evaluation of the child with tertiary frontal or tertiary parietal injury should continue through the elementary school years before a conclusion of no deficit is reached.

The final area of the brain to develop is the tertiary frontal area. This area generally develops in adolescence, with completion as late as age 17 or 18 in some children. Since the tertiary frontal area does not play a large role in behavior until adolescence, such injuries may be silent until age 14 or 15. For example, one such case involved a 10-year-old with an abscess localized quite clearly by computed tomography scan in the left tertiary frontal area. The child was given a full range of frontal lobe tests, as well as other assessment procedures, and no deficit could be documented. The child is currently scheduled for yearly reevaluations, and the parents have been apprised of the possible developmental problems which can occur.

In another case, a child with severe tertiary frontal injury as a result of head trauma at age 3 was pronounced cured because of the lack of symptoms. However, between ages 12 and 15, the child began to show many of the deficits characteristic of frontal lobe injuries; by age 20, a severe frontal lobe injury was evident. Unfortunately, the child at age 6 had been denied any compensation in a court case because of the testimony by a psychologist and neurologist that the child would have no problems due to the accident.

Thus, we must put off conclusions about tertiary frontal area injuries until at least mid-adolescence. With all of these deficits which may later develop, we must be sensitive to the need for regular reassessment over time, as well as the limitations of our predictive powers. Some have speculated that brain-damaged children may be at greater risk if the trauma involves brain areas which have not yet developed, since it is probably easier to disrupt development than it is to injure an already developed area. Some functions of the area may be spared, and other functional systems that do not involve the injured area as a component may help to compensate for the deficit. Clearly, children with significant neurologic disorders must be regarded as being at high risk for the development of these problems and should be followed as well as possible. In addition, anyone who evaluates children with these disorders should be familiar with what is known about brain development and the limitations regarding the prediction of neuropsychological deficits in children. Under no circumstances should the individual trained to assess adults assume that the techniques and interpretive strategies used with adults can be employed equally well with children.

Another important error made in these cases is to assume that the skills used by the child to do a given task are the same skills used by the adult. In general, because of the differences in child and adult brains, the child uses significantly different approaches to tasks, although this may be difficult to see when the child is simply observed in a standard test situation. For example, it is questionable whether the skills the child used to abstract similarities at age 6 are the same skills used at age 15. As a consequence, attempts to make predictions across this age span (and, more importantly, across neurologic stages of development) are subject to error in the case of a child whose development will not be normal because of brain injury or dysfunction.

In conclusion, intracranial infection and the subsequent brain abscess which can develop result primarily in injuries to the higher cortical centers of the brain and to the subcortical areas which deal primarily with memory functions. However, all degrees of impairment may be caused by abscesses, which will often result in severe, highly focal deficits throughout the brain. Infections may also cause the severe impairment characteristic of dementias, as discussed in the following chapters. In dealing with these and other disorders in children, care must be taken to interpret test results in the developmental context.

Chapter 5
Epilepsy

Epilepsy is the most common neurologic disease. Its importance to psychologists is predicated on the high incidence of behavioral and emotional disorders among individuals with the disease. A significant number of epileptic patients are hospitalized on psychiatric inpatient units. It is important for a clinician to be aware of the behavioral and psychologic problems of epileptic patients, although treatment of these problems may not be emphasized. In a review of the epidemiologic studies dealing with the incidence of psychiatric disturbances in epilepsy, Pond (1974) reported that at least 30% of all epileptics (children and adults) have psychiatric problems. Rodin (1977) reported an even higher figure of 50%. Neither of these studies showed any consistency in the type of psychiatric disturbance across the entire spectrum of disease, as this disturbance varies with the type of epilepsy. For example, in epilepsy originating in the temporal lobe, psychosis is more frequent. Epilepsy also must occasionally be differentiated from certain other disorders which simulate it.

DEFINITION

It is difficult to offer a completely satisfactory definition of epilepsy. The term *seizure disorder* is often applied to the syndrome. *Epilepsy* generally connotes a tendency to have recurring seizures together with a permanent or periodic cerebral dysfunction.

In 1870, Hughlings Jackson defined epilepsy as a group of disorders with paroxysmal and excessive neuronal discharge that caused a sudden disturbance in neurologic function. Brain (1955) defined epilepsy as "a paroxysmal and transitory disturbance of the functions of the brain which develops suddenly, ceases spontaneously, and exhibits a conspicuous tendency to recurrence." Alter, Masland, Kurtzke, and Reed (1972) proposed the definition of a sudden change in intellectual, sensory, motor, autonomic, or emotional activity, limited in length (usually under one hour) and presumably associated with neuronal overactivity.

Many attempts have been made to classify the different epilepsies, but no classification is widely accepted. Even the International Classification of Epileptic Seizures (Gastaut, 1970; Merlis, 1970) has not been accepted or endorsed uniformly by workers in the field. For purposes of discussion, a modification of the International Classification will be used (Wells & Duncan, 1980), which is illustrated in Table 5–1.

GENERALIZED SEIZURES

Seizures for which there is no evidence to suggest a focal origin are termed *generalized*. In these seizures there is no prodrome or aura to indicate abnormal function of any particular portion of the brain, and there is no focal electroencephalographic abnormality. The electroencephalogram (EEG) records a seizure pattern developing in a generalized distribution, appearing in leads from both hemispheres at the same time. It is not known whether the abnormal voltage pattern appears in both hemispheres after projection from a deeper midline source or if there is a humoral or systemic abnormality that causes simultaneous discharge, but the former theory is currently in favor.

Tonic/Clonic Seizures (Grand Mal)

The most familiar type of generalized seizure is the grand mal, which can serve as a model in describing the components of other types of seizures. Although not all elements are found in every seizure, a grand mal seizure may contain the following: prodrome, aura, ictus, and postictal state. For several hours, or in some instances several days, the epileptic may feel vague anxiety or discomfort which is usually sufficiently similar to past episodes to indicate an impending seizure. This period is called the *prodrome* and is incompletely understood. Although its precise cause is not known, the prodrome is not thought to result from abnormally increased electrical activity in the brain. The *aura* is the period at the beginning of the paroxysmal discharge before consciousness is lost. In this state, the patient may describe an unusual sensation of numbness rising from the upper abdomen, a sensation of faintness, or turning of the head and eyes. The aura is thought to be the consciously remembered portion of the seizure and should therefore be considered a part of the seizure. Specific characteristics of the aura are most likely related to the anatomic site of origin of the seizure, suggesting a possibly focal origin. Only about half of the patients with grand mal seizures, however, report such an aura.

Table 5-1
Classification of Seizures

Generalized seizures
    Tonic and/or clonic seizures (grand mal)
    Absence seizures (petit mal)
    Bilateral myoclonus
    Infantile spasms
    Atonic seizures

Partial seizures
    Simple partial seizures
        Pure motor (including Jacksonian) seizures
        Pure sensory seizures
        Affective seizures
    Complex partial (psychomotor seizures)

The seizure itself, or *ictus*, begins with tonic extension of all four extremities and frequently with arching of the back and neck. This muscular activity coincides with a paroxysm of spikes on the EEG. Shortly thereafter, the tonic phase is followed by clonic activity, which may be thought of as tonic extension rapidly alternating with relaxation of the muscles. During this phase the EEG shows alternating spikes and slow waves. Relaxation of the urethral and anal sphincters usually occurs, with resultant incontinence. The ictus, during which the patient remains unconscious, usually lasts for 1 or 2 minutes but may be prolonged.

Following the seizure, the postictal period begins. Some individuals return to consciousness almost at once, with only minimal symptoms of headache or fatigue; others pass through a period of unconsciousness or stupor, which can last for minutes or hours, often followed by confusion, headache, and fatigue. After regaining consciousness, the patient may remember the aura but does not recall the ictal period. Often, if the patient was asleep or alone during the entire period of the seizure, the only evidence of its occurrence may be soiled clothing or a bitten tongue.

Absence Seizure (Petit Mal)

Absence seizures are seen almost exclusively in children. They usually first appear between the ages of 5 and 7 and in most cases cease by puberty. The typical absence seizure consists of a brief interruption of consciousness during which the patient abruptly stops current activity and loses awareness of the surrounding environment. During the seizure, the patient may blink or make lip-smacking movements but does not collapse or have convulsive movements. After 2−10 seconds, the spell ends.

A characteristic EEG pattern is usually present during this type of seizure, which consists of repetitive, regular spike-and-wave complexes at a frequency of 3/sec. This pattern of discharge can be elicited during the interictal period by hyperventilation or photic (stroboscopic) stimulation. The spike-and-wave complexes appear symmetrically and simultaneously on both sides of the brain and are believed to be initiated by a discharge focus in the diencephalon.

In a few patients, the seizure disorder continues into adulthood. Rarely, it appears in late adult life, creating diagnostic confusion. When absence seizures arise in this age group, the episodes may be atypical, appearing as an acute psychosis, delirium, or a prolonged confusional state. EEG records may show continuous, diffuse spike-and-wave activity at a rate of 3/sec, but prolonged, generalized 1.5−2.0 Hz spike-and-wave activity can occur (Ellis & Lee, 1978). Wells (1975) suggested the following features which lead to suspicion of an epileptic etiology: (1) abrupt onset of psychosis in an individual previously believed to be psychologically healthy; (2) unexplained delirium; (3) similar past episodes with abrupt, spontaneous recurrences and remissions; and (4) a history of fainting spells. Since effective treatment with anticonvulsants is available, correct diagnosis is important.

PARTIAL SEIZURES

A partial seizure is one which is thought to have a focal origin. The epileptic activity may remain restricted to the general area of origin, with the patient remaining conscious. On other occasions, the epileptic activity may spread to involve the entire brain, becoming, by clinical and EEG examination, a generalized seizure. The period between onset of the focal paroxysm and its generalized spread varies widely. In some cases, when observers can describe the occurrence of two distinct phases, diagnosis of a focal seizure with generalized spread is relatively easy. With others, the interval between focal onset and diffuse spread may be so short that they cannot be distinguished by observation. The EEG often provides evidence of focal origin in these cases.

Simple Partial Seizures

Simple partial seizures exhibit primary neurologic symptoms of a motor or sensory nature. The ictal manifestations are the result of their site of origin. Commonly seen is a focal motor seizure which originates from an epileptic focus in the motor strip of the contralateral frontal lobe. The ictus may consist of convulsive movements that are limited to a limb or part of a limb, or of movements that may spread from their initial focus to involve the entire limb, the entire body on the same side, and the contralateral side as well. This progressive seizure has been named the *Jacksonian seizure* (after Hughlings Jackson, who first described the syndrome). The patient will usually lose consciousness by the time both sides of the body have become involved. Alternatively, motor signs may be limited to turning of the head and eyes to the side opposite to that of the epileptic focus. These focal seizures can become prolonged.

Other simple partial seizures, although less common, may also occur. Epileptogenic foci in the anterior parietal lobe produce focal sensory seizures. With these seizures, patients experience such unusual sensations as paresthesias or numbness. With a site of origin in the language area, there may be speech arrest or muteness. In rare instances, paraphrasic speech may occur. Epileptic foci in the visual cortex produce nonformed visual sensations such as lines, colors, and lights, whereas foci in the visual association areas of the posterior medial temporal lobe produce more highly formed images. Olfactory hallucinations occur with a focus in the uncinate region of the inferior medial aspect of the temporal lobe. Vertiginous sensations and auditory hallucinations, although rare, probably result from temporal lobe foci.

Complex Partial (Psychomotor) Seizures

This group of partial seizures is termed *complex* because of the elaborate symptoms they produce. These focal seizures involve alterations of autonomic, behavioral, intellectual, somatomotor, and sensory functions. An alternative term is *psychomotor seizure*. Most complex partial seizures originate in the temporal lobe, although some arise from foci in the frontal lobe, especially on its inferior surface.

Complex partial seizures usually have four components: sensory, psychic, autonomic, and somatomotor. The sensory symptoms are usually vague, described as giddiness, auditory distortions, visual aberrations, and unusual or disagreeable tastes and odors. The autonomic manifestations include palpitations, piloerection ("goose bumps" on the skin), nausea, increased salivation, dry mouth, hunger pangs, and abdominal pain.

Psychic symptoms tend to differentiate this type of seizure from others. Among the many symptoms described are feelings of impending doom, altered states of awareness accompanied by apparent alertness, dreamy and twilight states, forced thoughts, hallucinations, and sensations of dejà vu and jamais vu. Taylor (1977) and others have called attention to the apparent resemblance between these symptoms and those of schizophrenia.

The somatomotor signs consist largely of automatisms (movements or acts without conscious intent). Frequently, there are repetitive movements of the facial muscles such as blinking, grimacing, lip smacking, chewing, spitting, or swallowing. Other stereotyped movements such as gesturing, rubbing, patting, undressing, or wringing of the hands may occur. This phase is difficult to recognize as an ictal phenomenon and may also be difficult to separate from psychogenic disorders. The somatomotor period is usually brief, lasting for a few seconds to 1 or 2 minutes. The movements rarely fit together to make up complicated acts; usually they are fragmented and inappropriate. Aggressive behavior, especially directed acts as ictal events, are extremely rare.

In a typical seizure, the sensory components are experienced initially and are often well remembered. The psychic phase follows, varying widely from patient to patient, and is usually remembered, but not as clearly. Visual and auditory hallucinations and distortions, as well as confusion, may occur. Affective states ranging from happiness to rage can also develop. Following the psychic stage, the patient may return to consciousness, develop generalized convulsions, enter a somatomotor phase, or become unresponsive in the postictal period.

The postictal period of the complex partial seizure may last for minutes to hours after a generalized convulsion. During this time the patient is variably unresponsive, disoriented, and confused, with amnesia for the postictal period common. If a generalized convulsion does not occur, the postictal period is usually brief. Rarely, complex motor phenomena such as driving have been reported during seizures, although this is unlikely to be a cause of most fugue states.

BEHAVIORAL ABNORMALITIES IN EPILEPTICS

The majority of clinicians agree that patients with complex seizures have behavioral abnormalities which are related to the occurrence of seizures as well as to their site of origin. Behavioral problems do occur in patients with simple partial and generalized seizures, but they are attributed largely to cognitive defects and the psychosocial problems to which epileptics are subject. This attribution may not be entirely correct, as the cognitive defects and the epilepsy may be of common origin. However, the literature regarding behavioral abnormalities in eplepsy tends to stress complex partial seizures, particularly those of the temporal lobe, and associated behavioral changes. Two major types of change have been reported: (1) interictal personality and behavioral changes, and (2) interictal schizophreniform psychoses.

Interictal Personality Changes

Interictal personality changes tend to appear several years after the onset of temporal lobe epilepsy. Patients seem to develop a deepening of all emotions. They begin to take everything seriously, become unusually concerned with morality and often excessively religious, and lose all sense of humor. They tend to grow preoccupied with details. In this they acquire "viscosity," a quality of hanging onto others with details, which tends to create uneasiness in those around them. Despite these personality changes and the problems they create for others, the patients are frequently described as good-natured, warm, and worthy of tolerance. These individuals often have no sexual drive. Those who develop temporal lobe epilepsy before puberty often fail to become interested in sex, and those who develop the disorder after puberty often lose the interest they had.

Irritability and impulsivity often play a part in the behavior of these patients. Angry outbursts develop in many, and at times they may be verbally abusive and physically destructive. Such explosions tend to occur after periods of increasing anger and envy. Blumer (1975) has stated that these outbursts of violence (1) occur on provocation, however slight; (2) are directed toward the environment; 3) lack stereotypy; (4) are unassociated with other seizure phenomena; (5) are remembered; and (6) are often viewed in retrospect with remorse. These episodes therefore have none of the characteristics suggesting complex partial seizures which were previously noted.

Bear and Fedio (1977) studied personality characteristics of temporal lobe epileptics both by the patients' self-description and by observation. Temporal lobe epileptics believed themselves to be humorless, dependent, and obsessional, whereas observers rated them as circumstantial, philosophical, and angry. Bear (1977) suggested the term *syndrome of temporal hyperconnection in epilepsy* to describe the observed personality changes.

Seizure control appears to have little to do with most of the personality changes. Most studies, however, have been made of patients whose seizures are relatively poorly controlled. However, global hyposexuality appears to be strongly related to poor seizure control, with adequate control often leading to normalization of sexual activity. On the other hand, good control of complex partial seizures has been reported to lead to increased irritability and aggressiveness in some cases, almost as if the seizures acted as release mechanism. However, this belief is purely speculative at present.

It has not been established whether these interictal changes are peculiar to patients with temporal lobe epileptic foci. Rarely do patients with temporal lobe epilepsy display all the qualities described above, and many may display no abnormal behavioral characteristics.

Schizophreniform Psychosis

The incidence of schizophrenia or schizophreniform psychosis is several times greater in temporal lobe epileptics than in the population as a whole. These psychotic episodes typically begin 15 years or more after the onset of temporal lobe epilepsy. Pincus and Tucker (1978) have noted that the almost universal history of long-term use of anticonvulsant medication in these patients raises the question of anticonvulsant use as an etiologic factor.

Although these patients exhibit many symptoms associated with schizophrenia, they differ in several ways from the majority of schizophrenics. Their psychotic changes develop later in life. They lack a family history of psychosis, maintain good social rapport, show a normal affective range, and in general do not deteriorate as schizophrenics do. Slater and his associates (1963) noted that in their follow-up studies many patients with temporal lobe epilepsy began to appear more organic and less like schizophrenics with the passage of time.

Taylor (1977) and Flor-Henry (1969a) have stated that these schizophreniform psychoses do not simply occur at random among patients with temporal lobe epilepsy. Psychosis is more likely to occur in women and in those with left temporal lobe foci. Flor-Henry also emphasized the "epileptic" nature of the psychosis. In a carefully controlled study he noted that the frequency of temporal lobe psychomotor seizures was inversely correlated with the presence of psychosis, which suggested that these patients were most psychotic when their seizures were best controlled. Glaser (1964), however, found such an inverse relationship in only a few of his patients. Still another view is offered by Kristenson and Sindrup (1978), who observed that epileptiform abnormalities on EEG were more extensive and severe in their psychotic than in their nonpsychotic group. They believed deep temporal lobe dysfunction to be a significant factor in the development of psychosis in temporal lobe epilepsy.

DIFFERENTIAL DIAGNOSIS

Not infrequently, it is necessary to distinguish between epilepsy and psychogenic causes of fainting spells. The clinician should not allow a bizarre clinical presentation to argue too strongly for a functional diagnosis, as epileptic seizures are often bizarre. Nor should the influence of environmental events militate against a diagnosis of epilepsy. Environmental events with affective significance can precipitate an epileptic seizure or affect its clinical manifestations. However, Liske and Forster (1964) have observed that pseudoseizures should be considered when the seizure itself or its precipitants are unusual.

The EEG is often helpful in the differential diagnosis, especially when discharges typical of epilepsy are present. A negative EEG is less helpful, as single routine EEG records may be normal in 20–30% of epileptic patients (Kiloh, McComaas, & Osseltow, 1972). Although a variety of techniques (sleep recordings, sphenoidal electrodes) can be used to increase the yield of positive EEGs, in some epileptic patients an abnormal EEG is never obtained. This occurs either because the EEG is never recorded at a time when epileptic discharges are present or because the electrodes are too remote from the abnormal electrical activity. Despite this, a normal EEG taken during a spell is strong evidence against an organic etiology.

ETIOLOGY

Overall, seizures are considered to be the result of a primary disorder of the brain (idiopathic epilepsy) or to be symptomatic of and secondary to some other illness (Table 5-2). Seizures may be further separated into those in

Table 5-2
Etiology of Seizures

Idiopathic (autosomal dominant inheritance?)

Symptomatic
    Structural: neoplasm, stroke, trauma, arteriovenous malformation, abscess, congenital deficit, birth injury, degenerative disease
    Metabolic: hypoglycemia, hyperglycemia, drug or alcohol withdrawal, acute anoxia, uremia, hypocalcemia, hypomagnesemia
    Occult

---

which the brain is structurally altered by some disease process and those in which brain function is disturbed by a metabolic disorder.

Idiopathic epilepsy generally includes seizures occurring in any age group without an apparent etiology. A more restricted definition refers to those seizures which begin in childhood and puberty and are most likely inherited. This group includes the generalized tonic-clonic and absence seizures. Although most clinicians agree that these disorders must involve an actual brain lesion, none has yet been identified. When generalized or partial seizures begin after the teenage years, they are considered to be symptomatic and a thorough diagnostic evaluation must be undertaken. If no cause can be found, an occult lesion should be suspected and the patient reevaluated in the future.

The genetics of epilepsy remain unclear. Commonly recognized forms of inheritance do not explain the high incidence of seizures in relatives of epileptics. Large-scale EEG studies of the relatives of a group of patients with absence seizures have revealed that EEG abnormality is inherited in an autosomal dominant pattern, but the incidence of clinical seizures is comparatively low (Metrakos & Metrakos, 1961). This discrepancy between EEG abnormality and its expression is not presently understood.

The actual mechanisms involved in epilepsy remain unclear. Although all epilepsy is caused by abnormal discharges in the neurons in a specific area of the brain or the brain in general, there is often no known cause. In some cases, a specific irritant to the brain can be identified—such as a scar that develops after bleeding in the brain caused by trauma or a cerebrovascular disorder—but these factors are not known to be present in the idiopathic seizure disorders. Epileptic seizures may also be induced by high fever, especially in infants. Also, various metabolic/biochemical changes in the brain may be associated with epileptic foci. Chusid (1973) indicates that there may be a change in acetylcholine metabolism at the focus of a seizure, along with changes in the serum level of ammonia and potassium. In addition, a variety of drugs which interfere with other metabolic functions may induce seizures experimentally. Such seizures have been associated with phenothiazine use as well.

The main causes of epilepsy are (1) genetic predisposition; (2) birth factors, including birth trauma, infection, anoxia, and prematurity; (3) infectious disorders, including meningitis, brain abscess, encephalitis, fever, and parasites; (4) toxic factors, including poisoning with carbon monoxide, lead, mercury, other metals, alcohol, various drugs, allergies, toxemia of pregnancy, and many other toxic medical conditions; (5) trauma; (6) various cerebrovascular disorders; (7) metabolic and nutritional disturbances, including electrolyte imbalance, disorders of carbohydrate, protein, or fat metabolism, vitamin deficiency, and various endocrine disorders (e.g., disorders of menstruation); (8) various tumors; and (9) degenerative and inherited diseases, including multiple sclerosis (Chusid, 1973).

IMPLICATIONS FOR NEUROPSYCHOLOGICAL TESTING

A common referral problem for neuropsychologists concerns the discrimination of suspected seizures from psychiatric disorder. However, as the foregoing description of seizures indicates, it is not possible to diagnose the existence of a seizure disorder from neuropsychological or personality test results. Neuropsychological testing can determine whether there are cognitive deficits or personality changes which might be associated with the various types of epilepsy, but all of these deficits can and do exist in the absence of epilepsy and epilepsy may exist without any detectable neuropsychological changes.

Seizure disorder must be diagnosed eventually on the basis of a clear history and a description of a seizure episode or, more ideally, by direct observation of the phenomenon. Even the EEG cannot be used to decide definitely the existence of seizure disorder in all cases. In many cases the EEG is normal between seizures, although characteristic EEGs associated with the various types of seizures are considered diagnostic. In regard to psychological testing, one may ask whether the test results are consistent with a hypothesized brain location of the seizure. If they are, the presence of such seizures appears more likely. Even test results, however, are considered to be only one sort of evidence which is not necessarily pathognomonic of the seizure disorder. Since many seizure disorders may exist despite other findings within normal limits, the absence of psychological findings does not rule out a seizure disorder. This result only makes it less likely, especially when other findings (using related psychiatric evaluations) provide an adequate alternative explanation for the behavioral phenomenon under investigation.

Sometimes none of these techniques offers a firm conclusion. In these cases, medication trials may be given to see if the seizures disappear or if there is a general change in the patient's cognitive abilities or personality style. Pre- and postmedication psychological testing can be quite useful when there is a suspicion that subtle deficits in arousal or attention may be due to a subclinical epileptic phenomenon. If the medication brings the problems under control, the patient may show significant gains on test measures. Tests must be used which do not show large test—retest effects or for which the demensions of such effects are well known. This test—retest methodology is also useful in studying the effects of medication in general, including cases of hyperactivity or schizophrenia treated with medication.

In general, the findings on neuropsychological testing reflect the underlying cause of the epilepsy rather than the epilepsy itself. Thus, very severe neuropsychological deficits may exist in the absence of epilepsy, and one learns more about the etiologic agents than about the seizure disorder itself. Since the underlying cause may be located anywhere in the brain, may reflect various neurologic disorders, may be acute or chronic, and so on, test results can vary as much as those of any general neuropsychological population.

In addition, seizures may result from very mild disorders which cause no neuropsychological symptoms. They may also be associated with variable disorders which are active only when the seizures are occurring, so that both neuropsychological testing and EEG results between seizures may be normal. These temporary causes may include metabolic disruption or an acute syndrome such as an aneurysym which grows only when the patient's blood pressure becomes very high under severe stress. Children may have transient seizures when they develop high fevers which never recur, although seizure disorder onset in childhood in the absence of fever is prognostically less favorable. As with other childhood disorders, however, the psychological effects of the damage causing the seizure disorder may not become evident for many years after the seizure pattern itself.

There is one important exception to the above discussion. In some cases, frequent or severe seizures may cause additional damage to the brain through electrical discharge, either at the site of the original seizures focus or elsewhere in the brain. For example, brain damage may develop at the same spot as the original focus but in the opposite hemisphere. This is commonly called a *mirror focus*. Such additional damage is one reason why it is so important to control seizures. This complication does not necessarily occur in all cases, and the degree of neuropsychological impairment which accompanies such phenomena varies considerably.

Thus, psychological evaluation of the epileptic patient can be used in diagnosis to see if the results are consistent with a given possible disorder rather than as a direct diagnostic device. Testing is much more useful in describing the cognitive and personality deficits found in the patient and in relating these deficits to problems in vocational or personal adjustment. The seizure patient may have little or no impairment and may be able to work in all situations if the seizures are controlled; others have deficits which require informed counseling and recommendations. Since most seizure patients seen by the neuropsychologist are only mildly impaired, most of them have important and useful skills which can contribute to their own satisfaction as well as to society. Unfortunately, many of these individuals are not able to show their spared skills because of incomplete or improper evaluations. This may encourage patients either to avoid activities or to attempt activities that are beyond their skills, which surely leads to failure. However, the use of psychological testing to confirm the presence or absence of seizures is quite improper, and psychologists must resist the attempts of referral sources to have them make this diagnostic distinction.

Chapter 6

Aging and Dementia

With William MacInnes

A relatively complex area in the study of neuropathologic processes is the relationship between the various dementing diseases and the normal aging process. Researchers have held widely varying views on the relationship between normal aging and dementia. Moreover, these questions become extremely important in the neuropsychological analysis of the patient. This chapter will therefore evaluate not only common pathologic forms of aging but also the normal aging process.

Several cross-sectional studies on the similarities and differences between normally functioning elderly persons and various brain-damaged populations have discerned apparently distinct patterns of test results in each group (Goldstein & Shelly, 1975; Overall & Gorham, 1972; Reed & Reitan, 1963a). These studies imply that the consequences of the aging process differ in important ways from the effects of chronic, diffuse, or acute brain damage. Although it appears that age plays an important role in determining one's level of performance on tests of higher and more complex cognitive functions, the relationship between age, brain structures, and higher cognitive functions is still not well understood. Although cognitive changes in the elderly seem to accompany known structural declines in the aging brain, no direct or causative relationship has been established.

One of the major questions underlying all clinical neuropsychological research on aging is whether "some of the changes in psychological functioning observed in these people may be attributed to changes that are known to occur in brain structures and functions during aging?" (Klisz, 1978, p. 78) This question is difficult to answer. As Jernigan, Zatz, Feinberg, and Fein

(1980) have noted, one of the more difficult problems in neuropsychological assessment is the lack of safe, useful, and widely available anatomic validation criteria for theories of brain—behavior relationships. Recently, two noninvasive methods of providing anatomic validation of brain—behavior relationships have been developed. These are (1) computed tomography (CT) scanning, a pictorial and numerical representation of the structures of the brain, and (2) regional cerebral blood flow (rCBF), a method for estimating the actual blood flow in various areas of the brain, which reflects active metabolic processes rather than anatomic structures. The minimal radiation exposure associated with both of these techniques allows their use with normal populations. The data from these techniques have been used to examine the contributions that different brain structures make to various neuropsychological functions (Jernigan et al., 1980).

Numerous cross-sectional studies have examined the relationship of age to CT scan measurements. These studies have consistently found significant age—related effects (Barron, Jacobs, & Kinkel, 1976; Gyldensted, 1977; Jacobs, Kinkel, Painter, Murawski, & Heffner, 1978; Jacoby & Levy, 1980; Jernigan & Zatz, 1981. For example, Barron et al. (1976) found a gradual but progressive increase in the ratio of ventricular area to total brain area from the first through the sixth decade followed by a dramatic increase in the eighth and ninth decades. These results and other related measures have been cross—validated in other more recent studies (Gyldensted, 1977; Jacobs et al., 1978; Jernigan & Zatz, 1980).

Several CT scan studies have also detected significant differences between demented patients and age—matched controls. Huckman, Fox, and Topel (1975) were some of the first investigators to report such differences. They found the demented group to have an increased incidence of brain atrophy and ventricular enlargement. However, they noted that not all of their demented patients exhibited cerebral atrophy or ventricular enlargement. Similarly, not all of their patients with atrophy or ventricular enlargement were demented.

More recently, Naeser, Gebhardt, and Levine (1980) found Alzheimer's disease patients to have lower brain density in the centrum semiovale CT slice than medical control patients. Brinkman, Sarwar, Levin, and Morris (1981) found Alzheimer's disease patients to have abnormal ventricular brain ratios much more frequently than elderly community volunteers. They also found evidence of more cerebral atrophy as measured by the CT scan in the Alzheimer's group.

Hughes and Gado (1981) found no relationship of ventricular and sulcal sizes to mental status in a mixed group of demented patients. Bondareff, Baldy, and Levy (1981) found that the mean CT numbers or Hounsfield units (Hu) were significantly lower bilaterally in the medial temporal lobe, anterior frontal lobe, and head of the caudate nucleus in a group of patients at risk for Alzheimer's disease when compared to elderly community volunteers.

Another radiologic measure that has been employed in such research is rCBF. This research is based on the assumption that the brain will have greater blood flow to focal cerebral areas depending upon which task is being performed. Numerous studies in the past 30 years have also examined the relationship between aging and cerebral circulation.

Early studies reported a decline in cerebral blood flow (CBF) and a decrease in oxygen utilization with advancing age (Fazekas, Kleh, & Finnerty, 1955; Scheinberg, Blackburn, Rich, & Saslaw, 1953). Others (Shenkin, Novak, Goluboff, Soffe & Bortin, 1953) argued that age was not the critical variable. They suggested that correlations occurred only when hypertension or arteriosclerosis was present. Kety (1956) reviewed early studies that examined the effects of age on CBF and concluded that marked declines in CBF and metabolism of oxygen in the brain occurred beginning in adolescence. This followed by more gradual declines during adulthood and old age (Thompson, 1976). However, most of these studies were done using patients who had vascular diseases or who were hospitalized for other medical reasons. The likelihood that these subjects are representative of a healthy or normal aged group seems very questionable. Similarly, an early comprehensive study of healthy aging concluded that changes in CBF during senescence probably depend on pathologic processes other than age (Dastur, Lane, Hansen, Kety, Butler, Perlin, & Sokoloff, 1963).

The above studies refer to measurements of average CBF using the nitrous oxide method, a technique which requires the injection (usually in the carotid artery) of a radioactive material. With the development of the noninvasive [133] Xe inhalation method of measuring regional cerebral blood flow (rCBF), comparisons between hospitalized patients and healthy volunteers living in the community became more practical. The [133] Xe inhalation method requires subjects to breathe a small amount of radioactive xenon, which poses no serious danger to them. Using this method, several recent studies have found a progressive decline in cortial blood flow, but in general have detected no decrease in subcortical blood flow in the aged (Ingvar, Brun, Hagberg, & Gustafson, 1978; Lavy, Melamed, Bentin, Cooper, & Rinot, 1978; Meyer, Ishihara, Deshmuka, Naritomi, Sakai, Hsu, & Pollock, 1978; Naritomi, Meyer, Sakai, Yamaguchi, & Shaw, 1979).

Since age appeared to be related to CBF in some of the above studies, other investigators have attempted to examine more thoroughly the relationship between pathologic processes, age, and rCBF. Several studies have focused on the link between dementia and rCBF (Obrist, 1980; Obrist, Thompson, Wang, & Wilkins, 1975; Wang & Busse, 1975; Yamaguchi, Meyer, Yamamoto, Sakai, Shaw, & Meyer, 1980). In general, these studies reported that patients with senile dementia had lower blood flow in the gray matter than age-matched normals.

Obrist (1980) has presented the best synthesis of data on rCBF and aging to date. He combined the data from two earlier studies (Obrist et al., 1975;

Wang & Busse, 1975) and found that the elderly volunteers exhibited a 28% reduction in blood flow when compared to young controls. He also demonstrated a significant decrease when comparing the dementia subjects with the normal elderly. This finding is especially noteworthy because the dementia patients were on the average 20 years younger than the normal elderly controls.

In general, studies have shown that demented patients have lower rCBF than age-matched controls. However, none of the past studies have been able to differentiate the various dementing illnesses (such as Alzheimer's disease versus multi-infarct dementia) from each other on the basis of rCBF alone, nor reliably make a normal/abnormal distinction in a single individual.

It should be emphasized that although numerous studies have suggested that the physical structures of the brain change with advancing age, the relationship of these structural changes to the aging process is not entirely clear. Most of these studies have important methodologic limitations, such as small sample size, poor reliability of measures, or sampling error. For example, many CT scan studies have used as their control group medical patients who had no history of brain disorder. Medical patients may not be a fully satisfactory normative group because they may have subtle or unrecognized factors which affect their brain structures in addition to the normal aging process. Possibly what was thought to be the result of growing old is, in fact, due to an undetected or poorly understood pathologic process.

Although knowledge regarding the effects of age on the structure and function of the human brain has increased dramatically in the past decade, many questions remain unanswered. The results of past studies suggest that there are significant age-related changes in neuropsychological functioning. These changes appear to be qualitatively different from deficits exhibited by younger brain-damaged groups. Conclusions from these studies must be tentative because the older control groups employed were usually nonneurologic medical patients who may not function as well as healthy persons. Many deficits which were previously associated with the aging process may reflect medical illness, personality variables, and/or sociocultural effects (Butler, 1978).

These potential influences on functioning suggest the need to separate the effects of the healthy aging process from the cumulative effects of various physical insults to the brain (e.g., disease processes, physical trauma, poor diet, heavy alcohol consumption) which occur over an individual's life span. Similarly, numerous disease processes commonly occur with old age (e.g., hypertension, arthritis, diabetes) which, in addition to the aging process, may significantly affect an elderly individual's test performance. Thus, it appears that if one wants to examine the effects of age on test performance, a strong argument can be made for using homogeneously healthy samples (Benton, 1981). These individuals do not represent the population of elderly adults as a whole; however, they do have the least number of environmental and physiologic insults to their central nervous system.

THE SYNDROMES OF DEMENTIA

The dementias are diseases of the brain that result in the progressive loss of cognitive functions, including memory, learning, attention, and judgment. Although some forms of dementia are treatable, most are not. In time, the dementing process erodes all aspects of thought, feeling, and behavior; it eventually results in death (National Institutes of Health, 1981).

Contrary to what many people believe, dementing illnesses are not the fate that awaits us all with advancing age. These disorders are not a normal part of the aging process. Rather, they are diseases with a variety of causes, including intrinsic changes in the cells of the brain, vascular insufficiency, multiple infarcts, metabolic disturbances, hormonal inbalances, and medication side effects. Few of the elderly actually develop dementing disorders. An estimated 5% of the population over age 65 years in the United States are thought to be severely demented. Another 10% of the elderly are thought to be mildly to moderately demented (National Institutes of Health, 1981).

Although it is clear that the vast majority of the elderly do not develop dementing disorders, the 5% who develop severe dementias total approximately 1 million individuals. In addition, there is a small but unfortunate group of individuals who develop dementing disorders relatively early in life. Most of these early dementias are due to Alzheimer's disease, a progressive degenerative disease of the brain. Most neurologists now believe that disorders called senile dementia and chronic organic brain syndrome are probably Alzheimer's disease which appears later in life (National Institutes of Health, 1981). The terms senile and presenile dementia have been used rather loosely to refer to a variety of disease processes, including chronic organic brain syndrome, senility, hardening of the arteries, and Alzheimer's disease. Rather than use such terms such as senility or organic brain syndrome, this chapter will later describe the more common causes of dementing illnesses which occur with increasing frequency as one ages.

Dementing disorders are probably one of the most overdiagnosed and misdiagnosed disorders in the elderly. Part of the problem is that the symptoms of numerous other disorders resemble those of the senile or presenile dementias, including all of the disorders discussed previously in this book. The critical difference is that many of these disorders, unlike the various dementing disorders such as Alzheimer's disease, may be successfully treated. However they must be identified, and not dismissed as one of the senile or presenile dementias.

In addition to the misdiagnosis of other brain disorders, depression can also be confused with various dementing illnesses. Depressed patients are frequently passive and unresponsive to others around them. They may appear confused, have memory difficulties, and be easily agitated. Depression, however, unlike the true dementing disorders, can be treated successfully using such therapies as medication, psychotherapy, or electroconvulsive therapy. Because many disorders can be mistaken for various dementing illnesses, a comprehensive evaluation is essential. This assessment should include a thorough medical checkup, as well as a neurologic, neuropsychological, and psychological evaluation.

ALZHEIMER'S DISEASE

Alzheimer's disease, first described by Alzheimer (1907), has been repeatedly shown to account for at least 50% of all cases of dementing illnesses (Jellinger, 1976; Tomlinson, Blessed, & Roth, 1968, 1970). The prevalence of Alzheimer's disease has varied widely depending upon which study one reads (Akesson, 1969; Nielson, 1962). However, it is generally believed by many authorities that 5−7% is a good estimate of the prevalence for individuals above the age of 65 years (Kay, Beamish, & Roth, 1964).

Etiology

Several hypotheses have been suggested to explain the etiology of Alzheimer's disease. Schneck, Reisberg, and Ferris (1982) have done an extensive review of this literature. One current theory is that Alzheimer's disease results from a slow-acting virus. A second hypothesis has focused on the effects of a toxic agent, such as aluminum. A third concerns a defect in the immune system of patients suffering from Alzheimer's disease. Each of these hypotheses has supporting and contradicting evidence. It may be that each result is true and responsible for some subset of all cases.

Genetics has also been implicated in the etiology of Alzheimer's disease. Most cases occur in families with no history of the disease; however, particular families with multiple occurrences have been reported. According to Heston, Mastri, Anderson, and White (1981), these families are characterized by relatively youthful onset of illness, rapid progression, and an apparently autosomal dominant transmission. Heston et al. also presented strong evidence of a genetic link between Alzheimer's disease, Down's syndrome, lymphoma, and immune disease. They found that the risk to relatives decreased sharply as the severity of the proband's symptoms lessened.

Clinical Features

The onset of Alzheimer's disease usually occurs between the ages of 50 and 70 years, although cases have been reported in much younger and older individuals. It is difficult to pinpoint the exact age of onset of this disorder because its initial symptoms (usually mild, short-term memory difficulties) are often compensated for by the individual or the spouse. In some cases, the symptoms go unnoticed by the individual or the family or are explained as the result of normal aging. Relatives of the patient with Alzheimer's disease often note that onset seems to follow a significant stressor such as a head injury, operation, or hospital admission for other reasons. However, a detailed history typically demonstrates the preexistence of the illness, whereas the apparent aggravating insult served primarily to call attention to the cognitive loss. Alternatively, the person who functioned adequately in a familiar environment may be overly stressed in new surroundings, or additional mild brain damage from trauma, anesthesia, or infection may have emphasized the cognitive deficits.

Heston et al. (1981) report that Alzheimer's disease patients with a relatively early age of onset have a tendency to have shorter courses and to die more quickly than individuals who develop the disease later in life. This tendency appears to hold with the exception of the very old, for whom Heston et al. concluded that death may be due to competing causes toward the end of the expected life span. Survival after the onset of Alzheimer's disease can vary quite widely. Heston et al. report most survival times in the 5–10-year range.

Evidence for sex differences in the development of Alzheimer's disease appears to be equivocal. It is generally believed that women develop the disorder more often than men. However, women also live longer than men and thus may be at increased risk. Heston et al (1981) found that the percentage of women in the Alzheimer's disease population was not significantly different from the percentage of women in older age groups in the general population.

Clinical Stages

Three main stages are commonly described for the disease Lishman, 1978). The first, frequently lasting for 2–3 years, is characterized by failing memory, mild confusion, inefficiency in everyday tasks, and spatial disorientation. Mood disturbances may be prominent, but psychoses are rare. The disorder of mood may be one of perplexity, agitation, and restless hyperactivity. In other cases, aspontaneity and apathy may appear even in this early stage (Sjogren, Sjogren, & Lingren, 1952).

The second stage is marked by more rapid progression of intellectual and personality decline, with the appearance of focal symptoms. The parietal lobes are often involved, producing dysphasia, apraxia, agnosia, and acalculia. Extrapyramidal disorders are also common, with disturbance of posture and gait, increased muscle tone, and other parkinsonian features. Signs of parkinsonism appeared in nearly two-thirds of Pearce and Miller's (1973) patients. Extensor Babinski responses may occur, as well as facial weakness. Florid psychosis with delusions or hallucinations can appear, but typically it occurs only when the dementia has become severe.

A profound apathetic dementia, in which the patient becomes incontinent for urine and feces and is bedridden, appears in the third or terminal stage. Severe neurologic disability, such as spastic heiparesis or marked striatal rigidity and tremor, is likely to develop. Forced grasping and groping may be seen, along with infantile rooting and sucking reflexes. Grand mal seizures are common. Bodily wasting may be amazingly rapid even with an adequate appetite as death approaches. Prior to this stage, however, somatic manifestations are usually minimal regardless of the severity of the dementia. In addition, during the first two stages of the dementing process, patients can develop a variety of psychiatric symptoms. These secondary behavioral features can include paranoid states, agitation, hostility, depression, impulsivity, mania, schizophreniform psychotic symptoms, sleep disturbance, nocturnal delirium, and many other symptoms. These symptoms are often treatable with psychopharmacologic agents or psychosocial therapies.

Pathologic Findings

Typically, the affected brain is grossly atrophied, without obvious variation from one area to another. Microscopically, there is extensive loss of neurons, with degenerative changes in those remaining and secondary glial proliferation. Senile plaques and neurofibrillary tangles are widespread. The vascular system is usually only minimally changed at most.

Although cortical atrophy is diffuse, it usually involves the frontal and temporal lobes to a greater extent than the parieto-occipital area. This greater involvement can range from restricted lobar atrophy, like that in Pick's disease, to minimal gross shrinkage despite severe microscopic degeneration. Neuronal degeneration is most pronounced in the outer three layers of the cortex. Somewhat increased degeneration is frequently found in the limbic system, especially the hippocampus and the amygdala. Affected neurons may show lipofusin accumulation or granulovacuolar degeneration. Axonal degeneration, astrocytic hyperplasia, and fibrous gliosis appear in the white matter.

Senile plaques are almost always seen in Alzheimer's disease. They occur densely in all parts of the cortex. The hippocampus and amygdala are more severely affected, and the amygdala is perhaps more affected than any other region of the brain (Corsellis, 1970). The subcortical gray matter is much less involved, and the white matter contains no plaques at all. Nonmyelinated neuronal processes, including synaptic boutons, have been identified by electron microscopy in the plaques (Terry & Wisniewski, 1977).

Neurofibrillary tangles are also present and are commonly considered essential in making the diagnosis. They occur diffusely in the gray matter, particularly the hippocampus. They lie within the neurons themselves, in contrast to the extracellular senile plaques.

Detailed study of both plaques and tangles has been undertaken in an attempt to find their origin. Electron microscopy shows that the tangles may be derived from normal microtubules or possibly result from synthesis of an abnormal protein (Iqbal, Wisniewski, Shelanski, Brostoff, Liwinicz, Terry, 1974). The latter could result from a genetically mediated change in cell metabolism or from an obscure infectious agent or toxin. Along this line of reasoning, under experimental conditions aluminum has been shown to cause similar neurofibrillary changes, and Crapper, Kirshman, and Dalton (1973) have found areas of increased aluminum content in the brains of patients with Alzheimer's disease.

Increased oxidative metabolic activity in and around the margins of senile plaques has been suggested by histochemical assays. Terry and Wisniewski (1970, 1972) regard diseased neuronal processes as the focus of this activity. Electron microscopic studies tend to suggest that aggregation of small groups of deteriorating terminal dendrites containing large numbers of mitochondria may be the first stage of plaque formation. Amyloid material, an immunoglobulin-related protein, then appears as wisps between the dendrites which condense to form a central core. In this mechanism, the neurofibrillary tangles with their twisted tubules may be the primary structural defect, disturbing cell function and causing degeneration of dendritic processes by disrupting axoplasmic flow, leading to plaque formation. Although the details remain unclear, it now appears that plaques and tangles reflect metabolic disturbances in the neuron and neuronal processes.

Biochemical studies of autopsy samples, primarily from individuals with senile dementia, have shown changes in brain structural proteins and enzymes. Bowen, Smith, and Davison (1973) found a lack of specific brain protein in the cortices of dementia patients, and Bowen, White, Flack, Smith, and Davison (1974) demonstrated deficiencies of enzymes involved in synaptic transmission.

The pathologic changes of Alzheimer's disease occurring outside of the brain have not been studied in much detail. The terminal weight loss, which seems unaffected by food intake, remains a mystery. The possible contribution of hypothalamic and neuroendocrine factors is undetermined.

PICK'S DISEASE

Pick's disease is much less common than Alzheimer's disease, although it was discovered a few years earlier. It is now recognized as a separate disease entity with a distinct hereditary pattern and characteristic neuropsychological findings. Nothing is known of its etiology except that it seems to be the result of a single autosomal dominant gene, possibly accompanied by other genes which color its manifestations (Sjogren et al., 1952).

There is a distinct tendency for this illness to begin with changes suggesting frontal lobe damage. The early abnormalities often involve changes in character and social behavior rather than impairment of memory and intellect. Drive tends to diminish, and incidents of tactless or grossly insensitive behavior may occur. Lack of restraint and errors in judgment may occur and may lead to alcoholism, stealing, or sexual misadventures. Early in the course, the expression becomes vacant and fatuous, manners deteriorate, and lack of motivation may become severe. Foolish jocularity and pranks may be noted, and insight is severely impaired.

As the disease progresses, intellectual and memory impairment appear and slowly increase. The patient's mood is likely to remain one of fatuous euphoria, or apathy may alternate with spells of restless hyperactivity. Delusions and hallucinations are rather rare; epileptic seizures are also uncommon.

Speech becomes extremely perseverative, with stereotyped repetition of brief words or phrases (Lishman, 1978). Dysphasic disturbances may progress to jargon, and periods of mutism may occur. Apraxia and agnosia may be seen, but less commonly than with Alzheimer's disease. Gait and muscle tone are also less frequently affected. In the late stages, the widespread deterioration of personality and intellect is little different from that found in Alzheimer's disease.

Pathologic Findings

In those cases which fit the classic description, a characteristic picture appears on gross inspection. A moderate degree of generalized atrophy is combined with severe shrinkage of the frontal and temporal lobes. In the frontal lobes the convexity or the orbital surface alone may be affected, and in the temporal lobe the posterior half of the superior temporal gyrus may be relatively spared. The distribution of atrophy tends to vary widely; however, major involvement of the parietal lobes is unusual, and occipital atrophy is very rare. The ventricles are enlarged, often with great dilatation of the lateral ventricular horn beneath the region of maximal cortical atrophy.

Histologic study reveals neuronal loss, along with dense proliferation of astrocytes and fibrous gliosis in the cortex and underlying white matter. The loss of neurons is seen primarily in the outer layers of the cortex, and a notable feature may be the close proximity of normal neurons to severely degenerated cells. In most cases, senile plaques and neurofibrillary tangles are conspicuously absent. Changes in the vasculature are uncommon. The white matter of affected lobes is usually extensively reduced.

FEATURES DISTINGUISHING BETWEEN PICK'S AND ALZHEIMER'S DISEASES

Certain genetic and pathologic characteristics that distinguish between Pick's and Alzheimer's diseases have already been mentioned. In addition, specific clinical differences have traditionally been employed. Most cases, however, are diagnosed for certain only at autopsy. In Pick's disease, changes in character and disposition are frequently noted from the onset, whereas in Alzheimer's disease, memory disturbance is usually the presenting problem. Incontinence, which appears early in the course, has been more commonly ascribed to Pick's disease and may reflect the greater frontal lobe involvement. Much less common in Pick's disease are parietal lobe symptoms such as dysphasia, apraxia, and agnosia, as well as extrapyramidal signs such as gait disturbances. In addition, some investigators have contrasted the facile hilarity and aspontaneity of Pick's disease to the depression, anxiety, and overactivity of Alzheimer's disease (Lishman, 1978). Clinical differentiation, then, when it can be made, depends on the mode of onset and the early neurologic signs. In later stages of illness, the boundaries between the disorders tend to become indistinct.

MULTI-INFARCT DEMENTIA

Until recently, it was widely believed that arteriosclerosis and other vascular problems were the major cause of dementia in the elderly. However, several autopsy studies have found that approximately 50–60% of all demented patients had Alzheimer's disease, approximately 12–20% exhibited purely vascular causes, and in another 16–20% a combination of the two disorders was detected (National Institutes of Health, 1981; Terry, 1978). Corsellis (1969) noted that autopsy evidence for multi-infarct dementia is rare in those who did not have marked hypertension. Roth (1981) also mentioned that in a majority of these patients, "the syndrome arises from multiple emboli that emanate from atheromatous plaques in a cerebral or extracerebral artery" (p. 31).

Clincial Features

Multi-infarct dementia appears to occur at a nearly equal rate in men and women. It typically begins during the late 60s and 70s, although cases have been seen in individuals in their 40s. Arteriosclerosis is frequently apparent in the peripheral circulation, and hypertension is usually severe. Lishman (1978) has outlined a clinical description, based on the work of Rothschild (1941) and Birkett (1972), which may be helpful in distinguishing multi-infarct dementia from the primary parenchymatous dementias.

The onset is often more acute in multi-infarct dementia, and a large number of cases come to medical attention when a frank cerebrovascular accident has occurred. When the onset is gradual, personality changes may precede definite evidence of memory and intellectual impairment. Other frequent early features may include somatic symptoms such as headache, dizziness, tinnitus, and syncope, which may remain the main complaints for some time.

Once they appear, the cognitive impairments tend to fluctuate in severity from day to day or even hour to hour. This may be due largely to episodes of clouding of consciousness which often begin early in the course. Strokelike features punctuate the progress of the disorder and are due to episodes of cerebral infarction. Usually they consist of attacks of hemiparesis, dysphasia, or visual difficulties. At first, they appear to be transient and are followed by gradual return of function, but each episode, especially later ones, leaves more evident permanent neurologic deficits. Each episode also produces an abrupt increase in the degree of dementia.

Other features suggesting multi-infarct dementia include the resultant patchy psychological deficits. As a consequence, the personality may remain well preserved until late in the disease, unlike the situation in other dementing illnesses. Judgment and insight often remain intact until well into the course of the illness. As a result, severe depression and anxiety are more likely in these patients than in those with Alzheimer's disease (Rothschild, 1941). Other emotional changes include lability, probably due to basal lesions of the brain, with a tendency toward explosive emotional outbursts. Episodes of weeping or laughing may occur with minor provocation.

Birkett (1972) found that neurologic abnormalities predicted multi-infarct dementia changes more accurately than any mental manifestation. Even in the absence of gross defects such as dysphasia or hemiparesis, there will frequently be minor focal signs. The tendon reflexes may be unequal or the pupil reactions impaired. Parkinsonian features or evidence of pseudobulbar palsy may develop. Epileptic seizures are seen in about 20% of cases.

The rCBF technique may prove useful in identifying multi-infarct dementia. Patchy reductions in blood flow have been reported as opposed to the diffuse reduction seen in Alzheimer's disease (Yamaguchi, Meyer, Yamamoto, Sakai, & Shaw, 1980).

Course and Outcome

The most reliable distinguishing feature of multi-infarct dementia may be its course. It is rarely smooth, unlike Alzheimer's disease, but rather tends to progress in abrupt steps. There may also be some degree of remission following the acute exacerbations of the disorder.

The length of illness prior to death varies widely. The course may sometimes be brief and stormy, but it can also last for many years. Death is usually listed as due to ischemic heart disease (50% of patients); other causes given are massive strokes or renal complications.

Pathologic Findings

The brain may show localized or generalized atrophy, with thickened, adherent meninges. The ventricles are enlarged. Scattered infarctions are seen, with softening and scarring of the brain substance. Occasionally, occlusion of a major vessel may affect the greater portion of a hemisphere.

Corsellis (1969) has summarized the picture in detail. Vessels of all sizes are affected by arteriosclerosis. The main arteries at the base of the brain are thickened, tortuous, and rigid, frequently with yellowish patches and modular expansions of the wall. Their lumens are greatly reduced or occluded. Small vessels within the brain are greatly thickened. The walls are often necrotic and disintegrated.

Microscopic examination reveals the effects of ischemia and infarction. Loss of neurons is extensive, sometimes occurring in streaks and patches within the cortex. Irregualr patches of demyelination may be seen in the white matter. Small, scattered infarcts are found with cyst formation and reactive gliosis. Small cystic softenings are especially common in the pons, and microinfarcts occur in the hippocampus. Larger areas of infarcted tissue show necrotic degeneration with masses of granular phagocytes, followed by sclerosis with dense glial and fibrocytic infiltration and distortion of brain substance.

Hachinski Lassen & Marshall (1974), noting that the evolution of dementia results from the accumulation of large and small infarcts apply the term *multi-infarct dementia* to the disorder. They also conclude that the majority of infarcts are due to thromboemboli from arteriosclerotic disease in the general circulation.

PSEUDODEMENTIAS

Pseudodementias are disorders which mimic the symptoms of dementia but are usually reversible with proper treatment. The most common pseudodementia is depression. Depressed elderly individuals often seem apathetic and unresponsive. They may appear forgetful, confused, even agitated. Separating depression and dementia may be complicated by the fact that they may be somewhat interdependent. People in the early stages of a dementing process may become depressed over the loss of their cognitive abilities. However, it is also possible that the depression experienced by many demented patients is caused directly by the damage to the brain tissue itself.

In attempting to distinguish depression from a dementing process, a careful interview with the patient and significant others is necessary. The clinician may find that the patient has had earlier bouts of depression, including symptoms such as insomnia, loss of appetite, and fatigue. Such a history tends to indicate depression. However, it is entirely possible for an individual with a previous history of clinical depression to become demented in later life.

The clinician may attempt to distinguish between depression and dementia by observing how the individual reacts to the symptoms. Before elaborating on this point, it must be emphasized that all elderly adults are not alike. All individuals react to the physical changes, role changes, and losses in social status, friends, family, and income that often occur in their lives in a uniquely personal way. However, depressed elderly patients often complain loudly about their symptoms, whereas demented patients often attempt to deny them. For example, we have found several depressed patients to report much greater memory and cognitive difficulties than they actually have. Many of our demented patients, in contrast, have denied any problems at all when it was readily apparent that they had serious memory and cognitive difficulties.

Another complication in the differential diagnosis of the dementias is reaction to drugs. Typically elderly persons take different medications for several chronic conditions. It is well known that medications have side effects and that most drugs will interact. Taken in combination, two or more drugs may be much more powerful than if either one is taken alone. In addition, there are significant age-related changes in the speed with which the body metabolizes drugs. A drug may persist in the body for a much longer time period in an elderly adult than in a younger one. Often the dosage for a 30-year-old is much too strong for a 70-year-old. Thus, it is critically important for the clinician to know what medications the elderly adult is taking, including the dosage, when attempting to assess dementia (National Institutes of Health, 1981).

Another cause of pseudodementia is chemical imbalance. For the brain to function properly, a critical balance of nutrients is necessary. Poor eating habits or the malabsorption of food may seriously affect the elderly individual's ability to function. Often mental dysfunction may occur earlier than physical problems when nutritional deficiencies are present. These biochemical imbalances are relatively easy to detect with a series of blood tests.

Another fairly common cause of pseudodementia is chronic cardiopulmonary disease. Just as the brain needs balanced nutrients, it also requires a constant high level of oxygen. Chronic lung or heart diseases can slowly starve the brain of oxygen, resulting in the symptoms of dementia. Thus, a complete physical examination should be performed to rule out reversible causes of dementia.

IMPLICATIONS FOR NEUROPSYCHOLOGICAL TESTING

Roth (1981) discussed some of the issues involved in the differential diagnosis of the dementias. He emphasized that the diagnosis of any type of dementia should not be based solely on one type of evidence. Rather, it should be made on "the strength of many lines of evidence" (p. 41). He recommended clinical evaluation, interview, careful history taking, and appropriate radiologic and laboratory tests.

Although the clinical interview and history are vitally important in the assessment of any disorder, both methods have significant limitations. First, the clinician may not interview individuals with the appropriate knowledge, either because they are not available or because the clinician may not know of their existence. Second, numerous studies have discussed the problems of reliability and validity of historic information obtained either from knowledgeable informants or from the patient. Third, significant cultural biases at work on the patient—examiner interaction may affect the assessment without the knowledge of the examiner.

Under such conditions, neuropsychological testing can be a useful adjunct to the patient's evaluation. One major question in this area is the relationship of neuropsychological test results to changes in the brain. Numerous studies have attempted to investigate this relationship (Blessed, Tomlinson, & Roth, 1968; Brinkman, Sarwar, Levin, & Morris, 1981; Earnest, Heaton, Wilkinson, & Manke, 1979: Fox, Topel, & Huckman, 1975; Huckman, Fox, & Jordan, 1975; Naeser, Gebhardt, & Levine, 1980; Roberts & Caird, 1976). Blessed et al. (1968) found a significant relationship between quantitative measures of senile dementia and degenerative brain changes. Later studies have also found CT scan measures of brain atrophy related to the symptoms of senile dementia (Brinkman et al., 1981; Fox et al., 1975; Huckman et al., 1975; Naeser et al., 1980; Roberts & Caird, 1976).

Another recent study found that cognitive test performance declined with increasing age, whereas measures of brain atrophy increased. However, atrophy revealed on the CT scan did not correlate directly with loss of mental function (Earnest et al., 1979). In a recent study, Jernigan et al. (1980) examined the relationship between several cortical atrophy measures and Wechsler Adult Intelligence Scale (WAIS) subtest scores. They discerned a significant correlation on only one comparison. They concluded by saying, "no evidence was found for an association between degrees of apparent cerebral atrophy and performance on many cognitive tasks" (p. 92).

Thus, some previous studies have found significant relationships between overall functional levels and CT scan measures of cortical atrophy. They have failed, however, to detect large correlations between specific measures of cognitive functions and measures of cortical atrophy. This disparity can be explained in several ways. First, studies which have discerned a relationship between overall cognitive functioning and CT scan measures of cortical atrophy have employed very disparate groups, such as normal elderly persons and patients with senile dementia. Studies which have not detected a significant correlation have used groups that are homogeneous with respect to cognitive abilities, such as groups of dementia or stroke patients. This approach restricts the range of possible values and thus limits the potential correlations. Second, the cognitive measures used in these studies range from intelligence tests to simple measures of specific skills (such as motor ability). These tests of cognitive functioning may not be the most sensitive measures for detecting specific changes in brain function. Finally, the measures of cortical atrophy employed may also be unable to determine impairment in specific functional abilities.

Another problem with many previous studies relating cognitive functioning to brain structure concerns and CT scan variable. In many studies, this measure consists of a subjective rating by a radiologist of the degree of pathology apparent on the CT scan. Other studies have measured dimensions of various structures, such as the lateral ventricles, and have correlated these measures with cognitive functions. Unfortunately, many brain abnormalities are not visually detectable. Since CT scan pictures are merely computer representations of numbers generated by the scanner, a more fruitful approach might be to examine directly the relationship between the density numbers and measures of cognitive functions. Golden and his colleagues have developed a technique for sampling the actual CT numbers from the entirety of a CT slice (Golden, Graber, Coffman, Berg, Bloch, & Brogan, 1980; Golden, Graber, Coffman, Berg, Newlin, & Bloch, 1981). A statistical analysis may be able to find subtle differences in brain density that are not detectable by visual analysis of the scan.

Obrist (1980) attempted to examine the relationship between rCBF and cognitive functioning. He divided patients into two categories using the median split according to high blood flow and low blood flow. He found that the two groups differed significantly on the performance scale of the WAIS. The low blood flow group performed more poorly than the high blood flow group. The verbal scale of the WAIS was also lower for the low blood flow group, but this finding was not statistically significant. It appears that rCBF declines significantly in the average (unselected) old person; however, the reduction occurs earlier and is of greater magnitude when accompanied by dementia.

The relationship between the structural integrity of the brain and higher cognitive functioning in the elderly may be inadequately understood partly because of oversimplified conceptualizations of brain–behavior relationships. One of the basic tenets of neuropsychology is that the structures of the brain are intimately linked to cognitive functioning. However, there are numerous explanations of this relationship. A strict *localizationst* would posit a direct one-to-one correspondence between certain structures of the brain and specific functional abilities. From this perspective, damage to a particular brain structure causes equal damage to the functions associated with that area. On the other hand, the *equipotentialist* would posit that most higher cognitive abilities are dependent upon the integrity of the entire brain. From this perspective, it is the quantity of destroyed or dysfunctional brain tissue, rather than the particular structures damaged, which determines functional losses. Thus, the more extensive the tissue damage, the greater the functional losses.

Both of these conceptualizations of brain–behavior relationships implicitly assume a simple relationship between the integrity of the physical brain and the individual's functional abilities at all ages. However, research has failed to find consistent, direct one-to-one correlations between the integrity of the brain and functional levels in the elderly. For example, Blessed, Tomlinson, and Roth (1968) found great overlap between normal and demented elderly individuals in the number of senile plaques and neurofibrillary tangles in their brains.

Luria (1966, 1973) has proposed a theory of brain–behavior relationships which incorporates elements of the localizationist and equipotentialist models. He does not share with either group the implicit assumption of a narrow or necessary one-to-one relationship between the integrity of the physical brain and a person's functional abilities. Luria accomplishes this integration by using the concept of *functional systems*. In his model, local cortical areas do mediate specific skills. However, these modality-specific skills are so limited that performing even the simplest behavior entails a variety of elementary skills, and hence requires the activity of multiple cortical sites. Thus, a given brain area (which under normal conditions mediates a specific skill component of a particular behavior) may be necessary but not sufficient to accomplish the behavior. Only when a number of brain areas cooperate can a given behavior occur. A functional system represents the patterns of interaction within the brain necessary for any given behavior (Golden, Ariel, McKay, Wilkening, Wolf, & MacInnes, 1982).

A corollary to the functional system hypothesis is that more than one functional system can underlie a behavior, since there can be more than one way to accomplish a task. If pathologic processes develop very slowly, such as the structural changes which occur in the brain over the course of a lifetime, the individual may compensate for the structural changes by developing different functional systems to maintain past abilities that formerly used other functional systems. From Luria's (1966, 1973) perspective, the relationship between structural and cognitive measures is complex and not necessarily obvious in the elderly.

Since it is generally assumed that intelligence is related to brain structures and functions, it follows that there should be some correlation between neuropsychological, neurologic, and intellectual functioning. However, using Luria's notion of functional systems, one might not expect a one-to-one relationship between all measures of intelligence, neuropsychological functioning, and structural measures of the brain, but one might expect to see relationships among various intellectual skills and particular neuropsychological functions.

It is clear that theoretical issues play an important role in how one views the elderly patient's performance on measures of higher cognitive functioning. However, there are also important methodologic factors which can significantly affect the results of assessment of the elderly. It is not safe to assume that a given test measures the same psychological construct in both young and old adults; errors may be made for different reasons (Schaie & Schaie, 1977). If a young adult misses an item on an intelligence test, it is generally assumed to be directly related to that person's intellectual ability. If an elderly individual misses the same item, however, it may be for a variety of reasons. For example, an elderly person may lose points on the arithmetic subscale of the WAIS not because of low arithmetic ability but because auditory acuity has decreased with age. Questions may be misunderstood or they may have to be repeated, which decreases the available response time and results in lower scores. Skills that may be a function of "crystallized" abilities in the young person may be a function of "fluid" abilities in the elderly (Schaie & Schaie, 1977). For example, items which may tap a young adult's cultural and educational background in the 1980s may reflect very different abilities in 80-year-olds. Octogenarians simply have not had the same life experiences as today's 20-year-olds. Questions reflecting the general knowledge of today's young adults may be more indicative of an adventurous elderly individual's current experience and personality style. Many questions relevant to the young adult may not be so for the elderly person.

Other significant methodologic factors may also affect the interpretation of the elderly person's performance on tests of higher cognitive functions. The application of psychological test norms derived from younger groups can lead to serious errors in interpretation of such test results. Not only do tests validated on one age cohort not necessarily measure the same constructs in another age cohort, but tests validated in an earlier time period may not be valid in a later one (Schaie & Schaie, 1977). Tests constructed for a given age cohort in young adulthood may not be valid for successive age cohorts. A measure of cognitive abilities for an 80-year-old when he or she was 20 may not be useful for today's 20-year-olds.

Similarly, tests which differentiate between normal and brain-damaged persons in young adulthood cannot be assumed to do so in the elderly as well (Schaie & Schaie, 1977). Support for this notion comes from a recent study which suggested that scores falling in a "brain-damaged" range may not have the same meaning for the elderly as they do for younger adults. In a study of 49 retired teachers, Price, Fein, and Feinberg (1980) found that many subjects scored in the brain-damaged range on the Halstead–Reitan Neuropsychological Test Battery even though they performed in the superior range on the WAIS and maintained a high level of functioning in their daily lives.

The need for age-related norms on neuropsychological, neurologic, and radiologic tests is clearly apparent, as the methodologic problems with generating and using normative data for the elderly suggest. Significant deviations from norms established by using healthy elderly people may be viewed as the result of "abnormal" processes which are separate from, although not totally independent of, age per se. The use of well-documented norms would help the clinician to differentiate between one individual who is exhibiting the normal aging pattern and another who is performing at an impaired level relative to his or her age peers. Age-determined norms allow a more accurate delineation of pathology by defining pathologic performance in the elderly on their own terms (Price et al., 1980).

In light of these issues, the finding of Roth (1981) that intelligence testing was not very useful in the diagnosis of dementia is not surprising. Intelligence tests are not designed as measures of brain dysfunction; they are meant to be estimates of IQ. Since any diffuse brain damage tends to lower IQ it is not surprising that IQ tests are not very useful in the differential diagnosis of dementia. Similarly, other tests which attempt to measure brain functioning using complex skills will also not be helpful for this task.

However, Luria's (1966, 1973) notion of functional systems may give us a more useful basis for measuring the numerous cognitive strengths and weaknesses of various groups of demented patients. In addition, the use of a standardized, comprehensive neuropsychological battery avoids the primary pitfalls of depending heavily upon the clinical interview and history of the patient; such a test battery is not dependent on the accuracy and availability of others to supply information. Although it is desirable to have an accurate history and a thorough interview with the patient, symptoms can sometimes be misleading when we rely too heavily on clinical judgment. A neuropsychological assessment can give the clinician other important information about the patient's functional abilities.

The studies cited above suggest that neuropsychological testing may be useful in the diagnosis of elderly individuals. However, the clinician must keep several factors in mind. Although various motivational and situational factors must always be considered in conducting an assessment, work with elderly individuals raises particular problems. For example, the high incidence of depression in elderly populations will sometimes lead to poor test performance, which is a consequence of the patient's low energy level or lack of interest rather than an indication of cerebral dysfunction. Peripheral auditory and visual deficits can result in similar interpretive difficulties. Also, compared to younger adults, many elderly individuals find test situations unfamiliar and threatening. In such cases, performance anxiety may increase to a level which negatively affects performance. Other factors also complicate assessment of some elderly persons. If testing must be conducted at the clinician's office because of bulky equipment, transportation can become a major problem to the disabled elderly person.

One difference between old and young individuals that can seriously affect the findings of a neuropsychological assessment is stamina. Typically, even healthy elderly individuals tire more quickly than younger adults, and when they become fatigued, they require a longer period for recovery. If testing continues despite fatigue, the patient's performance may well suffer. A clinician may then inaccurately attribute a poor performance to cerebral dysfunction when none is actually present.

Another factor to consider when assessing an elderly individual concerns the complexity of the test items. As stated by Miller (1980), although elderly individuals are not necessarily less cooperative than younger ones regarding test taking, they tend to be more cautious, perhaps because they expect to do poorly and receive negative feedback. Even highly functioning elderly individuals may find involved, complex tasks to be more difficult than they actually are. To the impaired elderly individual, experiences with long, difficult tasks can be discouraging and humiliating. In some cases, poor initial performances and negative experiences on tests can lower the patient's motivation and cooperation on all subsequent tasks. Thus, tests which contain simple, discrete items and can be answered correctly even by many seriously impaired individuals will tend to maximize the elderly person's performance. For example, on the Luria–Nebraska Neuropsychological Battery, many of the items are quite simple and can be answered correctly even by seriously impaired individuals. Difficult and simple items are interspersed throughout the test. This makes it less likely that an inordinate number of failures will be encountered consecutively, and therefore less likely that the test taker will become irritable or discouraged.

Another potentially serious complicating factor for the neuropsychologist who is assessing the functioning of elderly individuals is the high incidence of peripheral sensory and motor deficits in this population (Schaie & Schaie, 1977). Peripheral sensory deficits can lead to errors on test items that are intended to evaluate quite different cortical functions. For example, the patient may provide incorrect responses to memory function items simply because his poor hearing has prevented him from hearing the questions clearly.

Typically, a clinician who works frequently with elderly individuals is sensitive to such issues and will not conclude that test errors reflect actual cerebral dysfunction without first evaluating the possibility of impairment at the peripheral level. Nonetheless, these impairments can restrict the range of a clinician's assessment. For example, in an individual with severely impaired peripheral hearing, evaluation of cortical areas that are necessary for phonemic discrimination cannot be made. However, the extent to which such deficits restrict the assessment of other skills will depend upon both the nature and the flexibility of the assessment devices.

Similarly, the high incidence of strokes, progressive dementing diseases, and other serious neurologic disorders in elderly individuals increases the likelihood that the neuropsychologist will encounter serious motor, language, and higher intellectual deficits. If these deficits are pervasive, they can interfere with performance on items that are intended to tap other functional systems. For example, because of difficulties in comprehending instructions, the patient may perform a motor response incorrectly even with the ability to do it. Although the experienced clinician would not conclude that this incorrect response reflects impaired motor function, his or her capacity to draw any conclusions regarding this motor skill is restricted.

Ideally, when one conducts a neuropsychological assessment of the elderly patient, the approach should be flexible. Problems associated with peripheral motor and sensory deficits or pervasive cerebral deficits which inadvertently interfere with assessment of other unrelated skills should be avoided or minimized. Another important factor to consider is that many neuropsychological skills should be assessed using multiple input and output channels. For example, evaluation of the ability to speak should include stimulus words presented in both auditory and visual forms. A patient with impaired hearing may distort or substitute words when stimuli are presented in auditory form but speak perfectly when allowed to read them. The clinician can then draw conclusions regarding expressive speech abilities that would not have been possible if only one input channel had been used.

When testing phonetic discrimination, verbal, written, and motor responses may be required. Individuals whose articulation is poor as a consequence of badly fitting dentures or missing teeth can indicate the ability to discriminate sounds through accurate written responses. Similarly, in patients whose expressive speech and writing have been disrupted by a stroke, the ability to make phonetic discriminations can be indicated by hand signals. Again, the use of multiple output channels avoids the unnecessary restriction of skills assessed by the clinician and minimizes the chance that impairment in response channels (e.g., speech) will be mistaken for impairment in the skill being measured.

CONCLUSION

A neuropsychological examination is most useful in assessment of the elderly if the following factors are kept in mind: (1) standardization to allow the establishment of age norms; (2) brief testing to reduce fatigue in the elderly patient; (3) simple items to maximize the elderly patient's performance and reduce the number of false-positive results in diagnosis; (4) utilization of multiple input and output channels to minimize the difficulties in assessing individuals with serious peripheral motor or sensory impairments; and (5) "testing the limits" to provide a more detailed analysis of the patient's cognitive strengths and deficits.

Chapter 7

Parkinson's Disease

Parkinson's disease was originally described by James Parkinson, who noted the pattern of motor symptoms seen with the disease. Seen most often in individuals in their 50s and 60s, the disease also has been reported in people in their 30s and 40s. The disease may arise from many causes: as a long-term effect of encephalitis, as a result of a cerebrovascular disorder, after poisoning with carbon monoxide, after head trauma, after neurosyphilis, or for no apparent cause at all.

CLINICAL FEATURES

Parkinson's disease can be described by its three major clinical features: tremor, rigidity, and bradykinesia. The tremor of parkinsonism is seen primarily when the patient is resting or holding sustained postures, and is much less apparent during voluntary movements. For this reason, tremor, of the three primary symptoms, seems to create the fewest hindrances to willed body movements. Rigidity results from an increase in muscle tone and is greatest in the flexor muscles. This produces the characteristic posture of parkinsonism with stooping and slight flexion of the knees, hips, neck, and elbows. This state of increased tone in antagonistic muscle groups must be overcome in order for the patient to move, which especially limits extensor actions. The extra effort required to move may be regarded by the patient as weakness, although testing of individual muscle groups usually shows little or no decrease in strength. Bradykinesia in parkinsonism generally consists of difficulty in initiating and sometimes ceasing movement. Patients may have considerable difficulty in carrying out spontaneous movements such as arm swinging while walking. Walking often can begin only after a few seconds' attempt. It is not unusual for such a patient to use collision with a door or wall as a means of stopping. An associated inability to rapidly recover from postural changes may result in frequent falls.

Other clinical features of Parkinson's disease that are related to the major symptoms include expressionless, masklike features, a feeling of being lethargic and weak, flattening and weakness of the voice, micrographia, *marche à petit pas* (festinating, small-stepping gait), and cogwheel rigidity. Features not readily associated with the pathogenesis of parkinsonism are oily seborrheic skin, excessive salivation, constipation, difficulty in focusing the eyes, and sleep disturbances. All of these suggest overactivity of the parasympathetic division of the autonomic nervous system and were recognized long before anything substantial was known about the pathogenesis of the disorder.

The causes of parkinsonism are many. Tranquilizers such as the pheno-thiazines are perhaps the most common source of parkinsonian syndromes at present. The idiopathic and postencephalitic causes of Parkinson's disease are also rather common. In these forms, the individuals affected are over 50 years of age, and there is little familial tendency. Although, as the name implies, the etiology of idiopathic parkinsonism is in doubt, the idea that a slow virus may be responsible is stirring interest (Pincus & Tucker, 1978). Rare causes of Parkinson's disease include carbon monoxide poisoning, manganese intoxica-tion, hypocalcemia, and degenerative disorders of the nervous system which produce parkinsonian syptoms in their course.

Most other neurologic disorders are easily differentiated from Parkinson's disease. However, some diagnostic confusion can arise in cases of depression. Depressed individuals may complain of generalized weakness, constipation, and sleep disturbance, and exhibit slowed movements, expressionless features, a weakened voice, decreased frequency of spontaneous movements, and a halting gait. All of these signs and symptoms are not unlike those of Parkin-son's disease. In addition, Parkinson's disease patients appear depressed, espe-cially while at rest, although other features of depression are usually absent.

Idiopathic parkinsonism is typically a progressive disorder. Hoehn and Yahr (1967) found that 25% of the patients were severely disabled or dead within 5 years of onset, a figure that rose to 66% by 10 years. A few, however, experienced very slow progression and remained only moderately disabled 20 years after onset. Mortality is estimated to be three times that of the general population of the same sex and age. The prognosis is better for postencephalitic patients in terms of both progression and mortality rates.

PATHOPHYSIOLOGY

Parkinson's disease is associated with defects in the components of the extrapyramidal motor system. Cellular degeneration occurs in the globus pallidus, putamen, caudate, and associated nuclei and is consistently seen in the zona compacta of the substantia nigra in the brain stem (Greenfield, 1963). The melanin-containing cells of the substantia nigra are greatly affected, so much so that damage to this nucleus may be seen on gross inspection. Microscopically, the hyaline inclusion bodies attributed to Lewy can often be seen in the cells which remain, as well as in the pigmented cells of the locus ceruleus, dorsal motor vagal nucleus, and reticular formation. Glial scars are seen in the spaces left by the missing neurons. Tract lesions in the nigro-striatal tract, however, are usually slight. Scattered, nonspecific changes may be seen in other sites in the diencephalon, brain stem, spinal cord, and cerebral cortex. Diffuse cortical atrophy has been frequently reported; it is most pronounced in the frontal lobes and occurs to an unexpected degree for the patient's age (Alvord, 1971). In postencephalitic parkinsonism, the pigmented cells of the substantia nigra and locus ceruleus are similarly lost, but neurofibrillary changes rather than Lewy bodies are seen in the remaining neurons.

The biochemical basis for parkinsonism has become much better understood, leading to the recognition of neurotransmitter system abnormalities as the basic disturbance in the disease. In fact, the idiopathic disease can be regarded as specific degeneration of one neuronal system: the pigmented neurons of the brain stem which manufacture and utilize the catecholamine neurotransmitters dopamine and norepinephrine (Parkes & Marsden, 1973). In the normal individual dopamine is found in high concentration in the pigmented cells of the substantia nigra, the nigro-striatal tract, and its terminals in the caudate nucleus and putamen. Dopamine is found in much lower concentration in the brains of most parkinsonian patients of both the idiopathic and postencephalitic subgroups, and is sometimes reduced to 10% of the normal striatal level. This seems to result from loss of dopaminergic fibers passing from the substantia nigra to the striatum (Hornykiewicz, 1971; Vogt, 1970). It appears that dopamine and acetylcholine may be antagonistic in their effects on the striatum, so that any effect which tips the dopamine – acetylcholine balance in the direction of cholinergic dominance leads to the movement disorders of parkinsonism. This mechanism provides the framework for the present drug treatments of parkinsonism. The source of the original lesion in idiopathic parkinsonism continues to remain obscure.

INTELLECTUAL AND EMOTIONAL CHANGES

In his original description of the disease, James Parkinson excluded intellectual change as a discriminating symptom (Pincus & Tucker, 1978). Observers since his time have differed in their reports of the incidence and nature of cognitive impairment in the disease. Pollock and Hornabrook (1966) found that 20% of a large unselected group of patients showed significant mental deterioration, and only a minority of the group had clearly idiopathic parkinsonism. Mindham (1970) found that one-third of patients with Parkinson's disease admitted to a psychiatric hospital showed impaired intellect. Celesia and Wanamaker (1972) reported a high incidence of cognitive impairment, with an incidence of some 40 percent in a group of 153 patients with idiopathic parkinsonism. Their degree of impairment correlated with the duration and severity of the disease. On the basis of these clinical studies, an association between idiopathic parkinsonism and some degree of dementia seems to exist.

IMPLICATIONS FOR NEUROPSYCHOLOGICAL TESTING

A cursory reading of the psychometric literature suggests somewhat contradictory results. Talland (1962) tested 45 Parkinson's disease patients and 45 matched controls with a battery of tests said to represent a wide range of cognitive functions not dependent on motor skills. The only deficit reported by the author appeared in the area of long-term memory and complex problem-solving ability, although the author suggested that these deficits may have been due to medications the patients were receiving rather than the disease itself. The study concluded that there were no cognitive deficits characteristic of Parkinson's disease.

Asso (1969) examined Parkinson's disease patients on the Wechsler Adult Intelligence Scale (WAIS). The author found no deficits, although this test cannot be considered a measure of all relevant major cognitive functions. The deficits which did appear on the test were attributed to poor motor function.

Reitan and Boll (1971) reported a comparison of 25 parkinsonion patients with 25 normal controls in the Halstead—Reitan Neuropsychological Battery. The patients were compared on 32 cognitive, sensory, and motor measures. Statistically significant lower scores were found on 25 of the 32 measures employed, and the authors concluded that the patients showed deficits in problem solving, sensory skills, motor skills, memory, general cognitive skills, abstraction, and concentration skills.

Loranger, Goodell, McDowell, Lele, and Sweet (1972) found lower WAIS performance IQ as compared to verbal IQ in individuals with idiopathic parkinsonism but did not attribute the differences to motor impairment alone. In observing the patients' behavior, these authors concluded on a qualitative basis that the problems were in cognitive rather than motor areas. They suggested that the greatest impairment in their patients was in immediate memory and in the comprehension of unfamiliar material. On the other hand, verbal comprehension, fluency, long-term information retrieval, and practical social judgment (comprehension) were intact.

These results and their discrepancies are probably due to several important factors in the evaluation of the parkinsonian patient. The first factor is the degree to which the disease has progressed. This is not simply the duration of the illness, since the rate of development of neuropsychological symptoms varies greatly with the etiology of the disease. This factor must be considered in evaluating both general studies and individual patients. Unfortunately, few studies report either the type of parkinsonism their patients have or the duration of the disorder within each subtype.

A second problem is the role of general physical ability. Parkinsonian patients generally fatigue faster than normal controls, causing impairment on tests which require sustained activity over long periods or on tests which last for a long time without frequent breaks. It is important to recognize deficits due to fatigue when planning rehabilitation, evaluating vocational skills, and so on. However, deficits caused either by physical or mental fatigue that arises from the increased effort required to perform motor tests must not be confused with deficits due to brain injury. These factors should be carefully analyzed when one is evaluating the parkinsonian patient, since the patient is often able to perform at a much higher level than is suggested by some test results. Thus, a seemingly fully disabled patient may be able to return to limited or flexible vocational activity, which is often useful in treating the feelings of depression and uselessness which may occur with this type of neurologic disease. A third factor to consider is that parkinsonian patients are frequently older individuals who may have deficits similar to those seen in normal aging. Appropriate age norms are necessary, but these are not available for many commonly used neuropsychological tests. Again, the clinician must be sensitive to this issue, especially when using tests that do not have the appropriate norms for this population.

When brain damage extends beyond the motor symptoms in a parkinsonian patient, the deficits on neuropsychological tests are usually found to be associated with activities traditionally assumed to reflect the functioning of the right hemisphere (visual, spatial, and integration tasks) or the frontal lobes (abstracting, planning, evaluating, integrating or sequencing tasks). These observations most likely begin not with the cortex but with the subcortical tracts. The involvement of these structures causes deficits that are very similar to those we ascribe to the cortical areas. Consequently, one must be cautious in attempting to localize these disorders to specific areas of the cortex, since in at least some of the patients the cortex will appear intact on neuroradiologic measures such as computed tomography (CT) scan. The frontal lobe deficits may begin in very subtle ways, as described earlier. In general, overlearned skills will be intact in these patients, whereas new learning skills will be impaired.

Motor skills have traditionally shown deficits in the parkinsonian patient. However, the introduction of such medications as levodopa (L-dopa) has minimized the extent of these deficits. In the early stages, the treatment may be adequate to abolish any existing deficit; in later stages, the degree of deficit will be significantly reduced. It is important to know what medication the patient is receiving and how well it is working when one is conductiong an evaluation. Testing the patient before and after medication is begun can be useful in quantifying the improvement produced.

The existence of sensory deficits in Parkinson's disease is somewhat controversial. In general, there appear to be no significant losses in basic sensation (such as the level of deficit typically measured on the neurologic examination), although there may be impairment on more sophisticated tasks such as recognizing numbers written on the hands or fingers. These problems may reflect the inability of the patient to concentrate and integrate basic sensations, as is seen in frontal lobe patients with other disorders. Alternatively, this situation may reflect a very mild disorder in sensory integration. This hypothesis, however, has yet to be proven. Whatever interpretation is placed on the tests, it is not unusual to see these tasks missed by the parkinsonian patient.

Deficits are also seen on complex tasks involving sustained attention, concentration, and abstraction, with or without a significant motor component. Again, the exact etiology of these deficits is unclear in the sense that the real underlying skill deficits in these patients remain obscure. These deficits generally worsen as the disease progresses, and they can become especially severe in those patients who have other clear signs of cortical involvement. As noted above, however, none of these deficits can be considered pathognomonic of cortical involvement.

Depression is often acute and may reflect the patient's reaction to the disease. For example, Mindham (1974) showed that the severity of the primary symptoms of parkinsonism correlated significantly with the degree of depression shown by the patient. However, there is also some evidence that depression is more common in this disease than in other debilitating disorders, which suggests a more direct relationship between the disease and depression (Lishman, 1978). In light of the research that suggests some relationship between right hemisphere or subcortical injuries and depression, this is a plausible association (see the chapter on affective disorders), but it remains unproven at present.

Generally, parkinsonian patients can be given most standard personality tests, although as frontal lobe signs become more pronounced and symptoms of dementia appear, these tests probably measure the patient's cognitive disability rather than his or her personality style. As long as the cognitive disability is slight, however, there should be no problem with tests such as the Rorshach or Minnesota Multiphasic Personality Inventory (MMPI). Caution should be used when interpreting tests which require motor skills, such as drawing tests which are likely to appear immature or regressed from normal adult performance.

CONCLUSION

Parkinsonian patients generally show less cognitive impairment than those with many other disorders but more than that seen in multiple sclerosis. In the slower-onset forms of the disease, there are long periods in which the patient shows little impairment on tests that do not involve fatigue or motor control. At the other extreme, patients may later become significantly disabled, although the course of the disease is quite variable, depending on the etiology and on its progression in the individual patient. The primary symptoms seen in parkinsonism include motor symptoms (although these may be significantly reduced by medication), spatial integration symptoms, and frontal lobe signs. In many cases, these symptoms reflect subcortical rather than cortical damage.

Chapter 8

Multiple Sclerosis

Of all the demyelinating diseases, multiple sclerosis (MS) is by far the most common. Among diseases of the nervous system as a whole, it is one of the more frequently seen disease entities in temperate latitudes. Its chronicity makes the disease a major source of disability even though its incidence is not particularly great. The etiology of the disorder remains obscure even in the face of extensive study. Although a familial tendency is seen in about 5% of cases, no clear genetic pattern has been discovered. The possibility of an environmental influence is suggested by the familial tendency as well as the known geographic variation in incidence. Various theories have been proposed, including infectious, metabolic, dietary, and autoimmune mechanisms, although none has been recognized as the answer. Grinker and Sahs (1966) and Hallpike (1973) have discussed these varied theories.

Multiple sclerosis has its onset primarily in young adults 20–40 years old. Women are affected somewhat more often than men. Because of the protean neurologic manifestations of the disease, the diagnosis traditionally has been made by noting the multifocal and relapsing nature of the signs and symptoms. Over the course of the disease, evidence of disseminated lesions in the central nervous system usually emerges. These lesions, especially early in the course, tend toward a pattern of remission and exacerbation.

Some of the early signs of MS include retrobulbar neuritis (optic nerve demyelination), oculomotor disturbances producing diplopia or nystagmus, or lesions of the long tracts of the spinal cord producing paresthesias or spastic paraparesis. Difficulty in control of micturition, particularly with precipitant onset, may be an early symptom, as may ataxia or intention tremor due to a

111

cerebellar lesion. Retrobulbar neuritis is rather common and may occur with central visual field defect long before other signs appear.

The initial problems tend to subside within a few months and occasionally disappear completely, but they often leave some residual disability. Future attacks may intensify symptoms already present or may produce new ones. The interval between attacks is highly variable. Most cases follow a relapsing and remitting pattern which ultimately becomes a steady progression with an accumulation of deficits. Some cases show such steady progression from the beginning.

Early findings on examination include pallor of the temporal halves of the optic discs, nystagmus, mild intention tremor, exaggerated tendon reflexes, absent abdominal reflexes, extensor plantar responses, and impaired vibration and joint position sense. During early remissions, however, abnormal signs may be subtle. Later, evidence of multiple lesions affecting the optic nerves, cerebellum, brain stem, and long spinal cord tracts will probably show some combination of ataxia, intention tremor, dysarthria, dysconjugate eye movements, paraparesis, sensory losses in the extremities, and urinary incontinence. Psychological disturbances, some of which may result from lesions in the cerebrum, arise in a large number of cases. Epileptic seizures rarely occur (Lishman, 1978).

PATHOLOGY

The pathologic findings in MS consist of limited areas of demyelination which are followed later in the course of the disease by secondary degeneration of long axonal tracts. Macroscopically, these demyelinated areas or plaques appear as grayish, translucent areas which may be seen in any part of the central nervous system, mainly in the white matter, but on occasion in the gray matter of the cortex and spinal cord. In most cases that come to autopsy, the number of lesions is much greater than the clinical picture would have suggested. The cerebellum and periventricular areas of the cerebrum are especially prone to the disease process.

Microscopically, in the acute stages myelin sheaths appear degenerated, but the neuronal axes remain intact. The perivascular spaces in and near the lesion contain lymphocytes and macrophages with neutral fats in their vacuoles. Later, when the macrophages have completed their work, the damaged myelin is removed and astrocytes proliferate to form a glial scar. At this stage, axonal destruction is seen within the lesion.

PSYCHIATRIC CHANGES

Mental changes are commonly noted in MS patients. Intellectual and emotional changes have been observed. Some investigators have stated that a particular set of symptoms is characteristic of the disease, with euphoria frequently being stressed. However, a consistent pattern is lacking. In addition, a role has been suggested for psychological factors in precipitating relapses, although little clear-cut supportive evidence has been found.

Early investigators of MS frequently regarded personality deficits as the greatest disturbances produced by the disorder, and in the latter 19th century, numerous instances of psychosis were attributed to the disease. At the time of these reports, however, neurosyphilis could not be readily distinguished from MS. Cottrell and Wilson (1926) reported a series of 100 outpatients in whom emotional changes included increased cheerfulness, physical well-being, and optimism, all usually inappropriate to the severity of the handicaps present. On the other hand, intellectual impairment was minimal. For diagnostic value in multiple sclerosis, changes of mood with a feeling of physical well-being and impairment of emotional control were, as a syndrome, considered to be more important than any neurologic finding. In 1930, Brain suggested hysterical conversion symptoms as yet another characteristic of the disease. For some time afterward, hysteria and euphoria were regarded as part of MS in the English literature. The continental European literature took a different view. Ombredane (1929) continued to regard intellectual disorders as integral to MS, reporting abnormalities of memory and intellect in his patients. Affective changes appeared commonly in patients suffering from intellectual deterioration and consisted of unstable moods with rapid variations rather than constant euphoria or depression. Runge (1928) stated that depression was likely to occur early in the course of the disease, giving way to euphoria, with further progression as intellectual deterioration occurred.

In the intervening years, researchers have attempted to bridge the gap by careful study of the psychological changes in large groups of patients. Surridge (1969) reported a thorough study of 108 MS patients who were seen in their homes while separate informants were questioned regarding intellectual defects and mood and personality changes. For a control group, patients suffering from a different progressive neurologic disorder, muscular dystrophy, were used.

Some psychiatric problem was found in 75% of the MS group, compared to less than 50% of the controls. Sixty-one percent of the MS patients showed an intellectual deficit, ranging from mild to severe, whereas none of the controls did so. Mood changes were seen in 53% of the subjects and 13% of controls. Depression occurred in 27%, and euphoria was noted in 26%. Euphoria appeared primarily in association with intellectual impairment, and increasing euphoria correlated strongly with increasing impairment of intellect.

Personality changes were found in 40% of patients with multiple sclerosis and 33% of controls. MS patients tended to become more irritable, whereas muscular dystrophy patients often became more patient and tolerant.

INTELLECTUAL IMPAIRMENT

The major changes found by Surridge (1969) were loss of memory for recent events and impairment of conceptual thinking. When severe, these deficits were usually associated with confabulation, perseveration, excessive fatigability, and dysphasia. Seven percent of the patients showed profound global dementia. There was also a strong association between the degree of intellectual impairment and the severity of physical disability. Psychometric evaluation of this group supported the presence of general and specific intellectual dysfunction (Jambor, 1969). The most severe impairments were of general intellectual efficiency, nonverbal reasoning, and memory functions. Concrete abstractions and circumstantiality often appeared.

An earlier study (Canter, 1951) showed significant impairment early in the course of the disease. A group of 47 army veterans with MS showed declines on most subtests of the Wechsler Bellevue Intelligence Scale over a 6 month period compared with gains in normal controls. Comparisons in 23 patients with tests at the time of enlistment (Army General Classification Test) 4 years earlier showed highly significant losses, although the disease was still in a very early stage. Apparently, then, MS patients must not only adapt to progressive physical disability but must make these adaptations with progressively deteriorating intellectual capacity (Lishman, 1978).

The frequency of intellectual impairment is not surprising in light of the finding of widespread plaques throughout the brain. Brownell and Hughes (1962) found macroscopically visible plaques in 22 patients seen at autopsy, ranging in number from 3 to 225, with an average of 72 plaques per patient. Although all parts of the white matter appeared to be involved, the periventricular areas seemed to be especially prone. Pneumoencephalography has revealed a high incidence of ventricular dilatation and an increase of air over the cortical surface (Freeman, 1944). Computed tomography in MS has identified plaques within the brain that correspond to clinically suspected lesions, as well as some that are clinically silent. The duration of the disease was found to correlate with the number of plaques (Reisner and Maida, 1980).

Dementia can, on occasion, be the presenting symptom of MS, which raises diagnostic difficulties. Koenig (1968) reported 7 patients in whom dementia was the sole or major sign of disease. The mental symptoms in these cases were no different from those seen in other types of organic dementia, although the onset was often acute, with memory loss, confusion, disorientation, or personality change. Three patients progressively deteriorated, and only one had a partial remission. Neurologic symptoms of brain stem or spinal cord involvement preceded or accompanied the onset of the dementia in four cases, and all patients showed evidence of widespread central nervous system dysfunction on careful examination. Koenig suggested that unrecognized MS may be a more common cause of organic dementia than is generally believed.

MOOD CHANGES

Various affective changes are common in MS. Euphoria is generally thought to be typical, but it is now apparent that depression is at least as frequent. The picture may depend on the stage of disease in which the patient is seen and whether any intellectual deterioration has taken place. Depression is generally a logical and expected response to the patient's condition in the earlier stages, and euphoria is more frequent as the disease progresses.

Surridge (1969) found depression in 27% and euphoria in 26% of patients and Kahana, Liebowitz, and Alter (1971) reported depression in 6% and euphoria in 5% of MS patients studied. Clearly, these results have varied considerably across studies.

Depression seems to be reactive in origin in most cases, and there is little reason to suggest that it results from cerebral pathology. There was no special tendency among the depressed patients in Surridge's study toward intellectual dysfunction. It seems that the psychological impact of the patient's disability and his or her awareness of the situation are primary factors affecting the depression. Marked reactive depression can result when the patient learns and understands the diagnosis and prognosis. Sphincter dysfunction can be particularly traumatic, with the increased dependency and hampered sexual function which often result. Impotence, ataxia, and visual disturbances are also very distressing manifestations of the disease. Suicide is not uncommon, as the depression may be severe.

Euphoria in these patients has been defined by Surridge (1969) as cheerful complacency out of context with the patient's total situation. It is unlike the elation of hypomania in that it does not include motor restlessness, increased energy, or quickened thought processes. Surridge's euphoric patients, as stated before, tended to have intellectual disturbances. Damage to the central nervous system seems to be central to this euphoria. In addition, the initial impression of euphoria in these patients often changes as the interview continues. Of Surridge's 28 euphoric subjects, 8 confessed to feeling depressed and miserable. Perhaps some element of emotional lability tends to mask the true feelings of these patients. Along with the euphoria, there may be an impression of increased physical well-being. Changes of mood, as well as denial and impaired awareness of disability, probably lead to these feelings. The extent to which denial in these patients depends on mental deterioration or psychological factors remains to be clarified.

PSYCHOSIS

A number of authors have noted the rarity of mental hospital admissions among patients with MS (Malone, 1937; Pratt, 1951). This may be due to the behavioral restrictions resulting from their physical disabilities. Also, mental symptoms in MS may be altered as the disease progresses, which can obviate the need for hospitalization.

Malone (1937) reported 10 cases of psychotic complication in MS; some punctuated by rage and hypomania and others by paranoid schizophrenia. Langworthy, Kolb, and Androp (1941), in a follow-up study of 199 patients, found that 16 ultimately presented serious behavioral problems requiring their transfer to a psychiatric facility, and another 21 had obvious behavioral disturbances which were managed at home.

Davison and Bagley (1969) studied cases of schizophrenialike psychoses in MS and found 39 acceptable cases in the literature. The symptoms of these patients did not differ greatly from those of other schizophrenialike psychoses except that expansive delusional states seemed more prevalent and neurologic symptoms were often included in paranoid delusional symptoms. The psychosis tended to arise early in the disease, roughly concurrent with the first appearance of neurologic problems. Although this factor and the lack of a family history of schizophrenia suggest a possible link between the disease and psychotic symptoms, the incidence of schizophrenia in the MS group was no greater than that which is possible by chance.

HYSTERIA

A good deal of attention has been given to the possible relationship between hysteria and MS. In the early phase of the disease, the two disorders can be difficult to differentiate. Later in the course, some have stated that conversion reactions are common. Still others have suggested that they have a common origin or mechanism.

Brain (1930) believed that hysterical conversion symptoms were more frequent in MS than in any other organic disease of the nervous system. On the other hand, Pratt (1951) was unable to find any evidence that hysteria was characteristic of this disease.

Wilson (1940) downplayed any special tie between MS and hysteria and regarded the presence of conversion symptoms as mere coincidence. He did recognize a "subjective" or "predisseminated" type of MS in which symptoms predominated without unequivocal objective signs, a situation in which a diagnosis of hysteria could be made. Complaints included paresthesias, clumsiness of a limb, giddiness, and fatigability. Suspicion might be aroused by the presence of minimal signs such as a defective abdominal reflex, nystagmoid jerking of the eyes, or intermittent ankle clonus. New objective techniques such as computed tomography and visual evoked potential studies are offering means to make finer distinctions.

EMOTIONAL INFLUENCES ON THE DISEASE

Physical and emotional trauma are frequently believed to be precipitants of MS or at least provocative factors in the occurrence of relapses.

Pratt (1951) attempted to study the question in detail. Of his group of MS patients, 38 percent had suffered some emotional stress in the months prior to onset, as opposed to 26% of a control group with other neurologic disorders. The difference fell short of statistical significance. The incidence of relapses following stress was nearly identical to the rate of illness onset in the control group.

In the absence of major relapses, some MS patients found that emotional disturbance, frequently of a specific kind, produced transient exacerbation of the symptoms of a lesion already present. This situation was much more common than in the control group and was seemingly clear-cut. Some 18% of MS patients noted exacerbation with great reliability, within a few months of the emotional trauma. In different individuals, worry led to increased unsteadiness, anger to weakness of a leg, and self-consciousness to diplopia.

Phillipopoulus, Wittkower, and Cousineau (1958) found even more convincing evidence for emotional precipitation of both initial symptoms and later relapses. Eighty-eight percent of their patients had experienced traumatic life events prior to disease onset, compared with 17% of controls with neurologic disease. Relapses often seemed to be brought on by similar emotional problems, occasionally at so short an interval as to suggest a connection on that basis alone. In other patients, relapses occurred during flareups of chronic emotional difficulties.

If these findings can be further substantiated, a program of continuing social and psychological support may have some effect on the course of the disease. At any rate, the question deserves further study.

IMPLICATIONS FOR NEUROPSYCHOLOGICAL TESTING

Multiple sclerosis may have little effect on cognitive functions, although deficits on neuropsychological tests may still occur because of motor, visual, or tactile deficits that are commonly associated with this disorder. Specifically, tests of visual-motor skills (such as Digit Span on the Wechsler Adult Intelligence Scale), especially those which rely strongly on speed, may show impairment which is due solely to the motor or tactile sensory impairment. Deficits on visual tasks may also arise from involvement of the optic nerve. In each of these cases, misinterpretation may lead to a mistaken conclusion that cognitive deficits commonly attributed to the right hemispheres exist.

Psychometric study of the disorder has generally confirmed such interpretations. Ross and Reitan (1955) found that MS patients differed from other patients with brain injury on a measure of motor speed. Matthews, Cleveland, and Hopper (1970) compared 30 MS patients with a matched control group of 30 brain injured patients. They reported strong differences on several measures of motor speed, but failed to find differences on measures of intellectual skills. Reitan, Reed, and Dyken (1971) compared 30 MS patients and 30 normal patients. The authors found that the MS patients were impaired on all the variables studied, with statistically significant deficits on 25. The largest differences occurred on tests of motor skills, although deficits were also seen in auditory perception, indirect memory, and other cognitive skills although these deficits were considerably smaller and generally not severe.

Goldstein and Shelley (1974) replicated these studies but included a psychiatric control group. Among the three groups, there were significant differences on two measures of motor control showing deficits for the MS patients, but a measure of rhythm, concentration, and attention found the MS patients to be superior. Beatty and Gange (1977) have reported deficits on some measures of memory.

In a study employing a relatively small group of MS patients (24), Golden (1979) found sets of skills on which these patients performed better than brain-injured patients and another set on which they performed worse. The items on which the MS patients did better included a wide range of cognitive and intellectual skills. The items on which the patients did worse primarily included measures of motor speed, complex language function, and memory. These latter deficits suggest the possibility of some very mild frontal lobe or subcortical frontal lobe involvement in the disease. A more recent unreported study found that the cognitive deficits correlated significantly with the degree of ventricular enlargement seen on computed tomography, although again, the sample employed was small and the results must be considered tentative.

Multiple sclerosis patients may show much greater deficits than those reported in these studies, as advanced cases may proceed to dementia. On neuropsychological measures this type of dementia is generally indistinguishable from other types, although there has been little study on comprehensive batteries to make these differentiations in such areas as remote memory, which could possibly yield some differences. The diagnosis of MS-related dementia depends on the recognition that a dementia exists that is not due to other factors (see Chapter 6) and on the history of MS.

Another important consideration in the evaluation of the MS patient is the difference in testing profiles between the exacerbation and remission stages of the disease. In the remission stage, errors can be found in more complex motor tasks and, in some cases, on very high level intellectual tasks, but in general the patient may show only subtle symptoms, with few important deficits. As the disease progresses, the level of residual deficits during remission will increase. At the same time, during exacerbation the level of deficit does not predict the residual level of deficit after the acute stage has receded. Thus, one must be careful not to base conclusions about the patient's ability to function between episodes on the motor or cognitive dificits seen during exacerbation.

Because of the variable nature of the symptoms associated with MS, and because poor performance is often due to factors that are incidental to measurement of cognitive skills on neuropsychological tests such as attention, peripheral motor problems, peripheral visual impairment, and psychiatric disturbance, the performance of the MS patients is extremely variable and in general inconsistent. In many neurologic disorders, such inconsistency would lead one to consider that the problems were due to psychiatric factors or even malingering. In MS, however, such performance is expected over time and indeed is one of the diagnostic signs of the disease on neuropsychological testing. However, this variability must lead to caution in reaching any long-term conclusions from test results. In general, as the disease progresses and involves wider areas of the brain, there is a decrease in test –retest inconsistency.

Because of the widespread psychiatric problems which have been associated with MS, these patients are often referred for personality evaluations. On the Minnesota Multiphasic Personality Inventory (MMPI), MS patients show a typical pattern of results associated with high scores on scales 1 (hypochondriasis), 3 (hysteria), and 8 (schizophrenia). The elevations on hypochondriasis and schizophrenia are generally associated with the medical problems related to the disease. The schizophrenia scale is particularly sensitive to the consistent, often contradictory physical symptoms reported by the MS patient. The elevation on the hysteria scale is generally due to a combination of the patient's physical symptoms, a tendency to deny the extent to which the problems interfere with day-to-day life, and optimism that things will be better with a disease that goes through unpredictable stages of remission and exaceration.

During the exacerbation stage the Depression scale may become elevated, which is generally interpreted as a direct response to the additional disability caused by the exacerbation. MS patients may show other elevations, but these more likely reflect a unique response of the patient to the disease or a long-term psychiatric problem having nothing to do with MS.

On the Rorschach test, the patient's performance will be affected by a number of factors. One of the most important considerations is the presence of visual problems. The patient may have difficulty in properly seeing the cards, causing them to be misinterpreted or perceived as diffuse blobs. In these cases, the interpretation of the test is essentially meaningless. When vision is not a problem, the patient will often show an excess of anatomy-related responses, combined with symptoms of depression, when the disease is exacerbated. Other deficits found on the test should be considered psychiatrically significant, and will vary with any psychiatric disorder which may be present.

CONCLUSION

The MS patient generally shows much less cognitive disruption than does the average individual with another form of brain damage, although the level of functioning will vary greatly depending on the stage of the disease. Patients will show disruption of motor and sensory skills which can be quite severe in exacerbation or as the disease progresses. Psychiatric disorders must also be evaluated in this disease, but one must be careful not to interpret routinely traditional tests such as the MMPI or Rorschach without considering the ways in which the neurologic problems can change test responses. Caution must also be used when making assumptions about particular symptoms; this should be done only when the disease is in remission.

Chapter 9

Huntington's Chorea

Huntington's chorea is a rare, genetically mediated disorder usually characterized by choreiform movements in association with dementia. Either the
movement disorder or dementia may be absent in early phases of the disorder.
Since its original description in 1872 by Huntington, cases have been reported
throughout the world and in all races, although prevalence does vary
regionally.

The disease is the result of an abnormal gene inherited in an autosomal
dominant manner, with 50% of offspring affected. It has virtually 100%
expressivity. Therefore, about half of the offspring of an affected individual
can be expected to develop the disorder, with equal incidence in both sexes.
Only very rarely does it seem to skip a generation. Although a family history
of the disorder is usually characteristic, it may be lacking due to the early
death of a parent, illegitimacy, an inadequate history, or a new spontaneous
mutation.

At present, the only method available for curtailing the disease is genetic
counseling, which is imperative on humanitarian and economic grounds. Due
to the course of the disease, however, most of the reproductive period has
passed when the disorder is expressed. As the patient deteriorates, he or she
becomes less likely to practice contraception, and hypersexuality may occur
(Lishman, 1978). This finding, together with the social disorganization present in many Huntington's chorea families, makes effective prevention very
difficult. For example, Bolt (1970) reported that 15 children had been
produced by 3 patients since the onset of their disease.

At present, there are no useful guidelines for gene carrier identification prior to the onset of illness, and 50% probability of incidence is all that can be given to relatives at risk who are seeking advice. The probability of having the disease declines as an individual passes through the age of onset, but one cannot be sure of being free of the disease until approximately age 60.

Biochemical studies for carrier detection and the discovery of metabolic abnormalities in established cases have not been very fruitful until recently. Perry, Hansen, and Kloster (1973) found reduced levels of gamma-aminobutyric acid (GABA) in the basal ganglia and substantia nigra of 8 brains from patients with Huntington's chorea when compared with normal brains. GABA is a possible inhibitory synaptic transmitter, and its lack could be related to the movement disorder. Bird, MacKay, Rayner, and Iverson (1973) and Bird and Iverson (1974) have confirmed the GABA deficiency in 38 patients compared with controls and have also reported a severe reduction in glutamic acid decarboxylase (the GABA-synthesizing enzyme) in the putamen and globus pallidus. GABA levels in the frontal cortex of patients did not differ from normal levels, which suggests a selective loss of GABA-containing neurons in the basal ganglia. A dopamine–GABA imbalance in the basal ganglia could account for the movement disorder in the disease.

CLINICAL FEATURES

The onset of the disorder usually falls between the ages of 25 and 50, averaging in the mid-40s. However, onset in children and the elderly has been reported. There is evidence that the disease tends to follow a more severe course with an earlier onset, and also that emotional disturbance is often present just prior to onset in such cases. There may also be different manifestations of the disorder with different ages of onset, with striate rigidity prominent in the early 20s, choreic movements in middle age, and intention tremor after 60 (Lishman, 1978).

A great deal of variation may be seen in the interrelationship of neurologic and psychiatric features. Typically, involuntary movements precede dementia, although the reverse is seen. Their occurrence may be separated by several years or may coincide, and once both have become established, they tend to worsen together. On occasion, chorea or dementia may occur alone. Other variations involve the form of neurologic abnormality which emerges, progressive rigidity with parkinsonism substituting for chorea in nearly 10% of cases.

In a study by Heathfield (1967), presenting symptoms were fairly evenly divided between psychiatric and neurologic manifestations. Neurologic presentations usually included choreiform movements or, less frequently, unsteadiness of gait or stance or general clumsiness. Psychiatric presentations occasionally included symptoms of incipient dementia but, more frequently, changes of disposition, emotional instability, or paranoia.

Psychiatric changes are often present for some time prior to the development of chorea or intellectual impairment. A change in personality may be noted, the patient becoming moody and quarrelsome, or slowed, apathetic, and neglectful of personal appearance (Lyon, 1962). Paranoid changes, depression and anxiety may all herald the onset of illness.

The neurologic signs of the disorder are frequently unrecognized at first. The patient may be thought to be clumsy or fidgety. Choreic movements in the early stages may be little more than a twitching finger or a transient facial grimace, and thus may pass as mannerisms. The movements usually begin in the muscles of the face, hands, or shoulders, or they may produce a subtle change in gait. Slightly dysarthric speech may appear. The patient may successfully conceal these movements by making them appear to be part of a habitual activity such as stroking the chin.

As the condition worsens, the disturbance becomes more pathologic in appearance. Movements become abrupt, jerky, rapid, and repetitive, varying with the muscle group. They may occur spontaneously or may be enhanced by voluntary movement. The face shows constant changes of expression and grotesque writhing contortions. The fingers twitch, the arms move in an athetoid manner, and the shoulders shrug. The gait is sometimes altered by a strange, dancelike ataxia due to variable choreic influences on the lower extremities. The weight is often carried on the heels with the toes flexed upward, with the foot held off the ground longer than is usual in stride. Eventually, the patient develops a wide-based gait, increased lumbar lordosis, wide arm abduction, and a zigzag progression due to lurching motions of the trunk. Pauses and even backward steps interrupt the progress.

The dementia of Huntington's chorea often develops long before it is suspected. Inefficiency at work and in the management of daily affairs is a more common presenting problem than obvious memory impairment. As the dementing process continues, long-term memory may be spared in relation to the deterioration of other cognitive functions. This conclusion agrees with the pathologic finding of relatively intact limbic systems in affected brains. Personal disorientation is rare in comparison with other primary dementias (Bruyn, 1968). Insight is often retained far into the course of the illness. The patient is aware of the deterioration and may complain of mental slowing or dullness, forgetfulness, and muddled thoughts.

Distractibility is usually severe and somewhat characteristic, and may be interpreted as the counterpart of the disturbed motor patterns. Eventually, apathy or fatuous euphoria ensues and inertia becomes marked. However, there may be episodes of restlessness, irritability, or excitement. Depression may be severe, particularly while insight persists, with suicide a significant risk in the early stages.

Psychotic characteristics may become apparent in many patients, often very early in the course of the disease. A depressive psychosis is the most frequent, and, although occasionally recurrent, it is usually responsive to somatic therapies. A schizophrenic picture may be seen. Delusions of persecution can be marked by religiosity and in some, grandiosity. Ideas of reference may be aggravated by the attention drawn to the patient's bizarre movements and facial expressions (Lishman, 1978).

In general, the course of Huntington's disease is much longer than that of other primary dementing illnesses. Although its duration varies widely, the average course is between 13 and 16 years.

FEATURES OF ONSET IN CHILDHOOD

Although Huntington's disease may begin in childhood, the diagnosis may be clarified only at autopsy. In some respects, the childhood disease differs from the adult form, but the pathologic changes are characteristic and the same genetic mechanisms appear to be active. Muscular rigidity and tremor are more common than choreiform movement, mental decline occurs rapidly, and epileptic seizures appear in the majority of cases. The affected children die an average of 8 years after the onset.

PSYCHIATRIC ASSOCIATIONS

A high rate of psychiatric disorder, occasionally severe, has been noted in detailed studies of Huntington's disease families. These families seem to be severely disrupted by myriad pathologies involving the patients and their relatives. Epilepsy, schizophrenia, mental retardation, and a number of other degenerative brain diseases have been reported. The question of a common genetic basis remains unanswered.

Dewhurst, Oliver, and McKnight (1970) reported a study of 102 patients who clearly demonstrated the psychosocial effects of the disorder. Of this group, 10 had attempted suicide and 13 had mutilated themselves. In addition, 19 were alcoholics and 18 had been convicted of serious crimes. Thirty-eight percent of those who had married later became divorced or separated, usually due to social or intellectual deterioration in the affected partner. Sexual disturbances frequently occurred, including excessive demands, violence after a rebuff, sexual assault, sexual deviation, impotence, and frigidity. Sexual promiscuity with the production of illegitimate children was frequent. The children of affected individuals were found to be at high risk for abuse and neglect.

PATHOLOGIC FINDINGS

The affected brain is usually small and atrophied, although the degree of atrophy varies. The frontal lobes are usually the most severely affected regions. Marked ventricular enlargement, especially of the frontal horns, is characteristic. The caudate nuclei are usually greatly atrophied, and instead of bulging into the lateral ventricles, they may be represented by a tiny rim of tissue along the ventrolateral edge of the dilated frontal horns. Although the putamen is also shrunken, the globus pallidus is largely spared.

Microscopically, neuronal cell loss is replaced by gliosis. Even when cortical atrophy is mild, this condition is likely to be present. The defect is greatest in the frontal lobes. Severe cell loss and astrocytic proliferation are present in the caudate and putamen. Similar changes of a milder nature may be found in the globus pallidus, substantia nigra, or cerebellar nuclei. Fiber loss is marked in the white matter, with resultant narrowing of the corpus callosum. Vascular changes are not impressive and cannot be blamed for the disorder.

IMPLICATIONS FOR NEUROPSYCHOLOGICAL TESTING

In its advanced stages, Huntington's disease resembles a diffuse dementia, but it shows specific psychological patterns in the earlier stages. Many studies of this disease in neuropsychological laboratories have approached it as a single set of symptoms without considering the disease at different stages. For this reason, much of the research has failed to find any of the distinctive features which differentiate Huntington's disease from other disorders resulting in dementia.

In studies of the different stages of Huntington's chorea, recent-onset disease has generally been defined as disease that has been recognized within the past 12 months, usually from the onset of distinctive choreic movements in very mild form which may initially become apparent when the patient was under stress. Since the choreic movements are not the first real manifestions, these recent patients must be recognized as having had the disease for longer than 1 year, although the exact length of time is, of course, unknown. As yet, the authors are not aware of published data on long-term studies of patients at risk for Huntington's chorea who were tested early and later developed the disease, although such studies are being attempted and should be useful in delineating the neuropsychological course of this syndrome.

Much of the major work in this area has been the excellent series of studies published by Butters and his associates (Albert, Butters, & Brandt, 1981; Butters, Sax, Montgomery, & Tarlow, 1978; Butters, Tarlow, Cermak, & Sax, 1976). In an initial study, these authors found that patients with recent-onset Huntington's disease showed focal deficits in the area of memory, especially acquisition of new memory. These patients failed to show the general intellectual deterioration described in more advanced cases of the disease. In later studies, Butters and his colleagues found that the retrograde amnesia in the disease (i.e., forgetting events that occurred before the onset of the disease) was characterized by the lack of a temporal gradient. By this the authors meant that events were equally likely to be forgotten no matter how long ago they took place. This is similar to the pattern of forgetting in normals, except that normals remember a significantly higher percentage of events. This pattern of forgetting serves to differentiate Huntington's disease from the pattern seen in other disorders, such as Korsakoff's syndrome.

A study by Moses, Golden, Berger, and Wisiniewski (1981) found the same deficits in acquisition of new memory as did Butters and his associates. Moses et al. also described deficits in the ability of the patient to do mental spatial manipulations such as describing how a figure would look if it were rotated. Such problems are likely to be related to the inability of these patients to retain the visual information and process it without forgetting. This is probably a pervasive deficit which may affect the performance of these patients on many tasks for which memory is required. It is also likely that this deficit, as well as the retrograde amnesia, appears before the choreic symptoms, and may be useful for identifying patients who are in the very early stages of the disease.

In most studies, the test results with chronic patients who have had the disease for an average of 5−9 years are less specific. Aminoff, Marshall, Smith, and Wyke (1975) found results that are consistent with the general clinical impression of these patients: global deterioration on intellectual skills, with a pattern of decline similar to that seen in aging, but in a much more advanced stage than is appropriate for the patient's age. No focal symptoms were revealed in these patients, nor were selective memory losses discovered. These results have generally been supported by numerous other studies, including the work of Boll, Heaton, and Reitan (1974), Moses et al. (1981), and Norton (1975). Butters and his associates found similar results, and they again noted that the retrograde amnesia in long-term Huntington's disease patients showed no temporal gradient but was significantly greater than that seen in recent-onset Huntington's disease patient.

In the more advanced Huntington's disease patients, long-term overlearned skills are generally best preserved, as in other dementing disorders. The neuropsychological examination in such patients is best used to find areas of competency in order to aid in dealing with them as well as possible. However, it is very important not to mistake overlearned skills in such areas as reading recognition for the higher-level cognitive skills which they once represented. In the earlier stages, neuropsychological testing can be quite useful in describing the course of the disease and in assisting the family to minimize the early effects.

Another area in which neuropsychological testing can be quite useful is the identification of personality and other psychiatric disorders which accompany the disease process. As a diagnostic aid, the development of psychiatric disorders should be considered significant, increasing the likelihood that the patient at risk is likely to develop Huntington's disease. In these cases, extensive and detailed neuropsychological testing in the areas in which the disease is likely to be manifested is obligatory.

Chapter 10

Vitamin Deficiencies

Severe, chronic malnutrition is often accompanied by mental changes such as apathy, emotional instability, retardation, memory impairment, and, on occasion, frank psychosis. Helwig-Larsen, Hoffmeyer, Keiler, Thaysen, Thaysen, Thygensen, and Wulff (1952) reported such problems in former prisoners of war. A similar degree of malnutrition is rarely seen in Western industrial societies. There are, however, certain groups within generally well-fed populations who suffer from nutritional deficiencies. Some of the mentally ill and mentally retarded, who may live a marginal existence, may have their symptoms enhanced by vitamin deficiencies. The aged may fail to provide adequate diets for themselves, either as a result of degenerative illnesses which interfere with self-care or because of poverty. Alcoholics not only have poor dietary habits but, because of the requirements of ethanol metabolism, further tax their vitamin reserves. Chronic gastrointestinal diseases that cause malabsorption may produce vitamin deficiencies, and any illness, particularly those requiring hospitalization and intravenous fluids, may add to their nutritional requirements.

B-COMPLEX VITAMINS

The B-complex vitamins are most closely associated, through their deprivation, with pathologic changes in the nervous system. Many of the B vitamins have been shown to be essential to metabolic processes of the neuron, both centrally and peripherally. Thiamine pyrophosphate is a coenzyme involved in carbohydrate metabolism and may also be needed for proper nerve impulse transmission. Nicotinic acid and its amide derivative are constituents of coenzymes required for glucose metabolism, as is riboflavin. Pantothenic acid is involved in the production of acetylcholine. Pyridoxine is converted into a coenzyme central to several important metabolic pathways in the brain.

Prior to the 1930s, when the B vitamins were first isolated and identified, few psychiatric disorders were attributed to nutritional deficits, although psychiatric symptoms had long been recognized as part of the syndrome of pellagra. With the availability of the B vitamins, experimental studies showed mental symptoms due to deprivation long before systemic manifestations appeared elsewhere. Both acute and chronic vitamin reserve depletion were found to result in fulminating neuropsychiatric disorders previously not thought to be nutritional in origin.

Thiamine deficiency classically leads to beriberi with neuropathy, heart failure, or peripheral edema and results from severe, chronic deprivation. Shorter periods of depletion may produce a neurasthenic picture with fatigue, weakness, and emotional disturbance. Acute, severe deficiency, usually resulting from overwhelming demands on depleted reserves, can lead to the syndrome of Wernicke's encephalopathy, which includes confusion, nystagmus, and ataxia. The characteristics of Wernicke's encephalopathy may appear in the absence of changes outside the central nervous system.

Nicotinic acid deficiency also produces a range of disorders. Chronic deficiency causes pellagra with its gastrointestinal symptoms, skin lesions, and psychiatric disturbance. Early in the course, there may be only isolated neurasthenic symptoms. Acute, severe depletion can lead to an encephalopathy frequently without signs, which provides a clue to the source of the disturbance.

Pyridoxine deficiency can cause seizures in infants either through dietary deficiency or abnormally high requirements. Electroencephalographic (EEG) records are strikingly abnormal in these patients. Mental deterioration may follow. Both symptoms and EEG changes resolve rapidly with injection of the vitamin. Dietary deficiency in adults or the administration of substances which antagonize pyridoxine can lead to irritability, confusion, and lethargy.

Naturally occurring central nervous system disorders have not been found to result from deficiencies of the following two B vitamins. Pantothenic acid deficiency leads to the "burning feet" syndrome, and riboflavin deficiency produces oral lesions, tearing (crying), and photophobia.

Mental Changes in Pellagra

Although multiple vitamin deficiencies are probably responsible for pellagra, nicotinic acid appears to be the most important, as its administration rapidly relieves symptoms. Characteristic changes include gastrointestinal disturbance, psychiatric disorder, and skin changes such as roughening and reddening of the dorsum of the hands, pigmentation over bony prominences, and lesions of the mouth and tongue.

Prodromal changes are not unlike those seen in experimental thiamine deficiency. Most prominent are neurotic symptoms which include subjective feelings of incapacity for physical and mental effort coupled with vague complaints of anorexia, insomnia, nervousness, apprehension, dizziness, headache, palpitations, and paresthesias. These symptoms tend to fluctuate greatly from day to day. Irritability and emotional instability may be dominant features. Depression may become severe, with attendant suicide risk. Later stages are marked by general slowing of mental processes, faulty memory, and confabulation.

Although these changes are well known in regions where pellagra is endemic, they are frequently misdiagnosed where only sporadic cases arise. Spies, Aring, Gelperin, and Bean (1938) linked nicotinic acid deficiency to neurotic symptoms in the patients of a pellagra clinic in whom administration and withdrawal of the vitamin without the patients' knowledge led to remission and repeated exacerbation of symptoms, respectively.

Longer, more severe nicotinic acid deficiency leads to frank psychiatric manifestations of pellagra. These may develop without prodromal symptoms. Although they are frequently accompanied by skin and gastrointestinal changes, mental symptoms may occur alone. Most commonly, the acute picture includes disorientation, confusion, and memory impairment. Wild excitement, violent outbursts, depression, and paranoia with persecutory delusions may also be present. Chronic untreated pellagra may resemble Korasakoff's psychosis, or it may result in a slowly progressive generalized dementia. Acute psychotic symptoms often respond dramatically to nicotinic acid replacement within hours to days. Chronic manifestations are somewhat less likely to respond.

The early symptoms of nicotinic acid deficiency presumably are the result of reversible biochemical changes within neurons. These changes become less reversible as neurons are irreparably damaged. In advanced chronic pellagra, chromatolytic degeneration is seen in the Betz cells of the motor cortex, as well as in neurons of the brain stem and spinal cord. Degeneration of the posterior and lateral columns of the spinal cord may be notable (Spillane, 1947).

WERNICKE'S ENCEPHALOPATHY

Wernicke's encephalopathy is the acute neuropsychiatric result of severe thiamine deficiency. It is, in brief, an acute disorder characterized by nystagmus, lateral and conjugate gaze palsies, ataxia of gait, and a global confusional state (Victor, Adams, & Collins, 1971).

Association with Alcoholism

Alcoholism is one of the major causes of Wernicke's encephalopathy. It may produce a thiamine deficiency state by several mechanisms: replacement of thiamine-containing foods by alcohol, impaired absorption of thiamine from the gut, impairment of thiamine storage and utilization secondary to liver damage, and excessive consumption of thiamine due to the metabolic requirements of alcohol degradation. Conditions other than alcoholism may be responsible for Wernicke's encephalopathy even when alcoholism seems to be the most obvious cause. For instance, Rimalovski and Aronson (1966), in reporting a large autopsy series, found unequivocal evidence of alcoholism in only 50% of the patients. In the remainder, the cause appeared to be carcinoma, especially of the esophagus, or tuberculosis. In contrast, in a large study done in the United States, Victor et al. (1971) found that all but 2 of their 245 patients suffered from established alcoholism. Therefore, at least in American urban society, Wernicke's encephalopathy is primarily a disease of the alcoholic.

Association with Beriberi

Only recently has Wernicke's encephalopathy become associated with beriberi, as the classic neuritic and cardiac forms of the disease are rarely accompanied by encephalopathy despite their clear relationship with thiamine deficiency. World War II, with its prisoner-of-war camps, provided ample opportunity for the study of acute deficiency syndromes in large numbers of subjects. In such epidemic situations, psychological changes in beriberi were often found to be marked. DeWardener and Lennox (1947) reported 52 cases of Wernicke's encephalopathy among prisoners of war in Singapore, most of whom also had the neuritic, cardiac, or edematous symptoms of beriberi.

Thiamine treatment produced good responses in these and other similar cases, and gross examination of brains from fatal cases showed changes usually found in Wernicke's encephalopathy. The previously cited authors believed that although commonly described forms of beriberi generally resulted from a prolonged, less severe lack of thiamine, the symptoms of encephalopathy were more likely to occur with acute, severe thiamine depletion over and above a preexisting partial deficiency.

Differentiation from Korsakoff's Psychosis

Korsakoff first described the amnesic syndrome which bears his name in 1887. It consists of memory deficits that affect primarily recent memory and acquisition of new information, with some impairment of remote memory and time disorientation and relative sparing of other cognitive functions. The majority of cases were discovered in alcoholics and led to the belief that the syndrome was the result of some toxic effect of alcohol. Cases not involving alcohol began to appear in the late 1800s and early 1900s, and by the 1930s other known causes included gastric carcinoma, intractable vomiting, and severely deficient diet. Thiamine deficiency was considered the cause, and Bowman, Goodhart, and Jolliffe (1939) reported encouraging results with parenteral thiamine.

DeWardener and Lenox (1947) found memory deficits in patients with ataxia and ophthalmoplegia. In these acute cases, thiamine successfully cleared the memory defects. Malamud and Skillicorn (1956) established more clearly the relationship between these two syndromes by finding that the location of pathology in the brains of Wernicke's and Korsakoff's patients was identical, the only difference lying in the chronicity of the pathologic process in hippocampal and medial temporal lobe structures. Of course, processes other than thiamine deficiency can damage these regions, producing Korsakoff's syndrome.

Clinical Features

Wernicke's encephalopathy generally appears abruptly. Mental confusion or a staggering gait are the most frequent presenting features. In addition, the patient may have noted wavering or double vision. The characteristic triad of ataxia, confusion, and ophthalmoplegia is often seen, but all of its parts may not be present. Anorexia, nausea, and vomiting may precede the onset of the above symptoms. Accompanying memory defects are often present but are frequently underemphasized in clinical descriptions. Isolated lethargy and hypotension in the absence of other acute mental changes may mark the syndrome (Victor et al., 1971).

The patients are evenly distributed according to age, and men are twice as frequently affected as women. This ratio is much lower than the sex distribution of alcoholism and may reflect differences in drinking patterns. It appears that the pattern which leads to Wernicke's encephalopathy is one of steady drinking over months or years coupled with inadequate dietary intake. The signs found by Victor et al. (1971) on examination include abstinence syndrome (10%), peripheral neuropathy (82%), serious malnutrition (84%), ataxia (87%), mental abnormalities (90%) and ocular abnormalities (96%).

Abnormalities of mental function were present in 90% of the patients. The remaining 10% showed ataxia and ophthalmoplegia but otherwise appeared lucid. A state of quiet global confusion with disorientation, apathy, and memory disturbance was the most common derangement. Many of the patients were drowsy, occasionally falling asleep in midsentence, whereas others were indifferent and inattentive. However, almost all of them were easily roused, and severe impairment of consciousness was rare.

Typically, spontaneity of speech and activity was lacking, but when speech occurred, remarks were inconsistent and irrational. Awareness and responsiveness were much impaired. Misidentifications were very common and were made without hesitation. Physical and mental fatigability was marked, and concentration, even for a simple task, was difficult. In contrast, a small number of these patients were alert, responsive, and voluble despite memory impairment and obvious confusion. Mild delirium was occasionally seen in this alert group, with perceptual distortions, hallucinations, insomnia, agitation, and autonomic overactivity.

Although assessment of memory was frequently difficult, testable patients showed defective acquisition of new memory after confusion cleared. Separation of the period of confusion and the period of a predominant memory deficit alone was not easy to accomplish, as the two often merged during the course of the illness. The problem was complicated by the ease with which the memory deficit could be overlooked; these patients were hard to test when confused and later hid their defects in spontaneous, facile chatter. A few showed a Korsakoff-type memory deficit from the outset as their only mental abnormality.

Early in the disorder, confabulation was frequent although not universal, and even in those who showed it, it was not seen on all occasions. When confusion or perceptual disorders were present, confabulation became difficult to distinguish from misinterpretation and misidentification. As confusion declined, confabulation could more readily be attributed to a haphazard recollection of true past experiences. DeWardener and Lennox (1942) noted emotional abnormalities in two-thirds of their prisoner-of-war population. Usually, these abnormalities appeared after ocular disturbance had become established. Apprehension was common, with anxiety, insomnia and fear of the dark. This was replaced by apathy and later by depression and emotional lability. Some patients showed marked excitability. Hallucinations were more frequent in this group, as was progression to coma.

Course of the Disease with Treatment

A large number of the patients seen by Victor et al. (1971) were followed for some time, allowing clarification of the course of the disease after treatment. About 17% died in the acute stage of the illness, but more than half were seen for periods ranging from 2–13 years.

Palsies of lateral eye movement always resolved, often beginning within hours and completed in several days to weeks. Other ocular abnormalities followed a similar pattern, except for horizontal nystagmus, which remained in two-thirds of the patients. Ataxia typically began to improve in the first week, often taking a month or two to reach maximal resolution. In one-fourth of the patients the ataxia did not improve at all, and more than half were left with some residual unsteadiness. Persistent ataxia and nystagmus, then, can be clues to the origin of a chronic amnesic syndrome. Polyneuropathy tended to improve very slowly over several months, if at all, leaving some patients with permanently diminished or absent tendon reflexes.

The global state of confusion always disappeared in survivors, usually beginning in 2 –3 weeks and clearing fully in 1 –2 months. Memory deficits tended to become more noticeable as confusion decreased. Of 186 patients observed long enough to ascertain an amnesic syndrome, 84% developed a typical Korsakoff psychosis. Those who escaped had had comparatively brief illnesses and had overcome their confusion within a week. In addition, about 16% of the total patient group presented with Korsakoff's psychosis at the outset, with ocular signs and ataxia, and a small group seemed to have developed this condition without showing signs of ophthalmoplegia or ataxia.

Follow-up revealed complete recovery in one-fourth of the Korsakoff patients, partial recovery in half, and no change in the rest. Even in some severe cases, complete recovery occurred. Recovery usually began in several weeks or months and continued for up to 2 years.

In the chronic amnesic or Korsakoff's stage, anterograde and retrograde amnesia predominated, but continued mild impairment of perceptual and cognitive functions could usually be found on careful examination. The retrograde amnesia was frequently of several years' duration, although islands of preserved memory remained and there was no clearly defined beginning of the syndrome. Confabulation was rare in the chronic stage. These patients were usually inert, apathetic, and lacking in insight, even though they were fully alert and responsive. Most of them were neglectful of their appearance and tended to spend their time in idleness. A few were gregarious. Most were bland, placid, and emotionally detached. Sustained episodes of anxiety or depression were rare, although brief periods of irritability did occur.

Pathologic Findings

Pathologic changes in Wernicke's encephalopathy are remarkably confined to limited areas of the brain. The predominant lesions are found in a symmetric distribution in the vicinity of the walls of the third ventricle, the periaqueductal region, the floor of the fourth ventricle, certain thalamic nuclei (especially the paraventricular parts of the medial dorsal nuclei and the pulvinar), the mamillary bodies, the terminal portions of the fornices, the brain stem, and the anterior lobe and superior vermis of the cerebellum. In contrast, lesions are rare in the cerebral cortex, corpus striatum, subthalamic and septal regions, cingulate gyri, and hippocampal areas. However Victor et al. (1971) did find that convolutional atrophy was notable in 27% of cases coming to autopsy in their series.

Microscopically, all neural elements appear to be involved, including neurons, axis cylinders, blood vessels, and glia, with variability from case to case and from location to location. Generally, myelinated fibers seem to be more severely affected than the cell bodies of the neurons. Astrocytic and histiocytic proliferation occurs in the areas of parenchymal loss. Blood vessel proliferation and petechial hemorrhages may take place, although the latter may occur only terminally.

The distribution of lesions is almost identical in patients who die in the acute phase of Wernicke's encephalopathy and in those who die of chronic Korsakoff's psychosis. The only difference lies in the chronicity of the glial and vascular changes.

Victor et al. (1971) have attempted to find a relationship between symptoms and lesions suggesting that ophthalmoplegias result from lesions in the third and sixth cranial nerve nuclei and the adjacent midbrain tegmentum, nystagmus from lesions of the vestibular nuclei, and ataxia from vestibular lesions and injury to the anterior lobes and vermis of the cerebellum. Amnesia appeared to be closely associated with lesions in the medial dorsal nuclei and pulvinar of the thalamus, whereas mamillary body lesions, traditionally believed to be crucial to amnesic symptoms, were less frequent.

When the above structural changes become fixed and irreversible, the framework is present for enduring amnesic problems. Much of the early disturbance probably stems from biochemically mediated neuronal dysfunction, but the longer such a disturbance persists, the more likely it is to progress, with fiber degeneration and neuronal destruction. The degree and severity of thiamine depletion may also play a role. Alcoholics may often have a borderline deficiency for months or years, with previous minor attacks of Wernicke's encephalopathy going unnoticed. Metabolism of alcohol alone is likely to place heavy demands on thiamine reserves.

VITAMIN B_{12} DEFICIENCY

The neurologic complication of subacute combined degeneration of the spinal cord, as well as mental abnormalities, may accompany pernicious anemia. Depression or anergy may be the earliest manifestation of vitamin B_{12} deficiency, and apathy and somnolence may be marked when the anemia is severe.

Surveys of psychiatric populations have frequently shown a high (15–20%) incidence of low serum vitamin B_{12} levels. Both "organic" and "nonorganic" types of mental illness have been found among patients with low vitamin B_{12} values, although few showed pernicious anemia (Edwin, Holten, Norum, Schumpf, & Skaug, 1965). Carney and Sheffield (1970) found a similar low vitamin B_{12} level in newly admitted psychiatric patients. However, Henderson, Strachan, Beck, Dawwon, and Daniel (1966), in screening 1000 unselected psychiatric patients, found low vitamin B_{12} levels in only 9, a rate probably no different from that found in the population at large.

There is some fairly convincing evidence that a lack of vitamin B_{12} is related to organic psychiatric dysfunction. A prospective study by Shulman (1967a) found that three-fourths of patients with pernicious anemia showed objective impairment of memory on a simple learning test. Retesting after treatment showed that the majority returned to normal, some within 24 hours.

There is much evidence of cerebral disorder in vitamin B$_{12}$ deficiency to serve as a basis for organic psychiatric disturbance. Cerebral pathology is known to occur in pernicious anemia, similar to that which takes place in subacute combined degeneration of the spinal cord (Holmes, 1956). This consists of diffuse and focal areas of degeneration in the white matter, of diffuse and focal areas of degeneration in the white matter, with comparatively little gliosis or change in neurons. Theoretically, the deficits should be reversible, at least in the early phases. The EEG record in pernicious anemia is abnormal in over 60% of cases (Walton, Kiloh, Osselton, & Farral, 1954). Mild abnormalities appear as excessive theta activity, and severe abnormalities as delta activity which may be paroxysmal or focal. Such abnormalities appear to be unrelated to the severity of the anemia but do appear to be linked to a defect in cerebral metabolism. Most of these EEG abnormalities will resolve with treatment. Metabolic studies have also shown impaired uptake of oxygen and glucose, especially in the presence of such symptoms as disorientation, confusion, and forgetfulness, to be responsive to replacement therapy (Schein-berg, 1951). Similar metabolic disturbances may also occur in patients with low serum vitamin B$_{12}$ when no hematologic changes are present. Such observations make it important to consider vitamin B$_{12}$ deficiency in the differential diagnosis of patients with unexplained acute dementing syndromes.

FOLIC ACID DEFICIENCY

Due to the association of megaloblastic anemia with mental disorder, folic acid (lack of which leads to megaloblastic anemia) has been the subject of a number of studies. Several investigators have found a high incidence of subnormal folic acid levels in psychiatric patients (Carney, 1967; Read, Gough, Pardoe, & Nicholas, 1965; Shulman, 1967). In all such surveys, the causal significance of low serum folate is difficult to determine. Deficient nutrition is likely to be responsible for the depressed folate level and may be secondary to the mental illness itself. Barbiturates and alcohol are known to depress folate levels and are commonly used by the psychiatric population. Particular attention has been focused on the relationship of folate levels to depression, dementia, and epilepsy.

Depression

Carney (1967) found a significant rate of low folate levels in a group of depressed patients. Reynolds, Preece, Bailey, and Coppen (1970) have published supportive results. Of 100 severely depressed patients, one-fourth were found to have abnormally low folate levels. This condition could not be related to a history of barbiturate usage. A slight but significantly poorer response to therapy was noted in the low folate group. Reynolds et al. also noted that a causal relationship of folate deficiency and depression was not incompatible with the biogenic theories of affective disturbance, as folate deficiency could interfere with catecholamine and serotonin synthesis.

Dementia

The cerebrospinal fluid folate level is known to be two or three times greater than that in the serum (Wells, 1965), which suggests a possibly increased need for the vitamin in cerebral metabolism. However, only a few case reports have been offered to support such a relationship. These cases have in common folate deficiency, dementia, and a positive response to folate administration.

Sneath, Chanarin, Hodkinson, McPherson, and Reynolds (1973) studied 113 patients who were admitted consecutively to a geriatric unit, 14 of whom were diagnosed as demented. These 14 had significantly lower red cell folate levels than the remainder. There was also a slight correlation between poor results on objective tests of cerebral impairment and red cell folate levels in those patients with a low folate level. The most likely explanation is folate deficiency secondary to poor nutrition resulting from dementia, but folate deficiency could not be ruled out as a cause of the initial dementia.

Epilepsy

Anticonvulsant drugs used in the treatment of epilepsy can lead to folate deficiency. Moreover, folate levels seem to be lower in mentally abnormal epileptics than in those free from mental symptoms (Reynolds, Preece, & Chanarin, 1969; Reynolds, Preece, & Johnson, 1971). These differences have been found to be especially large in cases of dementia.

The significance of these findings remains unclear. Although uncontrolled trials of folate have been promising (Reynolds, 1967), controlled trials have found no significant effect of folate administration (Grant and Stores, 1970). Thus, although an association between lowered folate and mental disturbance in epileptics seems clear, any causal factors in that association remain indefinite.

IMPLICATIONS FOR NEUROPSYCHOLOGICAL TESTING

Because of the relative rareness of most of these conditions, there is almost no information which can be employed to describe their manifestations on neuropsychological testing. In general, it is anticipated that these disorders would interfere with new learning as well as more complex intellectual skills, especially in severe cases. Since many of these disorders are treatable, such findings are often transitory and will show remission after treatment has been instituted. As with several of the other diseases we have examined, deficits are exacerbated by the general physical effects of these disorders and the tendency of the patient to tire quickly and show impairment in continued attention and concentration.

The one exception to this general lack of data is Korsakoff's syndrome, which is a common sequela of chronic alcoholism. These cases have become somewhat more rare as treatment for alcoholism has recognized the possible causes of this disorder, but the syndrome can still be seen in Veterans Administration Hospitals and other settings in which old, long-term alcoholics are seen. The work of Butters and his associates (see the chapter on Huntington's disease) has been instrumental in helping to define the characteristics of the amnesic syndrome which accompanies this disorder. Specifically, these patients show an impairment in new learning, as do Huntington's disease patients, but Korsakoff patients show a remote memory deficit with a clear temporal gradient: recent long-term memory is more impaired than earlier memories of the individual's life. In addition, cues for forgotten material do not aid recall, as they often do in Alzheimer's disease patients. This pattern appears to be diagnostic of Korsakoff's syndrome and probably also of disorders with a similar etiology, although this has yet to be proven.

It is difficult to discuss Korsakoff's syndrome without considering the effects of alcohol in general. There is a controversy in the literature about whether the pattern in Korsakoff's syndrome is simply an extension of the deficits seen in the alcoholic, that is, a more severe form of the same problem. Alternatively, Korsakoff's syndrome may be seen as a qualitatively different disorder in which the symptoms are not simply an extension of the problems seen in the alcoholic. One of the major problems in answering this question has been the difficulty of defining exactly the underlying deficits in alcoholism, which presents a vast but confusing, conflicting, and highly confounded literature. These controversial data are discussed in the following chapter. Although a survey of the literature clearly does not answer the question posed above, it appears most useful at present to view Korsakoff's syndrome and the general effects of alcoholism as two different disorders.

CONCLUSION

It is clear that a wide variety of cognitive and psychiatric deficits can arise from vitamin deficiencies, especially when the B-complex vitamins are involved. Thus, it is important to consider these disorders in cases of otherwise unexplained psychosis, especially in individuals with a history of malnutrition from any source.

PART II

Research Review

Chapter 11

Assessment of Neuropsychological Impairment and Brain Damage in Problem Drinkers

William R. Miller and Carlos F. Saucedo

PROBLEM DRINKING

The term *alcoholism* has been used in several descriptive senses. In the most general sense, it describes the full continuum of life and health problems that can accompany the excessive use of ethyl alcohol. Thus, the World Health Organization (1952) has defined as an *alcoholic* any person who is experiencing life problems related to alcohol use or who has shown prodromal signs of such problems. A more restructive definition, such as that presented in the Third Diagnostic and Statistical Manual of Mental Disorders (DSM-III: American Psychiatric Association, 1980), requires that additional criteria be met. The DSM III defines a general category of "Alcohol Abuse" and a more restrictive category of "Alcohol Dependence (Alcoholism)" that requires the presence of either substantial tolerance to ethanol or signs of the alcohol withdrawal syndrome. Miller and Caddy (1977) have advocated the use of the generic

The authors wish to express their appreciation to the following persons for their ongoing consultation and assistance in the preparation of this chapter: Dennis Feeney, Ph.D., Gordon Hodge, Ph.D., and James A. Moses, Jr., Ph.D.

term *problem drinking* to describe the full spectrum of alcohol-related disorders, reserving *alcoholism* for the upper end of the continuum, which represents more advanced and severe problems characterized by the DSM-III category "Alcohol Dependence."

At the present time, there is no adequate estimate of the prevalence of alcoholism in this more restricted sense. Because of the extensive and careful sociologic research of Calahan (1970), however, we do have reasonable estimates of the incidence of problem drinking. Calahan's random survey of the U.S. population suggested that approximately 9% of the adult population—15% of men and 4% of women—report enough alcohol-related life problems to be meaningfully termed *problem drinkers*. Among the problem categories used by Calahan, the closest to classic alcoholism was *symptomatic drinking*, which was modeled on Jellinek's (1960) description of gamma alcoholism, and which encompassed 8% of all men and 3% of all women over the age of 21. Based on projected 1980 U.S. adult population figures, this would suggest that there are approximately 10.5 million male and 2.9 million female problem drinkers, of whom about 5.6 million men and 2.2 million women are alcoholic. These statistics should be interpreted with caution: nevertheless they represent the best current estimates based upon scientifically acceptable research methods.

Applied to any other disease, these incidence data would represent nothing less than a health threat of epidemic proportions. Is problem drinking a health risk? It is now generally recognized that excessive drinking increases the risk of a wide variety of health problems, including disorders of the heart, liver, and gastrointestinal tract. Problem drinkers are also at higher risk of untimely death from a wide range of causes, including suicide, homicide, and vehicular and other accidents. Perhaps the largest percentage of problem drinkers, however, are affected not by these problems but by impairment of the system most sensitive to the effects of alcohol—the central nervous system (CNS). Recent studies of alcoholic populations have found significant cognitive impairment (ranging from poor performance on a few neuropsychological tests to cortical atrophy and dementia) in up to 84% of patients, with an average of 68% impaired (Cala, Jones, Mastaglia, & Wiley, 1978; Carlsson, Cloeson, & Petterson, 1973; Claeson & Carlsson, 1970; Draper, Feldman, & Haughton, 1978; Horvath, 1975; Marshman, 1975). As will be discussed later, cognitive impairment and cerebral atrophy frequently occur long before the appearance of significant liver damage or other overt medical signs. Further, the type of cerebral impairment that occurs in problem drinkers is not immediately apparent in social or interview settings because verbal intelligence and motor skills are largely spared. Thus, until recently, the neuropsychological aspects of alcoholism and their implications for etiology and treatment tended to be overlooked, although not completely. Almost 25 years ago, Lemere (1956) averred that brain damage was frequently present: "It is my opinion that brain damage from alcoholism is not only more common than is supposed, but that it also explains to a large extent the essential pathology of alcoholism, namely, the permanent loss of control over drinking" (p. 361).

EFFECTS OF ALCOHOL UPON MEMORY

One area of neuropsychological functioning in which the effects of alcohol are clearly seen is in performance on memory tasks. Alcohol produces memory deficits that are both acute (those accompanying intoxication in normal subjects) and chronic (those seen in sober individuals after prolonged periods of heavy drinking). Although this chapter is devoted primarily to a review of chronic effects of alcohol ingestion, we will first carefully examine acute effects of alcohol upon memory because these appear to form a continuum with the results of prolonged alcohol abuse. Three types of memory phenomena attributable to acute intoxication will be considered: state-dependent learning, storage and retrieval deficits, and the alcohol blackout. We will then turn to chronic memory deficits before reviewing of other types of impairment.

Alcohol State-Dependent Learning

State-dependent learning (SDL) is a phenomenon in which information learned in a particular psychological or drug state is more completely retrieved in a similar state than in a dissimilar one. Thus, in alcohol SDL, information that is learned while the individual is intoxicated is recalled better when the person is again intoxicated than when he or she is sober.

Evidence for the SDL effect comes from two sources—animal and human learning experiments. Overton (1972, 1978) has reviewed the animal literature and found substantial evidence that animals trained in a drugged state do remember their training better in a comparable drugged state than in a nondrugged condition. Likewise, SDL has been demonstrated with humans using moderate doses of a variety of drugs that act on the central nervous system, including ethyl alcohol, marijuana, barbiturates, amphetamines, physostigmine, and anesthetics. Alcohol, in particular, has been shown to produce SDL on verbal learning tasks (Cowan, 1976; Goodwin, Powell, Bremer, Hoine, & Sterne, 1969a: Hinrichsen, Kathan, & Levenson, 1974; Keane & Lisman, 1976; Madill, 1967; Petersen, 1977; Storm Caird, & Korbin, 1965; Storm & Caird, 1967; Tarter, 1970; Weingartner, Adefris, Eich, & Murphy, 1976; Weingartner & Faillace, 1971; Young, 1979), as well as on motor and physiologic responses (Crow & Ball, 1975; Madill, 1967; Powell, Goodwin, Janes, & Hoine, 1971). Storm and Smart (1965) have suggested that SDL may play an important role in the etiology and treatment of alcoholism, but their thesis has received little empirical support to date (Birnbaum, Parker, Hartley, & Noble, 1978; Lisman, 1974).

With further research, it has become clear that SDL does not occur under all conditions and that a variety of factors influence this phenomenon. Eich (1977) and Weingartner (1978) have marshaled evidence that SDL is most likely to occur when two conditions prevail: (1) moderate alcohol doses (blood alcohol concentration, or BAC, near 100 mg%). and (2) tasks requiring sequential processing and retrieval of information, as in free recall learning or serial learning. With regard to dose level, it appears that lower levels of intoxication may be insufficient to produce a main effect on acquisition or retrieval, whereas higher levels of intoxication may obstruct memory so completely as to obliterate the subtle SDL phenomenon. Thus, the dose must be strong enough to produce some decrement in retention (Goodwin, Powell, Hill, Lieberman, & Viamontes, 1974; Swanson & Kinsbourne, 1979) but not high enough to produce major deficits such as blackouts (Lisman, 1974). With regard to processing, current data suggest that SDL is less likely to be observed when the difficulty of retrieval is decreased by providing external cues during acquisition or retrieval stages, as in cued free recall or recognition tasks.

Some aspects of the memory task may also affect the occurrence of SDL. Weingartner and his colleagues (1976) have argued that SDL is most likely to occur when the material to be remembered is not very meaningful. The literature in general, however, offers little consistent support for this contention. Numerous studies have failed to find SDL with low-meaning stimuli (Miller, Adesso, Fleming, Gino, & Laverman, 1978; Saucedo, 1980) or, conversely, have demonstrated SDL effects with highly meaningful stimuli (Keane & Lisman, 1976; Storm & Caird, 1967; Weingartner & Faillace, 1971). Other studies have partially supported Weingartner's hypothesis, presenting a mixed picture (Parker, Birnbaum, & Noble, 1976; Storm et al., 1965). Several studies have suggested that memory for nonverbal pattern information is less susceptible to SDL than is verbal information (Cowan, 1976; Goodwin et al., 1969; Lisman, 1974; Parker et al., 1976). Weingartner (1978) has proposed that episodic information (presented only once) is more likely to show SDL than is overlearned information (utilizing semantic memory), but again, the literature as a whole does not support this contention. Most studies of SDL have involved two or more learning trials (Goodwin et al., 1969; Hinrichsen et al., 1974; Keane & Lisman, 1976; Lisman, 1974; Miller et al., 1978; Parker et al., 1976; Saucedo, 1980; Storm et al., 1965; Storm & Caird, 1967; Tarter, 1970; Weingartner & Faillace, 1971; Young, 1979), whereas few have employed the single learning trial strategy (Goodwin et al., 1974; Weingartner et al., 1976). Goodwin et al. (1974) failed to find SDL with a single presentation, and others have demonstrated SDL on tasks requiring trials to criterion or one errorless trial (Goodwin et al., 1969a; Storm et al., 1965; Storm & Caird, 1967; Tarter, 1970). Thus, SDL is not restricted to episodic memory, nor are there sufficient data at present to indicate that SDL is more likely to occur in episodic than in semantic memory processes.

In summary, SDL is a well-documented phenomenon, but the conditions under which it occurs are less than clear. Methodologic and sample differences among studies may account for some of the inconsistencies observed. It appears that few factors other than alcohol dose produce clear main effects, and that SDL may rely upon the superimposition of critical levels of two or more factors that interact to influence memory. SDL occurs both in normal subjects (Goodwin et al., 1969; Hinrichsen et al., 1974; Keane & Lisman, 1976; Storm et al., 1965; Tarter, 1970; Weingartner et al., 1976; Young, 1979) and in alcoholics (Storm & Caird, 1967; Weingartner & Faillace, 1971), and although drinking history variables may be related to memory and cognitive performance in general (to be discussed later), two studies in our own laboratory have failed to find a relationship between the occurrence of SDL and a wide range of drinking variables (Saucedo, 1980). It appears, then, that SDL is not unique to individuals with chronic drinking histories and does not itself represent a long-term effect of alcohol abuse.

Acute Effects of Alcohol on Memory

In 1971, Ryback proposed that short-term memory (STM) disruption by alcohol was the underlying defect common to a continuum of memory effects seen in social drinkers, alcoholics, and Korsakoff syndrome patients. In this article, STM disruption was defined as an inability to retain a memory-span amount of information for more than 1 or 2 minutes. Whether this impairment, however, was a function of alcohol-disrupted rehearsal (encoding), storage, or retrieval processes had not been adequately investigated at that time. What was known was that moderate BAC levels (up to 100 mg%) minimally disrupted STM capacity as measured by an immediate memory task such as digit span. Findings also suggested that alcoholic blackouts, occurring at BACs ranging from 150 to 200 mg%, resulted from storage problems perhaps mediated by STM deficits.

Since that time, an appreciable body of research bearing on these mechanisms has accumulated (Birnbaum & Parker, 1977). Information-processing approaches have increasingly been used to study the acute effects of alcohol on memory. As such, this section reviews the most current or relevant evidence on alcohol and memory as seen from a multistore model of memory (Crowder, 1976, and Horton & Turnage, 1976, review such models of human memory) and a levels-of-processing approach (Craik & Lockhart, 1972). It also reviews the available evidence on how other factors (e.g., age, sex, expectancy) may interact with alcohol to produce memory impairments. We will then turn our attention to the phenomenon of alcoholic blackouts.

In basic terms, a multistore memory model assumes information is processed and then transferred sequentially from one memory store to another.

Typically, incoming information is initially processed or registered at a large capacity sensory store, where iconic images of very short duration exist before being transferred via attention processes to STM, a store of limited capacity. From STM, the information can be further processed via a variety of encoding or organizational strategies which enable the stimuli to be consolidated into a long-term memory (LTM) of presumably infinite capacity.

Effects of alcohol on initial sensory processing have been recently reviewed by Mello and Mendelson (1978) and will not be detailed here. However, it is important to note that alcohol does not appear to alter the rate of decay of information from iconic memory but rather impedes acquisition of such information or its retrieval from iconic storage (Moskowitz & Murray, 1976).

STM has usually been defined as memory for a small amount of information that is rapidly lost after 30 seconds unless rehearsed. This short-term store has also been referred to as *primary memory*. It is clear that this definition differs markedly from that employed by Ryback (1971), who measured STM as existing from 1 to 2 minutes after stimulus presentation. Such differences, of course, make it difficult to assess whether alcohol affects STM.

It is also clear that not all aspects of primary memory can be considered equivalent. For example, although immediate memory can be broadly considered part of primary memory, it has not been found to correlate with the primary memory component in free recall (Martin, 1978). For this reason, primary memory as reflected by immediate memory span is discussed separately from studies assessing STM via other tasks.

First, since Ryback's review (1971), only a few studies have investigated the effect of alcohol on digit span. Both Parker et al. (1974) and Rosen and Lee (1976) found that digit span was impaired relative to sober conditions. At first, this finding may appear inconsistent with Ryback's review, wherein alcohol was described as having minimal effects on immediate memory tasks. In both of the latter studies, however, mean differences, although statistically significant, were really quite small. Overall, then, immediate memory is relatively resistant to alcohol-induced impairments until BAC levels approach 150 mg% (Lisman, 1974).

Another method of studying STM has been via free recall learning. Serial position curves obtained from free recall permit analysis of primacy effects reflecting items in LTM and recency effects reflecting items in STM (Glanzer, 1971). Several studies (Jones, 1973; Jones & Jones, 1976a) utilizing this procedure found that alcohol (BAC = 100 mg%) exerted a depressing effect on the primacy but not the recency component of the serial curve. From this finding, they concluded that alcohol disrupts storage of new information in LTM. Next, Miller et al. (1978) found that although immediate recall of a 16-word list was impaired by alcohol, serial position effects were independent of alcohol drug state or drug state change. This is not entirely inconsistent with the finding of Jones (1973), however, because in one experiment there was a trend showing that alcoholic subjects have a smaller primacy effect than sober subjects.

These studies, then, provide support for the notion that alcohol impedes the transfer of information from STM to LTM, but not the recall of STM items. Why might this be? Perhaps STM scanning is greatly reduced under alcohol, and some information is thus lost prior to greater processing. This latter explanation is not supported for normal subjects, because two studies (Roth et al., 1977; Tharp, Rundell, Lester, & Williams, 1974) have found no reduction in STM scanning (Sternberg, 1966) under alcohol. A population of alcoholics (Mohs, Tinklenberg, Roth, & Kopell, 1978) and Korsakoff syndrome alcoholics (Naus, Cermak, & De Luca, 1977), however, have shown slowing of STM scanning rates even when persons are sober. This particular deficit may thus reflect more chronic than acute effects of alcohol on STM.

Another possibility is that the elaborative processes in STM are disrupted by alcohol such that stimuli are poorly encoded and thus do not enter LTM; alternatively, perhaps information does enter LTM but retrieval processes fail under acute alcohol intoxication. These and other storage/retrieval issues are addressed in the following section.

Finally, a study by Riege, Miklusak, and Buchhalter (1976) suggests that the sensory modality in which stimuli are presented may influence retention. These investigators studied verbal recall as well as recognition of visual, auditory, and tactual stimuli. They found that alcoholics, relative to controls, were deficient in verbal recall and in visual and tactual recognition but showed no deficit in recognition of nonverbal auditory stimuli (bird calls).

Memory Storage Versus Retrieval

A number of studies have concluded that memory storage is much more susceptible to impairment by alcohol than is retrieval. Storage deficits have been demonstrated by having groups learn while sober or intoxicated and recall while sober another day. Jones (1973) and Miller et al. (1978), using this procedure, found no differential forgetting for sober versus intoxicated groups during retention tests on day 2. One criticism of these studies, however, is that intoxicated versus sober groups were not equivalent on the amount of original learning, and therefore later retention losses were not exactly comparable. One study that controlled for equivalence of original learning was that of Birnbaum et al. (1978). In this study, subjects first performed while sober on a paired associate learning and a free recall task, and then retrieved information in an intoxicated or sober state 1 week later. It was found that retention losses were equal for both the sober to intoxicated (S−I) and sober to sober (S−S) groups and that experimentally presented retrieval cues did not differentially alter the amount of retrieval for each group. From this study, then, it appears that information originally learned in a nondrug state is quite resistant to later retrieval deficits, even with moderate alcohol

intake. This finding is consistent with Ryback's review (1971) and with the SDL
literature in that asymmetric SDL from a sober to an intoxicated state is rarely
found (Weingartner, 1978). Before ruling out the effect of alcohol on later
retention, however, various retention intervals other than 24 hours or 1 week
should be tested. In addition, BAC levels higher than 70–80 mg% (Birnbaum et
al., 1978) may need to be used before alcohol impairs retrieval. Finally, a
comparison between intoxicated to intoxicated (I–I) and intoxicated to sober
(I–S) groups has not been conducted outside of SDL experiments, but such a
comparison may reveal retrieval differences due to the drug state on day 2.

Other investigators have studied the storage versus retrieval issue by
minimizing retrieval processes. Parker et al. (1976) found that alcohol disrupted initial learning but had no effect on later retention of the same material.
Wickelgren (1975) also showed that initial learning (recognition) was poorer
under alcohol relative to placebo conditions, but that forgetting curves obtained under sober states were equivalent for both groups. The findings of
both of these studies, then, suggest that alcohol impairs storage more than
retrieval.

Nevertheless, all the previously discussed studies involved retention or
retrieval tested after a period ranging from 1 day–2 weeks. By comparison,
other studies have examined learning and retrieval under alcohol within the
same 1-day session. In these studies (Gerrein & Chechile, 1977; Rosen &
Lee, 1976), there was evidence of both storage and retrieval deficits. Evidence
of retrieval deficit comes from the finding that retrieval cues greatly aided
alcohol groups, whereas alcohol disrupted storage purportedly by interfering
with semantic categorization of the stimuli (Rosen & Lee, 1976). Gerrein and
Chechile (1977), using a modified version of the Peterson paradigm (Peterson
& Peterson, 1959), which separates storage and retrieval, found that alcohol
impaired retrieval more than storage. Finally, Saucedo (1980) reported retrieval failure under initial alcohol intoxication; yet, when tested 24 hours later, a
significant number of subjects spontaneously recalled previously inaccessible
stimuli. This temporary retrieval deficit is also found with other CNS depressants. Adam (1979), for example, noted that recovery from an anesthetic
often brings about the emergence of temporarily inaccessible memory traces.

In sum, there is evidence that both storage and retrieval processes can be
affected by alcohol. More specifically, however, retention is less likely to be
disrupted by drugs or drug-state changes if the original learning is conducted
under sober conditions. On the other hand, if the original learning is
conducted under alcohol, short-term forgetting is a function of both storage
and retrieval (Gerrein & Chechile, 1977).

Locus of Alcohol Storage Deficit

Several researchers (Craik, 1977; Gerrein & Chechile, 1977; Rosen &
Lee, 1976) have suggested that alcohol-induced superficial encoding of information is the mechanism mediating storage deficits in alcohol studies. A

levels-of-processing approach (Craik, 1977) has not been borne out. Hartley, Birnbaum, and Parker (1978) reported that even when intoxicated subjects semantically encode information, storage deficits remain relative to sober subjects. Thus, the locus (loci) of alcohol-induced storage deficits remains undetermined, and continued research is needed to elucidate the mechanism(s).

Other Factors

This section presents a short survey of other factors (e.g., drinking history, age, sex, and expectancy) that may interact with each other or with acute alcohol intoxication to produce memory impairments. In one acute alcohol study (Rosen & Lee, 1976), the drinking history did not predict differential memory decrements. Parker et al. (1974), however, reported that alcoholics semantically categorize verbal material more poorly than do normals under intoxicating conditions. Recently, Jones and Jones (1980) demonstrated that middle-aged women who are moderate social drinkers are more impaired in STM under alcohol than are younger, lighter-drinking women. Whether this pattern holds for men is still untested.

The drinking history has also been found useful in predicting memory performance under sober conditions. For example, heavy social drinking in men correlates significantly with memory and organizational decrements in free recall learning (Parker & Noble, 1977). Even a history of a drunk driving offense may predict memory impairment as reflected in a visual STM (Memory for Designs) task (Fine & Steer, 1979).

The latter finding is consistent with the memory impairments seen in alcoholics. Miglioli, Buchtel, Campanini, & De Risio (1979) have shown that visual STM remains impaired in recovering alcoholics even after several months of abstinence. Parsons and Prigitano's (1977) suggestion that detoxified alcoholics may have nonverbal memory problems has begun to find support. Cutting (1978a, b) has also noted nonverbal memory deficits in alcoholics.

Another important variable is age. As reported earlier, STM is disrupted more severely under alcohol in older, moderate-drinking women than in younger, lighter-drinking women (Jones & Jones, 1980). Age—alcohol interactions were also noted by Robertson, Arenberg, and Vestel (1975); delayed recognition memory was more impaired in older intoxicated subjects that in younger ones. Finally, in a study conducted under sober conditions (Ryan & Butters, 1980b), young alcoholics outperformed older alcoholics on a verbal paired-associate learning task, a 4-word STM test, and a Symbol-Digit paired-associate learning task.

Gender is another important variable that can interact with alcohol. Women have been found to be more affected by alcohol during the premenstrual phase and, in comparison to men, show greater memory loss under delayed recall conditions (Jones & Jones, 1976b, 1977). The previously presented Jones and Jones (1980) study also relates gender and age to memory performance under alcohol.

One final variable that has recently been examined with respect to alcohol and memory is the expectancy of receiving alcohol (Marlatt, Demming, & Reid, 1973). Numerous phenomena once attributed to the pharmacologic actions of alcohol, including changes in sexual arousal, aggression, moods, and craving for alcohol, are now known to be partially if not primarily evoked by expectancy factors (Marlatt & Rohsenow, 1980). That such factors can influence cognitive performance has been demonstrated by Williams, Goldman, and Williams (1978), who found that subjects expecting alcohol but receiving tonic, or subjects expecting tonic but receiving alcohol made more errors on cognitive tasks than did subjects in expectancy-congruent groups. Miller et al. (1978) employed a balanced placebo design to study immediate and delayed recall of serial lists by heavy drinkers. They reported no effects of expectancy upon memory but a clear influence of moderate alcohol doses upon storage of information. Research in our own laboratory has supported their findings, with deficits in recall and recognition occurring almost exclusively in alcohol rather than placebo conditions. Thus, it appears that expectancy plays relatively little role in disrupting memory performance, although subjects who know they are receiving alcohol may be able to compensate to some extent (Williams et al., 1978).

Alcohol Blackouts

One of the most interesting memory anomalies is the alcohol blackout, an inability to recall while sober events that occurred and information that was learned while the individual was intoxicated (Goodwin et al., 1969, Goodwin, Powell, Bremer, Horne & Sterne, 1969). Relatively little experimental research has been devoted to this phenomenon. Early studies (Goodwin, 1971; Goodwin et al., 1969, 1970; Ryback, 1970; Tamerin, Weiner, Poppen, Steinglass, & Mendelson, 1971) attempted to explain alcohol blackouts as a disruption of STM which, in turn, would interfere with storage and consolidation into LTM. Subsequent evidence on this point has been mixed. Mello (1973; Mello & Mendelson, 1978), using a simple matching task and short (0−6 min) retention intervals, has failed to find STM deficits in alcoholics at blood alcohol levels as high as 200 mg%. Lisman (1974), on the other hand, has demonstrated STM deficits using a picture recall task and a 20-minute retention interval. It is clear that the length of the retention interval used to assess STM is a critical issue. Some researchers (Goodwin, Othmer, Kalikas, & Freeman, 1970; Goodwin, Hill, Hopper, & Viesselman, 1975) have defined immediate memory as encompassing intervals of 1−2 minutes. Others (Ryback, 1970; Tamerin et al., 1971) have used retention intervals of 1−5 minutes as indices of STM. Some have preferred to define STM in 20−30 minutes postpresentation intervals (Goodwin et al., 1970,

1975; Lisman, 1974). A further complication is that STM impairment and blackouts are probably related not only to the retention interval but also to BAC and type of task employed (e.g., recognition versus recall). Systematic studies of the conditions under which blackouts occur are needed.

SDL has been proposed as the mechanism underlying alcohol blackouts (Ryback, 1971), but research has failed to support this hypothesis (Lisman, 1974; Nathan, Goldman, Lisman, & Taylor, 1972). It appears that blackouts may be more similar to the retrieval deficits seen with acute intoxication (Adam, 1979). In partial blackouts, for example, a person may recall while sober a part of what he or she could not remember while intoxicated, reflecting a recovery of previously inaccessible stimuli rather than SDL. Goodwin and his associates (1975) have reported that providing recognition cues during the presentation of material while the subject was intoxicated prevented the occurrence of blackouts, whereas a noncued group experienced blackouts even when recognition cues were presented subsequently during the sober state. The cued group was able to use the cues to aid recall 24 hours later, suggesting that contextual cueing during initial learning even at very high BACs (near 300 mg%) may prevent blackouts by enhancing storage and retrieval. This study provides an interesting convergence with the finding that cueing may likewise obviate the SDL phenomenon, and it suggests a possible mechanism to explain the anecdotal reports of subjects in our laboratory that they could override the blackout effect if they "tried" during the intoxication phase.

Yet another possible explanation for blackouts is that alcohol alters the kind or quality of information processing (cf. Cermak, 1977). Recent research by Hartley et al. (1978) failed to support this explanation, but the BACs employed (70–80 mg%) were considerably lower than those needed to precipitate blackouts. Thus, the possibility remains that semantic processing may be impaired when the BAC exceeds 200 mg%.

Research with the balanced placebo design (Marlatt & Rohsenow, 1980) has pointed to the importance of controlling for cognitive expectancies in any study on the effects of alcohol. As indicated earlier, a wide range of effects previously attributed to the pharmacologic qualities of alcohol have been found to be related instead to subject beliefs and expectancies (e.g., when drinking a placebo beverage believed to contain alcohol). Pilot research in our laboratory employing a placebo condition has found the blackout phenomenon to be attributable to alcohol rather than to expectancies, replicating the findings of earlier studies (Miller et al., 1978; Vucinich & Sobell, 1978; Williams et al., 1978). These data suggest, not surprisingly, that memory anomalies observed with intoxication are almost completely the result of pharmacologic actions of alcohol.

Overall, then, the mechanisms which mediate alcohol blackouts remain to be delineated. Current research suggests that both storage and retrieval processes are important factors in producing blackouts. There is also a clear relationship to BAC, with concentrations in excess of 150–200 mg% being required to trigger a blackout. Recent data from our laboratory suggest two qualifying factors in this relationship, however. First, it appears that the onset of a blackout is a progressive process, with partial impairment occurring at BACs as low as 70 mg%. Second, it appears that there are large individual differences with regard to the blood alcohol threshold sufficient to induce a total en bloc blackout. The clinical literature (e.g., Goodwin et al., 1975) has reported the absence of blackouts in certain cases in which BACs approached 300 mg%, but in our laboratory we have observed total blocking of retrieval when information was presented at levels as low as 120 mg%. Clinical experience suggests that the critical threshold for blackouts may drop with progressive heavy drinking, but this remains to be verified by adequately controlled research.

Alcohol Amnestic Disorder

Ryback's (1971) review concluded that Korsakoff's syndrome represents the endpoint of a continuum of memory impairment and involves deficits in STM and LTM with sparing of immediate memory. Numerous thorough reviews of the Korsakoff or amnestic syndrome have since appeared (Butters, 1979; Butters & Cermak, 1974, 1975, 1976; Cermak, 1977, 1979; Cermak & Butters, 1973; Kinsbourne, 1976; Kinsbourne & Wood, 1975), along with a major definitive clinical and pathologic study (Victor, Adams, & Collins, 1971). The application of information-processing models to this disorder has proved fruitful, and the above-mentioned reviews have delineated the locus of deficits seen in the Korsakoff syndrome patient. Rather than repeat this extensive body of findings we will highlight past and recent trends in isolating various memory deficits related to alcohol amnestic disorder.

STM Impairment

Some researchers (e.g., Baddeley & Warrington, 1970) have presented evidence that STM functioning is normal in amnestic patients but that increased susceptibility to proactive interference causes failure of retrieval. Others (e.g., Cermak & Butters, 1973; Kinsbourne & Wood, 1975) have found that STM is greatly reduced in amnestic patients. Butters, Cermak, and Sax (1976) found that Korsakoff syndrome patients showed normal STM performance on a free recall task and that interference and distraction severely impaired STM performance (cf. Walker & Hunter, 1978). Differences among these studies in the population studied and in the stimulus exposure intervals probably account for this discrepancy. Baddeley and Warrington (1970), for example, studied a heterogeneous group that included non-Korsakoff amnestic patients. Current data suggest that different types of amnestic syndromes (e.g., postencephalitic versus Korsakoff) display differing patterns of memory impairment (cf. Butters, 1979; Butters & Cermak, 1976).

The mechanisms by which STM is impaired have been investigated in a number of studies. Cermak and Butters have argued that the rapid retention loss in STM is a function of problems in semantic encoding, and in a series of studies they have shown that amnestic patients tend to analyze both verbal and nonverbal information at a superficial level (Butters, 1979; Butters et al., 1976; Cermak, 1979; Cermak & Butters, 1973). A further finding supporting an encoding interpretation of this deficit was provided in a study showing that amnestic patients fail to show release from proactive inhibition (PI) with category shifts (Cermak, Butters, & Moreines, 1974). Another research team, however, has presented evidence that Korsakoff syndrome patients show release from PI and can process information semantically if given more than one trial (Kinsbourne & Wood, 1975), and further, that category cueing during encoding does not enhance retrieval (Wood & Kinsbourne, 1974). The latter study found that cueing at the time of the retention test did improve performance, suggesting a deficit in the retrieval process (cf. Cermak & Reale, 1978; Warrington, 1975). These findings have been supported by McDowell (1979). Cermak's most recent (1980) attempts to improve retention in amnestic patients by directed semantic coding have produced limited and temporary effects at best. This evidence, then, seems to support the view that a basic deficit in amnestic patients is retrieval of information from STM (Kinsbourne, 1976). This does not, of course, rule out encoding variables as significant factors. Kinsbourne (1976; Winocur & Kinsbourne, 1978), for example, has proposed that failure to encode contextual cues in learning new information may be a crucial variable in the amnestic syndrome. Finally, there is evidence that Korsakoff syndrome patients show impairment in STM itself, and not only in transfer from STM to LTM (Cermak, 1974; Huppert & Piercy, 1977; Kinsbourne & Wood, 1975; Naus et al., 1977).

LTM Impairment

Verbal LTM can be divided into episodic and semantic memory (Tulving, 1972). Episodic memory—recall of material presented once—is greatly disturbed in amnestic subjects. Semantic memory—memory for overlearned data, strategies, and so on—is relatively spared in amnestic patients (Kinsbourne & Wood, 1975). In this regard, Huppert and Piercy (1978) found that given additional time for encoding, Korsakoff syndrome patients forgot no faster than normal controls. This finding is consistent with that of several earlier studies that showed little differential forgetting for well-learned material when comparing normal with Korsakoff syndrome subjects (Cermak, Butters, & Goodglass, 1971; Warrington & Weiskrantz, 1970; Weiskrantz & Warrington, 1970). Retrieval from semantic memory in amnestic patients appears to be similar to normal processes, although the search process within semantic memory may be somewhat slower than normal (Cermak, 1979). In part, the profound deficits of Korsakoff syndrome patients may be due to the fact that semantic encoding appears to be a nonpreferred mode of operation in this group (Butters & Cermak, 1974, 1975, 1976). These findings suggest that directed semantic processing should be helpful in reversing the deficits of Korsakoff syndrome patients, but, as has been indicated, the results of such efforts have been disappointingly marginal (Cermak, 1980).

A Continuum of Alcohol-Related Memory Deficits

More than 10 years ago, Ryback (1971) proposed that the central problem in alcohol-related memory deficits was STM. Since then, memory research has become more·complex due to the use of information-processing approaches; in turn, interpretations of findings are often controversial due to differences between models. Nevertheless, these studies have yielded much new evidence with which to examine Ryback's original hypothesis.

In this regard, there are some new findings to support Ryback's hypothesis. First, Cermak and Ryback (1976) showed that recently hospitalized chronic alcoholics may perform as poorly as Korsakoff syndrome patients on an STM task but that such a deficit disappears after several weeks of abstinence. In addition, Illchysin and Ryback (1977) reported that alcoholics with a history of blackouts have STM impairments even after 3 weeks of abstinence. STM impairment may also extend to less pathologic populations. Jones and Jones (1980) found that under moderate doses of alcohol (BAC of 60 mg%), moderate-drinking, middle-aged women, relative to lighter-drinking, young women, had greater STM impairment.

In addition, in nonverbal STM, a continuum of deficits emerges. For example, nonverbal STM is poorer in young alcoholics than in young normals (Blucewicz, Dustman, Schenkenberg, & Beck, 1977). Middle-aged drunk-driving offenders, tested while sober on the Memory for Designs Test, also exhibited nonverbal memory impairments (Fine & Steer, 1979), and chronic alcoholics demonstrated nonverbal STM deficits even after several months of abstinence (Miglioli et al., 1979). In a study comparing normals, moderate drinkers, heavy drinkers, and chronic alcoholics, Cutting (1978a) found that on a picture memory task, normal subjects outperformed alcoholics and moderate drinkers outperformed heavy drinkers. Cutting (1978b) further reported that Korsakoff syndrome patients performed more poorly than did alcoholics on a picture recognition task.

Other STM processes have been shown to follow a continuum of alcohol pathology. Acutely intoxicated normals show no significant changes in their rate of STM scanning (Roth, Tinklenberg and Kopell 1977; Tharp et al., 1974). Yet chronic alcoholics, even when sober, do display greatly slowed STM search rates (Mohs et al., 1978), and in comparison to alcoholic controls, Korsakoff syndrome patients show even greater slowing of STM scanning processes (Naus et al., 1977). A continuum of impairment on the Wechsler Memory Scale (WMS) has been observed by Ryan and Butters (1980a) such that Korsakoff syndrome patients perform most poorly (Butters,

Cermak, Montgomery, & Adinolfi, 1977), followed by non-Korsakoff alcoholics, who in turn score more poorly than do psychiatric controls (Bauer & Johnson, 1957; Miller & Orr, 1980)—although some studies have found no significant differences between alcoholics and controls on the WMS (Bolter & Hannon, 1980; Butters et al., 1977).

Overall, this body of findings supports the notion of a continuum of STM deficits from social drinkers to alcoholics to Korsakoff syndrome patients. There are findings to suggest that continua involving other memory processes are important as well. For example, semantic encoding appears to be poorer in alcoholics than in normals (Parker et al., 1974), and alcohol interferes with such processing (Rosen & Lee, 1976). Korsakoff syndrome patients, as indicated above, prefer not to encode new information semantically (Cermak & Butters, 1973; Cermak, 1979). Despite these findings, depth of processing has not yet been causally linked to storage disruption seen in acutely intoxicated normals (Hartley et al., 1978) and in Korsakoff syndrome subjects (Cermak, 1980).

On the other hand, contextual encoding and retrieval mechanisms (Tulving & Thomson, 1973) may be part of another continuum of memory deficits. At one end of the continuum, both acute intoxication (Gerrin & Chechile, 1977) and alcohol SDL studies with normals (Weingartner, 1978) demonstrate instances of retrieval failure, although these may recover after intoxication wears off (Saucedo, 1980) or if retrieval cues are presented (Eich, 1977). In blackouts, however, retrieval of such amnesic information may not always be possible, although cueing during encoding and retrieval may help prevent blackouts (Goodwin, 1977). Finally, at the other, most pathologic end of the continuum are the Korsakoff syndrome patients, who have a notoriously difficult time encoding and generating contextual retrieval cues unless salient cues are presented (Winocur & Kinsbourne, 1978).

Thus, both STM and encoding/retrieval factors seem to be important all along the continuum of alcohol-induced memory deficits, and both deserve further attention and investigation. Further refinement and comparability of various memory models will help to clarify the developmental sequence and pattern of memory deficits occurring along this continuum of alcohol-related impairment.

IMPAIRMENT ON NEUROPSYCHOLOGICAL TESTS

We turn now from a consideration of the effects of alcohol on memory to a broader discussion of the long-term impact of problem drinking upon cognitive functions in general. Several generalizations seem to be justified by current research. It is now quite clear that heavy drinking can produce a predictable pattern of neuropsychological impairment, and that such deficits in brain function often precede the development of overt health problems (such as liver disease) by a number of years. The impairment appears not to be global, but rather is manifested in a selective pattern of deficits that may be difficult to detect in a standard interview. Further, it is clear that this pattern of impairment is, in many cases, at least partially reversible if the drinking problem is successfully resolved. Evidence for this pattern of cognitive dysfunction spans a broad literature, including studies of neuropsychological tests, to which we now turn, as well as biomedical research, which will be discussed in a later section. This literature also spans the international research community, with converging patterns of impairment being reported from a wide range of nations, including Norway (Løberg, 1980), Sweden (Amark, 1951; Bergman & Agren, 1974; Carlsson et al., 1973; Claeson & Carlsson, 1970), Holland (Boeke, 1970), Scotland (Guthrie & Elliott, 1980), Canada (Carlen, Wilkinson, & Kiraly, 1976; Carlen, Wilkinson, Single, Rankin, & Whiteside, 1977; Carlen, Wortzman, Holgate, Wilkinson, & Rankin, 1980; Sanchez-Craig, 1979), Ireland (Clarke & Haughton, 1975; Draper, Feldman, & Haughton, 1978), Chile (Ferrer, 1970), Germany (Götze, Kuhne, Hansen, & Knipp, 1978; Köhler, 1974), and England (Marshman, 1975).

Wechsler Adult Intelligence Scale (WAIS)

The WAIS has been used extensively to study cognitive functions in alcoholics and is perhaps the oldest instrument to be used for this purpose (Wechsler, 1941). Although findings have varied, there is an encouraging amount of consistency across studies. Table 11-1 summarizes the results of 17 controlled studies contrasting the WAIS performance of alcoholics to that of various comparison groups. Numerous uncontrolled studies have also been published (see the review by Miller and Orr, 1980), but their findings have been relatively consistent with those of controlled research. We will therefore focus on the latter studies.

Fitzhugh, Fitzhugh, and Reitan (1960, 1965) were among the first to observe that WAIS scores of alcoholics could be misleadingly normal in appearance. These authors found that although the alcoholics in their samples performed well on the WAIS, they showed substantial impairment on more sensitive neuropsychological measures from the Halstead—Reitan Battery (to be reviewed later). Similarly, other teams of investigators have reported normal performances of alcoholic samples across most subscales of the WAIS (Butters et al., 1977; Mohs et al., 1978; Peters, 1956; Plumeau, Machover, & Puzzo, 1960). Indeed, there has been considerable convergence of findings to suggest that at least on measures of verbal intelligence, alcoholics tend to produce normal scores. Only 25% of the studies reported in Table 11–1 found alcoholics to differ from controls in Verbal Intelligence (VIQ). One possible exception to this is the Arithmetic subscale, which was found in 42% of studies to differentiate alcholics from controls. Plumeau et al. (1960) found this to be the only subscale that differentiated their groups. Scores on the Vocabulary subscale are almost universally found to be normal in alcoholics (see Table 11 −1), consistent with findings of normal performance of problem drinkers on other vocabulary measures (Amark, 1951; Sharp, Rosenbaum, Goldman, & Whitman, 1977). Thus, Vocabulary appears to be a good "hold" measure in alcoholics and may be useful in judging the degree of relative impairment on other subscales.

On Performance subscales, by contrast, alcoholics have more often been found to be impaired relative to controls. Two-thirds of the studies reviewed found alcoholics' PIQ to be significantly lower than that of controls. Alcoholic samples almost universally show higher VIQ than PIQ (e.g., Goldstein & Shelly, 1971; Goldstone, Lhamon, & Nurnberg, 1977; Halpern, 1946; Holland & Watson, 1980; Köhler, 1974; Marshman, 1975; Miller & Orr, 1980; Teicher & Singer, 1946), although there are exceptions (Boeke, 1970; Smith, Burt, & Chapman, 1973). Smart (1965) has suggested the use of the VIQ − PIQ difference as a diagnostic guide, recommending a difference score of 18 as indicative of deterioration.

Perhaps the most consistently suppressed subscale is Block Design, found to be impaired in 79% of the studies we reviewed. It is often found to be among the most sensitive and discriminating indicators of impairment in alcoholics (Holland & Watson, 1980; Köhler, 1974; O'Leary, Donovan, Chaney, Walker, & Schau, 1979b; Overall, Hoffman, & Levin, 1978; Smith & Smith, 1977) and has been found to improve differentially in alcoholics who are successfully treated (Berglund, Leijonquist, & Horlen, 1977; Long & McLachlan, 1974). Of 12 diagnostic groups (including brain-damaged patients) studied by Overall et al. (1978), alcoholics showed the lowest score on Block Design.

Digit Symbol is also commonly found to be low among alcoholics and is often the lowest subscale of the WAIS profile (e.g., Dietvorst, Swenson, & Morse, 1978; Halpern, 1946; Kaldegg, 1956; Korboot, Naylor, & Soares, 1977; McLaughlin, Faillace, & Overall, 1979: Murphy, 1953; Overall et al., 1978; Page & Linden, 1974; Plumeau et al., 1960; Smith & Smith, 1977; Wechsler, 1941). This is not unique to alcoholism, however: Digit Symbol is a frequent low point in the profiles of any pathologic population (Holland & Watson, 1980). Nevertheless, Digit Symbol often proves to be a useful measure in discriminating alcoholic from control profiles (Butters et al., 1977; Holland & Watson, 1980; Köhler, 1974; O'Leary et al., 1979b). In an ingenious study, Kapur and Butters (1977) performed a task analysis of Digit Symbol performance in alcoholics in order to determine the reason for this common deficit. They found that visual search was not impaired in alcoholics, whereas digit/symbol paired associate learning, visuoperceptive analysis, and location learning were all deficient. Further, these investigators correlated Digit Symbol performance with each of these component abilities and found

Table 11-1

Summary of Studies of Alcoholics' Performance on the WAIS

Studies	Information	Comprehension	Arith.	Similarities	Digit Span	Vocab. IQ	Verbal IQ	Digit Symbol	Picture Completion	Block Design	Picture Arrangement	Object Assembly	Perform. IQ	Full Scale IQ
Wilkinson & Carlen, 1978	0					0							—	
Smith & Smith, 1977		—	—	—	—	0	—	—	—	—	—	—	—	—
Silberstein & Parsons, 1979		0		0				—	0	—				
Schau & O'Leary, 1977	0	—		0	0	0		—						
Ryan & Butters, 1980	0	0	0	0	0	0	0							
Plumeau et al., 1960	0	0	—	0	0	0	0	0	0	0	0	0	0	0
O'Leary et al., 1979	0	0	—	0	0	0	0	—	—	—	—	—	—	
O'Leary et al., 1977	0	—	—	0	0	0	0	—	—	—	—	—	—	—
Miller & Orr, 1980	0	—	—	—	0	0	—	—	—	—	—	—	—	—

158

Study													
Long & McLachlan, 1974	0	0	0	0	0	0	0	—	0	—	0	—	—	—
Loberg, 1980	+	0	0	+	—	0	0	—	0	—	—	—	—	—
Hewett & Martin, 1980	—		—											
Fitzhugh et al., 1965	0	0	0	0	0	0	0	0	0	—	0	0	0	0
Fitzhugh et al., 1960	0	0	0	0	0	0	0	0	0	0	0	0	0	0
Clarke & Haughton, 1975		0		—	0					—				
Butters et al., 1977	0	0	0	0	0	0	0	—	0	0	0	0	0	0
Blusewicz, 1975	—	—	0	0	—	—		0	—	—	—	—	—	—
Percent Impaired*	14%	36%	42%	25%	17%	07%	25%	69%	42%	79%	55%	67%	67%	56%

+ = alcoholics' performance significantly better than controls
0 = no significant difference between alcoholics and controls
− = alcoholics' performance significantly poorer than controls

*Percent Impaired = percentage of studies including the measure in which alcoholics' performance was found to be significantly poorer than that of controls

that whereas paired-associate learning ability predicted performance in normals, there was no such relationship among Korsakoff syndrome patients. Instead, performance in these patients depended upon their visuoperceptive analytic capabilities, as reflected on an embedded figures task. Thus, it appears that Korsakoff syndrome patients use a different cognitive strategy in approaching the Digit Symbol task. Non-Korsakoff alcoholics show an intermediate pattern, with performance on the Digit Symbol task being correlated both with paired-associate learning and with visuoperceptive abilities.

Overall, then, alcoholics tend to show deficits on Performance more than on Verbal subscales of the WAIS. Of the verbal subscales, Arithmetic may be most severely impaired. Block Design and Digit Symbol are the most typical low points of the profile, and Object Assembly is also frequently low. Relatively less impairment is seen on Picture Completion and Picture Arrangement, both of which may be less disrupted by the peripheral neuropathy commonly seen in alcoholics. Overall performance on intelligence tests may appear quite normal (Tarter, Buonpane, & Wyant, 1975), particularly if the tests used rely heavily upon verbal abilities, which are less affected by long-term alcohol abuse.

The Halstead—Reitan Tests

Perhaps the most extensively used battery of tests for neuropsychological assessment has been Reitan's modification of the Halstead measures (Halstead, 1947; Reitan & Davison, 1974). The Halstead—Reitan Neuropsychological Test Battery for Adults has been found to be respectably accurate in the identification and diagnosis of brain damage, comparing favorably with such traditional procedures as the electroencephalogram and the brain scan (Reitan, 1975; Tsushima & Wedding, 1979). This battery may be particularly useful in identifying cognitive impairment within alcoholic populations. Fitzhugh, Fitzhugh, and Reitan (1960, 1965) found that the Halstead—Reitan Battery detected a consistent pattern of impairment in alcoholics, whereas the WAIS reflected relatively normal performance. Wilkinson and Carlen (1980) reported that 50% of alcoholic cases found to be normal by a neurologist showed significant characteristic impairment when evaluated with the Halstead—Reitan battery, suggesting that these may be sensitive measures of earlier alcoholic deterioration.

In our survey of the literature, we identified 37 studies that have used some or all of the Halstead—Reitan Battery and have reported their findings in sufficient detail to permit independent evaluation. The results of these 37 studies are summarized in Table 11—2. A cursory examination of this table reveals that alcoholics are impaired on the majority of these measures, although not all. There is also an apparent difference in the percentage of studies that show impairment in alcoholics depending upon the criterion used. When the performance of alcoholics is judged against normative cutoff scores

(Russell, Neuringer, & Goldstein, 1970), a higher percentage are found to be impaired than in studies comparing the performance of alcoholics with control populations. As we shall see, one reason for this has been the relatively poor performance of certain control samples, who sometimes scored within the brain-damaged range, rather than normal performances by alcoholic samples.

We will consider briefly the current literature on each of the measures in the Halstead–Reitan Battery.

Category Test

The Category Test is a complex nonverbal learning task in which subjects, given continuous and immediate feedback, are asked to discover the rule or principle underlying each of seven series of stimuli. Discovery of the rule permits correct categorization of the stimuli into four classes. With impressive consistency, 23 of 24 studies using this measure have found alcoholics to score within the impaired range (51 or more errors) on the average. The one study that has reported normal performance of alcoholics on this measure (Grant, Adams, & Reed, 1979) employed extensive screening criteria to eliminate from their sample all alcoholics showing any sign of brain damage, making it understandable that no brain damage was found. In addition, in studies that have compared alcoholics with controls, 86% have found the alcoholics to be significantly more impaired on the Category Test. Of the two studies that failed to find such a difference, one was the report by Grant et al. (1979), and in the other (Goldstein & Chotlos, 1965) the performance of alcoholics was clearly in the impaired range but failed to differ from that of a control group of hospital employees whose mean score of 50 errors itself lies at the cutoff point between normal and impaired performance.

The meaning of this impairment is unclear because the Category Test, although a good indicator of brain damage in general, is of little use in localization of dysfunction. Nevertheless, this test has proven to be among the best discriminators of both male (Miller & Orr, 1980) and female alcoholics (Jones, Tarter, & Rosenberg, 1980b) from normal and patient control samples.

Jones and Parsons (1972) reported that the impairment of their alcoholic sample on this test was due largely to their poor performance on subscales 3 and 4, an interesting finding in that these two subscales require location learning, an ability found to be significantly impaired in alcoholics (Kapur & Butters, 1977; cf. our discussion to follow on Tactual Performance location score). To our knowledge, no other investigators have reported individual subtest scores, so that neither convergent nor discrepant findings have been published. To evaluate this hypothesis we reanalyzed, with the help of Dr. James A. Moses, Jr., data collected for a previous study (Miller & Orr, 1980). The subtest scores of alcoholic and brain-damaged groups from our study are reported in Table 11-3. Although the alcoholics did indeed make the largest number of their errors on subtests 3 and 4, so did our nonalcoholic brain-

Table 11-2
Summary of Studies of Alcoholics' Performance on the Halstead-Reitan Neuropsychological Test Battery

Studies	Categories		TPT dominant hand		TPT nondom. hand		TPT both hands		TPT total time		TPT memory		TPT location		Tapping dominant		Tapping nondom.		Trails A		Trails B		Aphasia Screening		Spatial Relations		Perceptual Errors		Seashore Rythm		Speech Perception		Impairment Index	
	I	D	I	D	I	D	I	D	I	D	I	D	I	D	I	D	I	D	I	D	I	D	I	D	I	D	I	D	I	D	I	D	I	D
Wilkinson & Carlen, 1980																																	–	
Templer et al., 1975	–																		–		–	0										–	–	
Tarter & Jones, 1971															–	–	–																	
Smith et al., 1973	–						–	–	–		0	0	–		0		0		0	0	0	0							0	0	0	0	0	
Silberstein & Parsons, 1979	–								0						0				–		–										–		–	
Shelly & Goldstein, 1976											0																	–						
Schau & O'Leary, 1977	–				–				–		–		0		–																			
Sanche-Craig, 1979																			–															
Prigitano, 1980	–								–		0		–		0														0					
Prigitano, 1977	–								–		0		–		–														–		0			
Page & Schaub, 1977	–		0		–		–																											
O'Leary et al., 1979	–	–	0	0	–	0	–		–		0	0	0		0		–		0		0		–						0		–		–	
O'Leary et al., 1977b																			–		–													
O'Leary et al., 1977a	–		0		0		–		0		0		–		–		–		0		–												–	
Miller & Orr, 1980	–	–	–	–	–		–		0		0		–		–		–		–		–		–		–	0	–		–		–		–	
McLaughlin et al., 1979	–														–		0																	
McLachlan & Levenson, 1974	–																																	
Marshman, 1975																			0															
Long & McLachlan, 1974	–		0	0	–		0		0		0		0		–		–		0		–						0	0	0	0	0	–	–	
Loberg, 1980	–		–		–		–		0		0				–		–										0					0		0

162

Jones & Parsons, 1972	–	–																																
Jones & Parsons, 1971	–	–														0																		
Jenkins & Parsons, 1979			–	0	–	–	–	–	–		0	0	–	0																				
Hill & Mikhael, 1979	–	–							–	–	–	–	–	–	–	–																		
Hester et al., 1980	–																																	
Grant et al., 1980	0	0		0		0		0	0	0	0	0	0	0	0	0		–		0	0	0		0		0		0	0	0	0	0	0	0
Goldstein & Chotlos, 1965	–	0																	–	–	–	–							–	0				
Fitzhugh et al., 1965		–								–		0		–						–		–								0		–		–
Fitzhugh et al., 1960		–								–		0		0		0				0		0								0		0		–
Eckardt et al., in press	–		0		–		–		–		0		–		–		–		–		–								–		–			
Eckardt et al., 1980	–		0		–		–		–		0		–		–		–		–		–								–		–			
Eckardt et al., 1979	–		0		–		–		–		0		–		–		–		–		–								–		–			
Eckardt et al., 1978	–								–		0		–		–				–		–								–		–			
Blusewicz, 1975	–	–							–	–	0	–	0	–	0	0					–	–							0	0			0	0
Bergman & Ågren, 1974																					–													
Barth et al., 1980	–								–		0		–		–						–								–		–		–	
Ayers et al., 1978																			–	0	–	0												
Percent Difference*		86%		17%		50%		67%		73%		18%		42%		44%		100%		42%		57%		50%		50%		50%		13%		50%		75%
Percent Impaired†	96%		40%		100%		100%		85%		06%		85%		73%		86%		84%		92%		50%		0%		50%		60%		67%		64%	

KEY: I = comparison of mean score for alcoholics with Reitan's normative cut-off scores
0 = alcoholics not impaired on this measure
– = alcoholics impaired on this measure
D = comparison of mean score for alcoholics with mean score for controls
0 = no significant difference between alcoholics and controls
– = alcoholics scored as significantly more impaired than controls on this measure

*Percent Difference = percentage of studies including this measure in which alcoholics' performance was found to be significantly poorer than that of controls. (Control groups varried — included normal subjects and psychiatric and medical patients.)

†Percent Impaired = percentage of studies including this measure in which alcoholics' mean performance was found to fall within the impaired range according to Reitan's normative cut-off scores.

Table 11-3
Mean Errors on Subtests of the Halstead Category Test

Subtest	Alcoholic Sample	Brain-Damaged Sample
I	0.3	0.2
II	1.0	0.8
III	23.3	25.9
IV	23.9	22.9
V	19.6	21.1
VI	13.9	16.0
VII	7.9	8.1

Note. Patient samples are described by Miller & Orr (1980). We wish to express our appreciation to James Moses, Ph.D., for his assistance in collecting and tabulating these data.

damaged group, suggesting that these subtests may simply be the most difficult of the series for individuals who manifest any degree of cognitive dysfunction. At any rate, the configuration of subtest scores for alcoholics is virtually identical to that for brain-damaged subjects in general.

Tactual Performance Test (TPT)

The TPT, another major component of the Halstead—Reitan Battery, likewise reflects a somewhat consistent pattern of impairment among alcoholics. In this test the subject is blindfolded and seated in front of a form board into which variously shaped blocks are to be placed. The subject first places the blocks into their respective spaces using only the dominant hand. The task is then repeated using only the nondominant hand, and again using both hands. Alcoholics are usually found to show little impairment in performance with the dominant (usually right) hand alone. By contrast, the performance of alcoholics using the nondominant (usually left) hand is consistently found to fall within the impaired range (100% of studies in Table 11-2) and to be significantly poorer than that of controls (50% of studies). In addition, performance with both hands is impaired in alcoholics (100% of studies), suggesting a deficit in learning with repeated trials on this task. Total time, the sum of these three performances, is found to be impaired in 85% of studies and is significantly poorer than that of controls in 73% of studies. Thus, although the time required to perform the first trial of the TPT is not markedly impaired in alcoholics, their performance on subsequent trials consistently falls within the impaired range.

Two further tasks complete the TPT assessment. The form board is removed from sight and then the blindfold is removed. The subject is then asked to draw from memory the board on which he or she has been working. With great consistency, alcoholics recall a normal number of shapes. With equal consistency, they demonstrate an inability to remember the correct position of those shapes on the form board. Thus, although the shapes are remembered, their former locations in three-dimensional space are not. Investigators using other measures have found that alcoholics have difficulty with tactual recognition (Riege et al., 1976) and with memory for location (Kapur & Butters, 1977).

In a fascinating study of tactual performance in alcoholics, Jenkins and Parsons (1979a) employed the TPT with two variations. Half of their subjects (all right-handed) performed their first trial using the right (dominant) hand, whereas the other half began with their left (nondominant) hand. Further, all subjects were tested on the standard TPT form board, which contains namable shapes (e.g., "star," "square") and on a second "nonverbal" form board consisting of irregular shapes to which names could not readily be attached. They found that the performance of alcoholics relative to controls was significantly poorer on the nonverbal form board and when the left hand was used first. On the other hand, the performance of alcoholics did not improve on the second trial, when the right hand was used first, whereas they did show improvement when the left hand was used first. Interestingly, there were no differences between these two groups in the time required to perform the first trial. Alcoholics who began the TPT with their left hand showed significantly greater deficits on memory and location scores in attempting to reproduce the form boards by recall.

Several studies have reported significant improvement of alcoholics on TPT measures after relatively brief periods of abstinence. Page and Schaub (1977) found that TPT performance improved between Week 1 and Week 3 of hospitalization but did not improve further by Week 25. Several other measures failed to show such improvement, so that the abilities tapped by the TPT may be unique in showing early reversal. Similarly, Prigitano (1980) found that the performance of alcoholics on the TPT improved over a period of 2 weeks, and Long and McLachlan (1974) found the TPT within normal limits at a 12-month follow-up.

Finger Oscillation (Tapping) Test

Findings regarding the performance of alcoholics on the Finger Oscillation task have been mixed. In Reitan's version of this task, the subject depresses a telegraph key as rapidly as possible over a span of 10 seconds. Repeated trials are used to obtain the subject's optimal speed using both the dominant and nondominant hands. Of the studies we surveyed, 73% found alcoholics' average tapping speed to fall within the impaired range for the dominant hand, although relative to controls, alcoholics were found to be significantly slower in only 44 percent of the studies. Tapping in the nondominant hand presents a more consistent picture. Impaired performance was found in 6 of 7 studies, and of 4 comparing alcoholics with controls, all 4 found alcoholics to be significantly slower. Fine motor dexterity has been found to be impaired in other studies as well (e.g., Kish & Cheney, 1969).

Trail Making Test

The Trail Making Test consists of two parts. Part A is a timed task in which the subject is asked to connect numbered circles with a continuous line, proceeding in numerical order as in a child's "follow-the-dot" task. Part B, also timed, is more complicated and requires the subject to draw a line connecting an alternating series of numbers and letters: 1-A-2-B-3-C and so on. Alcoholics have been found to score within the impaired range on Trails-A and Trails-B in 84% and 92% of studies, respectively. Fewer studies (42% and 57%) have found significant differences between alcoholics and controls, although this result has often been attributable to the poor performance of controls. A case in point is the study by Templer, Ruff, and Simpson (1975), which reported no difference in Trails performance between a group of alcoholics and a control group of "white males from various localities in western Kentucky who volunteered for this research" (p. 611). Based upon this finding, the authors concluded that the alcoholics definitely had psychological deficits. This seems a sweeping overstatement based upon one study employing a single measure of cognitive functioning, particularly since the authors failed to note that their "normal" controls scored well within the impaired range on both Trails-A and Trails-B.

Alcoholics show modest improvement in Trails performance over time, although their average scores tend to remain within the impaired range (Ayers, Templer, Ruff, & Barthlow, 1978). O'Leary and his colleagues (1977b) found improved performance on Trails at 1-year follow-up, but alcoholics' scores were still in the impaired range and remained significantly poorer than those of controls. This stability of deficit, combined with the simplicity and validity of the Trail-Making Test, recommend it as a potential screening instrument for cognitive impairment in alcoholics, although no definitive statements regarding the presence or absence of brain damage can be made on the basis of this or any other single neuropsychological test (Radford, Chaney, O'Leary, & O'Leary, 1978).

Speech Sounds Perception Test (SSPT)

The SSPT requires the subject to identify which of several nonsense syllables printed on an answer sheet best corresponds to a spoken sound presented via a standardized tape recording. Two-thirds of the studies we surveyed found alcoholics to be impaired on this measure, and three of six studies found alcoholics to perform more poorly than controls. Prigitano (1977) has found that the SSPT is particularly impaired in patients being maintained on disulfiram (Antabuse), a prescription medication used to deter future drinking. In a further study, Prigitano (1980) reported that receptive speech abilities as reflected on the SSPT tended to recover in patients not receiving disulfiram, whereas those taking the medication showed further deterioration on this test.

The normal performance of alcoholics on Verbal subscales of the WAIS argues against a pervasive deficit in overlearned speech functions, but there may be a deficit in reception of novel speech sounds. Rada and his colleagues (1977) employed sensitive speech pathology measures including the Porch Index of Communicative Abilities. They found that alcoholics performed more poorly than did normal geriatric patients, but that the alcoholics' deficits were partially reversible over the period of detoxification.

Seashore Rhythm Test

Perhaps the largest discrepancy between normative and comparative studies is found for the Seashore Rhythm Test, an evaluation of auditory perceptual acuity with nonverbal stimuli. The subject is asked to listen to two rhythmic patterns presented in close temporal proximity and then to indicate whether these patterns were the same or different. In terms of normative performance, 60% of the studies surveyed found scores indicative of impairment in alcoholics. Only one study of eight, however, found the performance of alcoholics to be significantly worse than that of controls. No definitive conclusions can be drawn at present.

Impairment Indices

Both Reitan (Reitan & Davison, 1974) and Russell et al. (1970) have proposed impairment indices by which the subscales of the Halstead–Reitan battery can be combined in an actuarial manner to produce an overall indication of the degree of cognitive impairment and of the probability of brain damage. On these overall measures, 64% of the studies included in Table 11-2 found alcoholics to score within the impaired range, and 75% found significantly greater impairment among alcoholics than among control subjects. Thus, in spite of variations in the pattern of impairment, alcoholics present a consistent overall picture of cognitive dysfunction relative to normative standards and to controls.

One further impairment index that may be of particular interest for evaluating alcoholic clients is the Brain Age Quotient (BAQ) proposed by Michael O'Leary. The BAQ is an actuarial combination of four Halstead–Reitan scales (Category errors, TPT total time, TPT location score, and Trails-B) and two Performance subscales of the WAIS (Block Design and Digit Symbol). Alcoholics have been found to differ significantly from controls on the BAQ in spite of a lack of difference on verbal intelligence measures (Schau & O'Leary, 1977). The BAQ may represent a particularly good index of impairment for alcoholics because its components are those scales on which alcoholics are most consistently found to be impaired relative to normative data and matched controls.

Shipley–Hartford Institute of Living Scale

Another instrument commonly used to study cognitive functioning in alcoholics is the Shipley–Hartford Institute of Living Scale (SHILS). This scale provides two measures: a vocabulary score, somewhat analogous to the

WAIS Vocabulary subscale score, and an index of verbal abstraction ability. A total performance index is also available, combining scores on the two subscales. Several investigators have found no differences between alcoholics and controls on SHILS performance (Donovan, Quiesser, & O'Leary, 1976; Jones, 1971; Jones & Parsons, 1972; Tarter, 1973; Tarter & Jones, 1971). Others have found alcoholics to perform normally on the vocabulary scale (consistent with normal WAIS Vocabulary performance, as reviewed above) but to be impaired on verbal abstraction (Hatcher, Jones, & Jones, 1977; Jones, Jones, & Hatcher, 1980; Silberstein & Parsons, 1979; Smith, Johnson, & Burdick, 1971; Smith & Layden, 1972). Only Hewett and Martin (1980) have found alcoholics to be more impaired on both vocabulary and abstraction relative to controls. Thus, alcoholics are consistently found to show normal vocabulary skills, whereas verbal abstraction is found to be impaired among alcoholics in about half of these studies.

Information Processing

Further data point to alcoholic deficits in abstraction and in information processing generally. Klisz and Parsons (1977) and Oscar-Berman (1973) employed the Levine Hypothesis Test to study problem-solving skills in alcoholics while minimizing the necessity of relying upon memory. Both found alcoholics to be impaired on problem-solving and abstraction abilities even when memory requirements were minimized. Interestingly, humor appreciation—a specific information-processing skill—appears to be normal in alcoholics both on Picture Arrangement of the WAIS and in research by Levine and Zigler (1976). Other investigators have found deficits among alcoholics in the processing of spatial and temporal information (Goldstone et al., 1977; Gregson & Taylor, 1977; Gudeman, Craine, Golden, & McLaughlin, 1977). These difficulties in integrating new information are consistent with the reliable impairment of alcoholics on the Halstead Category Test and the Tactual Performance Test and on various memory tasks reviewed earlier.

Another task on which alcoholics show consistent impairment is the Wisconsin Card Sorting Test (Heilbrun, Tarbox, & Madison, 1979; Jenkins & Parsons, 1979b; Klisz & Parsons, 1979; McLaughlin et al., 1979; Tarter, 1973; Tarter & Parsons, 1971). In one negative report, Silberstein and Parsons (1979) found that women alcoholics performed as well as controls on the Wisconsin Card Sorting Task in spite of the fact that their performance was significantly poorer on a range of other measures from the WAIS and the Halstead–Reitan Battery. Tarter (1973) found that short-term alcoholics (less than 10 years) did not differ from controls in card-sorting performance, but that long-term alcoholics (more than 10 years) scored significantly more poorly than did either of the other two groups. Interestingly, the characteristic errors made by alcoholics included perseveration—not abandoning a prior problem-solving strategy—and failure to retain a cognitive set, commiting errors after making correct responses. These are similar to the kinds of errors made by alcoholics in responding to the Halstead Category Test (cf. Smith et al., 1973).

Visuospatial Performance Tasks

The poor performance of alcoholics on the WAIS Digit—Symbol and Block Design subtests points to possible deficits in visuospatial abilities. An acute dose of alcohol is known to impair visuospatial discrimination (Linnoila, Erwin, Cleveland, Logue, & Gentry, 1978) and visual search in nonalcoholic subjects (Chandler & Parsons, 1977). Bertera and Parsons (1978) found visual search in alcoholics to be slower than normal, particularly in the left visual field, but only when shapes as opposed to verbal stimuli were used. This provides an interesting convergence with the reported disproportionate impairment of visual search in the left visual field in nonalcoholics receiving alcohol doses (Chandler & Parsons, 1977). Here, as on other tasks, it appears that the effects of acute intoxication may recapitulate the progressive impact of chronic alcohol abuse.

Impaired performance of alcoholics is seen on other visuospatial tasks as well. Several investigators have found alcoholic deficits on the Benton Visual Retention Test, a design memory task (Berglund & Sonesson, 1976; Brewer, 1976; Brewer & Perett, 1971; Claeson & Carlsson, 1970; Guthrie, 1980; Page & Linden, 1974), although Hoy (1973) found alcoholics to be less impaired than a comparison group of psychiatric patients on this task.

Similarly, alcoholics are rather consistently found to be impaired on the Ravens Progressive Matrices, a nonverbal visuospatial task often used to assess nonverbal intelligence and abstraction abilities (Hatcher et al., 1977; Jones, 1971; Jones & Parsons, 1972; Jones et al., 1980; Page & Schaub, 1977), although again, not all studies find impairment relative to controls (Bauer & Johnson, 1957). Jones (1971) found that long-term alcoholics (mean of 15 years) were significantly impaired on the Raven's Matrices relative to short-term alcoholics (mean of 3 years) and controls, with no difference in performance between the latter two groups. Once again, the impairment in chronic alcoholics appears to be mirrored in the performance decrements accompanying acute intoxication. Interestingly, however, Williams, Goldman, and Williams (1978) reported that subjects who knew they had received alcohol showed less impairment on the Raven's Matrices and on other measures than did subjects given alcohol without their knowledge. They further found that the degree of this compensatory ability was related to the amount of experience that their subjects had had with alcohol.

Not all measures requiring visuospatial abilities are found to be impaired in alcoholics. On two very commonly used screening devices, the Graham—Kendal Memory for Designs Test and the Bender—Gestalt, alcoholics generally show relatively normal performance (Berglund & Sonesson, 1976; Donovan et al., 1976; Hirschenfang, Silber, & Benton, 1967; May, Urquhart, & Watts, 1970; Riege et al., 1976; Silber, Hirschenfang, & Benton, 1968), with the usual exceptions (Bean & Karazievich, 1975; Fine, and Steer, 1979; Silberstein & Parsons, 1979). The preponderance of evidence, however, supports a visuospatial deficit in alcoholics (Jones & Parsons, 1972). It appears, then, that the Bender—Gestalt and the Graham—Kendall are not sensitive measures of the particular deficits manifested in alcoholics and therefore do not represent promising screening devices for this population.

Field Dependence

Field dependence is a perceptual/personality dimension, derived in part from gestalt psychology, representing the extent to which an individual's perception of figure is dependent upon the surrounding context or ground. Field-dependent people are those who have difficulty in separating figure from ground; they cannot see the trees for the forest. The two most commonly used indices of field dependence are variations on the Rod and Frame Test (RFT) and on the Embedded Figures Test (EFT).

On the RFT the subject is asked to adjust a rod to the true vertical position while ignoring a tilted frame within which the rod is encased. Field-dependent subjects are those who tilt the rod away from vertical in the direction of the frame. Alcoholics consistently score as field dependent on this task (Bergman & Agren, 1974; Goldstein, 1976; Goldstein & Chotlos, 1965; Goldstein & Shelly, 1971; Karp & Knostadt, 1965). Performance on the RFT is found with equal consistency to be unrelated to the degree of impairment on a wide range of measures of general intellectual and neuropsychological functioning (Bergman & Agren, 1974; Donovan et al., 1976; Goldstein & Chotlos, 1965; Goldstein & Shelly, 1971; Pisani, Jacobsdon, & Berenbaum, 1973).

The EFT, on the other hand, has been found to be significantly correlated with the severity of impairment on a variety of neuropsychological measures (Donovan et al., 1976; Goldstein, 1976; O'Leary et al., 1977). This task differs from the RFT, requiring the subject to find figures hidden within a larger geometric matrix. Alcoholics are generally (Goldstein, 1976), although not always (Jones & Parsons, 1972), found to score as more field dependent than controls on the EFT. The fact that EFT performance appears to determine the degree of cognitive dysfunction in alcoholics may make it a relatively simple screening device (Donovan et al., 1976).

Although field dependence has usually been interpreted as a personality variable, various researchers have suggested that the field-dependent status of alcoholics is more likely the result of alcohol-related organicity than of any pre-existing personality organization (Bailey, Hustmeyer, & Kristofferson, 1961; Goldstein & Chotlos, 1965). This view is supported both by the relationship between the EFT and measures of cognitive impairment and by the fact that the degree of field dependence has been found to decrease following detoxification (Goldstein, 1976; Smith et al., 1971). Likewise, Bergman and Agren (1974) found the degree of field dependence to be greater in patients who had experienced delirium tremens than in earlier-stage problem drinkers.

Finally, it should be noted that field dependence appears to be less than a unitary concept. Patterns of dependence and of impairment vary depending upon which measure is chosen. The EFT appears to differentiate impaired from nonimpaired alcoholics more successfully than does the RFT (e.g., Goldstein, Neuringer, & Klappersack, 1970). The RFT may show greater change over the course of detoxification than does the EFT, perhaps because RFT performance may be influenced by the impairment of balance common among alcoholics (Goldstein, 1976; Goldstein et al., 1970). Further, both the RFT and the EFT appear to be unrelated to other presumed measures of field dependence such as the Stroop Test and delayed auditory feedback tasks (Goldstein, 1976; Goldstein et al., 1970).

Luria–Nebraska Neuropsychological Battery

A relatively recent addition to the armamentarium of the neuropsychologist is the standardized Luria–Nebraska Battery pioneered by Golden and his colleagues (Golden, Hammeke & Purish, 1978, Golden, Purish & Hammeke, 1979). The first controlled investigation of the performance of alcoholics on the Luria–Nebraska Battery has been reported by Chmielewski and Golden (1980). Their findings provide an encouraging amount of convergence with previous research. Alcoholics showed significant impairment (relative to controls) on 6 of 14 scales. The impaired scales included Visual (converging with findings of visuospatial impairment on other measures), Receptive Language (consistent with impairment on the Speech Sounds Perception Test and on the Porch Index), Arithmetic (also the most severely impaired of the verbal WAIS measures; cf. numerical impairment on the General Aptitude Test Battery reported by Kish and Cheney, 1969), Memory (summarizing a range of memory tasks), Intellectual (consistent with abstraction and concept formation deficits found on other tests), and the summary Pathognomonic scale (similar to Reitan's Impairment Index). The authors interpret these findings to reflect a general deficit in complex analysis and integration of information, suggesting that the "associative areas" within Luria's conceptual model of the brain are most strongly affected. As in prior research, verbal abilities other than Receptive Speech (Expressive, Reading, Writing) were found to be unimpaired. Further, alcoholics were found to be unimpaired on Motor and Tactile functions, a series of tests similar to the basic sensory-perceptual and aphasia screening tasks of the Halstead–Reitan Battery. Finally, no impairment was found on the Rhythm scale, a set of tasks somewhat more comprehensive than the Seashore Rhythm Test, requiring perceptual judgments of both rhythm and pitch.

PHYSIOLOGIC DATA

A large body of physiologic evidence has now accumulated to document further the untoward effects of chronic alcohol abuse on the CNS. We now turn our attention to a review of this literature.

Neuronal Level

The effects of ethanol on the nervous system are clear even at the neuronal level. Alcohol has been shown to slow conduction along both sensory and motor pathways (e.g., D'Amour, Shahani, Young, & Bird, 1979; Silber et al., 1968). At least two mechanisms for this inhibition of conduction have been identified. The first is the demyelinating effect of alcohol. Demyelination of nerve fibers has been observed in the peripheral nervous system (with overt symptoms manifested as peripheral neuropathy), in the pyramidal cells of the motor cortex, in the Purkinje cells of the cerebellum, in the corpus callosum, and in the pons (D'Amour et al., 1979; Lynch, 1960; Neuburger, 1957; Poser, 1973). A second mechanism whereby neural transmission may be impaired is by direct action of alcohol upon the neural membrane, a phenomenon documented in acute intoxication (e.g., Holman, 1977). Degeneration of neural pathways may account for some of the common symptoms observed in alcoholics (e.g., peripheral neuropathy, tremor), as well as for certain well-documented sequelae of long-term excessive drinking such as Marchiafava–Bignami disease, attributed to deterioration of the corpus callosum (Neuburger, 1957). This may also be the cause of observed deficits in processing of sensory information (Goldman, Whitman, Rosenbaum, & Vande Vusse, 1978; Goldstone et al., 1977) and in cortical evoked potentials.

Electroencephalography

Alcohol in both acute and chronic doses appears to have a marked and consistent effect on cortical evoked potentials following various kinds of sensory stimulation. Lewis, Dustman, and Beck (1969) observed that an acute dose of alcohol significantly reduced the amplitude of visual evoked responses (VER) in the right but not in the left hemisphere (consistent with Bertera and Parsons' [1978] finding of selective impairment in the left visual field), whereas the amplitude of somatosensory evoked responses (SER) was reduced in both hemispheres. In a subsequent study, these investigators found that the inhibition of visual evoked responses (VER) and SER is restricted to potentials recorded from central areas, and consists primarily of a reduction in later components of the evoked response, a pattern similar to that produced by anesthetics and other CNS depressants (Lewis, Dustman, & Beck, 1970). Schenkenberg, Dustman, and Beck (1972) found no difference between alcoholics and two control groups on visual or auditory evoked potentials, but the SER (evoked by an electric pulse to the right index finger) was found to be highly abnormal in alcoholics. This same research group later reported amplitude and latency abnormalities in alcoholics' VER and SER patterns (Cannon, Dustman, Beck, & Schenkenberg, 1975). The primary locus of amplitude changes was found to be in the late wave components of the evoked potentials, a pattern resembling that of elderly normal subjects.

The implications of this late wave amplitude decrease are not yet fully understood. Such abnormalities of evoked responses are consistent with deficits of information processing and associational functions (Cannon et al., 1975). Lewis et al. (1969, 1970) have speculated that a reduction in later components of the evoked response may point to disruption of the ascending reticular activating system, and that observed patterns of cortical disruption may be attributable to the absence of organized electrical impulses ascending from the brain stem.

More general abnormalities of the electroencephalogram (EEG) are commonly observed in alcoholics. Among the anomalies reported are fast activity in the frontal and parietal regions (Bennett, Doi, & Mowrery, 1956; Bennett, Mowrey, & Fort, 1960; Tumarkin, Wilson, & Snyder, 1955), paroxysmal changes (Fleming & Guthrie, 1980), and abnormally low voltage levels for alpha in particular and for EEG in general (Hudolin & Gubarev, 1967). EEG abnormalities have been reported in a high percentage of alcoholics examined (Bennett et al., 1956; Tumarkin et al., 1955), but the diagnostic value of such findings is questionable. Although the types of EEG abnormalities reported in alcoholics are consistent with cerebral atrophy, the EEG can appear quite normal even in the presence of significant atrophy (Newman, 1978). Dymond, Coger, and Serafetinides (1980) reported no differences in EEG bending between alcoholics and normals, although both groups differed significantly from schizophrenics. Brewer has found EEG records to be unhelpful in evaluating the presence and extent of organic brain syndromes in alcoholics (Brewer 1976, Brewer & Perett, 1971). On the other hand, the improvement in the EEG during the early weeks of treatment may reflect the extent of improvement in cognitive functioning in general. Carlen, Wilkinson, Singh, Rankin, and Whiteside (1977) found that increases in alpha wave patterns predicted overall reversibility of cognitive impairment.

Finally, EEG abnormalities have obvious implications for the sleep disturbances that are so common among alcoholics. Benson, Cohen, and Zarcone (1978) observed persistent deficits in low-wave and rapid eye movement (REM) sleep even after months of abstinence. They found that the persistence of abnormalities in REM sleep was related to poor performance on the Digit Span test, particularly the inability to recite digits backward. This supports the finding of Carlen et al. (1977) that reversal of EEG abnormalities is related to the degree of overall cognitive deficits.

Cerebral Blood Flow

Recent technology permits the measurement of patterns of blood flow within the cerebrum. Berglund and Sonesson (1976) reported overall decreased cerebral blood flow among alcoholics, with particular reductions in the anterior-temporal region. Similar findings have been reported by Heiss, Kufferle, and Demel (1974). Berglund and Ingvar (1976) found reduced blood flow to the anterior temporal and frontal-basal areas in older alcoholics (over age 45). By contrast, younger alcoholics showed reduction in blood flow within the parietal lobes.

Cerebral Atrophy

Data from a variety of sources converge to support the presence of cerebral atrophy in an alarmingly high percentage of alcoholics. In a study employing air encephalography, Haug (1968) found significant enlargement of the ventricles, particularly the third ventricle, in 44 of 60 alcoholics versus 3 of 25 controls. Ventricular enlargement has been verified by other investigators using this same technique (Brewer & Perett, 1971; Horvath, 1975; Tumarkin et al., 1955). Brewer and Perett (1971) reported frontal atrophy to be most common (28 of 30 alcoholics), followed by parietal atrophy (21 of 30). By contrast, Tumarkin et al. (1955), studying a group of young alcoholics, found parietal atrophy to be more common (6 of 7) than frontal atrophy. This is an interesting parallel to Berglund and Ingvar's (1976) finding of decreased cerebral blood flow to the parietal region in younger alcoholics.

Computed tomography (CT), a somewhat more sensitive and sophisticated procedure, has provided similar results. Significant cerebral atrophy has been found in approximately 60% of the alcoholics examined by numerous research teams (Cala, Jones, Mastaglia, & Wiley, 1978; Epstein, Pisani, & Pawcett, 1977; Fox, Ramsey, Huckman, & Proske, 1976; Götze et al., 1978; Lusins, Zimberg, Smokler, & Gurley, 1980; Newman, 1978; Von Gall, Becker, Lerch, & Nemeth, 1978; Wilkinson & Carlen, 1980). Ventricular enlargement is commonly reported in these studies (Fox, Ramsey, Huckman, & Proske, 1976; Newman, 1978; Wilkinson & Carlen, 1980). Cortical atrophy is even more common than ventricular enlargement, a fact which converges with other data to suggest that subcortical atrophy of significant proportions is associated with more advanced stages of alcoholism, whereas cortical atrophy occurs even at early stages (Cala et al., 1978; Newman, 1978). The largest degree of cortical atrophy has been reported to occur in the frontal lobes (Cala et al., 1978; Von Gall et al., 1978), with particular atrophy in the region of the cingulate gyrus (Cala et al., 1978). Temporal lobe atrophy has also been reported by Von Gall et al. (1978), who found evidence of such deterioration in 37 of 46 patients (versus 40 of 46 patients showing frontal lobe atrophy). Cerebellar atrophy has also been reported in 16 of 26 cases studied by Cala et al. (1978), confirming Horvath's (1975) report of cerebellar atrophy associated with alcoholic dementia.

In a novel approach to the use of CT data with alcoholics, Golden et al. (1980) used the density numbers rather than the traditional linear measurements of the CT scan output. Whereas normal subjects showed a slight density advantage for the left hemisphere, 11 chronic alcoholics showed the opposite pattern, producing a significant difference in left (but not right) hemispheric density between alcoholics and normals.

Autopsy data provide yet another type of information regarding cerebral changes in alcoholics. In the most comprehensive report of its kind, Courville (1955) reported pathology findings indicating frontal (especially dorsolateral) lobe atrophy and ventricular enlargement in chronic alcoholics. More recently, Kariks (1978) has reported disproportionate degeneration of the substantia nigra in all 40 alcoholics studied by autopsy. We will return to this finding in our subsequent discussion of dopamine.

It appears, then, that a majority of alcoholics may show significant cerebral atrophy. The rather high incidence estimate of 50−60% (cf. Parsons, 1977) suggests that brain atrophy is among the most common medical disorders resulting from alcohol abuse. Indeed, studies have consistently found substantial cortical atrophy in the absence of significant liver disease, one of the former hallmarks of alcoholic deterioration (Brewer & Perett, 1971; Cala et al., 1978; Carlen et al., 1978; Horvath, 1975). Consistent correlations have been found, however, between the amount of cerebral atrophy and the duration of alcoholism (Cala et al., 1978; Götze et al., 1978; Lusins et al., 1980). Cerebral atrophy has also been reported to be related to performance on 6 of the 14 subscales of the Luria−Nebraska Battery (Zelazowski, Golden, Graber, Moses, Stahl, Osmon & Pfefferbaum 1980), to performance on the Category Test (Matthews & Booker, 1972), and to scores on the Digit Symbol, Block Design, and Object Assembly subscales of the WAIS—three subscales that are rather consistently impaired in alcoholics (Cala et al., 1978). Haug (1968) found that in patients with a history of delirium tremens, only 1 of 22 had a normal pneumoencephalogram (as compared with 22 of 25 controls). It is likewise clear, however, that substantial neuropsychological impairment can occur without any evidence of cortical atrophy. Hill and Michael (1979) studied 15 young alcoholics and reported that whereas 12 showed clinical elevations on the Average Impairment Index of the Halstead−Reitan Battery, only one showed enlarged ventricles and none showed widening of the cortical sulci, a phenomenon observed in later stages of alcoholic deterioration (Horvath, 1975; Wilkinson & Carlen, 1980). It appears, then, that the incidence of cerebral atrophy among alcoholics may underestimate the percentage actually suffering significant neuropsychological impairment.

Finally, it is noteworthy that cerebral atrophy is also a characteristic of children with fetal alcohol syndrome, a continuum of birth defects occurring in children of alcoholic mothers who drank during gestation (Abel, 1980;

Streissguth, Landesman-Dwyer, Martin, & Smith, 1980). Low brain weight has also been demonstrated in neonate rats exposed to alcohol (Diaz & Samson, 1980). The mechanisms by which alcohol brings about low brain weight in neonates and cerebral atrophy in adults may be quite different, but the deleterious effects of prolonged exposure of the brain to ethanol are quite plain.

Dopaminergic Pathways

Some recent findings point to the possible importance of dopaminergic pathways in understanding the impact of alcohol upon cognitive functions. Kariks (1978) reported disproportionate degeneration in alcoholics of the substantia nigra, a primary area of origin for dopamine pathways. Further work by Kariks (1980) has suggested that damage to the substantia nigra is more prevalent in persons who have indulged in increased alcohol consumption up to the time of their death. Hunt, Majchrowicz, Dalton, Swartzwelder, and Wixon (1979) found that a low dose of ethanol produced an increase in striatal dopamine release, whereas higher doses suppressed release of dopamine in the stratum. Black, Hoffman, and Tabakoff (1980) demonstrated a persistent suppression of dopamine and sensitivity to dopamine antagonists following chronic alcohol ingestion. Alcohol ingestion has also been demonstrated to be related to levels of other neurotransmitters, including serotinin.

There are several ways in which these influences upon neurotransmitters in general and on dopamine in particular may be related to the symptoms of alcoholism. The first of these is related to recent research linking the substantia nigra and the dopaminergic pathways to both normal and premature aging. Dopamine levels have been found to be suppressed in elderly normal subjects, particularly in the caudate nucleus and the putamen (Carlsson & Winblad, 1976). Marshall and Berrios (1979) recently reported that doses of either apomorphine (a dopamine agonist) or L-dopa (levodopa) reversed impairment of swimming ability in aged rats. This is of interest because of the widespread description of alcoholics as prematurely aged (see the discussion in the section below). That dopamine depletion can also affect higher associative functions has been demonstrated by Brozoski, Brown, Rosvold, and Goldman (1979), who applied a catecholaminergic toxin to the dorsolateral surface of the frontal cortex of rhesus monkeys, an area hypothesized by Luria (1966, 1973) to be involved in memory and attentional processes and in spatial abilities. A profound local depletion of dopamine followed, accompanied by a very marked impairment of performance on a spatial delayed alternation problem that had been previously learned. This deficit was found to be reversible with administration of L-dopa or, to a lesser extent, with apomorphine. The parallel with alcoholic deficits in spatial abilities is interesting in light of the impact of ethanol on dopaminergic pathways.

Second, some of the symptoms of alcoholic withdrawal and alcoholic deterioration resemble parkinsonism, the cardinal syndrome associated with degeneration of the substantia nigra. The most obvious of these symptoms is tremor, but there are other interesting parallels. Parsons et al. (1972), for example, have reported a deficit in inhibitory control of movement not attributable to the tremor and muscle weakness also common among alcoholics. A deficit in motor inhibition is seen in the parkinsonian symptom of obstinate progression, a type of motoric perseveration.

Third, changes in neurotransmitters may be at least partially responsible for the affective disorders that are now frequently diagnosed in relation to alcoholism (Weissman & Myers, 1980). The biphasic effect of ethanol on striatal dopamine (Hunt et al., 1979) provides a striking parallel to the biphasic changes in mood generated by increasing blood alcohol levels (Allman, Taylor, & Nathan, 1972; McNamee, Mello, & Mendelson, 1968; Mendelson, LaDow, & Solomon, 1964; Steffen, Nathan & Taylor, 1974; Tamerin & Mendelson, 1969).

Finally, dopamine pathways may be involved in the etiology of alcoholism. Aldehyde dehydrogenase, an enzyme required in the metabolism of acetaldehyde (the first metabolite of alcohol) is likewise used in the metabolism of dopamine. The metabolism of alcohol apparently takes precedence, however, so that in the presence of alcohol abnormal metabolites of dopamine may be produced. One of these metabolites in turn, may interact with other dopamine molecules to produce a new compound: tetrahydropapaveroline (THP). This molecule resembles morphine and, when injected into the brain of rats, elicits differential preferences for alcohol consumption (Myers & Melchior, 1977). This biochemical pathway for addiction remains highly speculative, but it is one more phenomenon pointing to the dopaminergic pathways as critical keys to understanding the effects of alcohol on the brain.

PREDICTORS OF IMPAIRMENT

Several drinking history variables have been studied as predictors of impairment in alcoholics. These are of importance both in predicting the probability of impairment in specific cases and populations and in evaluating the extent of the potential causal relationship between drinking variables and cognitive impairment.

An obvious and easily obtained predictor is the number of years that an individual has been drinking (usually measured from the time of the first drink or from the onset of regular drinking). The length of drinking is reportedly related to the degree of cerebral atrophy (Cala et al., 1978) and to the degree of impairment on the Category Test (Jones & Parsons, 1971, 1972) and tapping speed (Long & McLachlan, 1974). Other studies have found no significant relationship between years of drinking and impairment on the

Shipley—Hartford Test (Jones, 1971; Tarter & Jones, 1971) or on vocabulary learning (Sharp, Rosenbaum, Goldman, & Whitman, 1977). Discrepancies among studies may be attributable to the different measures used; it is likely that some measures are related to drinking history and others are not. Another problem, however, is the confounding of years of drinking with age (e.g., Jones & Jones, 1980; Parker & Noble, 1980). The age of alcoholic subjects has been found to be related to cerebral atrophy (Cala et al., 1978) and to impairment on a variety of measures, including the Halstead—Reitan and WAIS subscales (Bertera & Parsons, 1978; Goldman, Williams, Dickey, & Weintraub, 1980, Jones & Parsons, 1971, 1972; Parker & Noble, 1980), although again, some investigators have found age to be unrelated to impairment in alcoholics (Draper et al., 1978; Kish & Cheney, 1969; Løberg, 1980). Age may also function as a moderator variable, creating more complex relationships. Parker and Noble (1980) found a higher correlation between alcohol consumption variables and impairment on the Wisconsin Card-Sorting Test among older than among younger subjects. Eckardt, Ryback, and Pautler (1980) studied the relative amounts of variance in impairment accounted for by individual predictors. Whereas age of the subject accounted for approximately 20% of variance in impairment, drinking history variables accounted for 70%. This is consistent with the contention of other investigators that the organicity observed in alcoholics is not attributable to normal aging (Miller & Orr, 1980; Williams, Ray, & Overall, 1973).

If age or years of drinking predict small amounts of variance, perhaps length of alcoholism or of heavy drinking would be a still better predictor. Indeed, duration of alcoholism has been found to be related to impairment on physiologic (Götze et al., 1978; Haug, 1968; Lusins et al., 1980) as well as neuropsychological measures (Bolter & Hannon, 1980b; Guthrie & Elliott, 1980; Jones, 1971; Løberg, 1980; McLaughlan et al., 1979; Miller & Orr, 1980; Tarter & Jones, 1971). Jones (1971; Tarter & Jones, 1971) has found cognitive impairment to be related to duration of alcoholism but not to duration of drinking. Several studies have reported that individuals with less than 10 years of alcoholism do not differ significantly from normal controls, whereas alcoholics of more than 10 years' duration show significantly greater impairment than either normal controls or short-duration alcoholics. On the other hand, a large number of studies have failed to find the duration of alcoholism to be predictive of either physiologic (Wilkinson & Carlen, 1980) or neuropsychological impairment (Bergman & Agren, 1974; Guthrie, 1980; Hatcher et al., 1977; Jones et al., 1980, Klisz & Parsons, 1977, 1979; Page & Linden, 1974; Tarter & Jones, 1971). Discrepancies here may again be due to differences in the cognitive measures employed, although positive and negative studies have somtimes used the same variables. Another more likely reason for variation in the findings is the manner in which duration of alcoholism is defined. If years of heavy drinking is the criterion, how is *heavy* defined and how is its onset determined in retrospect? If occurrence of the first alcohol-related problem is the criterion, whose definition of *problem* is to be used? Even pharmacologic addiction represents a continuum of symptoms, so that the onset of "dependence" is not a simple matter. These criterion differences, combined with variations in the tone and carefulness of interview procedures, can produce substantial variance in "length of alcoholism."

"Duration of alcoholism" may simply be an inefficient way of measuring two other dimensions: alcohol consumption and severity of symptoms of alcoholism. To what extent are these related to impairment? With regard to the symptoms of alcoholism, findings have been consistent and somewhat surprising. The presence or number of classic symptoms of alcoholism (e.g., delirium tremens, blackout, withdrawal tremor or seizure) has been found to be unrelated to the extent of cerebral atrophy (Lusins et al., 1980), EEG abnormality (Fleming & Guthrie, 1980), or neuropsychological impairment (Eckardt, Parker, Noble, Feldman, & Gottschalk, 1978; Eckardt et al., 1980; Guthrie, 1980; Jones, 1971; Rada et al., 1977). Berglund and Leijonquist (1978) reported an inverse relationship between cognitive impairment and periods of mental disorder. A significant exception to this trend may be liver disease, which would logically increase the impact of alcohol upon the brain because of slowed metabolism and failure to filter toxins. Smith and Smith (1977) reported that alcoholics with cirrhosis showed significantly greater deficits on the WAIS. On the other hand, psychometric impairment (Guthrie, 1980), and EEG anomlies (Fleming & Guthrie, 1980) have been found to be unrelated to liver function tests but significantly related to an index of malnutrition.

Alcohol consumption variables again present a mixed picture. Some investigators have attempted to determine lifetime alcohol consumption—the total volume of alcohol that a person has consumed during his or her entire life. Cutting (1978a) and Eckardt et al. (1978) have reported relationships between impairment and lifetime consumption, but others have found no such relationship (Parker & Noble, 1977; Parker, Birnbaum, Boyd, & Noble, 1980; Wilkinson & Carlen, 1980). Periodic drinkers have been found to be less impaired on the Trail-Making Test (Sanchez-Craig, 1979) and to show less cerebral atrophy relative to steady drinkers (Haug, 1968). Simple comparisons of periodic versus steady drinkers fail, however, to control for the total amount of alcohol consumed (e.g., periodic drinkers may drink less than steady drinkers in a given year). Eckardt et al. (1978, 1980) have employed more careful definitions of drinking history variables with quite fruitful results, finding that (1) alcohol consumption variables can account for 70% of the variance in cognitive impairment of alcoholics; (2) about half of this variance is attributable to chronic drinking patterns and the other half to recent drinking; (3) some cognitive measures (e.g., Tactual Performance memory) are primarily related to chronic consumption variables, whereas others (e.g.,

Object Assembly, Seashore Rhythm Test) are more strongly determined by recent consumption; and (4) amount of alcohol consumed per drinking occasion is a better predictor of impairment than is the frequency of drinking occasions (cf. Parker et al., 1980). It seems likely that future researchers will need to employ such careful and specific definitions of drinking variables in order to discover the ways in which alcohol consumption influences cognitive abilities.

REVERSIBILITY OF DEFICITS

A significant and controversial issue in the current literature is the reversibility of the now well-documented cognitive deficits observed in alcoholics. To what extent are these deficits reversed over time with or without treatment?

Recovery of function has been reported in alcoholics over the initial weeks and months of treatment, with significant improvement reported on the Category Test and Tactual Performance Test (Long & McLachlan, 1974; Prigitano, 1980), Bender–Gestalt (Farmer, 1973), Shipley–Hartford (Ornstein, 1977; Smith & Layden, 1972), tapping speed (Long & McLachlan, 1974), language functions (Ellenberg, Rosenbaum, Goldman, & Whitman, 1980; Rada et al., 1977), reaction time, color vision, and hand steadiness (Smith & Layden, 1972), vocabulary learning (Sharp et al., 1977), and verbal memory (Goldman & Rosenbaum, 1977; Guthrie, 1980; Weingartner et al., 1971). Likewise, improvement has been observed on physiologic measures including the EEG (Bennett et al., 1960; Fleming & Guthrie, 1980) and cerebral atrophy as measured by CT scans (Carlen et al., 1978).

Improvement, however, is almost always judged against the patients' performance level at admission or shortly thereafter. Early performance levels may have been particularly poor if the patient was tested during the detoxification process. Practice effects must also be considered because some of the measures employed are not intended for repeated testing within brief time intervals. With designs that have controlled for practice effects it has been found that some of the "reversal of deficits" shown by alcoholics is due to simple practice effects on the tests (e.g., Eckardt et al., 1979). Clarke and Haughton (1975) found that alcoholics did "improve" over time on a variety of performance measures, but that controls showed similar improvement and that alcoholics continued to perform more poorly than controls (in spite of "improvement") at follow-up. This is consistent with the most frequently reported finding in the literature: that alcoholic populations typically show some improvement over the course of weeks or months of treatment and follow-up, but that performance does not return to normal limits and significant differences remain between alcoholics and controls (Boeke, 1970; Carlsson et al., 1973; Clarke & Haughton, 1975; Eckardt et al., 1979; Jenkins &

Parsons, 1979b; Jonsson, Cronholm, Izikowitz, Gordon, Rosen, 1962; O'Leary et al., 1977; Page & Linden, 1974; Page & Schaub, 1977; Smith et al., 1971).

General statements that alcoholic deficits do, do not, or partially recover are overgeneralizations, however (Goldman, in press). The truth appears to be that some measures can recover almost completely in some individuals. Variables that must be considered include (1) which measures, (2) what kinds of alcoholics, and (3) over how long a period of recovery time. Certain measures appear to be relatively resistant to recovery (or to return to normal levels), although they may show some improvement over initial levels. These include the Trail-Making Test (Long & McLachlan, 1974; O'Leary et al., 1977b; Sanchez-Craig, 1979), certain memory measures (Ryan, Brandt, Bayog, & Butters, 1980), and Digit-Symbol (Jonsson et al., 1962; Page & Linden, 1974). Other measures, including the Category, Tactual Performance, and Finger Oscillation Tests, have been found to recover to within normal limits at 12-month follow-up (Long & McLachlan, 1974). The timing of pre- and postmeasures is also critical. Some measures show improvement over the first 2 or 3 weeks of sobriety but little change thereafter (Page & Linden, 1974; Page & Schaub, 1977). Other measures may require a longer period of time to show recovery (Carlen et al., 1976; Fleming & Guthrie, 1980; Guthrie, 1980; Tomsovic, 1968).

Individual difference variables also play a role in predicting recovery of functions. Younger and less severe alcoholics have been found to show greater reversal of cognitive deficits than do their older and more symptomatic counterparts (Bennett, 1960, 1967; Ellenberg et al., 1980; Fehrenbach, 1980; Goldman, in press; Goldman et al., 1980; Tarter & Jones, 1971). Prigitano (1977, 1980) has reported that patients taking disulfiram may show selective failure to improve on certain measures relative to patients not taking the medication. This provides a noteworthy convergence with recent findings of disulfiram's ability to interfere with biochemical and neurophysiologic functions (Burnett & Reading, 1970; Kwentus & Major, 1979; Van Thiel, Gavaler, Paul & Smith, 1979. Bennett (1960, 1967) has suggested that the initial occurrence of blackouts precedes irreversible brain damage by 1−2 years, although objective data to support this contention are lacking at present. Treatment outcome has also been found to be related to the degree of reversal in cognitive deficits, such that individuals who abstain or reduce their drinking show greater improvement than do those who continue to drink heavily (Guthrie, 1980; Guthrie & Elliott, 1980; Hester, Smith, & Jackson, 1980; McLachlan & Levenson, 1974). The direction of causality in this latter relationship is unclear, however, because as we shall see shortly, those individuals with less initial cognitive impairment (or perhaps those with less permanent, more reversible impairment) are more likely to sustain successful drinking outcomes.

INTEGRATIVE HYPOTHESES

Various hypotheses have been proposed to account for the pattern of deficits and anomalies reviewed above. We will consider five hypotheses that have been commonly discussed in the literature: (1) premature aging, (2) global impairment, (3) right hemisphere deficit, (4) frontal lobe deficit, and (5) etiologic deficit. We will also present evidence for three additional formulations that have emerged from recent findings but that have not been previously elaborated as ways of integrating alcoholics' cognitive deficits: (6) left hemisphere deficit, (7) hierarchical impairment, and (8) subcortical deficit. It should be mentioned that none of these hypotheses accounts for all of the data at present, and that these alternative formulations are not mutually exclusive.

Premature Aging

Courville (1955) first observed that the cerebral deterioration of alcoholics resembles that of the normal elderly brain. This premature aging hypothesis—that the type of damage inflicted on the brain by alcohol is essentially that of accelerated senescence—has come to be one of the most common integrative statements regarding the cognitive dysfunctions of alcoholics. Indeed, the patterns of deficits displayed by normal elderly subjects (Reed & Reitan, 1962, 1963a,b) bear a rather striking resemblance to the "selective" deficits of alcoholics (Blusewicz, 1975; Blusewicz et al., 1977; Fitzhugh et al., 1965; Kleinknecht & Goldstein, 1972; Korboot, Naylor, & Soares, 1977; Miller & Orr, 1980; Williams et al., 1973). Smith et al. (1971) reported that the sleep paterns of alcoholics resemble those of elderly individuals. Reed and Reitan (1963a) found that the deficits typical of older subjects were primarily in adaptive abilities rather than in tasks dependent on prior experience and long-term memory. The four most discriminating subscales of the Halstead—Reitan Battery and the WAIS were found to be the Category Test, Tactual Performance Test (TPT), location score, TPT total time, and Object Assembly, all of which are also typically found to be impaired in alcoholics. On the other hand, normal elderly subjects failed to show deficits on several measures commonly impaired in alcoholics (e.g., tapping speed, Speech Sounds Perception, Seashore Rhythm Test, Arithmetic) and were relatively deficient on other measures not usually impaired in alcoholics (e.g., Tactual Performance memory score, Picture Completion). Thus, the patterns of deficits shown by elderly and alcoholic subjects are not identical. Nevertheless, the resemblance is of interest, particularly in light of evidence reviewed earlier that alcoholics may show selective deterioration in the substantia nigra and depressed activity in dopaminergic pathways.

Global Impairment

Closely related to the premature aging hypothesis is the global impairment view—that prolonged exposure to alcohol induces uniform impairment of cognitive functions. At its simplest level, this hypothesis is clearly incorrect. The preceding review has documented the presence of deficits in some areas of cognitive functioning and the relative absence of impairment in others. Other reviewers have discounted the global impairment hypothesis on this basis (Bolter & Hannon, 1980a; Tarter, 1975a). No drug or brain insult produces consistent deficits in all cognitive functions, however (Fisher, 1958; Geschwind, 1978), and one could question whether alcoholic impairment resembles the pattern of deficits generated by the most diffuse of organic brain syndromes. In this regard, the premature aging hypothesis is relevant, and as we have seen, there is a strong though less than identical resemblance between alcoholic and senescent processes. Likewise, attempts to discriminate alcoholics from brain-damaged samples via discriminant function analyses have been less than successful, although both groups are easily discriminated from normal or psychiatric controls (Holland & Watson, 1980; Miller & Orr, 1980; O'Leary et al., 1979b). This suggests a similarity between the effects of alcohol and those of other kinds of generalized brain damage, and questions whether alcohol does indeed produce selective damage to a unique set of loci.

Right Hemisphere Deficit

Another commonly proposed integration of findings is that alcoholics show a selective impairment of right hemispheric functions and that alcohol somehow selectively damages the right more than the left cerebral hemisphere. The most commonly cited evidence in support of this hypothesis is the deficit of alcoholics on Performance subscales of the WAIS relative to their own Verbal subscale scores. Spatial orientation and analysis deficits have also been interpreted as pointing to a right hemisphere impairment.

Other more specific data do exist to support this viewpoint. Cutting (1978b) reported that the poor pattern recognition performance of alcoholics relative to intact verbal skills resembles the impairment of patients with right but not left temporal lobectomies. Goodglass and Peck (1971) found a selective left ear impairment in alcoholics on a dichotic listening task, and further observed that the imbalance was even more marked in Korsakoff syndrome patients. Jenkins and Parsons (1979a) found that alcoholics who used their right hand first showed poorer performance on the second (left hand) trial of the Tactual Performance Test relative to patients who started with their left hand. They interpreted this finding as supporting selective impairment of the right hemisphere (left hand). Further, this research group has reported poorer motor inhibition in the left hand (Parsons, Tarter, &

Edelberg, 1972) and a left ear disadvantage on dichotic listening (Chandler, Vega, & Parsons, 1973). As indicated earlier, alcoholics' tapping speed is more often found to be impaired in the left than in the right hand. Bertera and Parsons (1978) reported that alcoholics required more time and made more errors in the left visual field relative to controls, echoing the effect of acute doses of alcohol.

Not all evidence, however, supports this view (Bolter & Hannon, 1980a). Right hemisphere functions may simply be more sensitive to brain injury of any kind, as suggested by the similarity of alcoholic impairment configurations to those of elderly and general brain-damaged populations (Klisz, 1978). Asymmetries observed in alcoholics may not be unique to this population. Chandler et al. (1973), for example, found a right ear advantage on dichotic listening in all populations tested, not only in alcoholics. Chmielewski and Golden (1980) found no selective elevation of alcoholics on either the right of the left hemisphere lateralization scales of the Luria–Nebraska Battery, and Goldstein and Shelly (1982) failed to find support for a lateralization hypothesis using a multivariable strategy, particularly when sensorimotor variables were included. Finally, there is a body of literature, to be reviewed below, supporting selective damage to the left hemisphere in alcoholics. Thus, evidence does not consistently support lateralized damage to the right hemisphere as a function of excessive alcohol consumption.

Frontal Deficit

Another integrating hypothesis posits the primary locus of damage in alcoholics to be the frontal lobes, with impairment in other functional areas being attributable to insufficient or abnormal integration from the frontal cortex. Tarter, in his numerous reviews of this literature (1975a,b, 1976a,b), has proposed a primary deficit in a functional system involving frontal, limbic, and diencephalic units, with primary damage localized to the anterior basal region of the frontal cortex. Numerous investigators have found alcoholics to be impaired on tests of functions believed to be localized to the frontal lobes (Bolter & Hannon, 1980b; Chmielewski & Golden, 1980; Chelune & Parker, 1981; Cutting, 1978a; Hatcher et al., 1977). Differential atrophy of the frontal cortex has also been found in radiologic (Brewer & Perett, 1971) and pathology investigations (Courville, 1955), and Berglund and Ingvar (1976) found decreased blood flow in the frontal basal region in alcoholics. Various researchers have suggested that frontal lobe impairment may even account for the alcoholic syndrome itself: loss of volitional control over drinking behavior, poor problem-solving skills, failure to learn from experience (Brewer & Perett, 1971; Goldstein, 1976; Lemere, 1956; Ron, 1977).

This hypothesis is not without its problems, however. The detection of localized frontal lobe dysfunction is not an easy matter, and many of the indices impaired by frontal lobe damage are affected by insult to other brain areas as well (Bolter & Hannon, 1980a). Goldstein and Shelly (1982) found that the performance of alcoholics on diverse neuropsychological measures did not resemble that of patients with known brain damage localized to the cortex. Rather, alcoholic impairment most closely resembled that of patients with diffuse lesions. Nevertheless, Tarter's hypothesis remains viable in that it accounts for many of the current data, and there is no substantial body of research refuting this explanation. Further, there is at least preliminary support for the frontal lobe hypothesis from neuroanatomic and radiologic investigations.

Etiologic Deficit

Some investigators have suggested that a minimal brain damage syndrome may actually precede the development of alcoholism and may contribute to the etiology of this disorder (Tarter, 1976a). To the extent that frontal lobe dysfunction, as discussed above, may interfere with volitional control and problem-solving skills, a pre-existing impairment of frontal lobe functions might predispose an individual to alcohol abuse.

Several lines of research support this hypothesis. Retrospective studies have found that individuals who report having shown symptoms of hyperactivity (minimal brain dysfunction) as children are at higher risk of alcoholism in adulthood (Morrison, 1979). Tarter, McBride, Buonpane, and Schneider (1977) developed a 9-point scale of "primary alcoholism"—a severe pattern of alcohol abuse including early onset and pathologic drinking from the individual's first drink. In contrasting primary alcoholics to less severe drinkers, and to psychiatric and normal controls, these investigators found that the severe alcoholics reported having had substantially more symptoms of minimal brain dysfunction as children. Longitudinal studies following individuals from early childhood through adulthood have provided similar results. Both Jones (1968) and McCord (1972; McCord & McCord, 1962) found that children who would later become alcoholics had been rated as less controlled, and more aggressive and hyperactive, and showed higher rates of antisocial behavior in childhood.

Is there a more severe subtype of alcoholism characterized by childhood hyperacitivity and perhaps hereditary predisposition? Tarter et al. (1977) found that their primary alcoholics showed a higher family history of alcoholism than did the comparison groups, including less severe problem drinkers. Miller and Joyce (1979) found that problem drinkers with a family history of alcoholism were more likely to be successful as abstainers and less likely to be able to sustain moderate drinking, whereas those with a less prominent family history of alcoholism showed the opposite pattern. Possibly the minimal brain dysfunction of prealcoholic children may be a subclinical form of the fetal alcohol syndrome in cases in which the parents were heavy drinkers prenatally. Hyperactivity has been reported to be one of the symptoms of the fetal alcohol syndrome in developing children (Abel, 1980; Streissguth et al., 1980).

Another interesting etiologic hypothesis posits a deficit in sensitivity to internal cues as predisposing individuals to alcohol abuse. Heilbrun et al.

(1979) found an "internal scanning" factor to be associated with treatment outcome. Individuals scoring low on internal scanning—a factor including performance on the Wisconsin Card Sorting Test and the ability to discriminate the volume of beverage consumed—showed a poorer prognosis in treatment. These investigators postulate a general deficit in internal scanning and in behavior control as a potential precursor of chronic alcoholism. Converging data are provided by a fascinating series of studies conducted by Nathan (1980) and his colleagues demonstrating that alcoholics show selective inability to discriminate their own blood alcohol concentration from internal cues after biofeedback training, a skill that is readily learned by nonalcoholics. Further, these investigators found that this skill of internal cue discrimination is poorer in individuals with a family history of alcoholism and in those who show a higher tolerance for ethanol. To date, however, no longitudinal study has demonstrated the presence of differential cognitive impairment in children who will later become alcoholics.

Still another etiologic deficit hypothesis was first proposed by Petrie (1967). She described a continuum of perceptual responses to sensory stimuli, with the two extremes labeled *augmenters* and *reducers*. Augmenters are those whose nervous systems essentially augment or amplify sensory input so that it is perceived as being more intense (louder, larger, etc.) than it really is. Reducers, by contrast, dampen incoming sensory information. Petrie posited that augmenters would prefer sedating drugs, whereas reducers would choose drugs such as stimulants or hallucinogens that heighten sensory experience. Whereas Petrie's operational definitions of the augmentation−reduction dimension were based on psychophysical measures, Von Knorring (1976) used visual evoked response (VER) potentials to study this question. Subjects who showed decreased VER amplitude when stimulus intensity was increased were defined as reducers, whereas those with increased VER amplitude were called augmenters. Of 26 alcoholics studied, 22 (85%) were augmenters, as compared with 21 (53%) of 40 depressed patients and 13 (46%) of 28 normals. The percentages within the two control populations approximated 50%, which would be expected from a normally distributed individual difference variable. Alcoholics, by contrast, showed disproportionate augmentation. Is augmentation a neuroperceptual trait predisposing the individual to alcohol abuse, or does alcohol abuse change perceptual processes in the direction of augmentation? Again, prospective studies are lacking, but the question is an intriguing one.

Left Hemisphere Deficit

Although the most popular lateralization view regarding alcoholic brain damage has been the right hemisphere deficit hypothesis, a case can also be made for a lateralized left hemisphere deficit in alcoholics. Golden et al.

(1980) studied the density numbers of alcoholic and normal CT scans as an index of cell density within the cerebral hemispheres. Whereas controls showed a normal density advantage for the left hemisphere, alcoholics showed the opposite pattern, with a slightly lower density on the left side. This resulted in a lack of significant difference between alcoholics and controls in right hemisphere density but a significant difference in density on the left side.

Motor functions have shown a right hemisphere advantage in alcoholics in several studies. Tarter and Jones (1971b) found alcoholics to be impaired in tapping speed in the right but not in the left hand. Løberg (1980) found right hand performance of alcoholics to be poorer than that of the left hand on four of six tests, with significant differences on two of these measures: tapping speed and static steadiness. These differences remained after Løberg had corrected for normal differences due to lateral dominance.

Certain findings that have been interpreted as supporting right hemisphere lateralization could equally support a left hemispheric lateralization if given a different interpretation. Jenkins and Parsons (1979a), for example, compared alternative procedures for administering the Tactual Performance Test. They had normal and alcoholic subjects perform the task by starting with either the right or the left hand on the first trial. They found that on the second trial, subjects using their right hand (and therefore having begun with their left hand on the first trial) showed improvement in performance, whereas those using their left hand on the second trial did not. This finding was interpreted as supporting a right hemisphere deficit because of the poorer performance of the left hand. An alternative view, however, would be that subjects who used their right hand on the first trial learned significantly less than did those who used their left hand first. Therefore, left-hand-first subjects showed greater transfer of learning to the second trial. Further, it is noteworthy that although control subjects in this study showed a normal right hand advantage on the first trial, alcoholic subjects failed to do so. Equal performance times were observed in alcoholics regardless of which hand was used on the first trial. Viewed in this way, then, these data would support a left hemisphere deficit. Similarly, the fact that alcoholics are found to show a right ear advantage on certain auditory tasks, such as dichotic listening (Goodglass & Peck, 1971), has been interpreted as supporting a lateralized right hemisphere deficit. A right ear advantage is also characteristic of normal subjects, however, and the simple absence of a right ear advantage in alcoholics as observed in other studies (e.g., Chandler, Vega, & Parsons, 1973) could be interpreted as reflecting a left-hemisphere disadvantage. This underlines the importance of comparing the performance of alcoholics with normative data rather than simply contrasting right with left hemisphere performance within alcoholics alone.

The normal performance of alcoholics on verbal subscales of the WAIS might call into question the validity of a left hemisphere deficit hypothesis. More sensitive measures of receptive speech, however, do often reflect mild aphasic symptoms in alcoholics. As indicated earlier, deficits on the Speech Sounds Perception Test are not uncommon among alcoholics. Chmielewski and Golden (1980) found alcoholics to be impaired on the Receptive Speech subscale of the Luria—Nebraska Battery. Rada and his colleagues (1977) likewise found alcoholic deficits (relative to geriatric controls) on the Porch Index of Communicative Ability. Weingartner et al. (1976) have postulated that acute doses of alcohol affect the left hemisphere more markedly than the right. Alcohol disrupts semantic organization (Parker, Alkana, Birnbaum, & Noble, 1974; Rosen & Lee, 1976) and serial processing of information (Moskowitz & Murray, 1976), processes attributed to left hemispheric function (Kimura, 1967; Sperry, 1962, 1967).

Nevertheless, the case for left lateralization is less than complete. In spite of their finding of a receptive speech deficit, Chmielewski and Golden (1980) failed to find an elevation of alcoholics' on the Left Hemisphere lateralization scale of the Luria—Nebraska Battery. Other scales that are normally suppressed in lateralized left hemisphere disorders—including the verbal WAIS—do not show deficits in alcoholics. It is our opinion that although a case can be made for both right and left lateralization in alcoholics, the type of damage inflicted by chronic alcohol abuse is not adequately explained by a lateralization hypothesis. Rather, the impairment appears to affect a larger functional system involving both hemispheres. Tarter's frontal-limbic-diencephalic hypothesis represents a more comprehensive model of this kind. Another model with integrative potential involves *disconnection syndromes* (Geschwind, 1965). Alcohol may produce long-term impairment of interhemispheric connections at the corpus callosum and other commissures. In the advanced stages of Marchiafava-Bignami disease, there is a clear selective deterioration of the corpus callosum, producing symptoms of the disconnection syndrome. Callosal degeneration appears to be a continuum within alcoholics, however, ranging from mild (Neuburger, 1957) to colossal (Poser, 1973). Partial interference with interhemispheric communication could produce decrements in certain right hemisphere functions that are dependent upon left hemispheric language or sensory input (Geschwind, 1965). This may account in part for what appears to be an odd combination of frontal and postcentral deficits.

Subcortical Deficit

An alternative hypothesis may comprehensively account for the diffuse pattern of higher cortical deficits characteristic of alcoholics. This hypothesis posits the primary disruption of cerebral functioning to be at subcortical levels. The often observed enlargement of cerebral ventricles supports the presence of subcortical atrophy in alcoholics. The specific differential atrophy of the substantia nigra and the disruption of dopaminergic pathways in alcoholics have been previously discussed, along with data demonstrating that dopaminergic depletion can lead to disruption of higher cortical functions. Korsakoff's syndrome is known to involve damage to the mamillary bodies and to thalamic functions (Butters & Cermak, 1976; Victor et al., 1971). Short-term as well as chronic changes in subcortical structures and in pathways of neural transmission projecting to the cortex may account for some of the dysfunctions observed in higher associative and integrative processes.

Several lines of data, however, question the primacy of subcortical deficits in alcohol brain damage. Substantial degrees of subcortical dysfunction should be detectable in neurologic examinations. Yet it is not uncommon for alcoholics to be found normal when examined by a neurologist. Further, Wilkinson and Carlen (1980) examined alcoholics who had been found to be neurologically normal and detected significant neuropsychological impairment in 50% of this sample (using the Halstead—Reitan Battery). Neuroradiologic research has also reported ventricular enlargement to be a concomitant of more advanced alcoholism, following rather than preceding atrophy of the cortex. These data suggest that subcortical damage may not be a necessary prerequisite for the types of cognitive dysfunction observed in alcoholics. Again, it seems unlikely that alcoholic brain damage is attributable to specific loci, and that examination of functional systems within the brain may provide a more fruitful avenue to understanding the deficits suffered by alcoholics.

Hierarchical Impairment

If alcohol produces a progressive impairment of cognitive functions, it might be possible to identify a consistent sequence in which specific functions tend to be impaired. The functions most frequently found to be impaired, for example, might be those which are affected earliest (e.g., Trail-Making Test, Category Test, Block Design). Measures on which findings are more mixed might be those affected only after longer periods of alcoholism (e.g., speech functions). Clarke and Haughton (1975) sought such a hierarchy of impaired functions in their sample of Irish alcoholics but failed to find a consistent progression. Similarly, Miller and Orr (1980) employed a statistical modeling procedure to evaluate the extent to which alcoholic impairment on WAIS and Halstead—Reitan measures would simulate a Guttman Scale. They found no progression of impairment resembling a Guttman model. Further, they found that although alcoholics and brain-damaged patients could be readily discriminated from psychiatric controls, the former two groups could not be adequately differentiated from each other.

These findings suggest that cognitive deficits in alcoholics do not occur in any unique sequence. Whatever progression exists appears to be one of steadily increasing impairment across a broad range of measures. The pattern of deficits closely resembles that attributable to normal aging and to other kinds of diffuse brain dysfunction, and although there appear to be some differences it is difficult to differentiate alcoholics from brain damaged patients statistically. It is possible that the relatively new Luria—Nebraska Battery, still largely untested with alcoholics, may succeed where other batteries have failed in producing either a predictable progression of deficits or a reliable discriminant function to differentiate alcoholics from patients who have sustained other kinds of brain injury.

RESEARCH SUMMARY

The overwhelming weight of current research evidence points to a clear and rather diffuse pattern of cognitive deficits in alcoholics, with approximately 60% showing significant impairment on the average. Studies that have reached optimistic conclusions regarding the absence of significant brain damage in alcoholics have done so either by overgeneralizing from one or two tests—inadequate to sample a comprehensive range of adaptive abilities (e.g., Hoy, 1973; Templer, Ruff, & Simpson, 1975)—or by studying good prognosis populations (e.g., Dietvorst, Swenson, & Morse, 1978) or using exclusion criteria so extensive as to eliminate *a priori* any patients showing significant brain damage of any etiology (e.g., Grant, Adams, & Reed, 1979). A very extensive literature including controlled and longitudinal research designs now documents the presence of significant cognitive impairment and cerebral abnormalities in alcoholic populations drawn from a wide range of treatment settings and nations. To be sure, the specific etiology of these deficits has not been established, and some may be attributable to indirect consequences of alcohol abuse (e.g., head injuries, poor nutrition). Nevertheless the deleterious effects of alcohol alone upon the central and peripheral nervous systems are no longer open to reasonable doubt.

Memory functions are quite sensitive to alcohol in both acute and chronic doses. A continuum of impairment in short-term memory processes and in transfer from STM to LTM is apparent among alcoholics. These deficits appear to be largely reversible in alcoholics with shorter durations of alcohol abuse (under 10 years), with impairment abating within 2—3 weeks of abstinence. STM deficits may be less reversible in long-duration alcoholics and in those who have experienced frequent blackouts. Memory impairment appears to be greater with nonverbal (e.g., faces, patterns) than with verbal stimuli, and less with regard to retrieval of overlearned material previously stored in long-term memory.

A variety of other higher cognitive processes also show rather consistent impairment. These include spatial and visuoperceptual analysis, location learning, and problem solving abilities. Verbal abilities, on the other hand, are relatively spared within the alcoholic syndrome so that an individual's deficits may be difficult to detect within a standard interview. Psychometric intelligence of alcoholics is usually found to be within normal limits, particularly to the extent that the measurement device relies upon verbal skills.

In addition to a large body of neuropsychological evidence, neuropathologic and radiologic data exist to document alcohol's impact upon the brain. Cerebral atrophy has been observed in alcoholics by pneumoencephalography, computerized tomography, and autopsy. Electroencephalograms often show abnormal brain wave patterns. Ventricular enlargement and cerebellar atrophy are also common observations.

Prediction of the degree of impairment is a complicated process. Older and more advanced alcoholics tend, not surprisingly, to show greater overall deficits. Certain adaptive abilities appear to be more influenced by recent alcohol consumption whereas others seem to be more affected by chronic excess. The amount of alcohol consumed per drinking occasion appears to be a better predictor of impairment than is frequency of drinking. The presence or absence of classic symptoms of addiction appear to be unrelated to the degree of cognitive impairment, although the presence of liver disease or malnutrition may be associated with more severe deficits. The absence of liver disease is not predictive of cognitive normality, however, and significant brain impairment often precedes the development of other signs of medical deterioration. Indeed, brain damage may be one of the first serious effects of chronic heavy drinking.

Reversibility of deficits is likewise a complex issue. Impairment on some measures (such as the Category Test and tapping speed) appears to be largely reversible except in the most deteriorated cases. Deficits on other measures (e.g., Trail-Making and Digit-Symbol) appear to be more permanent once established. The latter therefore may represent "negative hold" measures, providing indices of prior and present impairment after the individual has been sober for some time. Younger and less advanced alcoholics appear to show not only fewer deficits but also better reversal of existing deficits with successful treatment. The latter correlation, however, may be due to the fact that patients with less cognitive impairment show better prognosis for successfully coping with their drinking problems.

No current integrative hypothesis adequately accounts for all of the data on alcoholic brain damage. It is clear that a wide range of areas and functions are affected and that dysfunction is probably not localized to any one particular site. Both right and left hemispheres are impaired, and arguments for lateralization of deficit are inconclusive. Subcortical and cerebellar as well as cortical areas are affected, at least in more deteriorated cases. The type and pattern of deficits shown by alcoholics are not clearly distinguishable from the deficits of brain damaged individuals in general or from an extrapolation of deficits occurring with normal aging of the brain, although the alcoholics are clearly distinguishable from normal and from psychiatric controls when an adequate battery of tests of adaptive abilities is employed.

IMPLICATIONS FOR DIFFERENTIAL DIAGNOSIS
AND TREATMENT

The incidence of cognitive deficits is sufficiently high within an alcoholic population so that any program offering diagnostic and treatment services to alcoholics should at least screen patients for such impairment. The degree of identified deficits may play an important role in treatment planning (Carlsson, Claeson, & Petterson, 1973). Recent research has indicated that treatment outcome is associated with both degree of impairment at intake (Berglund, Leijonquist, & Horlen, 1977; Gregson & Taylor, 1977; Guthrie & Elliott, 1980; O'Leary & Donovan, 1979; O'Leary, Donovan, Chaney, & Walker, 1979a) and the degree of improvement in neuropsychological measures over the course of treatment (Farmer, 1973; Ornstein, 1977; Shelly & Goldstein, 1976). Litman, Eiser, Rawson, & Oppenheim (1979) found that patients using cognitive self-control strategies were least likely to show immediate relapse upon discharge. Patients with less minimal impairment appear to be more likely to complete treatment as well (O'Leary et al., 1979a). Longer and more intensive treatment programs may be of differentially greater benefit to patients with a higher degree of cognitive impairment (Guthrie & Elliott, 1980; Miller & Hester, 1980; O'Leary & Donovan, 1979). Certain patterns of impaired abilities may also provide differential diagnostic cues for a more severe or primary form of alcoholism, as discussed above with regard to the etiological impairment hypotheses. Although current findings are far from conclusive, current data suggest that primary alcoholics may benefit maximally from different treatment approaches than those which succeed with earlier stage problem drinkers (Miller & Hester, 1980; Miller & Joyce, 1979).

Treatment decisions should also be made with awareness of the fact that the cognitive deficits of alcoholics may impair their ability to respond to certain therapeutic approaches (Allen, Faillace, & Reynolds, 1971; Bennett, 1960; Eckardt, Parker, Noble, Feldman, & Gottschalk, 1978; Gottschalk, 1979). Treatment approaches requiring insight or complex associative or abstraction processes may be particularly inappropriate for alcoholics with cognitive deficits (Chelune & Parker, 1981; O'Leary & Donovan, 1979), perhaps one reason for the relatively poor efficacy of such approaches in alcoholism treatment (Miller & Hester, 1980). The fact that alcoholics show marked improvement in some adaptive abilities during the first 2 to 3 weeks of sobriety has led some to recommend that treatment interventions be delayed for at least 2 weeks after detoxification (Allen et al., 1971; Page & Linden, 1974; Weingartner, Faillace, & Markley, 1971). Retention for presented verbal material tends to improve over early weeks of treatment as do some adaptive abilities. Eckardt et al. (1979) found little improvement on several measures over the early weeks of treatment and therefore recommended that cognitive therapies could begin immediately after withdrawal symptoms subside. The alcoholic and the medical control subjects of that study both scored within the impaired range on most measures, however, and one might question the appropriateness of complex and abstract verbal therapies with such a population at all. If treatment interventions are delayed, early weeks could be spent in full resolution of the detoxification process and perhaps in retraining of cognitive abilities that are found to be impaired (e.g., Hansen, 1980). Presentation of new information within treatment programs should be planned in light of the fact that once-presented material is quickly lost, whereas repeated material may be more likely to be retained by alcoholics, particularly if opportunities for active rehearsal are provided. Finally, recent data suggest that careful consideration should be given to the appropriateness of prescribing disulfiram for patients with cognitive deficits, especially deficits of receptive speech (Burnett & Reading, 1970; Kwentus & Major, 1979; Prigitano, 1980). This is of particular concern because patients with the most severe cognitive impairment may also be those for whom disulfiram is most likely to be prescribed (Prigitano, 1977; 1980).

One unresolved question of some importance is the advisability of treatment approaches whose goal is moderation rather than abstinence, given various degrees of cognitive deficit (Eckardt, in press). Miller and Hester (1980) have reviewed recent research on the effectiveness of "controlled drinking" therapies, and findings in general have been encouraging. It is unclear, however, what changes if any occur in initial cognitive impairment levels of individuals who attain and maintain a pattern of moderate drinking. Outcome studies have tended to compare abstainers with *all* individuals still drinking, regardless of amount (e.g., Eckardt, Parker, Pautler, Noble, & Gottschalk, 1980; McLachlan & Levenson, 1974). Reyes and Miller (1980) have reported improvement in liver function values of problem drinkers who became controlled drinkers, but few data are available to evaluate analogous effects on neuropsychological functions. Eckardt et al. (1980) found that when "moderate drinker" was defined in terms of frequency of drinking (moderate = drinks 1–6 times per week, regardless of amount!) abstainers showed significantly less post-treatment impairment than did "moderate" drinkers. When, on the other hand, moderation was defined in terms of amount of consumption (moderate = up to 6 drinks per day, by which standard the heaviest drinker in the sample was considered "moderate"), abstainers and moderates did not differ from each other and both were found to be less impaired than heavy drinkers. Neither definition of moderation seems quite adequate, and Miller and Hester (1980) have proposed more conservative standards for judging moderation by taking into account both quantity and frequency. Parker and Noble (1977) suggested that even moderate drinking brings about cognitive impairment on the basis of their findings of correlations between alcohol consumption data and certain neuropsychological measures within a moderate drinking population. Unfortunately no performance means were reported so that degree of impairment could not be judged against normative standards. Further, the correlations reported, though statistically significant, accounted, on the average, for less than 5% of the variance in impairment. In a subsequent study (Parker & Noble, 1980) these same investigators again reported significant correlations between alcohol consumption quantity and neuropsychological performance within a social drinking population (cf. Parker, Birnbaum, Boyd, & Noble 1980). Only one correlation of nine exceeded .30, however, so that once again the variance accounted for was quite small. Mean data were again omitted. Quantity of consumption was also confounded with age in this study because older subjects tended to drink larger amounts of alcohol, a fact that could well account for the small amounts of shared variance (cf. Jones & Jones, 1980). Thus to date no adequate evaluation of neuropsychological functioning related to moderate drinking patterns has been reported. Longitudinal studies of neuropsychological functioning in problem drinkers who abstain or who drink moderately (preferably with more conservative definitions of "moderately") would also be of interest. The only report of this kind to date is the finding of Guthrie and Elliott (1980) that all patients who reduced their drinking (abstainers and moderate drinkers pooled) showed improvement on cognitive measures. It seems likely that a continuum will be discerned in future research whereby the goal of moderation is found to be inadvisable for patients whose cognitive dysfunction has progressed beyond a certain point (cf. Miller & Caddy, 1977). An evaluation period of abstinence may also be advisable prior to the pursuit of a moderation goal, permitting assessment of the degree of impairment and reversal therein (Sanchez-Craig, 1980).

For programs serving individuals convicted of driving while intoxicated, neuropsychological assessment may be particularly important. Several investigators have suggested that the visuospatial and visuomotor deficits of alcoholics may render them hazardous drivers even when sober (Alcohol and the Brain, 1976; Clarke & Haughton, 1975; Draper, 1978), and that visuospatial functions may recover more slowly than do other adaptive abilities (Goldman & Rosenbaum, 1977). Standard neuropsychological screening of drunk drivers would seem advisable (Brewer, 1976), both to assist in choosing appropriate interventions for individuals and to assess degree of risk to society. Fine and Steer (1979), using the Memory for Designs test to screen drunk driving offenders, found 33% to score in the borderline range and an additional 24% to score within the critical range.

Even beyond such considerations there are good reasons to consider inclusion of screening measures within the intake procedures for any program serving problem drinkers (cf. Wood, 1978). Because neuropsychological impairment is among the first of medical sequelae to appear with chronic drinking, screening for such impairment may improve and increase validity of attempts to detect problem drinking in earlier stages (Eckardt, Ryback, &

Pautler, in press). The potential importance of measures of cognitive function in treatment planning has already been discussed. Feedback regarding level of impairment may also be of use in motivating clients for treatment. In using relatively simple blood tests to assess liver function within our clinic population (Reyes & Miller, 1980) we have found that clients express a great deal of interest in and concern for the results of these objective measures of alcohol damage. The detection and documentation of early phases of alcohol brain damage may increase the motivation of clients to enter and cooperate with interventions designed to modify their drinking patterns (Miller & Orr, 1980). We find that arguments as to whether or not a given client is "alcoholic" accomplish little except to increase drop-out rate, whereas "objective" data presented in a relatively dispassionate fashion are rather persuasive and difficult to refute.

CONCLUSION

Research completed over the past 20 years makes it clear that cognitive impairment in alcoholics is genuine and a phenomenon of considerable importance. Significant deficits are likely to be manifested at intake by a majority of the patients of most alcoholism treatment programs. To ignore this critical dimension of individual differences in the course of assessment and treatment is to overlook a health variable with major implications for the patient's life. More effective individualized treatment plans may be developed if neuropsychological variables are considered, and even motivation for treatment—a notorious problem in alcoholism treatment—may be aided. Both future research and therapeutic endeavors with alcoholics need to address the relationships between cognitive dysfunction and treatment process and outcome.

Chapter 12

Assessing Brain Damage in Schizophrenia

With David Newlin

Assessing brain damage in schizophrenic populations has been a controversial and problematic issue. The clinical neuropsychologist is frequently faced with the differential diagnosis of schizophrenia and brain damage or the assessment of brain damage in addition to schizophrenic illness. In these instances, a number of neuropsychological instruments are commonly employed, most notably the Wechsler Adult Intelligence Scale (WAIS), the Halstead–Reitan Neuropsychological Battery, and, more recently, the Luria–Nebraska Neuropsychological Battery.

A large body of research has been reported in which the ability of these and other tests to discriminate between schizophrenic and brain-damaged neurologic patients has been evaluated. Heaton, Baade, and Johnson (1978) reviewed this research through 1977 and concluded that neuropsychological instruments show significant discriminatory power in most psychiatric populations other than chronic schizophrenics. However, they noted a number of serious methodologic problems with this literature, including the representativeness of the neurologic and psychiatric populations, the reliability of diagnoses, and the effects of age, chronicity, and premorbid intellectual level of the subjects. Malec (1978), in an additional review of this literature, noted methodologic problems concerning the effects of medication and subtypes of both schizophrenia and brain damage, and the common failure to report separate hit and miss rates for the schizophrenic and neurologic groups.

Although the present authors also view these as important methodologic problems that limit the validity of many of these studies, we consider several additional problems to be more fundamental. Previous reviews have not attempted to evaluate different neuropsychological tests in their separate abilities to discriminate between diagnostic groups. Neuropsychological batteries have different properties, and it is improbable that disparate tests would yield comparable hit rates, or that they would be interpreted either actuarially or clinically in similar ways. This discussion focuses upon three commonly used standardized batteries (WAIS, Halstead–Reitan, and Luria–Nebraska), and their effectiveness is evaluated separately.

Second, the severity of pathology of any patient population, including brain-damaged patients and schizophrenics, can vary from mild to severe. Thus, comparison of severely brain-damaged patients with acute schizophrenic patients whose symptoms were well controlled clinically would enable clear neuropsychological differentiation of groups. Similarly, minor head trauma patients may be very difficult to distinguish from chronic, institutionalized schizophrenics. The severity of the psychiatric disturbance of the patient samples employed in these studies has frequently been noted and evaluated, whereas the severity of brain damage in the neurologic patients has been generally ignored. Yet it is entirely possible that hit rates are more a function of the severity of brain damage in the neurologic sample than of psychiatric impairment in the schizophrenic sample.

A third consideration, which we feel is by far the most important, is the question of brain damage associated with schizophrenia itself. The underlying assumption in neuropsychological comparisons of schizophrenic and neurologic populations is that schizophrenia is a functional as opposed to an organic disorder, that is, schizophrenia is not intrinsically associated with brain damage. Thus, the criterion in these studies for the presence or absence of brain damage is simply the diagnostic group. The assumption that schizophrenia is a purely functional disorder has a long history. However, recent evidence leads us to question seriously the assumptions underlying this functional label.

This last issue is basic to any discussion of neuropsychological assessment in schizophrenia. For this reason, the recent literature concerning neurologic evidence of brain damage among schizophrenic patients is first discussed in detail. Studies comparing neuropsychological performance of schizophrenics and brain-damaged performance on the WAIS, Halstead–Reitan, and Luria–Nebraska batteries are then reviewed. It is concluded that a new approach to the neuropsychological assessment of brain damage in schizophrenic patients is needed in which subtypes of neurologically normal and abnormal schizophrenics are evaluated separately.

NEUROLOGIC ASSESSMENT OF BRAIN DAMAGE IN SCHIZOPHRENIA

Several studies have reported a greater frequency of hard and soft neurologic signs of central nervous system damage in schizophrenics. Pollin and Stabenau (1968) found that 72.5% of schizophrenics had at least one neurologic sign of impairment, and Rochford, Detre, Tucker, and Harrow (1970) reported that 65% of 26 schizophrenics had such signs. Mocher, Pollin, and Stabenau (1971) studied monozygotic twin pairs discordant for schizophrenia. Of the index twins, 11 of 15 (73%) showed neurologic signs compared to two normal twins. Quitkin, Rifkin, and Klein (1976) found significantly more neurologic signs in schizophrenics with premorbid asociality.

These studies are difficult to evaluate since the judges were not blind to diagnosis in the Rochford et al. (1970) and Mocher et al. (1971) studies. Neurologic signs, particularly "soft" or behavioral signs, are difficult to interpret without clear information concerning reliability, which was provided only in the study of Quitkin et al. (1976). Finally, neurologic signs are measured at a behavioral level and may not reflect cerebral damage.

A number of new radiologic techniques, most notably the computed tomography (CT) scan, have been applied to the assessment of brain damage in schizophrenic populations. Behavioral or neuropsychological evidence, although complementary, is subject to interpretation in terms of cognitive deterioration secondary to chronic psychosis. However, the application of radiologic techniques to schizophrenic populations is a relatively new approach, with some limitations. First, these techniques have most often been applied to assessment of global indications of brain damage, such as general brain atrophy, rather than being used to localize the brain dysfunction in schizophrenic patients. Second, in most cases, these techniques do not suggest the etiology of the brain damage. Despite these problems, research in which radiologic assessment is applied to schizophrenic populations provides striking evidence of an association between brain damage and schizophrenia.

The first controlled investigation of brain abnormalities in schizophrenia was Haug's (1962) pneumoencephalographic analysis of 101 schizophrenic patients who had been screened to exclude those with histories of head trauma, alcoholism, leukotomy, and old age. Fifty-eight percent of these patients had abnormal pneumoencephalograms, with evidence of ventricular enlargement and cortical atrophy. This percentage was only slightly below the 72% of organic dementia patients with abnormal pneumoencephalograms. Repeated pneumoencephalograms showed increased atrophy in those schizophrenic patients who demonstrated a declining clinical course. Ventricular size was greater in the schizophrenic group than in a group with nonorganic mental disorders. Young and Crampton (1974) also found comparable percentages of atrophy determined by pneumoencephalography in mixed psychiatric and neurologic patients.

Bryant, Eiseman, Spencer, and Lieber (1965) used bilateral carotid arteriography and aortic injection of dyes to evaluate extracranial cerebrovascular disease in 65 schizophrenics. Of this group, 22% had evidence of cerebrovascular disease compared to 22% of organic brain syndrome patients. Surgical operations were performed in 5 schizophrenic patients with arteriographic occlusion, with no subsequent change in mental status in any of the cases. Bryant et al. (1965) concluded that cerebrovascular disease was not a significant factor in schizophrenia, although they failed to explain the comparable prevalence of extracranial vascular disease in the schizophrenic and organic groups.

Interpretation of these studies using pneumoencephalographic and arteriographic techniques is hampered by the failure of Haug (1962), Young and Crampton (1974), and Bryant et al. (1965) to indicate whether judgments of abnormality were made by individuals blind to the psychiatric status of the patients, and the failure to include normal control groups.

The advent of the computed tomography (CT) scan marked an important new development in the neurologic study of schizophrenia. The CT scan allows comprehensive, noninvasive cerebral evaluation of both schizophrenic and normal individuals. The only major limitation of the CT scan is that it is a relatively new technique, and normative data have not been clearly established. The CT scan is normally evaluated qualitatively on the basis of films, which are actually analogue representations of digital density data that are represented at a higher resolution than is possible in the analogue film medium. It may be expected that further developments in the standardization and analysis of CT scan data, including numerical density data, will enhance the research value of this technique.

Johnstone, Crow and Associates (Johnstone, Crow, Frith, Husband, & Kreel, 1976; Johnstone, Crow, Frith, Stevens, Kreel, & Husband, 1978) measured ventricular size using CT scan films in 14 chronic schizophrenics and age-matched controls. The chronic schizophrenics without leukotomy had a larger ventricular area but a comparable sulcal size compared to controls. This research was criticized by Jellinek (1976) and Marsden (1976), who argued that Johnstone et al.'s (1976) chronic schizophrenics were older individuals in whom cortical atrophy might be expected, and that they had been institutionalized for many years. Trimble and Kingsley (1978) made similar criticisms, and offered evidence showing no ventricular enlargement (using a different measurement procedure) in the CT scans of 11 young schizophrenic patients.

Nevertheless, a series of CT scan studies by Weinberger and his associates (Weinberger, Bigelow, Kleinman, Klein, Rosenblatt, & Wyatt, 1980; Weinberger, Torrey, Neophytides, & Wyatt, 1979a,b) has confirmed the earlier results of Johnstone et al. (1976, 1978). Weinberger et al. (1979a) found that 58 chronic schizophrenics under 50 years of age had larger mean ventricular areas than 56 age-matched controls. Ventricular area was uncorrelated with duration of illness and length of hospitalization, and slightly inversely related to a history of electroconvulsive shock treatment. In the same sample (plus 2 additional subjects), Weinberger et al. (1979b) noted increased width of the sylvian and interhemispheric fissures or widened sulci in 19 of 60 chronic schizophrenic patients. Again, these structural abnormalities were unrelated to duration of illness or length of hospitalization. Interestingly, ventricular enlargement was also unrelated to these other indices of cortical atrophy, so that a total of 67% of the chronic schizophrenic sample showed some structural abnormality. In a further analysis of this patient sample, Luchins, Weinberger, and Wyatt (1979) examined patterns of brain asymmetry in the CT scans of these patients. The 51 right-handed chronic schizophrenics showed more reversals from the normal pattern of wider right frontal and left occipital lobes than 80 normal right-handers. Again, this type of structural abnormality (reversal of normal asymmetry) was more common in chronic schizophrenics without evidence of cortical atrophy (ventricular enlargement, widening of the sulci or fissures, or cerebellar atrophy).

Weinberger et al. (1980) studied the response to neuroleptic medication of 10 of the chronic schizophrenics from this larger sample who showed ventricular enlargement and 10 who did not. The schizophrenics with atrophy did not respond to phenothiazines, whereas those without atrophy showed substantial clinical improvement under medication compared to a drug-free period.

In additional replications of the finding of cerebral atrophy in schizophrenics, Rieder, Donnelly, Herot, and Waldman (1979) noted sulcal prominence and widening of the interhemispheric fissure in 4 of 17 young chronic schizophrenics. A recent review by Weinberger (1982) at a conference sponsored by the National Institute of Mental Health on the relationship of CT scan studies to schizophrenia found a current population of about 16 published or unpublished studies comparing schizophrenics to control subjects. Of these studies, all but two have found indications of CT scan deficits in the schizophrenic patients, a remarkable rate of agreement when one considers the degree to which the question of brain injury has been hotly debated for the past century.

As was noted above, the CT scan film image is simply an analogue representation of digital density values. In a series of studies using the numerical density data, Golden and his collegues (Golden, Graber, Coffman, Berg, Bloch, & Brogan, 1980; Golden, Graber, Coffman, Berg, Newlin, & Bloch, 1981) compared CT scan density in 21 chronic schizophrenics and 22 age-matched normal controls. Golden et al. (1980) found lower overall brain tissue density in the schizophrenic subjects. This effect was found at almost all horizontal and vertical levels of the brain, and therefore appears unrelated to previous findings of sulcal and ventricular enlargement. The effect was uncorrelated with age, suggesting independence from factors such as duration of illness, length of hospitalization, and length of medication treatment.

In a second study, Golden et al. (1981) found that lower density values were localized to left anterior areas in the brains of 23 chronic schizophrenics compared to 24 normal controls. Again, the effect was uncorrelated with age, suggesting that the reduction in left anterior brain density may be an early developmental phenomenon rather than the effect of a chronic, degenerative process associated with schizophrenic symptomatology. Finally, additional CT scan density research (Lyon, Wilson, Golden, Graber, Coffman, & Block, 1981) found that medication and drug usuage was associated with lowered posterior density rather than the general anterior reduction found in schizophrenics by Golden et al. (1981). Thus, it appears unlikely that the reduced left anterior CT scan density found in schizophrenia was a residual effect of medication history.

The CT scan studies have been remarkably consistent in showing structural and density abnormalities in the brains of some schizophrenic subjects. The most consistent effect has been enlargement of the lateral ventricles (Golden et al., 1980; Johnstone et al., 1976, 1978; Weinberger et al., 1979a), an effect strongly indicative of cortical atrophy. Evidence supporting the interpretation of atrophy has been obtained with measures of sulcal and interhemispheric fissure enlargement, although the latter effects were uncorrelated with ventricular enlargement. Weinberger et al. (1979b) suggested that ventricular and sulcal enlargement could represent different forms of atrophy since they were independent. In addition, the reversal of normal asymmetry was found in chronic schizophrenic subjects who did not show atrophy in the sample of Weinberger et al. (1979a,b), and might therefore reflect an additional independent form of structural abnormality in schizophrenia.

Including all of the types of structural abnormalities identified in the Weinberger et al. (1979a,b; Luchins et al., 1979) sample of 60 young chronic schizophrenics, approximately 83% had some form of CT scan abnormality. This must be considered a remarkably high estimate that stands in direct contrast to earlier (and current) assumptions that schizophrenia is a functional rather than an organic disorder. Using these estimates, it must be concluded that a substantial subset of schizophrenics show clear evidence of brain damage, although the etiology and ultimate effects of this damage have not yet been elucidated.

The criticisms leveled by Jellinek (1976), Marsden (1976), and Trimble and Kingsley (1978) that the CT scan results showing cortical atrophy were actually due to age, institutionalization, or medication history have been effectively rebutted by empirical research. Weinberger et al.'s (1979a,b) sample was under age 50, and the atrophy was unrelated to these factors. Golden et al. (1980) and Rieder et al.'s (1979) samples of chronic schizophrenics were under age 45, and the reduced CT scan density effects reported by Golden et al. (1980) were uncorrelated with age.

One limitation of the CT scan technique is that it identifies static anatomic effects rather than dynamic physiologic aspects of brain function.

The advent of regional cerebral blood flow (rCBF) techniques, in which a radioactive isotope is injected into the carotid arteries or inhaled in the form of radioactive xenon gas, allows examination of dynamic brain function. Scintillation counters on the scalp measure washout curves of the radioactivity, allowing regional assessment of brain activity. In a series of studies, Ingvar and Franzen (1974; Franzen & Ingvar, 1975a, 1975b) examined left hemisphere rCBF in chronic schizophrenic patients. Ingvar and Franzen (1974) initially found that older schizophrenics had clearly reduced flow at rest in left frontal lobe areas, and Franzen and Ingvar (1975a) replicated this effect in a larger sample of schizophrenic patients that included younger subjects. They also studied the pattern of regional activation during a psychological task that normally elicits increased frontal lobe flow; schizophrenics failed to show this increased left frontal activation (Franzen & Ingvar, 1975b).

In a more recent study, Ariel, Golden, Berg, Quaife, Dirksin, Forsell, Wilson, and Graber (in press) examined 29 schizophrenics and 22 normal controls. They found a general decrease of cerebral blood flow (CBF), but specifically found the greatest decrease in the anterior half of the left hemisphere, consistent with the CT scan density findings. Further support for an anterior left hemisphere deficit has come from recent research using positron emission tomography (PET) (Buchsbaum, 1982). This technique studies glucose uptake in each area of the brain. The major finding of this research to date has pointed to a frontal lobe deficit in the left hemisphere. Thus, we find that the three disparate techniques of CT scan, rCBF, and PET all point to a focus in the anterior half of the left hemisphere in schizophrenics.

Schizophrenics show a host of research signs indicating left hemisphere overactivation and impairment. This research has employed a number of experimental techniques, including assessment of motor and sensory deficits, electrophysiologic parameters, and neuropsychological characteristics. A parallel literature presents evidence that functioning of the corpus callosum is impaired in schizophrenic patients.

The strongest evidence of left hemisphere overactivation in schizophrenia stems from research on lateral eye movements (LEM) in response to reflective questions. Following the work of Kinsbourne (1972), a tendency to look left following a reflective question might be interpreted as indicating right hemisphere activation. Gur (1978) found that schizophrenic patients tended to look right in response to reflective questions, a finding that she interpreted as indicating left hemisphere overactivation in schizophrenia. This finding was replicated by Schweitzer, Becker, and Welsh (1978) in a comparison of schizophrenics with normal controls, and Schweitzer (1979) again found this effect in comparing schizophrenics with normals and manic-depressive patients; the affective disorder patients tended to look in the opposite direction, indicating right hemisphere overactivation. However, Sandel and Alcorn (1980) found that a small sample of schizophrenics had a tendency toward left

LEM, a finding contradictory to those of Gur (1978) and Schweitzer (1979: Schweitzer et al., 1978), although Sandel and Alcorn had no normal comparison group.

The interpretation of LEM in terms of contralateral hemispheric activation was criticized by Erlichman and Weinberger (1978), although recent evidence using rCBF techniques strongly supports this interpretation. Gur and Reivich (1980) found a relationship between the tendency toward right or left LEM and differential hemispheric blood flow that would be predicted by the contralateral hemisphere activation hypothesis.

Further evidence of left hemisphere overactivation in schizophrenia has been obtained using electrophysiologic techniques. Studying autonomic laterality, Gruzelier (1973) found unilateral nonresponding and underresponding of electrodermal activity on the left hands of schizophrenic patients. Gruzelier and Venables (1974) replicated this effect, and also found an opposite pattern of results for depressive patients. Uherick (1975) reported a further replication of this effect, noting that schizophrenics showed greater electrodermal activity on their right hands. Gruzelier and Hammond (1976) again found left-hand underresponding in schizophrenics and noted that medication abolished this electrodermal laterality in two schizophrenics. In a larger sample of schizophrenic patients, Gruzelier and Hammond (1977) again found that medication abolished or reversed the left-hand electrodermal underresponding in schizophrenics.

Although the electrodermal data have been remarkably consistent in showing a deficit in electrodermal responding of the left hand in schizophrenics, questions remain concerning interpretation of this effect. Gruzelier (1973) reviewed evidence that electrodermal activity is controlled by the ipsilateral hemisphere and subcortical areas, and he interpreted the left-sided effect in terms of left temporal—limbic dysfunction in schizophrenia (Gruzelier, 1973; Gruzelier & Hammond, 1976). In contrast, Myslobodsky and Rattok (1975, 1977) have reported evidence that electrodermal activity is contralaterally controlled.

The electrocortical evidence has also been consistent in showing left-sided abnormalities in schizophrenia, and this evidence may be unequivocally interpreted in relation to the affected hemisphere. Rochford, Swartzburg, Chowdhrey, and Goldstein (1976) reported a lower right—left coefficient of variation in the electroencephalograms (EEG) of schizophrenic patients. Similar effects were found by Etevson, Pidoux, Rioux, Peron-Magnon, Verdeaux, and Dencker (1979) and Goldstein, Temple, and Pollack (1976). Greater left hemisphere EEG variability suggests either overactivation or dysfunction of the left hemisphere in schizophrenia since right hemisphere variability was comparable to that of normals (Rochford et al., 1976).

Flor-Henry (1976) presented evidence of greater high-frequency (20—30 Hz) power in the left temporal EEG of schizophrenics compared to control subjects, and Coger, Dymond, and Serafetinides (1979) found a similar effect of greater high-frequency activity in left precentral sites for schizophrenics. Using integrated voltage of the EEG (a function of both frequency and amplitude), Serafetinides (1972, 1973) found greater left hemisphere integrated voltage in the EEG of schizophrenics, and this effect was reduced by treatment with chlorpromazine. Finally, Abrams and Taylor (1979) found more left temporal EEG abnormalities for schizophrenic patients and more right parieto-occipital abnormalities for manic-depressive patients.

Roemer and his colleagues (Roemer, Shagass, Straumanis, & Amadeo, 1978, 1979) found similar results using average evoked potential techniques. There were no lateralized amplitude differences between schizophrenics and normals, although schizophrenics had more variable left hemisphere visual evoked potentials than normals or personality disorder patients. Roemer et al. (1979) also found lower stability of left hemisphere auditory evoked potentials in the schizophrenic group.

Similar results suggesting left hemisphere abnormality, usually involving greater EEG variability on the left hemispheric side, have been obtained using a broad range of EEG techniques. As noted above, the results can be interpreted as clearly indicating that left hemisphere EEG activity tends to be abnormal in schizophrenia, although the nature of this abnormality and localization of the effect within the left hemisphere remain unclear.

A number of reports suggest the presence of left hemisphere dysfunction in schizophrenia, an effect which may be related in some ways to overactivation of the left hemisphere. This evidence was also obtained with a broad range of techniques, all converging on left hemisphere dysfunction in schizophrenia. Early reports (Fleminger, Dalton, & Standage, 1977; Gur, 1977; Lishman & McMeekan, 1976; Walker & Birch, 1970) consistently reported increased incidence of sinistrality among schizophrenic adults and children, particularly males, although this has not been unanimous. The inconsistency of these data may potentially be related to different subforms of schizophrenia. Boklage (1977) found that among monozygotic twins discordant for schizophrenia, the schizophrenic twin was more likely to be sinistral. In an analysis of similar data, Luchins, Weinberger, and Wyatt (1979) noted that the sinistral members of monozygotic twin pairs discordant for schizophrenia were more likely to be schizophrenic than the dextral members, although dextral schizophrenics tended to have a more severe form of the disorder. Finally, Metzig, Rosenberg, Ast, and Krashen (1976) found greater "pure-dominant" characteristics (i.e., hand dominance and maximum thumb rotation on the same side) among schizophrenic patients compared to normals. The full implications of the data concerning handedness are not yet clear, due to the inconsistency and complexity of the results, although these data suggest the importance of lateral asymmetries in the study of schizophrenia.

Other authors have studied "soft" neurologic signs of impairment in schizophrenia using different sensory modalities. In the tactual modality,

Torrey (1980) found significant neurologic impairment in a schizophrenic group using graphesthesia and face—hand tactile tests, with predominant impairment in the right hand. This was interpreted in terms of the left hemisphere dysfunction. In the visual modality, Gur (1978) found that schizophrenics had left hemifield superiority on both verbal and spatial tasks, and Gur (1979) reported that schizophrenics showed performance on a simultaneous and successive presentation of a visual task that was similar to a right hemisphere brain-damaged group. She argued that this pattern of results suggested left hemisphere hyperexcitability and dysfunction in schizophrenia, although other interpretations may be possible.

A number of studies have been done concerning lateralized perception in the auditory modality. Alpert, Rubenstein, and Kesselman (1976) found that schizophrenics differentiated good from poor semantic structure with the left rather than the right ear (i.e., the right rather than the left hemisphere), a result suggestive of preferential right hemisphere processing of semantic stimuli and left hemisphere dysfunction. Gruzelier and Hammond (1976) found that schizophrenics had more right ear omissions on a temporal discrimination task, an effect that was reduced by chlorpromazine administration.

Two auditory threshold tasks have yielded contradictory results. Bahzin, Wasserman, and Jonkonogii (1975) found that schizophrenics had increased right ear (i.e., left hemisphere) thresholds for short tones, although Gruzelier and Hammond (1976) found a right ear superiority among schizophrenics for high tones. However, since Gruzelier and Hammond (1976) found that this effect was labile and decreased with clinical improvement, and since Hammond and Gruzelier (1978) found that right ear auditory performance improved with chlorpromazine rather than placebo medication, this opposite result was also interpreted as indicating left hemisphere dysfunction.

Two studies have been performed in which lateralized deficits in schizophrenia were found using traditional neuropsychological tests. Taylor, Greenspan, and Abrams (1979) found that schizophrenics had more errors on an aphasia screening test indicative of left temporal and left temporal—parietal lobe impairment. Flor-Henry (1976) found evidence of left frontal—temporal lobe dysfunction in schizophrenia using a battery of neuropsychological tests.

Several reports have raised the possibility of simulation of schizophrenic symptomatology from brain lesions. Thompson (1970) reported 4 clinical cases, 3 of them involving left anterior brain lesions, that simulated schizophrenia. Flor-Henry (1969a,b) evaluated the seizure foci of epileptic individuals showing psychiatric symptomatology and found that schizophrenic subjects were more likely to have left-sided epileptic foci. Therefore, the few studies investigating the ability of brain dysfunction to mimic schizophrenic symptomatology have emphasized left-sided lesions or epileptic foci in patients showing schizophrenic symptoms. These studies, although hardly conclusive, raise the question of whether schizophrenia may be effectively simulated by brain lesions, particularly left hemispheric lesions, as well as the implications of this effect for the etiology of schizophrenia.

Studies of hemispheric asymmetry in schizophrenia consistently indicate left hemisphere overactivation and/or dysfunction in schizophrenic patients. Although important methodologic problems plague some of this research (Newlin, Carpenter, & Golden, 1981), converging evidence clearly implicates left hemisphere involvement in schizophrenia. However, the strongest evidence supporting left hemisphere dysfunction remains the data on CT scan density parameters (Golden et al., 1980) and rCBF techniques (e.g., Franzen & Ingvar, 1975b). It may be expected that further research using sophisticated neurologic techniques will clarify the implications of this research for the etiology of schizophrenia.

A parallel literature has suggested that callosal function, including interhemispheric transfer of information, is impaired in schizophrenia. This literature was also reviewed by Newlin et al. (1981). The basis for this research approach was a report by Rosenthal and Bigelow (1972) of autopsied schizophrenic patients in whom significant enlargement of the corpus callosum was noted. However, these investigators examined only the right halves of the brains of these subjects, leaving open the possibility that significant right–left morphologic differences might have been missed.

A number of studies have been performed to test the hypothesis that interhemispheric transfer of information, a presumed callosal function, is impaired in schizophrenic patients. Green (1978) found that schizophrenics did poorly on a two-handed tactual problem, as well as on the same task when relearning with the opposite hand was required. Dimond, Scammel, Pryce, Huws, and Gray (1979) found more left-hand object-naming errors in a schizophrenic group. In two other studies using the tactual modality, Carr (1980) found that schizophrenics did more poorly on a cross-hemispheric stereognostic (object recognition) task, and Dimond, Scammell, Pryce, Huws, and Gray (1980) noted deficits in tasks requiring localization of touches to the body when the contralateral hand was used to indicate the location of the touch.

In the visual modality, Beaumont and Dimond (1973) found that schizophrenics did more poorly on matching of visual stimuli presented to opposite hemifields. However, the schizophrenics also showed poorer right-hemifield letter matching than controls, an effect suggestive of left hemisphere dysfunction. Tress and Kugler (1979) found superior interocular transfer of movement aftereffects, a result that was interpreted as evidence against the callosal dysfunction hypothesis. However, hemifield viewing would more clearly involve the hemispheres differentially, so this may not be a strong test of the hypothesis.

In the auditory modality, Green and Kotenko (1980) found that schizophrenics showed deficits in left ear speech comprehension and poorer comprehension with binaural than monaural listening conditions. Both effects were interpreted in terms of impaired interhemispheric transfer of information and callosal dysfunction.

Newlin, Carpenter, and Golden (1981) argued that this literature was seriously flawed by methodologic problems. The most basic problem is a failure to demonstrate a differential deficit in schizophrenic patients. In almost all cases, tasks devised to require interhemispheric transfer of information are more difficult or complex than those not requiring transfer. Thus, poorer schizophrenic performance may simply reflect degenerated performance in the psychotic, usually chronically ill group. An adequate test of the callosal dysfunction hypothesis would require the comparison of equally difficult tasks and the demonstration of a differential deficit in the schizophrenic group on the task requiring interhemispheric transfer of information.

A second problem concerns Luria's (1973) argument that coordination of the two sides of the body is primarily a left hemisphere function. Many of the tasks reviewed above that were designed to require interhemispheric transfer of information also involve bilateral coordination, so that impairment on these tasks could reflect primary left hemisphere dysfunction.

Conclusions

The literature on brain damage in schizophrenics strongly supports the presence of brain dysfunction in schizophrenia. The CT scan research yields very high estimates of the prevalence of structural brain abnormalities in schizophrenic patients, and these estimates have been partially cross-validated. Other research, including CT scan density and rCBF studies (Golden et al., 1980; Ingvar & Franzen, 1974), supports the conclusion that left-hemispheric abnormalities are particularly associated with schizophrenia. This conclusion is supported by a large body of electrophysiological and sensory research (Newlin et al., 1981).

Major questions remain concerning the interpretation of these results. It is possible that schizophrenia produces brain damage in a subset of schizophrenics as part of a degenerative process associated with psychosis. This interpretation has not been supported by findings that atrophy and lowered density are uncorrelated with measures of institutionalization and chronicity (Weinberger et al., 1979a,b) or age (Golden et al., 1981). However, this can be fully evaluated only by using prospective methodology, and data are not available concerning CT scan parameters of acute schizophrenics. A second possibility is that in many cases the etiologic agent in schizophrenia produces both schizophrenic symptomatology and brain damage. This hypothesis is consistent with the available literature, but again, it can be tested only prospectively. A third possibility is that schizophrenia is one of several sequelae of brain damage; that is, brain lesions resulting from any number of factors may produce a form of organic impairment associated with the psychiatric symptomatology of schizophrenia.

These possibilities are not mutually exclusive, and a sample of schizophrenic patients might include those with etiologies of any of these other types. The second hypothesis, that schizophrenia is an illness with both psychological and organic features, seems most plausible on the basis of the present evidence, although more research is needed that specifically addresses this issue. The application of advanced radiologic techniques to the question of brain damage in schizophrenia is in its infancy, although the initial results indicate that it is a very fruitful approach.

WECHSLER ADULT INTELLIGENCE SCALE

A small number of studies have evaluated the ability of WAIS pattern rules and performance levels to discriminate brain-damaged neurologic patients from chronic schizophrenic patients. These studies are summarized in Table 12-1. DeWolfe (1971) reported that decision rules based on the Comprehension, Digit Span, and Vocabulary subtests of the WAIS achieved a 75% overall hit rate among 50 chronic schizophrenic and 50 diffusely brain-damaged patients. The rules were that Digit Span greater than Comprehension indicated schizophrenia, and Comprehension greater than Digit Span indicated organicity, with ties broken by comparisons of Digit Span with Vocabulary rather than Comprehension. Watson (1972) attempted to cross-validate these pattern rules, and found 74% overall discriminability in one sample of 40 chronic schizophrenics and 40 organic brain syndrome patients, but the hit rate was not significant in another sample of 50 chronic schizophrenics and 50 organic brain syndrome patients.

In retrospect, it seems curious that pattern rules might have been developed using these particular subtests since Digit Span and Block Design have traditionally been viewed as being associated with impairment due to brain damage (Golden, 1979). Also, Digit Span is sensitive to distractability and inattention, features commonly associated with schizophrenia (and brain damage). Golden's (1977) optimized hit rates for the WAIS in a schizophrenic population have slightly lower cutoffs for Comprehension than Digit Span, which is consistent with DeWolfe's (1971) hypothesis, although the difference is only 1 scale score point. Golden (1977) also has lower recommended cutoffs for Arithmetic, Digit Span, and Picture Arrangement.

In a final study of the effectiveness of the WAIS in discriminating schizophrenic from brain-damaged patients, Chelune, Heaton, Lehman, and Robinson (1979) achieved a nonsignificant hit rate of 60% using WAIS level-of-performance scores, which increased to a significant 68% when WAIS deficit pattern scores were added. The deficit pattern scores were not significant discriminators by themselves, and the pattern rules used were not reported.

The literature concerning assessment of brain damage in schizophrenic patients with the WAIS is of limited scope and success. On the basis of

Table 12-1
Studies of the Discriminatory Power of the WAIS

Experiment	Schizophrenic (Sx) Sample	Neurologic Sample	Statistical Procedure	Overall Hit Rate	Sx Hit Rate	Neurologic Hit Rate
DeWolfe (1971)	50 chronic Sx	50 mixed neurologic patients	Pattern rules	75%	72%	78%
Watson (1972)	40 chronic Sx	40 mixed neurologic patients	Pattern rules from DeWolfe (1971)	74%	73%	75%
	50 chronic Sx	50 mixed neurologic patients	Pattern rules from DeWolfe (1971)	ns*	ns	ns
Chelune et al. (1979)	24 chronic Sx	48 diffuse neurologic patients	Optimal level of performance scores	60%	na†	na
			Optimal pattern rules and level of performance	68%	na	na

*ns — not significant.
†na — not available.

present information, it must be concluded that the WAIS should not be used alone as a test of brain damage with schizophrenics, although the data of Chelune et al. (1979) suggest that it may add significant discriminatory power when used in combination with the Halstead—Reitan Battery. A review of the WAIS was included in this discussion because this combination is frequently used clinically. However, there are no cross-validated pattern rules for use in schizophrenic populations, and WAIS subtest scores should be interpreted cautiously even when used in combination with the Halstead—Reitan Battery.

HALSTEAD—REITAN NEUROPSYCHOLOGICAL BATTERY

Neuropsychological assessment in schizophrenic populations with the Halstead—Reitan Neuropsychological Battery has been a controversial topic. Different investigators have reported grossly discrepant results. A number of factors concerning the patient populations selected for these studies could have accounted for the disparate findings, including age, acute versus chronic schizophrenic classification, screening of schizophrenics for neurologic abnormalities, and the severity of brain damage in the populations selected. It is not possible to control or systematically vary all of these factors in any single study, so that the conclusions drawn from each study are to some extent limited to the patient populations that were chosen.

This discussion focuses upon studies in which the Halstead—Reitan Battery was given in its entirety, or in which a sufficient number of the tests were administered so that an Impairment Index could reasonably be computed. These studies are summarized in Table 12-2. A number of other studies have been reported comparing schizophrenic with brain-damaged populations on various subtests of the Halstead—Reitan, and these have been adequately reviewed by Heaton et al. (1978). Given the controversy and the difficulties in this area, it was concluded that use of the full Halstead—Reitan Battery was more informative than the use of its subtests for these purposes.

In an early attempt to discriminate schizophrenic from brain-damaged patients using the Halstead—Reitan Battery, Watson, Thomas, Anderson, and Felling (1968) reported a very low (54%) overall correct classification (hit rate) using Reitan's (1955) cutoff scores. Watson et al. found that the Impairment Index value was related to the chronicity of both neurologic and schizophrenic illnesses but did not significantly discriminate between the two diagnostic groups. Watson, Thomas, Felling, and Anderson (1968) reported some success in discriminating recent-admission schizophrenics from neurologic patients using double simultaneous auditory stimulation results, as well as both recent-admission and long-term patients with right—left hemisphere differences in simultaneous auditory stimulation. Watson, Thomas, Felling, and

Table 12-2
Studies of the Discriminatory Power of the Halstead–Reitan Battery

Experiment	Schizophrenic (Sx) Sample	Neurologic Sample	Statistical Procedure	Overall Hit Rate	Sx Hit Rate	Neurologic Hit Rate
Watson et al. (1968)	50 first admission and chronic Sx	50 mixed neurologic patients	Standard cutoff, Impairment Index	54%	16%	92%
Levine and Feirstein (1972)	18 chronic Sx	18 severe, diffuse neurologic patients	Optimal Halstead–Reitan summary and Bender–Gestalt	73%	67%	78%
Klonoff et al. (1970)	53 older, chronic Sx	13 organic Sx	standard cutoff, Impairment Index	36%*	na*	na
Lacks et al. (1970)	27 chronic Sx; 19 medical controls	19 severe, diffuse neurologic patients	Standard cutoff, Impairment Index	69%	62%	84%
Chelune et al. (1979)	23 chronic Sx	48 diffuse neurologic patients	Optimal discriminant analysis, Halstead–Reitan (without WAIS)	68%	na	na
Golden (1977)	50 acute Sx	50 mixed neurologic patients	Optimal discriminant analysis, Halstead–Reitan (with WAIS)	97%	100%	94%
Kane et al. (1981)	23 Sx	23 mixed neurologic patients	Expert clinical judgment	78%	na	na

*na — not available.

212

Anderson (1969) also reported some success in this patient sample with right−left grip strength differences on the hand dynamometer.

Levine and Feirstein (1972) criticized the Watson et al. studies, arguing that their schizophrenic sample was more chronic than their organic sample. Levine and Feirstein reported a 73% overall hit rate with optimal cutoff scores combining the Halstead Impairment Index, Trail-Making Tests, Bender−Gestalt, and two Wechsler subtests. However, Watson (1974) noted that Levine and Feirstein (1972) employed only severe, diffusely lesioned neuro-logic patients, who would be expected to show severe neuropsychological impairment, and that schizophrenics were excluded who were unable to complete the battery, whereas neurologic patients were not excluded for this reason. It may be added that the hit rates might have been more useful if they had been based on the Halstead−Reitan or the Bender−Gestalt separately, rather than combined.

Watson (1974) answered Levine and Feirstein's criticism concerning differential chronicity by reporting a comparison of schizophrenic and neuro-logic patients matched for chronicity; there were no significant differences between these groups on the Halstead−Reitan Battery.

Klonoff, Fibiger, and Hutton (1970) obtained results similar to those of Watson et al. (1968) in a group of 53 schizophrenics who had been diagnosed and pensioned 20 years earlier during World War II. Using Reitan's cutoffs, the Impairment Index correctly classifed approximately 36 percent (estimate from Heaton et al., 1978) of the subjects, a result far below the 50% chance level. This result is best attributed to the advanced age and long-term hospitalization of the patient sample.

Lacks, Colbert, Harrow, and Levine (1970) evaluated the ability of the Halstead−Reitan and Bender−Gestalt tests to discriminate 19 diffusely brain-damaged patients from a combined group of 27 schizophrenic and general medical patients. The Reitan cutoff for the Impairment Index correctly classified 84% of the organic patients but only 62% of the schizophrenic and medical patients. The Bender−Gestalt outperformed the Impairment Index in overall correct classifica-tions, primarily because it was less likely to classify the schizophrenic and medical patients as organic. The results of this study might have been more useful had they been reported separately for the schizophrenic and medical patients.

Fredericks and Finkel (1978) evaluated the performance of 44 acute, recently hospitalized schizophrenic patients against Reitan's (1955) original sample of normals and brain-damaged patients. Although no hit rates were reported, the schizophrenics performed better than the neurologic patients on all tests but Category and worse than normals only on Category, Tactual Performance Test (TPT) Memory, and TPT Localization. There were no effects of medication on Halstead−Reitan Battery performance.

One study has been reported in which Kane, Sweet Golden, Parsons & Moses (1981) evaluated the ability of expert clinicians to discriminate between a psychiatric (primarily schizophrenic) sample and a neurologic group using the Halstead–Reitan Battery. The experts obtained a 78% overall hit rate, but actuarial hit rates were not reported. Although this research is of considerable value in the sense that it more closely approximates the clinical decision-making process, it may reflect the acumen of the expert clinician rather than the actuarial quality of the neuropsychological test.

Chelune et al. (1979) found an overall hit rate of 68% comparing 23 short-term schizophrenics in a Veterans Administration Hospital with 48 diffusely brain-damaged patients using optimized discriminant analysis of Halstead–Reitan subtest scores (without intellectual scores). This is not a high percentage considering the use of optimized discriminant analysis and selection of diffusely brain-damaged neurologic patients.

In a final study of the effectiveness of the Halstead–Reitan Battery in discriminating between schizophrenic and neurologic patients, Golden (1977) reported excellent success using an optimal discriminant analysis employing all of the Halstead–Reitan subtest scores. Golden compared 50 acute schizophrenic patients (including a small number of nonschizophrenic psychotic patients) who had been screened to rule out organicity with 50 neurologic patients. He reported an overall hit rate of 97%, with 100% correct classification of the psychiatric patients and 94% of the neurologic patients. The use of a large number of variables in the discriminant analysis indicates that considerable shrinkage would be expected with cross-validation. Golden (1977) also established optimal cutoff scores for use of the Halstead–Reitan Battery in diagnosis of brain damage in a psychiatric population.

It is quite apparent that studies concerning the ability of the Halstead–Reitan Battery to classify correctly schizophrenic and neurologic patients have reported conflicting results. However, examination of the characteristics of the patient samples and the statistical procedures used to classify patients suggests a possible resolution of the discrepancies. The two studies in which acute schizophrenics were studied (Fredericks & Finkel, 1978; Golden, 1977) reported high discriminability from the neurologic sample, and the lowest discriminability was reported using a sample of very long-term, institutionalized schizophrenic patients (Klonoff et al., 1970). This may reflect a lower frequency of acutal brain damage among acute than chronic schizophrenics, and/or the debilitating effects of chronicity. Goldstein and Halperin (1977) found that the long- versus short-term classification of schizophrenics yielded the highest correct classification rate using discriminant analyses of Halstead–Reitan data, with lower hit rates associated with paranoid versus nonparanoid and neurologically normal versus abnormal classifications.

Second, moderately successful discriminability was reported in two studies (Lacks et al., 1970; Levine and Feirstein, 1972) in which severe, diffusely brain-damaged dementia patients were selected for the neurologic group. In both studies, the Halstead—Reitan Impairment Index more accurately classified the neurologic than the schizophrenic sample. This may mean only that severely organic patients are neuropsychologically more impaired than schizophrenics, a conclusion that is relatively unremarkable. In these studies, as well as that of Chelune et al. (1979), the neurologic patients were not representative of the population normally encountered in clinical settings.

A third consideration involves the statistical procedures used to classify patients according to the Halstead—Reitan Battery. It is not surprising that optimized cutoffs yielded consistently higher discriminability rates than standard cutoffs; this follows on purely statistical grounds. However, it is also possible that the standard cutoffs, developed using a medical rather than a psychiatric population (Reitan, 1955), are not applicable to the schizophrenic patients. Golden (1977) is the only researcher to advance recommended cutoffs in a schizophrenic population, and these values differ considerably from those of Reitan (1955) based on a normal population.

It should be noted that Golden's (1977) cutoff scores were based on an acute schizophrenic sample, and optimal values in a chronic population might be different. In addition, these cutoff scores were designed to maximize discriminability between patients according to the diagnosis, without full consideration of possible organicity using sophisticated radiologic techniques (such as cortical atrophy measured by CT scan, lowered CT scan brain density, and decreased rCBF). Thus, they may be applicable only to the assessment of extrinsic brain damage unrelated to the schizophrenic process. New values may be needed in order to evaluate intrinsic brain damage in schizophrenics as measured by new radiologic techniques.

There was a strong tendency in the data for neurologic patients to be classified more accurately than schizophrenics. This may simply reflect the fact that schizophrenics tended to be impaired relative to a medical control group. However, it might also represent accurate labeling of some of the schizophrenics as organically impaired. Further research is needed in which assessment of subtle structural brain abnormalities in the schizophrenic samples is employed to describe the samples more accurately in terms of the criterion of neurologic deficit.

There has been one significant preliminary study in this area. Donnelly and his associates (1980) examined 15 chronic schizophrenics using the Halstead—Reitan Battery and attempted to predict the presence or absence of CT ventricular abnormality according to the criteria of Weinberger et al. (1979a). Of the 15 subjects, 12 (80%) were classified correctly, which suggests a much higher hit rate than has been achieved by the other studies described above. Although this sample is too small for widespread generalization, it clearly indicates the potential of the Halstead—Reitan Battery in a properly screened population.

LURIA – NEBRASKA NEUROPSYCHOLOGICAL
BATTERY

The Luria – Nebraska Neuropsychological Battery (LNNB) is a standardized test battery developed by Golden, Hammeke, and Purisch (1980) on the basis of the work of Luria (1966, 1973) and Christensen (1975). The Luria – Nebraska Battery has demonstrated high effectiveness in discriminating between normal and brain-damaged populations, with overall correct classification (hit) rates based upon optimal discriminant analyses of 93% (Hammeke, Golden, and Purisch, 1978), and 93% (Moses and Golden, 1979).

Validation and cross-validation studies have shown the ability of the LNNB differentiate chronic schizophrenic from brain-damaged (neurologic) patients (see Table 12-3). Purisch, Golden, and Hammeke (1978) examined the LNNB performance of 50 neurologic and 50 schizophrenic subjects who did not differ in age or education. Discriminant analysis using the 14 scale scores yielded an 88% hit rate for diagnoses of brain damage and schizophrenia, with the neurologic patients scoring significantly higher on 9 of the 14 scales.

In a cross-validation of the LNNB in a schizophrenic population, Moses and Golden (1980) found an overall hit rate of 90% using an optimized discriminant analysis of the 14 scale scores, which shrunk to 87% using the discriminant function from the Purisch et al. (1978) study. In this study, the schizophrenics were carefully screened to exclude those with positive neurologic signs of brain damage. In both experiments, the Rhythm, Receptive Speech, Memory, and Intelligence scales failed to discriminate schizophrenic from neurologic patients, and the Pathognomonic scale was the best discriminator. The Pathognomonic scale, which was originally composed of those items most sensitive to acute brain damage (Golden et al., 1979), was notably higher in the neurologic than in the schizophrenic patients. In both studies, the LNNB scale scores (excluding those 4 scales that did not discriminate between groups) were elevated to T scores of approximately 60, suggesting significant impairment relative to a normal population. However, the effectiveness of the LNNB in discriminating between neurologic and schizophrenic patients indicated that the degree of severity or the type of impairment was different in the two populations.

It must be noted that both of the schizophrenic samples employed by Purisch et al. (1978) and Moses and Golden (1980) were chronic, with an average of more than four previous hospitalizations, and significantly longer durations of illness than the neurologic groups in both studies. Thus, it appeared that institutionalization was not associated with severe impairment on the LNNB.

Table 12-3
Studies of the Discriminatory Power of the LNBB

Experiment	Schizophrenic (Sx) Sample	Neurologic Sample	Statistical Procedure	Overall Hit Rate	Sx Hit Rate	Neurologic Hit Rate
Purisch et al. (1978)	50 chronic Sx	50 mixed neurologic patients	Optomized discriminant analysis, 14 scale scores	88%	92%	84%
Moses and Golden (1980)	50 chronic Sx	50 mixed neurologic patients	Optimizeddiscriminant analysis, 14 scale scores	90%	85%	95%
			Discriminant function from Purisch et al (1978)	87%	86%	88%
Kane et. al. (1981)	23 chronic Sx	23 mixed neurologic patients	Expert clinical judgment	83%	na	*na

*na — not available.

In order to evaluate more fully the effects of institutionalization of schizophrenic patients on the LNNB, Lewis, Golden, Purisch, and Hammeke (1979) evaluated the relationship between length of hospitalization and duration of illness on LNNB scale scores. Multivariate techniques revealed no significant effects of either variable on LNNB performance, although small correlations were found between length of hospitalization and selected scale scores. The schizophrenic subjects scored significantly higher than the normal control groups of the original validation study (Golden et al., 1978) on all 14 scale scores, which again suggested significant neuropsychological impairment in the schizophrenic population.

Since impaired performance of the schizophrenic subjects did not appear to be attributable to institutionalization, Golden et al. (1980) investigated the relationships between LNNB scores and ventricular enlargement on CT scans. A multiple correlation of .72 was found between ventricular area and scaled scores, and 8 or 14 scales were significantly positively correlated with ventricular enlargement, with the Pathognomonic scale showing the highest correlation. Interestingly, these scales did not include the 4 scales that failed to discriminate schizophrenic from neurologic patients in the experiments of Purisch et al. (1978) and Moses and Golden (1980). It would appear that these 4 scales are particularly sensitive to psychotic symptoms (such as distractability) that are not associated with ventricular enlargement, although elevations on these scales were related to CT scan density effects (Golden et al., 1980). Using optimized actuarial rules, the LNNB correctly classified 85% of the schizophrenics according to the presence or absence of ventricular enlargement (Golden, 1980).

Golden concluded that in most young chronic schizophrenics, the LNNB scales are elevated because of actual brain damage rather than the effects of distractability or institutionalization. This brain damage appears to be associated with schizophrenia itself, rather than with head trauma or other extrinsic factors. Assessment of brain damage resulting from extrinsic factors in addition to schizophrenia may also be conducted using the LNNB, as long as allowance is made for the expected scale elevations in a schizophrenic population.

One study has been reported in which the Halstead—Reitan Battery and the LNNB were compared in their ability to discriminate schizophrenic from neurologic patients. Kane, Sweet Golden, Parsons, and Moses (1981) had expert clinicians blindly rate 23 mixed psychiatric (including 18 schizophrenic and 5 nonpsychotic patients) and 23 mixed neurologic protocols. The clinician using the LNNB correctly classified 83% of the protocols, and the clinician using the Halstead—Reitan Battery achieved a hit rate of 78%; this was not a significant difference. It would appear that the Halstead—Reitan Battery and the LNNB were essentially equivalent in their ability to discriminate these diagnostic groups, although it is not possible with this experimental design to evaluate the effect of the expert clinicians separately from the tests themselves since actuarial hit rates were not reported.

Conclusions

Hit rates for the classification of schizophrenic and neurologic patients have varied widely with different tests, patient samples, and methods of analysis. However, several conclusions are in order:

1. The WAIS does not appear to be a satisfactory test for assessing brain damage in schizophrenic populations. It may be helpful when used in conjunction with the Halstead–Reitan Battery, or in the (unlikely) event that premorbid WAIS levels are known.

2. The Halstead–Reitan Battery appears to discriminate schizophrenic from neurologic patients well only when the schizophrenic sample is acute (or has not been hospitalized for a long period) and when optimal cutoffs are used (Golden, 1977). This implies that subtle cerebral dysfunction in the schizophrenic population, if present, is qualitatively or quantitatively different from that of neurologic patients.

3. The Halstead–Reitan Battery cutoffs recommended by Golden (1977) require cross-validation and extension to a chronic schizophrenic population.

4. In a chronic schizophrenic population, the Halstead–Reitan Battery does not (in the studies conducted to date) discriminate schizophrenic from neurologic patients at a significant level. However, this failure may result from the deterioration of performance in chronic schizophrenics which accurately reflects structural brain impairment.

5. The LNNB appears able to discriminate neurologic from schizophrenic samples (Moses and Golden, 1980); Purisch et al., 1978) and schizophrenic samples with and without brain atrophy (Golden, 1982; Golden et al., 1980). The LNNB appears to be relatively insensitive to chronicity (Lewis et al., 1979), although more research is needed on this question.

6. Initial evidence suggests that the LNNB and Halstead–Reitan Battery yield roughly comparable clinical results in a psychiatric population (Kane, Sweet, Golden, Parsons & Moses 1981). Comparison of actuarial performance on these two comprehensive batteries is needed.

7. There is growing evidence that many schizophrenic patients show neurologic impairment on CT scans and other neuroradiologic measurement devices. These data have not been available in most studies of the discriminative ability of the above tests, indicating that the criteria for the absence of neurologic impairment in the schizophrenic samples were inadequate. It is probable that a substantial proportion of the schizophrenic patients in these samples would show CT scan evidence of atrophy or structural abnormality. This conclusion signals the need for a new research approach in which schizophrenic populations are evaluated in terms of both intrinsic and extrinsic brain damage. In this context, the neuropsychological test may be used to evaluate the interplay between neurologic and psychiatric factors in schizophrenia, rather than simply to rule out organicity in schizophrenic patients.

A second issue is the heterogeneity of schizophrenic populations. It is possible that the presence or absence of CT scan abnormalities and/or neuro-psychological impairment may reflect an important subclassification of schizo-phrenic populations. This subtyping may bear a critical relationship to the etiology or to clinical variables such as the response to medication (Wein-berger et al., 1980) and the clinical course (Haug, 1962). The basic evidence (reviewed above) showing that neurologic abnormalities are present in a substantial proportion of schizophrenics is sufficiently strong that reasearch relating these factors to etiology and clinical symptomatology must be consid-ered important avenues for further research.

We expect that the Halstead—Reitan Battery and the LNNB, will play an essential role in this research. In order for this to occur, we view as essential the development of neuropsychological norms and decision rules for discriminating brain damage resulting from intrinsic and extrinsic factors in schizophrenic populations. This approach goes far beyond the issue of simply establishing hit rates for classifying schizophrenic and brain-damaged neurolog-ic patients, an approach with which the literature has been preoccupied over the last 10—15 years (cf. Heaton et al., 1978; Malec, 1978). Initial steps in this direction have been taken with the LNNB (Golden, 1982), with some success. We believe that the employment of conjunctive neurologic—neuro-psychological techniques involving CT scan structural abnormalities, CT scan density parameters, rCBF analyses, and other advanced techniques will pro-mote further progress in this area.

Chapter 13

Neuropsychological Examination of the Affective Disorders

With Bruce N. Carpenter

Recent research has increasingly implicated the brain and neural functioning in the so-called functional disorders, especially the psychoses. Research findings in the area of the affective disorders has generally been consistent with this trend. Although we are still in the early stages of investigation of this topic, there is sufficient convergence of evidence to draw some tentative conclusions. Neuropsychological techniques have already played an important role in developing our present knowledge of the affective disorders and appear to be a promising approach for gaining greater understanding of their neural correlates.

NONNEUROPSYCHOLOGICAL EVIDENCE

Many studies which have used techniques other than neuropsychological measures have indicated abnormal brain functioning in individuals suffering from affective disorders. The studies presented here represent only a small sample of those in the area. Also, it should be remembered that although there does appear to be some convergence of evidence, it is unclear what the findings mean and whether they are reliable. In general, there are only a limited number of studies in each area, and few replications have appeared to date.

Electrophysiologic Studies

Much interest in the brain functioning of persons with affective disorders has centered on the use of the electroencephalogram (EEG) and evoked potential measures. Using power spectrum EEG, Flor-Henry (1976) found that manic-depressives, as compared to normal controls, demonstrated predominantly right temporal lobe abnormalities on various tasks. Shagass, Roemer, Straumanis, and Amadeo (1978) found that the evoked potential of depressives and manics differed from that of normals in that later evoked potential events were significantly attenuated. Abrams and Taylor (1979) compared manics, depressives, and schizophrenics on EEG abnormalities. They found that about 27% of the manics and 13% of the depressives had abnormal EEGs. About 30% of the abnormal records were classifed as having a diffuse, temporal, or parietal-occipital location, with the remaining 10% being frontal. They also found a nonsignificant trend toward lateralization of affective abnormalities to the right hemisphere and of schizophrenic abnormalities to the left hemisphere. Gruzelier and Venables (1974) and Myslobodsky and Horesh (1978) have found lateralized skin conductance abnormalities in depressives, opposite to those found in schizophrenics, which they have interpretated as indicating nondominant temporal lobe dysfunction.

Neuroradiologic Studies

Neuroradiologic research has only just begun, as most of the emphasis to date has been on schizophrenia. However, one published and one unpublished study have found enlarged cerebral ventricles in patients with affective disorders (Pearlson & Veroff, 1981; Scott, Golden, Ruedrick & Bishop, in press). Preliminary results from positron emission tomography (PET) scanning have indicated a right frontal lobe deficit in affective disorders, as have initial findings with regional cerebral blood flow (Buchsbaum, 1982; Golden, 1982). All of these results must be considered tentative at present because of the generally small samples currently available and the lack of cross-validation.

Case Studies

A number of case studies appearing in the literature have addressed the possibility of misdiagnosis. Affective symptoms may appear without organic symptoms, but seizure disorder or organic symptomatology may appear later under careful examination (e.g., Hambert & Willén, 1978; Hellekson, Buckland, & Price, 1979; Strauss, 1955). Alternatively, organic symptoms may be manifested in the absence of affective features, but treatment for depression would result in the alleviation of symptoms (e.g., Cavenar, Maltbie, & Austin, 1979). Both of these approaches fail to recognize the possibility of overlap in the two classes of disorder. A case study by Jamieson and Wells (1979) supports this possibility of a relationship between cerebral dysfunction and affective difficulties by reporting the case of a 45-year-old man who developed a manic psychosis at the same time as the appearance of several metastatic lesions. Although the tumors could not be removed, the psychosis responded to lithium treatment.

Analogue Studies

Temporal lobe epileptics have occasionally been compared to schizophrenic or manic-depressive populations because the considerable emotional disturbance seen in these epileptic patients parallels that found in schizophrenia or affective disorder. Dongier (1959) found that psychotic episodes were approximately twice as frequent in temporal lobe epilepsy as in other epilepsies. In a controlled study of psychoses in temporal lobe epilepsy, Flor-Henry (1969a,b) found that of individuals with primarily affective symptoms, 44% had a right-sided focus and only 22% had a left-sided focus; the remainder showed bilateral impairment.

DIFFERENTIATING INDIVIDUALS WITH ORGANIC VERSUS AFFECTIVE DISORDERS

It has been repeatedly demonstrated that many neuropsychological techniques used to detect organic disorders cannot effectively discriminate neurologic patients from schizophrenics. The usual reasons suggested for these failures are the inability of the measures to make fine discriminations, the generalized poor performance of schizophrenics on most measures, the possibility that schizophrenics do have organic impairment, or some combination of these reasons. There have been very few attempts to use neuropsychological measures to differentiate neurologic from affective patients. Typically, it is expected that a generalized deficit plays less of a role in impairing the performance of affectives compared to schizophrenics. Performance deficits tend to be more specific and less severe in affective disorders than in schizophrenia, except perhaps in more severe, psychotic affective cases.

Donnelly, Dent, Murphy, and Mignone (1972) compared temporal lobe epileptics and depressives or manic-depressives on subtests from the Halstead–Reitan Battery. Most of the affectives had been diagnosed as psychotic. Only the Category, Tactual Performance, Seashore Rhythm, Speech Perception, and Tapping tests were administered. A cutoff score (not given) was applied to each of the 7 scores derived from these measures, with scores above the cutoff considered characteristic of brain damage. Scores above the cutoff contributed to an Impairment Index score for each subject, which could range from .00 to 1.00, with scores above .50 considered characteristic of brain damage. It was found that 69% of the affectives and 54% of the epileptics scored in the mild to severe brain damage range. The average Impairment Index was .59 for each group. It appears, then, that this global measure of brain dysfunction has difficulty in differentiating severely disturbed affectives from temporal lobe epileptics, who generally show less neuropathology than other neurologic patients.

Watson, Davis, and Gasser (1978) compared a mixed group of neurologic patients and a mixed group of depressives on several ability measures and on the Minnesota Multiphasic Personality Inventory (MMPI) Depression Scale. The ability measures included the Benton Visual Retention Test, the Halstead Category Test, the Smith Symbol—Digit Modalities Test, Gorham Proverbs, and the Wechsler Adult Intelligence Scale (WAIS) Digit Span, Block Design, and Object Assembly subtests. They found that initially the organics were more impaired on several tests including Category, Symbol—Digit Modalities, Gorham Proverbs, Block Design, and Object Assembly tests, and less deviant on the MMPI Depression Scale. However, after subjects were excluded to equate the groups for age, education, and estimated intelligence, all differences on ability measures became nonsignificant, leaving the groups differing only on the Depression Scale. Thus, the expected finding emerged that depressives report symptoms characteristic of depression more than do neurologic patients. Unfortunately, Watson et al. did not report whether or not the neuropsychological scores of the depressives fell within the ranges generally considered characteristic of brain damage.

Orme, Lee, and Smith (1964) compared a mixed organic group to several psychiatric groups on three measures that they believed should distinguish the brain-damaged patients from others. The measures were the Modified Word Learning Test, which measures trials to criterion in learning new words; a design recall test, in which the subject must reproduce from memory several briefly exposed Bender—Gestalt figures; and a verbal/nonverbal discrepancy measure modeled after "hold—don't hold" indices, which consists of Mill Hill Vocabulary Scale scores minus Colored Progressive Matrices scores. The cutoff for the modified Word Learning Test classified 81% of brain-damaged patients as brain-damaged and 23% of melancholics as brain-damaged, whereas the cutoff for the design recall measure correctly classified 83% of brain-damaged patients, but misclassified 40% of the melancholics as brain-damaged. Only chronic schizophrenics had more misclassifications on both measures. On the verbal/nonverbal discrepency score, only slightly more neurologic patients (53%) than melancholics (40%) had positive scores, which were assumed to suggest brain damage. Although these measures did tend to differentiate the neurologic patients from the psychiatric groups other than the schizophrenic group, there were many false-positive cases of brain damage in the melancholic group, especially on the measures of nonverbal abilities. The percentage of melancholics classified as brain-damaged tended to fall about midway between the number of schizophrenics and the number of persons from other psychiatric groups classified as brain-damaged.

Summary

Researchers who have attempted to distinguish accurately between brain-damaged patients and affectives have generally been unable to do so. Although the results have been variable, it appears that nonverbal tasks are least suited for this discrimination and that global measures, such as the Impairment Index of the Halstead—Reitan Battery, are also poor discriminators. This difficulty with global indices may be due in part to the inclusion of nonverbal measures. However, the elimination of such measures greatly reduces the number of tools available to the neuropsychologist, as they currently play a central role in neuropsychological assessment. These findings across measures and studies indicating the similarity between brain-damaged patients and affectives add to the data supporting organic deficits in affective disorders, although they do not rule out alternative explanations.

THE NATURE OF NEUROPSYCHOLOGICAL DEFICITS IN AFFECTIVE DISORDERS

Most researchers have been less concerned with the practical aspects of diagnosis and have examined instead the nature of the deficits seen in affective disorders. In general, these studies have compared affectives with normal control groups and have focused on the meaning of the deficits in terms of the disorder.

Taylor, Greenspan, and Abrams (1979) compared the functioning of schizophrenics, affectives, and normals on Reitan's modification of the Halstead—Wepman Aphasia Screening Test. The affectives made significantly more total errors than controls, although less than the schizophrenics. After classifying items according to the area of the brain primarily involved in the task, they found that affectives made most of their errors on items requiring functioning of the nondominant parietal area and, to a lesser degree, the frontal areas. However, the affectives did not make more of such errors than did the schizophrenics. The affective group's performance was like that of normals for items involving the dominant temporal/temporal-parietal and dominant parietal areas.

Weckowicz, Tam, Mason, and Bay (1978) compared depressed and nondepressed female psychiatric patients on unspeeded power tests of intelligence and on speeded psychomotor tests. They found that the depressed subjects were significantly impaired on the speeded tests, but that the two groups did not differ on the power tests.

Kronfol, Hamsher, Digre, and Waziri (1978) examined the functioning of 18 depressed patients prior to electroconvulsive therapy. Using several performance measures that reportedly assess the functioning of primarily one hemisphere, such as a sentence repetition test and the Judgment of Line Orientation Test, they examined the number of defective performances by their depressed patients. Their criterion for defective performance was that less than 4% of the population of nonpsychiatric medical patients free of neurologic problems scored at or below the cutoff. They found that their depressives had three times as many defective performances on tasks considered primarily right hemisphere as they did on tasks considered primarily left hemisphere, and that over half of the subjects had such defective performances on right hemisphere tasks.

Probably the most complete neuropsychological investigation of affective disorders to date has been done by Flor-Henry and Yeudall (in press), comparing manic-depressives (including schizoaffectives) and schizophrenics. This study is essentially an extension and amplification of a previous study by Flor-Henry (1976), which found essentially the same results. In the Flor-Henry and Yeudall study, subjects were administered the Halstead—Reitan Battery, the WAIS, and several additional tests. Although the schizophrenics were significantly more impaired than the affectives overall, the affectives had considerable deficits, primarily on nondominant hemisphere tasks. However, it was not uncommon to find mild dominant hemisphere deficits for the affectives as well. In comparing the performance of right-handed subjects on frontal—temporal lobe tasks, experienced neuropsychologists found that all but 1 of 49 affectives had scores in the brain-damaged range, and that about 90% had performance deficits indicating predominantly right hemisphere dysfunction. None of the affectives were classified as having predominantly left hemisphere dysfunction, but nearly all of the schizophrenics were so classified. When only depressives were compared to a normal control group, they were found to be impared on Trails B and Trails A + B, Memory for Designs, Tactual Performance Test (TPT) Localization and Memory, Purdue Pegboard, and nonpreferred hand Finger Oscillation, strongly indicating dysfunction of the nondominant frontal—temporal lobe system. Manics, as compared to controls, were impaired on both the preferred and nonpreferred hands for Finger Localization, Finger Oscillation, TPT, and Purdue Pegboard. They also showed deficits on Memory for Designs and TPT Localization and Memory. Thus, deficits in manics appear to be somewhat more bilateral and extensive than those in depressives, even though the groups were not significantly different from each other on the neuropsychological measures. These differences between affectives and controls remained essentially unchanged when the effects of age and Full Scale IQ were controlled by analysis of covariance.

In a study of dichotic listening, Yozawitz, Bruder, Sutton, Sharpe, Gurland, Fleiss, and Costa (1979) found that a mixed affective group had more trouble separating two clicks presented closely together when the second click was presented to the left ear than when it was presented to the right ear. That is, they tended to *suppress* the stimulus to the nondominant hemisphere. This asymmetry is similar to that found in controls with right temporal lobe lesions whereas schizophrenics and normal controls showed no such asymmetries.

Schweitzer (1979) studied the lateral eye movements of a group of psychotic depressives. He found that this group made an excessive number of eye movements to the left, as compared to controls, whereas schizophrenics were excessive in the opposite direction. Evidence appears to support somewhat the hypothesis that lateral eye movements in a particular direction during a reflective task tend to indicate greater relative activity of the hemisphere contralateral to the direction of eye movement. Hence, Schweitzer interprets his results as indicative of overactivation and dysfunction of the right hemisphere of psychotic depressives.

Taylor, Abrams, and Gaztanaga (1975) compared manic-depressives and schizophrenics on the Aphasia Screening Test and the Trail-Making Tests. They reported that for the affective group, 46% on Trails A and 71% on Trails B had abnormal speed, and 4% on Trails A and 38% on Trails B had abnormal performance. The schizophrenics performed slightly but not significantly worse than the affectives. On the Aphasia Screening Test, 13% of the affectives had abnormal performance, compared to 67% of the schizophrenics; this is a significant difference. For the Aphasia Screening Test, the affectives missed only 1% of the dominant hemisphere items and only 3% of the nondominant hemisphere items. However, most nondominant hemisphere items on this measure tend to depend primarily on functioning of more posterior areas of the brain.

Several studies (Covi, Lipman, Alarcon, & Smith, 1976; Donnelly & Waldman, 1977, 1978) have found either a significant or a nearly significant relationship between intelligence (IQ) and response to imipramine or lithium carbonate in affective patients. Apparently, responders to these medications tend to have lower IQs than do nonresponders, although IQ seems to be a poor predictor of responsivity to these drugs.

In a study of factors affecting performance on the Halstead–Reitan Battery in middle-aged, normally functioning individuals, Dorosh (1978) found that scores on Zung's Self-rating Depression Scale were significantly correlated with Impairment Index scores. He also concluded that the results offered no support for a view of right hemisphere deficits in depressives, but his subjects were not clinically depressed.

Summary

In the few reports published to date, researchers have consistently found affectives to have performance deficits on neuropsychological measures. Depending on the measure used, affectives have typically performed better than schizophrenics. Most deficits for affectives appear on tasks that reportedly measure primarily right or nondominant hemisphere functioning. At the same time, dominant hemisphere tasks frequently show deficits in affectives, although these are usually milder than the nondominant hemisphere deficits. Impaired performance on nondominant hemisphere tasks is not limited to affectives, however; schizophrenics appear to have nondominant deficits as severe or nearly as severe as those of affectives, although the major deficits in schizophrenia are on dominant hemisphere tasks. Various reviews of the literature, which have also considered findings not based solely on neuropsychological measures, have also tended to conclude that a right hemisphere focus of impairment exists for affectives and a left hemisphere focus of impairment exists for schizophrenics (Newlin, Carpenter, & Golden, 1981; Newlin & Golden, 1980; Wexler, 1980).

Although they are less systematic in approaching the topic, the studies appear to suggest that the focus of impairment in the brain tends to be more anterior. This is not surprising, considering the marked emotional component seen in many injuries to the right frontal—temporal lobe area. Thus, deficits tend to be subtle and related to organization, coordinated responding, and speed of performance, with some impairment of tactile—motor performance. There is also some very tentative evidence that deficits seen in mania are less lateralized than those seen in depression. Two studies by Taylor and his collegues (Taylor, Abrams, & Gaztanaga, 1975; Taylor, Greenspan, & Abrams, 1979) have emphasized parietal dysfunction, but this could be due, at least in part, to the limited measures they used.

METHODOLOGIC AND INTERPRETIVE CONSIDERATIONS

Several considerations are important in evaluating these studies and designing future ones. Comparison across studies is difficult because of the variability in the way subject populations are defined. Some researchers have used rigid criteria, whereas others have accepted diagnoses of psychiatrists or used other nonstandard criteria. The populations studied are often quite mixed, including the mixing of schizoaffectives with affectives (Flor-Henry & Yeudall, in press). Not only does this make comparison of studies difficult, but evidence suggests that various ways of defining diagnostic subdivisions may be meaningful for predicting differences in patterns of neurologic and neuropsychological deficts (e.g., Flor-Henry & Yeudall, in press; Kadrmas & Winokur, 1979; Sandel & Alcorn, 1980; Shagass, 1975). It is apparent that in general affectives show impaired performance on neuropsychological measures. The greater refinement and understanding of these deficits that is now needed will likely occur only as attention is given to subject characteristics.

This same care must be given to the selection of neurologic patient samples. Whether or not affectives have deficits similar to those of brain-damaged patients depends very much on the types of brain-damaged patients considered, simply because performance varies with the location and nature of the brain lesion. Thus, failure to find similarity of performance between affectives and brain-damaged patients with left posterior lesions would not be too surprising, given the currently available evidence. The demonstration that affectives have deficits similar to those of brain-damaged patients with right hemisphere lesions but not similar to those of patients with left hemisphere lesions offers considerably more information than a comparison with a mixed brain-damaged group.

The selection of an appropriate control group is also important. Comparison of affectively disturbed patients to schizophrenics or other psychiatric populations alone is probably inappropriate because it may be unclear whether findings are due to impairment of the affective group or the other psychiatric control group or both. Many neuropsychological measures have normative data which can facilitate interpretation, but ratings based solely on such norms are usually less informative than comparisons to a normal control group.

The selection of appropriate neuropsychological measures is another important consideration. One can find that affectives do or do not appear impaired, depending on the measures one selects. Currently, it seems nearly as important to know the measures on which affectives perform well as it is to know those on which they perform poorly. This is because the pattern of performance on a variety of measures, especially within subjects rather than across studies, will best clarify the nature of the deficits and what they mean. Most valuable will be studies with carefully (and probably somewhat narrowly) defined populations, employing multiple measures that are logically chosen to answer specific questions. Preferably, the measures selected for use will be those that have already been adequately researched and related to neurologic functioning, so that conclusions can be based on previous empirical findings.

As we make greater advances in this area, we will probably focus on those deficits that are most evident. Care must be taken to ensure that these differential deficits represent real differences in abilities and not just differences in the effectiveness of the measures used to discriminate true abilities. Apparent differences in various deficits can be due to differences in the measures rather than in the abilities the measures are intended to assess. (For a complete discussion of this methodology, see Chapman and Chapman, 1973.)

Another source of confusion is that studies have addressed the the issue of neuropsychological performance in affectives with very different questions in mind. Traditionally, it has been asked what measures can differentiate functional from brain-damaged patients. Failures generally have been considered to be due to poor discrimination of the measure or misdiagnosis of the patient. Only recently has much attention been paid to the possibility that some affectives may have subtle neurologic impairment. The fact is that organic-like deficits in performance can be due either to neurologic impairment in affectives or to the inability of the measure to control for other patient characteristics that lower the performance level, such as low motivation. Rather than simply continuing to demonstrate a lowered level of performance, we must begin to rule out alternative reasons for it.

Some of the data appear to suggest that differences between groups can be due to only certain neuropsychological deficits. Perhaps the presence of certain types of performance can provide valuable clues about how best to divide affectives into meaningful subcategories. There is already some evidence that a measure as global as IQ has some relationship to treatment. This is an area that neuropsychology needs to address.

Another important question that has rarely been asked is whether any neurologic impairment is causal in affective disorders, whether any neurologic impairment is a result of an affective disturbance, or whether both the disorder and the neurologic deficit are caused by some other variable. Although attempting to answer such a question is premature until the presence of neurologic impairment is better established, neuropsychological measures appear to be promising tools for addressing preliminary questions about cognitive–behavioral changes over time and over treatments.

CONCLUSION

Although this area of research is still very new, some tentative conclusions appear warranted:

1. Affectives have lowered performance on many neuropsychological measures. This makes them difficult to distinguish from many brain-damaged patients, especially those who are mildly impaired.
2. The performance deficits of affectives occur primarily on tasks considered dependent on nondominant, frontal–temporal lobe functioning. However, mild impairment on other tasks is not uncommon: Some evidence suggests parietal lobe involvement, but this remains to be demonstrated using other measures. Thus, performance on tasks requiring speed, organization, higher spatial functioning, and sensorimotor abilities of the nonpreferred body side are frequently impaired.
3. Affectives perform most like brain-damaged patients on tasks measuring anterior, nondominant hemispheric functioning. The affectives' performance on these measures is generally better than that of brain-damaged patients but worse than that of normals, depending possibly on the makeup of the neurologic group.
4. Schizophrenics appear to be more impaired than affectives on many neuropsychological measures, but on measures of nondominant, anterior brain functioning, the two groups appear to be about equally impaired.
5. It is currently unclear whether these performance deficits in affectives actually represent neurologic impairment. The convergence of evidence, including data from fields outside of neuropsychology, favors such an interpretation.

It is expected that interest in this area of overlap between neuropsychology and psychopathology will continue to grow, and that any neurologic correlates with the affective disorders will become clearer. Neuropsychology has the potential to play an important role in the progress made in understanding the affective disorders.

References

Abel, E. L. Fetal alcohol syndrome: Behavioral teratology. *Psychological Bulletin*, 1980, *87*, 29–50.

Abrams, R., & Taylor, M. A. Differential EEG patterns in affective disorder and schizophrenia. *Archives of General Psychiatry*, 1979, *36*, 1355–1358.

Adam, N. Disruption of memory functions associated with general anesthetics. In J. F. Kihlstrom & F. J. Evans (Eds.), *Functional disorders of memory*. Hillsdale, N.J.: Lawrence Erlbaum, 1979.

Adler, A. Mental symptoms following head injury. *Archives of Neurology and Psychiatry*, 1945, *53*, 34–43.

Aita, J. A. Follow-up study of men with penetrating injury to the brain. *Archives of Neurology and Psychiatry*, 1948, *59*, 511–516.

Albert, M. S., Butters, N., & Brandt, J. Patterns of remote memory in amnesic and demented patients. *Archives of Neurology*, 1981, *38*, 495–500.

Akesson, H. O. A population study of senile and arteriosclerotic psychoses. *Human Heredity*, 1969, *19*, 546–566.

Alcohol and the brain. *British Medical Journal*, 1976, *1*, 1168.

Allen, I. M. A clinical study of tumors involving the occipital lobe. *Brain*, 1930, *53*, 194–243.

Allen, R. P., Faillace, L. A., & Reynolds, D. M. Recovery of memory functioning in alcoholics following prolonged alcohol intoxication. *Journal of Nervous and Mental Disease*, 1971, *153*, 417–423.

Allman, L. R., Taylor, H. A., & Nathan, P. E. Group drinking during stress: Effects on drinking behavior, affect, and psychopathology. *American Journal of Psychiatry*, 1972, *129*, 669–678.

Alpert, M., Rubenstein, H., & Kesselman, M. Asymmetry of information processing in hallucinators and non-hallucinators. *Journal of Nervous and Mental Disease*, 1976, *162*, 258–265.

Alter, M., Masland, R. L., Kurtzke, J. F., & Reed, D. M. Proposed definitions and classifications of epilepsy for epidemiological purposes. In M. Alter & W. A. Hauser (Eds.), The epidemiology of epilepsy: A workshop. National Institute of Neurological Disease and Stroke, Mongraph No. 14. Washington, D.C. U.S. Dept. of Health, Education, and Welfare, 1972.

Alvord, E. C. The pathology of parkinsonism. Part II. An interpretation with special reference to other changes in the aging brain. In F. H. McDowell & C. H. Markham (Eds.), Recent advances in Parkinson's disease (Part II). Oxford: Blackwell, 1971.

Alzheimer, A. Über eine eigenartige erkrankung der hirnrinde. Centraeblatt Nervenheilk Psychiatry, 1907, 18, 177.

Alzheimer, A. Uber eine eigenartige Erkrankung der Hirnrinde. Allegemeine Zeitschrift fur Psychiatrie, 1907, 64, 146−148.

Alzheimer, A. Über eigenartige Krankeirsfalle des spateren Alters. Zeitschrift fur die Gesamte Neurologie und Psychiatrie, 1911, 4, 356−385.

Amark, C. A study in alcoholism: Clinical, social-psychiatric and genetic investigations. Acta Psychiatrica et Neurologica, 1951, 70, 1−283.

American Psychiatric Association. Diagnostic and statistical manual of mental disorders (3rd ed.). Washington, D.C.: American Psychiatric Association, 1980.

Aminoff, M. J., Marshall, J., Smith, E. M., & Wyke, M. A. Pattern of intellectual impairment in Huntington's chorea. Psychological Medicine, 1975, 5, 169−172.

Ariel, R. N., Golden, C. J., Berg, R. A., Quaife, M. A., Dirksen, J. W., Forsell, T. Wilson, J., & Graber, B. Regional cerebral blood flow in schizophrenia with the 133-xenon inhalation method. Archives of General Psychiatry (in press).

Aring, C. D. Observations on multiple sclerosis and conversion hysteria. Brain, 1965, 88, 663−674.

Asso, D. WAIS scores in a group of parkinsonian patients. British Journal of Psychiatry, 1969, 115, 555−556.

Ayers, J. L., Templer, D. I., Ruff, C. F., & Barthlow, V. L. Trail Making Test improvement in abstinent alcoholics. Journal of Studies on Alcohol, 1978, 39, 1627−1629.

Baddeley, A. D., & Warrington, E. K. Amnesia and the distinction between long- and short-term memory. Journal of Verbal Learning and Verbal Behavior, 1970, 9, 176−189.

Bahzin, E. G., Wasserman, L. I., & Jonkonogii, I. M. Auditory hallucinations and left temporal lobe pathology. Neuropsychologia, 1975, 13, 481−487.

Bailey, W., Hustmeyer, F., & Kristofferson, A. Alcoholism, brain damage, and perceptual dependence. Quarterly Journal of Studies on Alcohol, 1961, 22, 387−393.

Ballenger, J. C., Goodwin, F. K., Major, L. F., & Brown, G. L. Alcohol and central serotonin metabolism in man. Archives of General Psychiatry, 1979, 36, 224−227.

Barron, S. A., Jacobs, L., & Kinkel, W. R. Changes in size of normal lateral ventricles during aging determined by computerized tomography. Neurology, 1976, 26, 1011−1013.

Barth, J. T., Sandler, H. M., & Anchor, K. N. Cerebral dysfunction and self-concept in chronic alcoholics. Clinical Neuropsychology, 1980, 2, 28−32.

Bauer, R. W., & Johnson, D. E. The question of deterioration in alcoholism. Journal of Consulting Psychology, 1957, 21, 296.

Bean, K. L., & Karazievich, G. O. Psychological test results of three stages of alcoholism treatment. *Journal of Studies on Alcohol*, 1975, *36*, 838–852.

Bear, D. The significance of behavioral change in temporal lobe epilepsy. *McLean Hospital Journal*, special issue, June 1977, 9.

Bear, D., & Fedio, P. Quantitative analysis of interictal behavior in temporal lobe epilepsy. *Archives of General Neurology*, 1977, *34*, 454–467.

Beatty, P. A., & Gange, J. J. Neuropsychological aspects of multiple sclerosis. *Journal of Nervous and Mental Diseases*, 1977, *164*, 42–50.

Beaumont, J. G., & Dimond, S. S. Brain disconnection and schizophrenia. *British Journal of Psychiatry*, 1973, *123*, 661–662.

Beck, E., Daniel, P. M., Gajdusek, D. C., & Gibbs, C. J. Similarities and differences in the pattern of the pathological changes in scraple, kuru, experimental kuru and subacute presenile polioencephalopathy. In C. W. M. Wittey, J. T. Hughes, & F. O. MacCallum (Eds.), *Virus diseases and the nervous system*. Oxford: Blackwell, 1969.(a)

Beck, E., Daniel, P.M., Matthews, W.B., Stevens, D.L., Alpers, M.D., Asher, D.M., Gajdusek, D.C., & Gibbs, C.J. Creutzfeld-Jakob disease: The neuropathology of a transmission experiment. *Brain*, 1969, *92*, 699–716. (b)

Bennett, A. E. Diagnosis of the intermediate stage of alcoholic brain disease. *Journal of the American Medical Association*, 1960, *172*, 1143–1146.

Bennett, A. E. Treatment of brain damage in alcoholism. *Current Psychiatric Therapies*, 1967, *7*, 142–146.

Bennett, A. E., Doi, L. T., & Mowery, G. L. The value of electroencephalography in alcoholism. *Journal of Nervous and Mental Disease*, 1956, *124*, 27–32.

Bennett, A. E., Mowery, G. L., & Fort, J. L. Brain damage from chronic alcoholism: The diagnosis of an intermediate stage of alcoholic brain disease. *American Journal of Psychiatry*, 1960, *116*, 705–711.

Benson, K., Cohen, M., & Zarcone, V., Jr. REM Sleep time and digit span impairment in alcoholics. *Journal of Studies on Alcohol*, 1978, *39*, 488–498.

Benton, A. *Aspects of the Neuropsychology of Aging*. Paper presented at the meeting of the American Psychological Association, Los Angeles, August, 1981.

Berg, R. A., & Golden, C. J. Identification of neuropsychological deficits in epilepsy using the Luria–Nebraska Neuropsychological Battery. *Journal of Consulting and Clinical Psychology*, 1981, *49*, 745–747.

Berglund, M., & Ingvar, D. H. Cerebral blood flow and its regional distribution in alcoholism and in Korsakoff's psychosis. *Journal of Studies on Alcohol*, 1976, *37*, 586–597.

Berglund, M., & Leijonquist, H. Prediction of cerebral dysfunction in alcoholics. *Journal of Studies on Alcohol*, 1978, *39*, 1968–1974.

Berglund, M., Leijonquist, H., & Horlen, M. Prognostic significance and reversibility of cerebral dysfunction in alcoholics. *Journal of Studies on Alcohol*, 1977, *38*, 1761–1770.

Berglund, M., & Sonesson, B. Personality impairment in alcoholism: Its relation to regional cerebral blood flow and psychometric performance. *Journal of Studies on Alcohol*, 1976, *37*, 298–310.

Bergman, H., & Agren, G. Cognitive style and intellectual performance in relation to the progress of alcoholism. *Quarterly Journal of Studies on Alcohol*, 1974, *35*, 1242–1255.

Bertera, J. H., & Parsons, O. A. Impaired visual search in alcoholics. *Alcoholism: Clinical and Experimental Research*, 1978, *2*, 9–14.

Bingley, T. Mental symptoms in temporal lobe epilepsy and temporal lobe glioma. *Acta Psychiatrica et Neurologica Scandinavica*, 1958, supplement *120*, 1–151.

Bird, E. D., & Iverson, L. L. (1974) Huntington's chorea—postmortem measurement of glutamic acid decarboxylase, acetyl-transferase and dopamine in basal ganglia. *Brain*, 1974, *97*, 457–472.

Bird, E. D., MacKay, A. V. P., Rayner, C. N., & Iverson, L. L. Reduced glutamic-acid decarboxylase activity of post-morten brain in Huntington's chorea. *Lancet*, 1973, *1*, 1090–1092.

Birkett, D. P. The psychiatric differentiation of senility and arteriosclerosis. *British Journal of Psychiatry*, 1972, *120*, 321–325.

Birnbaum, I. M., & Parker, E. S. Acute effects of alcohol on storage and retrieval. In I. M. Birnbaum & E. S. Parker (Eds.), *Alcohol and human memory*. Hillsdale, N.J.: Lawrence Erlbaum, 1977.

Birnbaum, I. M., Parker, E. S., Hartley, J. T., & Noble, E. P. Alcohol and memory: Retrieval processes. *Journal of Verbal Learning and Verbal Behavior*, 1978, *17*, 325–336.

Black, R. F., Hoffman, P. L., & Tabakoff, B. Receptor-mediated dopaminergic function after ethanol withdrawal. *Alcoholism: Clinical and Experimental Research*, 1980, *4*, 294–297.

Blessed, G., Tomlinson, B. E., & Roth, M. The association between quantitative measures of dementia and of senile change in the grey matter of elderly subjects. *British Journal of Psychiatry*, 1968, *114*, 797–811.

Blumer, D. Temporal lobe epilepsy and its psychiatric significance. In D. F. Benson & D. Blumer (Eds.), *Psychiatric aspects of neurologic disease*. New York: Grune & Stratton, 1975.

Blumer, D. Treatment of patients with seizure disorder referred because of psychiatric complications. *McLean Hospital Journal*, Special Issue, June 1977, 53.

Blusewicz, M. J. *Neuropsychological correlates of chronic alcoholism and aging*. Unpublished doctoral dissertation, Pennsylvania State University, 1975.

Blusewicz, M. J., Dustman, R. E., Schenkenberg, R., & Beck, E. C. Neuropsychological correlates of chronic alcoholism and aging. *Journal of Nervous and Mental Disease*, 1977, *165*, 345–355.

Boeke, P. E. Some remarks about alcohol dementia in clinically-treated alcoholics. *British Journal of Addiction*, 1970, *65*, 173–180.

Boklage, C. E. Schizophrenia, brain asymmetry development, and twinning: Cellular relationship with etiological and possibly prognostic implications. *Biological Psychiatry*, 1977, *12*, 19–35.

Boll, T. S., Heaton, R., & Reitan, R. Neuropsychological and emotional correlates of Huntington's disease. *Journal of Nervous and Mental Diseases*, 1974, *158*, 61–69.

Bolt, J. M. W. Huntington's chorea in the West of Scotland. *British Journal of Psychiatry*, 1970, *116*, 259–270.

Bolter, J. G., & Hannon, R. Cerebral damage associated with alcoholism: A re-examination. *Psychological Record*, 1980, *30*, 165–179. (a).

Bolter, J. G., & Hannon, R. *A neuropsychological examination of localization of brain damage in early and late stage alcoholics*. Paper presented to the annual meeting of the International Neuropsychological Society, San Francisco, January 1980. (b).

Bondareff, W., Baldy, R., & Levy, R. Quantitative computed tomography in senile dementia. *Archives of General Psychiatry*, 1981, *38*, 1365–1369.

Botez, M. I., & Wertheim, N. Expressive aphasia and amnesia following right frontal lesion in a right-handed man. *Brain*, 1959, *82*, 186–202.

Bowen, D. M., Smith, C. B., & Davison, A. N. Molecular changes in senile dementia. *Brain*, 1973, *96*, 849–856.

Bowen, D. M., White, P., Flack, R. H. A., Smith, C. B., & Davison, A. N. Brain decarboxylase activities as indices of pathological change in senile dementia. *Lancet*, 1974, *1*, 1247–1249.

Bowman, K. M., Goodhart, R., & Jolliffe, N. Observations on the role of vitamin B[1] in the etiology and treatment of Korsakoff psychosis. *Journal of Nervous and Mental Disease*, 1939, *90*, 569–575.

Brian, W. R. Critical review: Disseminated sclerosis. *Quarterly Journal of Medicine*, 1930, *23*, 343–391.

Brian, W. R. *Diseases of the nervous system* (5th ed.). New York: Oxford University Press, 1955.

Brewer, C. Alcohol and the brain. *British Medical Journal*, 1976, *1*, 1468–1469.

Brewer, C., & Perett, L. Brain damage due to alcohol consumption: An air-encephalographic, psychometric and electroencephalographic study. *British Journal of Addiction*, 1971, *66*, 170–182.

Brinkman, M. A., Sarwar, M., Levin, H. S., & Morris, H. H. Quantitative indexes of computed tomography in dementia and normal aging. *Radiology*, 1981, *138*, 89–92.

Brownell, B, & Hughes, J. T. The distribution of plaques in the cerebrum in multiple sclerosis. *Journal of Neurology, Neurosurgery, and Psychiatry*, 1962, *25*, 315–320.

Brozoski, T. J., Brown, R. M., Rosvold, H. E., & Goldman, P. S. Cognitive deficit caused by regional depletion of dopamine in prefrontal cortex of rhesus monkey. *Science*, 1979, *205*, 929–931.

Bruyn, G. W. Huntington's chorea—historical, clinical and laboratory synopsis. In P. J. Vinken, & G. W. Bruyn (Eds.), *Handbook of clinical neurology* (Vol. 6). Amsterdam: North Holland, 1968.

Bryant, L. R., Eiseman, B., Spencer, F. C., & Lieber, A. Frequency of extracranial cerebrovascular disease in patients with chronic psychosis. *New England Journal of Medicine*, 1965, *272*, 12–17.

Burnett, G. B., & Reading, H. W. The pharmacology of disulfiram in the treatment of alcoholism. *British Journal of Addiction*, 1970, *65*, 281–288.

Buchsbaum, M. *Positron Emission Tomography*. Paper presented at the Laterality Conference, Banff, 1982.

Busch, E. Psychical symptoms in neurosurgical disease. *Acta Psychiatrica-Neurologica Scandinavica*, 1940, *15*, 257–290.

Butler, R. N. The National Institutes of Mental Health study. In R. Katzman, R. D. Terry, & K. L. Bick (Eds.), *Alzheimer's disease: Senile dementia and related disorders (aging)* (Vol. 7). New York: Raven Press, 1978.

Butters, N. Amnesic disorders. In K. M. Heilman & E. Valenstein (Eds.) *Clinical Neuropsychology*. New York: Oxford University Press, 1979.

Butters, N., & Cermak, L. S. The role of cognitive factors in the memory disorder of alcoholic patients with the Korsakoff syndrome. *Annals of the New York Academy of Sciences*, 1974, *233*, 61–75.

Butters, N., & Cermak, L. S. Some analysis of amnesic syndrome in brain damaged patients. In K. Pribram & R. Isaacson (Eds.), *The hippocampus*. New York: Plenum Press, 1975.

Butters, N., & Cermak, L. S. Neuropsychological studies of alcoholic Korsakoff patients. In G. Goldstein & C. Neuringer (Eds.), *Empirical studies of alcoholism*. Cambridge, Mass.: Ballinger/Lippincott, 1976.

Butters, N., & Cermak, L. S. *Alcoholic Korsakoff's syndrome: An information processing approach to amnesia*. New York: Academic Press, 1980.

Butters, N., Cermak, L. S., Montogmery, K., & Adinolfi, A. Some comparisons of the memory and visuoperspective deficits of chronic alcoholics and patients with Korsakoff's disease. *Alcoholism: Clinical and Experimental Research*, 1977, *1*, 73−80.

Butters, N., Cermak, L. S., & Sax, D. A comparison of the information processing deficits of patients with Huntington's chorea and Korsakoff's syndrome. *Cortex*, 1976, *12*, 134−144.

Butters, N., Sax, D., Montgomery, K., & Tarlow, S. Comparison of the neuropsychological deficits associated with early and advanced Huntington's disease. *Archives of Neurology*, 1978, *35*, 585−589.

Butters, N., Tarlow, S., Cermak, L., & Sax, D. A comparison of the information processing deficits of patients with Huntington's chorea and Korsakoff's syndrome. *Cortex*, 1976, *12*, 134−144.

Cala, L. A., Jones, B., Mastaglia, F. L., & Wiley, B. Brain atrophy and intellectual impairment in heavy drinkers—a clinical, psychometric and computerized tomography study. *Australian and New Zealand Journal of Medicine*, 1978, *8*, 147−153.

Calahan, D. *Problem drinkers: A national survey*. San Francisco: Jossey-Bass, 1970.

Cannon, W. G., Dustman, R. C., Beck, E. C., & Schenkenberg, T. *Cortical evoked responses of young normal, young alcoholic and elderly normal individuals*. Paper presented at the annual meeting of the Western Psychological Association, Sacramento, April 1975.

Canter, A. Direct and indirect measures of psychological deficit in multiple sclerosis. *Journal of General Psychology*, 1951, *44*, 3−35.

Carlen, P. L., Wilkinson, A., & Kiraly, L. T. Dementia in alcoholics: A longitudinal study including some reversible aspects. *Neurology*, 1976, *26*, 355. (Abstract)

Carlen, P. L., Wilkinson, A., Singh, R., Rankin, J. G., & Whiteside, E. Alcoholic organic brain syndrome: Sensitive indicators of cerebral damage and later reversability. *Alcoholism: Clinical and Experimental Research*, 1977, *1*, 163. (Abstract)

Carlen, P. L., Wortzman, G., Holgate, R. C., Wilkinson, D. A., & Rankin, J. G. Reversible cerebral atrophy in recently abstinent chronic alcoholics measured by computerized tomography scans. *Science*, 1978, *200*, 1076−1078.

Carlsson, A., & Winblad, B. Influence of age and time interval between death and autopsy on dopamine and 3-methoxytyramine levels in human basal ganglia. *Journal of Neural Transmission*, 1976, *38*, 271−276.

Carlsson, C., Claeson, L. E., & Petterson, L. Psychometric signs of cerebral dysfunction in alcoholics. *British Journal of Addiction*, 1973, *68*, 83−86.

Carney, M. W. P. Serum folate values in 423 psychiatric patients. *British Medical Journal*, 1967, *4*, 512−516.

Carney, M. W. P., & Sheffield, B. F. Associations of subnormal serum folate and vitamin B^{12} values and effects of replacement therapy. *Journal of Nervous and Mental Disease*, 1970, *150*, 404−412.

Carr, S. Interhemispheric transfer of stereognostic information in chronic schizophrenics. *British Journal of Psychiatry*, 1980, *136*, 53–58.

Cavenar, J. O., Maltbie, A. A., & Austin, L. Depression simulating organic brain disease. *American Journal of Psychiatry*, 1979, *136*, 521–523.

Celesia, G. G., & Wanamaker, W. M. Psychiatric disturbances in Parkinson's disease. *Diseases of the Nervous System*, 1972, *33*, 577–585.

Cermak, L. S. The contribution of a "processing" deficit to alcoholic Korsakoff patients' memory disorder. In I. M. Birnbaum & E. S. Parker (Eds.), *Alcohol and human memory*. Hillsdale, N.J.: Lawrence Erlbaum Associates, 1977.

Cermak, L. S. Amnesic patients' level of processing. In L. S. Cermak & F. I. M. Craik (Eds.), *Levels of processing in human memory*. Hillsdale, N.J.: Lawrence Erlbaum, 1979. (a)

Cermak, L. S. The contribution of a "processing" deficit to alcoholic Korsakoff patients' memory disorder. In I. M. Birnbaum & E. S. Parker (Eds.), *Alcohol and Human Memory*. Hillsdale, N.J.: Lawrence Erlbaum, 1979. (b)

Cermak, L. S. Improving retention in alcoholic Korsakoff patients. *Journal of Studies on Alcohol*, 1980, *41*, 159–169.

Cermak, L. S., & Butters, N. Information processing of alcoholic Korsakoff patients. *Quarterly Journal of Studies on Alcohol*, 1973, *34*, 1110–1132.

Cermak, L. S., Butters, N., & Goodglass, H. The extent of memory loss in Korsakoff patients. *Neuropsychologia*, 1971, *9*, 307–315.

Cermak, L. S., Butters, N., & Moreines, J. Some analysis of the verbal encoding deficit in alcoholic Korsakoff patients. *Brain and Language*, 1974, *1*, 141–150.

Cermak, L. S., & Reale, L. Depth of processing and retention of words by alcoholic Korsakoff patients. *Journal of Experimental Psychology: Human Learning and Memory*, 1978, *4*, 165–174.

Cermak, L. S., & Ryback, R. S. Recovery of verbal short term memory in alcoholics. *Journal of Studies on Alcohol*, 1976, *37*, 46–52.

Chandler, B. C., & Parsons, O. A. Altered hemispheric functioning under alcohol. *Journal of Studies on Alcohol*, 1977, *38*, 381–391.

Chandler, C. C., Vega, A., & Parsons, O. A. Dichotic Listening in alcoholics with and without a history of possible brain injury. *Quarterly Journal of Studies on Alcohol*, 1973, *34*, 1009–1109.

Chapman, L. J., & Chapman, J. P. *Disordered thought in schizophrenia*. New York: Appleton-Century-Crofts, 1973.

Chelune, G. J., Heaton, R. K., Lehman, R. A. W., & Robinson, A. Level versus pattern of neuropsychological performance among schizophrenic and diffusely brain damaged patients. *Journal of Consulting and Clinical Psychology*, 1979, *47*, 155–163.

Chelune, G. J., & Parker, J. B. Neurological deficits associated with chronic alcohol abuse. *Clinical Psychology Review*, 1981, *1*, 181–195.

Chmielewski, C., & Golden, C. Alcoholism and brain damage: An investigation using the Luria–Nebraska Neuropsychological Battery. *International Journal of Neuroscience*, 1980, *10*, 99–105.

Christensen, A. L. *Luria's neuropsychological investigation*. New York: Spectrum, 1975.

Chusid, J. G. *Correlative neuroanatomy and functional neurology* (15th ed.) Los Altos, Calif.: Lange Medical Publications, 1973.

Claeson, L. E., & Carlsson, C. Cerebral dysfunction in alcoholics: A psychometric investigation. *Quarterly Journal of Studies on Alcohol*, 1970, *31*, 317–323.

Clarke, J., & Haughton, H. A study of intellectual impairment and recovery rates in heavy drinkers in Ireland. *British Journal of Psychiatry*, 1975, *130*, 178–184.

Coger, R. W., Dymond, A. M., & Serafetinides, E. A. Electroencephalographic similarities between chronic alcoholics and chronic nonparanoid schizophrenics. *Archives of General Psychiatry*, 1979, *36*, 91–98.

Connolly, J. H., Allen, I. V., Hurwitz, L. J., & Miller, J. H. D. Measles-virus antibody and antigen in subacute sclerosing panencephalitis. *Lancet*, 1967 *1*, 542–544.

Constantinidis, J., Garrone, G., & Ajuriaguerra, J. De l' heredité des demences de l'age avance. *Encephale*, 1962, *51*, 301–344.

Corkin, S. Tactually guided maze learning in man. Effects of unilateral cortical excisions and bilateral hippocampal lesions. *Neuropsychologia*, 1965, *3*, 339–351.

Corkin, S., Milner, B., & Tayler, L. Bilateral sensory loss after unilateral cerebral lesion in man. *Transactions of the American Neurological Association*, 1973, *98*, 118.

Corsellis, J. A. N. The pathology of dementia. *British Journal of Hospital Medicine*, 1969, *2*, 695–702.

Corsellis, J. A. N. The limbic areas in Alzheimer's disease and other conditions associated with dementia. In G. E. W. Wolstenholme & M. O'Connor (Eds.), *Alzheimer's disease and related condition. CIBA Foundation Symposium.* London: Churchill, 1970.

Cottrell, S. S., & Wilson, S. A. K. The affective symptomatology of disseminated sclerosis: A study of 100 cases. *Journal of Neurology and Psychopathology*, 1926, *7*, 1–30.

Courville, C. B. Coup-countercoup mechanism of craniocerebral injuries; Some observations. *Archives of Surgery*, 1942, *45*, 19–43.

Courville, C. B. *Effects of alcohol on the nervous system of man.* Los Angeles: San Lucas Press, 1955.

Covi, L., Lipman, R. S., Alarcon, R. D., & Smith, V. K. Drug and psychotherapy interactions in depression. *American Journal of Psychiatry*, 1976, *133*, 502–508.

Cowan, J. *Alcohol state dependent learning: Effects of repetition and recognition on retrieval of faces, names and words.* Unpublished doctoral dissertation, University of California, San Francisco, 1976.

Craik, F. I. M. Similarities between the effects of aging and alcoholic intoxication on memory performance, construed within the "levels of processing" framework. In I. M. Birnbaum & E. S. Parker (Eds.), *Alcohol and human memory.* Hillsdale, N.J.: Lawrence Erlbaum, 1977.

Craik, F. I. M., & Lockhart, R. S. Levels of processing: A framework for memory research. *Journal of Verbal Listening and Verbal Behavior*, 1972, *11*, 671–684.

Crapper, D. R., Kirshman, S. S., & Dalton, A. J. Brain aluminum distribution in Alzheimer's disease and experimental neurofibrillary digeneration. *Science*, 1973, *180*, 511–513.

Critchley, M. Psychiatric symptoms and parietal disease: Differential diagnosis. *Proceedings of the Royal Society of Medicine*, 1964, *57*, 422–428.

Crow, L. T., & Ball, C. Alcohol state-dependency and autonomic reactivity. *Psychophysiology*, 1975, *12*, 702–706.

Crowder, R. G. *Principles of learning and memory*. Hillsdale, N.J.: Lawrence Erlbaum, 1976.

Cutting, J. Patterns of performance in amnesic subjects. *Journal of Neurology, Neurosurgery and Psychiatry*, 1978, *41*, 278–282. (a)

Cutting, J. Specific psychological deficits in alcoholism. *British Journal of Psychiatry*, 1978, *133*, 119–122. (b)

D'Amour, M. L., Shahani, B. T., Young, R. R., & Bird, K. T. The importance of studying sural nerve conduction and late responses in the evaluation of alcoholic subjects. *Neurology*, 1979, *29*, 1600–1604.

Dastur, D. K., Lane, M. H., Hansen, D. B., Kety, S. S., Butler, R. N., Perlin, S., & Sokoloff, F. L. Effects of aging on cerebral circulation and metabolism in man. In *Human aging: A biological and behavioral study*. Public Health Service Publication #986. Washington, D.C.: U.S. Government Printing Office, 1963.

Davison, K., & Bagley, C. R. Schizophrenia-like psychoses associated with organic disorders of the central nervous system: A review of the literature. In R. N. Herrington (Ed.), *Current problems in neuropsychiatry*. Ashford, Kent: Headley Brothers, 1969.

Delay, J., Brion, S., & Derouesne, C. Syndrome de Korsakoff et etiologie tumorale. *Revue Neurologique*, 1964, *111*, 97–133.

Dencker, S. J. A follow-up study of 128 closed head injuries in twins using co-twins as controls. *Acta Psychiatrica et Neuropsychologica Scandinavica*, 1958, supplement 123, 1–125.

Dencker, S.J. Closed head injury in twins *Archives of General Psychiatry*, 1960, *2*, 569–575.

Dewhurst, K. The neurosyphilitic psychoses today: A survey of 91 cases. *British Journal of Psychiatry*, 1969, *115*, 31–38.

Dewhurst, K., Oliver, J. E., & McKnight, A. L. Socio-psychiatric consequences of Huntington's disease. *British Journal of Psychiatry*, 1970, *116*, 255–258.

DeWardener, H. E., & Lennox, B. Cerebral beriberi (Wernicke's encephalopathy). *Lancet*, 1947, *2*, 11–17.

DeWolfe, A. S. Differentiation of schizophrenia and brain damage with the WAIS. *Journal of Clinical Psychology*, 1971, *27*, 209–211.

Diaz, J., & Samson, H. H. Impaired brain growth in neonatal rats exposed to ethanol. *Science*, 1980, *208*, 751–753.

Dietvorst, T. F., Swenson, W. M., & Morse, R. M. Intellectual assessment in a midwestern alcoholism treatment population. *Journal of Clinical Psychology*, 1978, *34*, 244–249.

Dimond, S. J., Scammel, R. E., Pryce, I. G., Huws, D., & Gray, C. Callosal transfer and left-hand anomia in schizophrenia. *Biological Psychiatry*, 1979, *14*, 735–739.

Dimond, S. J., Scammel, R. E., Pryce, I. G., Huws, D., & Gray, C. Some failures of international and cross-lateral transfer in chronic schizophrenia. *Journal of Abnormal Psychiatry*, 1980, *89*, 505–509.

Direkze, M., Bayliss, S. G., & Cutting, J. C. Primary tumors of the frontal lobe. *British Journal of Clinical Practice*, 1971, *25*, 207–213.

Dodrill, C., & Wilkus, R. G. *EEG epileptiform activity and neuropsychological performance*. Paper presented at the 84th annual convention of the American Psychological Association, Washington, 1976.

Dongier, S. Statistical study of clinical and electroencephalographic manifestations of 536 psychotic episodes occurring in 516 epileptics between clinical seizures. *Epilepsia*, 1959, *1*, 117–142.

Donnelly, E. F., Dent, J. K., & Murphy, D. L. & Mignone, R. J. Comparison of temporal lobe epileptics and affective disorders on the Halstead–Reitan Battery. *Journal of Clinical Psychology*, 1972, *28*, 61–62.

Donnelly, E. F., & Waldman, I. N. IQ as a predictor of antidepressant responses to imipramine. *Psychological Reports*, 1977, *41*, 54.

Donnelly, E. F., & Waldman, I. N. IQ as a predictor of antidepressant responses to lithium. *Psychological Reports*, 1978, *42*, 898.

Donnelly, E. F., Weinberger, D. R., Waldman, I. N., & Wyatt, R. J. Cognitive impairment associated with morphological brain abnormalities on computed tomography in chronic schizophrenic patients. *Journal of Nervous and Mental Disorders*, 1980, *5*, 305–308.

Donovan, D. M., Quiesser, H. R., & O'Leary, M. R. Group Embedded Figures Test performance as a predictor of cognitive impairment among alcoholics. *International Journal of Addiction*, 1976, *11*, 725–739.

Dorosh, M. E. *The effects of age, depression, sex differences, and educational level on the Halstead–Reitan Neuropsychological Test Battery*. Unpublished doctoral dissertation, York University (Canada), 1978.

Draper, R. J. Evidence for an alcohol brain damage syndrome. *Irish Medical Journal*, 1978, *71*, 350–352.

Draper, R. J., Feldman, B., & Haughton, H. Undetected brain damage in Irish alcoholics. *Irish Medical Journal*, 1978, *71*, 353–355.

Duncan, G. W., Lees, R. S., Ojemann, R. G., & David, S. S. Concomitants of atherosclerotic carotid artery stenosis. *Stroke*, 1977, *8*, 665–669.

Duncan, G. W., Pessin, M., Mohr, J. P., & Adams, R. D. Tranisient cerebral ischemic attacks. *Advances in Internal Medicine*, 1976, *21*, 1–20.

Dymond, A. M., Coger, R. W., & Serafetinides, E. A. EEG banding and asymmetry in schizophrenics, alcoholics, and controls: An objective comparison. *Research Communications in Psychology, Psychiatry, and Behavior*, 1980, *5*, 113–122.

Earle, K. M. Metastatic brain tumors. *Diseases of the Nervous System*, 1955, *16*, 86–93.

Earnest, M. P., Heaton, R. K., Wilkinson, W. E., & Manke, W. F. Cortical atrophy, ventricular enlargement and intellectual impairment in the aged. *Neurology*, 1979, *29*, 1138–1143.

Eckardt, M. J. Central nervous system impairment in the alcoholic: A research and clinical perspective. *NIAAA Research Monograph*, in press.

Eckardt, M. J., Parker, E. S., Noble, E. P., Feldman, D. J., & Gottschalk, L. A. Relationship between neuropsychological performance and alcohol consumption in alcoholics. *Biological Psychiatry*, 1978, *13*, 551–565.

Eckardt, M. J., Parker, E. S., Noble, E. P., Pautler, C. P., & Gottschalk, L. A. Changes in neuropsychological performance during treatment for alcoholism. *Biological Psychiatry*, 1979, *14*, 943–954.

Eckardt, M. J., Parker, E. S., Pautler, C. P., Noble, E. P., & Gottschalk, L. A. Neuropsychological consequences of post-treatment drinking behavior in male alcoholics. *Psychiatry Research*, 1980, *2*, 135–147.

Eckardt, M. J., Ryback, R. S., & Pautler, C. P. Neuropsychological deficits in alcoholic men in their mid-thirties. *American Journal of Psychiatry*, 1980, *137*, 932–936.

Edwin, E., Holten, K., Norum, K. R., Schumpf, A., & Skaug, O. E. Vitamin B^{12} hypovitaminosis in mental diseases. *Acta Scandinavica*, 1965, *177*, 689–699.

Eich, J. E. State-dependent retrieval of information in human episodic memory. In I. M. Birnbaum & E. S. Parker (Eds.), *Alcohol and human memory*. Hillsdale, N.J.: Lawrence Erlbaum, 1977.

Ellenberg, L., Rosenbaum, G., Goldman, M. S., & Whitman, R. D. Recoverability of psychological functioning following alcohol abuse: Lateralization effects. *Journal of Consulting and Clinical Psychology*, 1980, *48*, 503–510.

Ellis, J. M., & Lee, S. I. Acute prolonged confusion in later life as an ictal state. *Epilepsia*, 1978, *19*, 119–128.

Epstein, P. S., Pisani, V. D., & Pawcett, J. A. Alcoholism and cerebral atrophy. *Alcoholism: Clinical and Experimental Research*, 1977, *1*, 61–65.

Erlichman, H., & Weinberger, A. Lateral eye movements and hemispheric asymmetry: A critical view. *Psychological Bulletin*, 1978, *85*, 1080–1101.

Etevson, P., Pidoux, B., Rioux, P., Peron-Magnon, P., Verdeaux, G., & Deniker, P. Intra- and interhemispheric EEG differences quantified by spectral analysis. *Acta Psychiatrica Scandinavica*, 1979, *60*, 57–68.

Falk, B., & Silfverskiold, B. P. Pneumoencephalographic changes in the chronic post-concussion syndrome and non-traumatic cephalgia. *Acta Psychiatrica et Neurologica Scandinavica*, 1954, *59*, 161–171.

Farmer, R. H. Functional changes during early weeks of abstinence, measured by Bender–Gestalt. *Quarterly Journal of Studies on Alcohol*, 1973, *34*, 786–796.

Fazekas, J. F., Kleh, J., & Finnerty, F. A. Influence of age and vascular disease on cerebral hemodynamics and metabolism. *American Journal of Medicine*, 1955, *18*, 477–485.

Fehrenbach, P. A., Chaney, E. F., & O'Leary, M. R. A comparison of cognitive deficit and recovery in younger and older middle-aged alcoholics. *Alcoholism: Clinical and Experimental Research*, 1980, *4*, 214. (Abstract)

Ferrer, S. *Complications neurologicas cronicas del alcoholismo*. Santiago: Editorial Universitaria, 1970.

Feuchtwanger, E. *Die Funktionen des Stirnhirns: Ihre Pathologie und Psychologie*. Berlin: Springer, 1923.

Fine, E. W. *Brain damage in early alcohol dependency*. Paper presented at the annual meeting of the Medical-Scientific Session of the National Alcoholism Forum, St. Louis, May 1–3, 1978.

Fine, E. W., & Steer, R. A. Short-term spatial memory deficits in men arrested for driving while intoxicated. *American Journal of Psychiatry*, 1979, *136*, 594–597.

Fisher, C. M. Observations of the fundus oculi in transient monocular blindness. *Neurology*, 1959, *9*, 337–347.

Fisher, C. M. Pure sensory stroke involving the face, arm and leg. *Neurology*, 1965, *15*, 76–80.

Fisher, C. M. Pathological observations in hypertensive cerebral hemorrhage. *Journal of Neuropathology and Experimental Neurology*, 1971, *30*, 536–550.

Fisher, C. M., Karnes, W. E., & Kubrik, C. S. Lateral medullary infarction—the pattern of vascular occlusion. *Journal of Neuropathology and Experimental Neurology*, 1961, *20*, 323–379.

Fisher, G. C. L. Selective and differentially accelerated intellectual dysfunction in specific brain damage. *Journal of Clinical Psychology*, 1958, *14*, 395–398.

Fitzhugh, L. C., Fitzhugh, K. B., & Reitan, R. M. Adaptive abilities and intellectual functioning in hospitalized alcoholics. *Quarterly Journal of Studies on Alcohol*, 1960, *21*, 414–423.

Fitzhugh, L. C., Fitzhugh, K. B., & Reitan, R. M. Adaptive abilities and intellectual functioning of hospitalized alcoholics: Further considerations. *Quarterly Journal of Studies on Alcohol*, 1965, *26*, 402–411.

Fleming, A. M. M., & Guthrie, A. *The electroencephalogram, psychological testing, and other investigations in abstinent alcoholics: A longitudinal study.* Unpublished manuscript, Ninewalls Hospital, Dundee, Scotland, 1980.

Fleminger, J. J., Dalton, R., & Standage, K. F. Handedness in psychiatric patients. *British Journal of Psychiatry*, 1977, *131*, 448–452.

Flor-Henry, P. Psychosis and temporal lobe epilepsy: A controlled investigation *Epilepsia*, 1969, *10*, 363–395. (a)

Flor-Henry, P. Schizophrenic-like reactions and affective psychoses associated with temporal lobe epilepsy: Etiological factors. *American Journal of psychiatry*, 1969, *126*, 148–152. (b)

Flor-Henry, P. Lateralized temporal–limbic dysfunction and psychopathology. *Annals of the New York Academy of Sciences*, 1976, *280*, 777–795.

Flor-Henry, P., & Yeudall, L. T. Neuropsychological investigation of schizophrenia and manic depressive psychoses. In J. Gruzelier & P. Flor-Henry (Eds.), *Hemisphere asymmetries of function and psychopathology*, in press.

Folstirn, M. F., Maiberger, R., & McHugh, P. R. Mood disorder as a specific complication of stroke. *Journal of Neurology, Neurosurgery, and Psychiatry*, 1977, *40*, 1018–1020.

Fox, J. H., Ramsey, R. G., Huckman, M. S., & Proske, A. E. Cerebral ventricular enlargement: Chronic alcoholics examined by computerized tomography. *Journal of the American Medical Association*, 1976, *236*, 365–368.

Fox, J. H., Topel, J. L., & Huckman, M. S. Use of computed tomography in senile dementia. *Journal of Neurology, Neurosurgery, and Psychiatry*, 1975, *39*, 203–211.

Franzen, G. & Ingvar, D. H. Abnormal distribution of cerebral activity in chronic schizophrenia. *Journal of Psychiatric Research*, 1975, *12*, 199–214 (a).

Franzen, G., & Ingvar, D. H. Absence of activation in frontal structures during psychological testing of chronic schizophrenia. *Journal of Neurology, Neurosurgery, and Psychiatry*, 1975, *38*, 1027–1032. (b)

Fredericks, R. S., & Finkel, P. Schizophrenic performance on the Halstead–Reitan Battery. *Journal of Clinical Psychology*, 1978, *38*, 26–30.

Freeman, W. Frontiers of multiple sclerosis: I. Pneumoencephalography, electroencephalography, morbid anatomy and pathogenesis. *Medical Annals of the District of Columbia*, 1944, *13*, 1–10.

Friedman, E. D. Head injuries: Effects and their appraisal. III. Encephalographic observations. *Archives of Neurology and Psychiatry*, 1932, *27*, 791–810.

Froshaug, H., & Ytrehus, A. A study of general paresis with special reference to the reasons for the admission of these patients to the hospital. *Acta Psychiatrica et Neurologica Scandinavica*, 1956, *31*, 35–60.

Gardner, E. *Fundamentals of neurology.* Philadelphia: Saunders, 1975.

Gastaut, H. Clinical and electroencephalographic classification of epileptic seizures.

Epilepsia, 1970, *11*, 102−113.

Gerrein, J. R., & Chechile, R. A. Storage and retrieval processes of alcohol-induced amnesia. *Journal of Abnormal Psychology*, 1977, *86*, 285−294.

Geschwind, N. Disconnection syndromes in animals and man. I. *Brain*, 1965, *88*, 237−294.

Geschwind, N. Organic problems in the aged: Brain syndromes and alcoholism. *Journal of Geriatric Psychiatry*, 1978, *11*, 161−166.

Gibbs, C. J., Gajdusek, D. C., Asher, D. M., Alpers, M. D., Beck, E, Daniel, P. M., & Matthews, W. B. Creutzfeldt-Jakob disease (Spongiform encephalopathy): Transmission to the chimpanzee. *Science*, 1968, *161*, 388−389.

Glanzer, M. Short-term storage and long-term storage in recall. *Journal of Psychiatric Research*, 1971, *8*, 423−438.

Glaser, G. H. The problems of psychosis in psychomotor temporal lobe epileptics. *Epilepsia*, 1964, *5*, 271−278.

Golden, C. J. Validity of the Halstead−Reitan Neuropsychological Battery in a mixed psychiatric and brain injured population. *Journal of Consulting and Clinical Psychology*, 1977, *45*, 1043−1051.

Golden, C. J. *Clinical interpretation of objective psychological tests*. New York: Grune & Stratton, 1979.

Golden, C. J. *Diagnosis and rehabilitation in clinical neuropsychology*. Springfield, Ill.: Charles C. Thomas, 1981. (a)

Golden, C. J. The Luria−Nebraska Neuropsychological Battery. In P. McReynolds (Ed.), *Advances in psychological assessment* (Vol. 5). Palo Alto, Calif.: Science and Behavior Books, 1981. (b)

Golden, C. J. *Cerebral Blood Flow*. Paper presented at the Laterality Conference, Banff, 1982.

Golden, C. J., Ariel, R., McKay, S. E., Wilkening, G. N., Wolf, B. A., & MacInnes, W. D. The Luria−Nebraska Neuropsycholgical Battery: Theoretical orientation and comment. *Journal of Consulting and Clinical Psychology*, 1982, *50*, 291−300.

Golden, C. J., Graber, B., Blose, I., Berg, R., Coffman, J. A., & Bloch, S. Difference in brain densities between chronic alcoholic and normal control patients. *Science*, 1981, *211*, 508−510.

Golden, C. J., Graber, B., Coffman, J., Berg, R., Bloch, S. & Brogan, D. Brain density deficits in chronic schizophrenia. *Psychiatry Research*, 1980, *3*, 179−184.

Golden, C. J., Graber, B., Coffman, J., Berg, R. A., Newlin, D. B., & Bloch, S. Structural brain deficits in schizophrenia: As identified by CT scan density parameters. *Archives of General Psychiatry*, 1981, *38*, 1014−1017.

Golden, C. J., Hammeke, T., & Purisch, A. Diagnostic validity of a standardized neuropsychological battery derived from Luria's neuropsychological test. *Journal of Consulting and Clinical Psychology*, 1978, *46*, 1258−1263.

Golden, C. J., Hammeke, T. A., & Purisch, A. D. *The Luria−Nebraska Neuropsychological Battery*. Los Angeles: Western Psychological Services, 1980.

Golden, C. J., Moses, J. A., Zelazowski, R., Graber, B., Zata, L. M., Horvath, T. B., & Berger, P. A. Cerebral ventricular size and neuropsychological impairment in young chronic schizophrenics: Measurement by the standardized Luria−Nebraska Neuropsychological Battery. *Archives of General Psychiatry*, 1980, *37*, 619−623.

Golden, C. J., Purisch, A., & Hammeke, T. *The standardized Luria−Nebraska Neuro-*

psychological Battery: A manual for clinical and experimental uses. Lincoln, Neb.: University of Nebraska Press, 1979.

Goldman, M. S. Reversibility of psychological deficits in alcoholics: The interaction of aging with alcohol. in A. Wilkinson (Ed.), *Symposium on cerebral deficits in alcoholism.* Toronto: Addiction Research Foundation, in press.

Goldman, M. S., & Rosenbaum, G. Psychological recoverability following chronic alcohol abuse. In F. Seixas (Ed.), *Currents in alcoholism* (Vol. 2). New York: Grune & Stratton, 1977.

Goldman, M. S., Whitman, R. D., Rosenbaum, G., & Vande Vusse, D. Recoverability of sensory and motor functioning following chronic alcoholic abuse. In F. Seizas (Ed.), *Currents in alcoholism* (Vol. 3). New York: Grune & Stratton, 1978.

Goldman, M. S., Williams, D. L., Dickey, J. H., & Weintraub, A. L. *Alcoholics' differential psychological recovery over three months as a function of age.* Paper submitted for publication, Wayne State University, 1980.

Goldstein, G. Perceptual and cognitive deficit in alcoholics. In G. Goldstein & C. Neuringer (Eds.), *Empirical studies of alcoholism.* Cambridge, Mass: Ballinger/Lippincott, 1976.

Goldstein, G., & Chotlos, J. W. Dependency and brain damage in alcoholics. *Perceptual and Motor Skills,* 1965, *21,* 135−150.

Goldstein, G., and Halperin, K. M. Neuropsychological differences among subtypes of schizophrenia. *Journal of Abnormal Psychology,* 1977, *86,* 34−40.

Goldstein, G., Neuringer, C., & Klappersack, B. Cognitive, perceptual, and motor aspects of field dependency in alcoholics. *Journal of Genetic Psychology,* 1970, *117,* 253−266.

Goldstein, G., & Shelly, C. H. Field dependence and cognitive, perceptual and motor skills in alcoholics: A factor analytic study. *Quarterly Journal of Studies on Alcohol,* 1971, *32,* 29−40.

Goldstein, G., & Shelly, C. H. Neuropsychological diagnosis of multiple sclerosis in a neuropsychiatric setting. *Journal of Nervous and Mental Disease,* 1974, *158,* 280−290.

Goldstein, G., & Shelly, C. H. Similarities and differences between psychological deficits in aging and brain damage. *Journal of Gerontology,* 1975, *30,* 448−455..

Goldstein, G., & Shelly, C. H. A multivariate neuropsychological approach to brain lesion localization in alcoholism. *Addictive Behaviors,* 1982, *7,* 165−176.

Goldstein, K. *After-effects of brain injury in war.* New York: Grune & Stratton, 1942.

Goldstein, K. The effect of brain damage on the personality. *Psychiatry,* 1952, *15,* 245−260.

Goldstein, L., Temple, R. J., & Pollack, I. W. EEG and clinical assessment of subjects with drug abuse problems. *Research Communications in Psychology, Psychiatry and Behavior,* 1976, *1,* 193−200.

Goldstone, S., Lhamon, W. T., & Nurnberg, H. G. Temporal information processing by alcoholics. *Journal of Studies on Alcohol,* 1977, *38,* 2009−2024.

Goldstein, G., Neuringer, C., & Klappersack, B. Cognitive, perceptual, and motor aspects of field dependency in alcoholics. *Journal of Genetic Psychology,* 1970, *117,* 253−266.

Goodglass, H., & Peck, E. Dichotic ear order effects in Korsakoff and normal subjects. *Neuropsychologia,* 1971, *10,* 211−217.

Goodwin, D. W. Blackouts and alcohol induced memory dysfunction. In N. K. Mello & J. J. Mendelson (Eds.), *Recent advances in studies of alcoholism*. Washington, D.C.: U.S. Government Printing Office, 1971.

Goodwin, D. W. The alcohol blackout and how to prevent it. In I. M. Birnbaum & E. S. Parker (Eds.), *Alcohol and human memory*. Hillsdale, N.J.: Lawrence Erlbaum, 1977.

Goodwin, D. W., Crane, J. B., & Guze, S. B. Phenomenological aspects the alcohol "blackout". *British Journal of Psychiatry*, 1969, *115*, 1033–1038.

Goodwin, D. W., Hill, S. Y., Hopper, S., & Viesselman, J. D. Alcoholic blackouts and Kosakoff's syndrome. In M. M. Gross (Ed.), *Alcohol intoxication and withdrawal: Experimental studies II*. New York: Plenum Press, 1975.

Goodwin, D. W., Othmer, E., Kalikas, J. A., & Freeman F. Loss of short-term memory as a predictor of the alcoholic "blackout." *Nature*, 1970, *227*, 201–202.

Goodwin, D. W., Powell, B., Bremer, D., Hoine, H., & Sterne, J. Alcohol and recall: State dependent learning in man. *Science*, 1969, *163*, 1358–1360.

Goodwin, D. W., Powell, B., Hill, S. Y., Lieberman, W., & Viamontes, J. Effect of alcohol on "dissociated" learning in alcoholics. *Journal of Nervous and Mental Disease*, 1974, *158*, 198–201.

Gordon, E. B., & Sim, M. The EEG in presenile dementia. *Journal of Neurology, Neurosurgery, and Psychiatry*, 1967, *30*, 285–291.

Gottschalk, L. A. Cognitive impairment associated with acute or chronic disease. *General Hospital Psychiatry*, 1979, *1*, 344–346.

Götze O., Kuhne, D., Hansen, J., & Knipp, H. P. Hirnatrophische Veranderungen bei chronischem Alkoholismus: Eine klinische und computertomographische Studie. *Archiv fur Psychiatrie and Nervendrankheiten*, 1978, *226*, 137–156.

Grant, I., Adams, K., & Reed, R. Normal neuropsychological abilities of alcoholic men in their late thirties. *American Journal of Psychiatry*, 1979, *136*, 1263–1269.

Grant, R. H., & Stores, O. P. Folic acid in folate deficient patients with epilepsy. *British Medical Journal*, 1970, *4*, 644–648.

Green, P. Defective interhemispheric transfer and schizophrenia. *Journal of Abnormal Psychiatry*, 1978, *87*, 472–480.

Green, P., & Kotenko, V. Superior speech comprehension in schizophrenia under monaural versus binaural listening conditions. *Journal of Abnormal Psychiatry*, 1980, *89*, 399–408.

Greenbaum, J. V., & Lurie, L. A. Encephalitis as a causative factor in behavior disorder in children. *Journal of American Medical Association*, 1948, *136*, 923–930.

Greenfield, J. G. In W. Blackwood, W. H. McMenemy, A. Meyer, R. M. Norman, & D. S. Russell (Eds.), *Greenfield's neuropathology* (2nd ed.). London: Edward Arnold, 1963.

Gregson, R. A. M., & Taylor, G. M. Prediction of relapse in men alcoholics. *Journal of Studies on Alcohol*, 1977, *38*, 1749–1760.

Grinker, R. R., & Sahs, A. L. *Neurology* (6th ed.). Springfield, Ill.: Charles C. Thomas, 1966.

Gruzelier, J. H. Bilateral asymmetry of skin conductance orienting activity and levels in schizophrenia. *Biological Psychology*, 1973, *1*, 21–41.

Gruzelier, J., & Hammond N. Schizophrenia: A dominant hemisphere temporal–Limbic disorder? *Research Communications in Psychology, Psychiatry, and Behavior*, 1976, *1*, 33–72.

246 References

Gruzelier, J. H., & Hammond, N. The effect of chlorpromazine upon bilateral asymmetries in bioelectrical skin reactivity of schizophrenics. *Studia Psychologia*, 1977, *19*, 40–50.

Gruzelier, J., & Venables, P. Bimodal and lateral asymmetry in patients with depression and disorders of personality. *Biological Psychiatry*, 1974, *8*, 55–73.

Gudeman, H. E., Craine, J. R., Golden, C. J., & McLaughlin, D. Higher cortical dysfunction associated with long term alcoholism. *International Journal of Neuroscience*, 1977, *8*, 33–40.

Gur, R. E. Motoric laterality imbalance in schizophrenia. *Archives of General Psychiatry*, 1977, *34*, 33–37.

Gur, R. E. Left Hemisphere dysfunction and left hemisphere dysfunction and left hemisphere over-activation in schizophrenia. *Journal of Abnormal Psychology*, 1978, *87*, 226–238.

Gur, R. E. Cognitive concomitants of hemispheric dysfunction in schizophrena. *Archives of General Psychiatry*, 1979, *36*, 269–274.

Gur, R. E., & Reivich, M. Cognitive task effects on hemispheric blood flow in humans: Evidence for individual differences in hemispheric activation. *Brain and Language*, 1980, *9*, 78–92.

Guthrie, A. *The first year after treatment: Factors affecting time course of reversibility of memory and learning deficits in alcoholism.* Unpublished manuscript, Tayside Area Alcoholism Unit, Sunnyside Royal Hospital, Montrose, Scotland, 1980.

Guthrie, A., & Elliott, W. A. The nature and reversibility of cerebral impairment in alcoholism: Treatment implications. *Journal of Studies on Alcohol*, 1980, *41*, 147–155.

Guttmann, E. Late effects of closed head injuries: Psychiatric observations. *Journal of Mental Science*, 1946, *92*, 1–18.

Gyldensted, C. Measurements of the normal ventricular system and hemispheric sulci of 100 adults with computed tomography. *Neuroradiology*, 1977, *14*, 183–192.

Hachinski, D., & Strich, S. J. Atypical Alzheimer's disease with dementia of acute onset. In G. E. Wolstenholme & M. O'Connor (Eds.), *Alzheimer's disease and related conditions. Ciba Foundation Symposium*. London: Churchill, 1970.

Hachiniski, V. C., Lassen, N. A., & Marshall, J. Multi-infarct dementia. *Lancet*, 1974, *2*, 207.

Hahn, R. D., Webster, B., Weickhardt, G., Thomas, E., Timberlake, W., Solomon, H., Stokes, J. H., Moore, J. E., Heyman, A., Gammon, G., Gleeson, G. A., Curtis, A. C., & Cutler, A. C. Pencillin treatment of general paresis (dementia paralytica). *Archives of Neurology and Psychiatry*, 1959, *81*, 557–590.

Hallpike, J. F. Multiple sclerosis: Problems of aetiology and pathogenesis. *British Journal of Hospital Medicine*, 1973, *9*, 625–642.

Halpern, F. Studies of compulsive drinkers: Psychological results. *Quarterly Journal of Studies on Alcohol*, 1946, *6*, 468–479.

Halstead, W. C. *Brain and intelligence*. Chicago: University of Chicago Press, 1947.

Hambert, G., & Willen, R. Emotional disturbance and temporal lobe injury. *Comprehensive Psychiatry*, 1978, *19*, 441–447.

Hammeke, T., Golden, C. J., & Purisch, A. A standardized, short and comprehensive neuropsychological test battery based on the Luria neuropsychological evaluation. *International Journal of Neuroscience*, 1978, *8*, 135–141.

Hammond, N., & Gruezelier, J. Laterality, attention and rate effects in the temporal discrimination of chronic schizophrenics: The effects of treatment with chlorpromazine. *Quarterly Journal of Experimental Psychology*, 1978, *30*, 91−103.

Hansen, L. Treatment of reduced intellectual functioning in alcoholics. *Journal of Studies on Alcohol*, 1980, *41*, 156−158.

Hartley, J. T., Birnbaum, I. M., & Parker, E. M. Alcohol and storage deficits: Kind of processing? *Journal of Verbal Learning and Verbal Behavior*, 1978, *14*, 635−647.

Hatcher, E. M., Jones, M. K., & Jones, B. M. Cognitive deficits in alcoholic women. *Alcoholism: Clinical and Experimental Research*, 1977, *1*, 371−377.

Haug, J. O. Pneumoencephalographic studies in mental disease. *Acta Psychiatrica Scandinavica*, 1962, supplement *165*, 100−104.

Haug, J. O. Pneumoencephalographic evidence of brain damage in chronic alcoholics. *Acta Psychiatrica Scandinavica*, 1968, supplement *203*, 135−143.

Heaton, R. K., Baade, L. E., & Johnson, K. L. Neuropsychological test results associated with psychiatric disorders in adults. *Psychological Bulletin*, 1978, *85*, 141−162.

Heathfield, K. W. G. Huntington's chorea. *Brain*, 1967, *90*, 203−232.

Hecaen, H., & Ajuriaguerra, J. De troubles mentaux au cours des tumeus intracraniennes. Paris: Masson, 1956.

Heilbrun, A. B., Jr., Tarbox, A. R., & Madison, J. K. Cognitive structure and behavioral regulation in alcoholics. *Journal of Studies on Alcohol*, 1979, *40*, 387−400.

Heiss, W. D., Kufferle, B., & Demel, I. Storungen der Hirndurchblutung bei chronischen Alkoholikern in Ahangiegkeit vom klinischen Bild. *Psychiatria Clinica*, 1974, *7*, 181−191.

Hellekson, C., Buckland, R., & Price, T. Organic personality disturbance: A case of apparent atypical cyclic affective disorder. *American Journal of Psychiatry*, 1979, *136*, 833−835.

Helwig-Larsen, P., Hoffmeyer, H., Keiler, J., Thaysen, E. H., Thaysen, J. H., Thygesen, P., & Wulff, M. H. Famine disease in German concentration camps: Complications and sequels. *Acta Psychiatrica Neurologica Scandinavica*, 1952, supplement 83, 1−460.

Henderson, J. G., Strachan, R. W., Beck, J. S., Dawson, A. A., & Daniel, M. The antigastric-antibody test as a screening procedure for vitamin B[12] deficiency in psychiatric practice. *Lancet*, 1966, *2*, 809−813.

Henry, G. W. Mental phenomena observed in cases of brain tumor. *American Journal of Psychiatry*, 1932, *89*, 415−473.

Hester, R. K., Smith, J. W., & Jackson, T. R. Recovery of cognitive skills in alcoholics. *Journal of Studies on Alcohol*, 1980, *41*, 363−367.

Heston, L. L., Mastri, A. R., Anderson, V. E., & White, J. Dementia of the Alzheimer type: Clinical genetics, natural history and associated conditions. *Archives of General Psychiatry*, 1981, *38*, 1085−1090.

Hewett, B. B., & Martin, W. R. Psychometric comparisons of sociopathic and psychopathological behaviors of alcoholics and drug abusers versus a low drug use control population. *International Journal of Neuroscience*, 1980, *15* 77−105.

Hill, S. Y., & Mikhael, M. A. Computerized transaxial tomographic and neuropsychological evaluations in chronic alcoholics and heroin abusers. *American Journal of Psychiatry*, 1979, *136*, 598−602.

Hillbom, E. After-effects of brain injuries. *Acta Psychiatrica et Neurologica Scandinavica*, 1960, *142*, 1–195.

Hinrichsen, J. J., Kathan, M., & Levenson, R. W. Alcohol-induced state-dependent learning in non-alcoholics. *Pharmacology, Biochemistry, and Behavior*, 1974, *2*, 293–296.

Hirschenfang, S., Silber, M., & Benton, J. G. Comparison of Bender–Gestalt reproductions by patients with peripheral neuropathy. *Perceptual and Motor Skills*, 1967, *24*, 1317–1318.

Hoehn, M. M. & Yahr, M. D. Parkinsonism: Onset, progression and mortality. *Neurology*, 1967, *17*, 427–442.

Holland, T. R., & Watson, C. G. Multivariate analysis of WAIS–MMPI relationships among brain-damaged, schizophrenic, neurotic, and alcoholic patients. *Journal of Clinical Psychology*, 1980, *36*, 352–359.

Hollander, D., & Stich, S. J. Atypical Alzheimer's disease with dementia of acute onset. In G. E. Wolstenholme & M. O'Connor (Eds.), *Alzheimer's disease and related conditions*. Ciba Foundation Symposium. London: Churchill, 1970.

Holmes, J. M. Cerebral manifestations of vitamin B^{12} deficiency. *British Medical Journal*, 1956, *2*, 1394–1398.

Holman, R. B. Alcohol: Biological mechanisms. In J. D. Barchas, P. A. Berger, R. D. Ciarnello, & G. R. Elliott (Eds.), *Psycho-pharmacology: From theory to practice*. New York: Oxford University Press, 1977.

Hornykiewicz, O. Neurochemical pathology and pharmacology of brain dopamine and acetylcholine: Rational basis for the current drug treatment of parkinsonism. In F. H. McDowell & C. H. Markham, (Eds.), *Recent advances in Parkinson's disease*. Oxford: Blackwell, 1971.

Horton, D. L., & Turnage, T. W. *Human learning*. Englewood Cliffs, N.J.: Prentice-Hall, 1976.

Horvath, T. B. Clinical spectrum and epidemiological features of alcoholic dementia. In J. G. Rankin (Ed.), *Alcohol, drugs and brain damage*. Toronto: Alcoholism and Drug Addiction Research Foundation, 1975.

Hoy, R. M. Alcoholism and brain damage: Some psychometric findings in addiction unit alcoholics. *British Journal of Addiction*, 1973, *68*, 201–204.

Huckman, M. S., Fox, J., & Topel, J. The validity of criteria for the evaluation of cerebral atrophy by computed tomography. *Radiology* 1975, *116*, 85–92.

Hudolin, V. I., & Gubarev, N. Characteristics of the alpha rhythm in chronic alcoholics. *British Journal of Addiction*, 1967, *62*, 55–60.

Hughes, C. P., & Gado, M. Computed tomography and the aging of the brain. *Radiology*, 1981, *139*, 391–396.

Hunt, W. A., Majchrowicz, E., Dalton, T. K., Swartzwelder, H. S., & Wixon, H. Alterations in neurotransmitter activity after acute and chronic ethanol treatment: Studies of transmitter interactions. *Alcoholism: Clinical and Experimental Research*, 1979, *3*, 359–363.

Huppert, F. A., & Piercy, M. Recognition memory in amnesic patients: A defect in acquisition? *Neuropsychologia*, 1977, *15*, 643–652.

Huppert, F. A., & Piercy, M. Dissociation between learning and remembering in organic amnesia. *Nature*, 1978, *275*, 317–318.

Illchysin, D., & Ryback, R. S. Short-term memory in non-intoxicated alcoholics as a function of blackout history. In F. A. Seixas (Ed.), *Currents in alcoholism* (Vol. 2.). New York: Grune & Stratton, 1977.

Ingvar, D. H., Brun, A., Hagberg, B., & Gustafson, L. Regional cerebral blood flow in the dominant hemisphere in confirmed cases of Alzheimer's disease, Pick's disease, and multi-infarct dementia: Relationship to clinical symptomatology and neuropathological findings. In R. Katzman, R. D. Terry, & K. L. Bick (Eds.), *Alzheimer's disease: Senile Dementia and Related Disorders (Aging)*, (Vol. 7). New York. Raven Press, 1978.

Ingvar, D. H., & Franzen, G. Abnormalities of cerebral blood flow distribution in patients with chronic schizophrenia. *Acta Psychiatrica Scandinavica*, 1974, *50*, 425–462.

Iqbal, K., Wisniewski, H. M., Shelanski, M. L., Brostoff, S., Liwinicz, B. H., & Terry, R. D. Protein changes in senile dementia. *Brain Research*, 1974, *77*, 337–343.

Jacobs L., Kinkel, W. R., Painter, F., Murawski, J., & Heffner, R. R. Computerized tomography in dementia with special reference to changes in size of normal ventricles during aging and normal pressure hydrocephalus. In R. Katzman, R. D. Terry, & K. L. Bick (Eds.), *Alzheimer's disease, senile dementia and Related Disorders (Aging)* (Vol. 7). New York: Raven Press, 1978.

Jacoby, R. J., & Levy, R. Computed tomography in the elderly: I. The normal population. *British Journal of Psychiatry*, 1980, *136*, 249–255.

Jambor, D. L. Cognitive functioning in multiple sclerosis. *British Journal of Psychiatry*, 1969, *115*, 765–775.

Jamieson, R. C., & Wells, C. E. Manic psychosis in a patient with multiple metastatic brain tumors. *Journal of Clinical Psychiatry*, 1979, *40*, 280–282.

Jellinek, E. M. *The disease concept of alcoholism*. Highland Park, N.J.: Hillhouse Press, 1960.

Jellinek, E. H. Cerebral atrophy and cognitive impairment in chronic schizophrenia. *Lancet*, 1976, *2*, 1202–1203.

Jellinger, K. Neuropathological aspects of dementia resulting from abnormal blood and cerebrospinal fluid dynamics. *Acta Neurologica Belgica*, 1976, *76*, 83–102.

Jenkins, R. L., & Parsons, O. A. Lateralized patterns of tactual performance in alcoholics. In M. D. Galanter (Ed.), *Currents in alcoholism* (Vol. 5). New York: Grune & Stratton, 1979.

Jenkins, R. L., & Parsons, O. A. Recovery of cognitive abilities in male alcoholics. *Alcoholism: Clinical and Experimental Research*, 1979, *3*, 181. (Abstract) (a)

Jenkins, R. L., & Parsons, O. A. Recovery of cognitive abilities in male alcoholics. *Alcoholism: Clinical and Experimental Research*, 1979, *3*, 181. (Abstract) (b)

Jennett, W. B. *Epilepsy after blunt head injuries*. London: Heineman, 1962.

Jernigan, T. L., Zatz, L. M., Feinberg, I., & Fein, G. Measurement of cerebral atrophy in the aged by computed tomography. In J. N. W. Poon (Ed.), *Aging in the 1980's*. Washington, D.C.: American Psychological Association, 1980.

Jernigan, T., & Zatz, L. *Normal adult variation on computerized CT measures: Comparisons with measures from clinical groups*. Pater presented at the meeting of the International Neuropsychological Society, Atlanta, February 1981.

Johnstone, E. C., Crow, T. J., Frith, C. D., Husband, J., & Kreel, L. Cerebral ventricular size and cognitive impairment in chronic schizophrenia. *Lancet*, 1976, *2*, 924–926.

Johnstone, E. C., Crow, T. U. J., Frith, C. D., Stevens, M., Kreel, L., & Husband, J. The dementia of dementia praecox. *Acta Psychiatrica Scandinavica*, 1978, *57*, 305–324.

Jones, B. M. Verbal and spatial intelligence in short and long term alcoholics. *Journal of Nervous and Mental Disease*, 1971, *153*, 292–297.

Jones, B. M. Memory impairment on the ascending and descending limbs of the blood alcohol curve. *Journal of Abnormal Psychology*, 1973, *82*, 24–32.

Jones, B. M., & Jones, M. K. Women and alcohol: Intoxication, metabolism, and the menstrual cycle. In M. Greenblatt & M. A. Schuckit (Eds.), *Alcoholism problems in women and children*. New York: Grune & Stratton, 1976. (a)

Jones, B. M., & Jones, M. K. Alcohol effects in women during the menstrual cycle. *Annals of the New York Academy of Sciences*, 1976, *273*, 576–587. (b)

Jones, B. M., & Jones, M. K. Alcohol and memory impairment in male and female social drinkers. In I. M. Birnbaum & E. S. Parker (Eds.), *Alcohol and human memory*. Hillsdale, N.J.: Lawrence Erlbaum, 1977.

Jones, B. M., Jones, M. K., & Hatcher, E. M. Cgnitive deficits in women alcoholics as a function of gynecological status. *Journal of Studies on Alcohol*, 1980, *41*, 140–146.

Jones, B. M., & Parsons, O. A. Impaired abstracting ability in chronic alcoholics. *Archives of General Psychiatry*, 1971, *24*, 71–75.

Jones, B. M., & Parsons, O. A. Specific vs. generalized deficits of abstracting ability in chronic alcoholics. *Archives of General Psychiatry*, 1972, *26*, 380–384.

Jones, B. M., Tarter, R. E., & Rosenberg, J. Neuropsychological deficits in women alcoholics. *Alcoholism: Clinical and Experimental Research*, 1980, *4*, 219. (Abstract)

Jones, M. C. Personality correlates and antecedents of drinking patterns in adult males. *Journal of Consulting and Clinical Psychology*, 1968, *32*, 2–12.

Jones, M. K., & Jones, B. M. The relationship of age and drinking habits to the effects of alcohol on memory in women. *Journal of Studies on Alcohol*, 1980, *41*, 179–186.

Jonsson, C. O., Cronholm, B., Izikowitz, S., Gordon, K., & Rosen, A. Intellectual changes in alcoholics: Psychometric studies on mental sequels of prolonged intensive abuse of alcohol. *Quarterly Journal of Studies on Alcohol*, 1962, *23*, 221–242.

Kadrmas, A., & Winokur, G. Manic depressive illness and EEG abnormalities. *Journal of Clinical Psychiatry*, 1979, *40*, 306–307.

Kahana, E., Liebowitz, U., and Alter, M. Cerebral multiple sclerosis. *Neurology*, 1971, *21*, 1179–1185.

Kaldegg, A. Psychological observations in a group of alcoholic patients; with analysis of Rorschach, Wechsler–Bellevue and Bender–Gestalt test results. *Quarterly Journal of Studies on Alcohol*, 1956, *17*, 608–628.

Kallman, F. J. Genetic aspects of mental disorders in later life. In O. J. Kaplan (Ed.), *Mental disorders in later life*. Palo Alto, Calif.: Stanford University Press, 1956.

Kane, R. L., Sweet, J. J., Golden, C. J., Parsons, O. A., & Moses, J. A., Jr. Comparative diagnostic accuracy of the Halstead–Reitan and standardized Luria–Nebraska Neuropsychological Batteries in a mixed psychiatric and brain damaged population. *Journal of Consulting and Clinical Psychology*, 1981, *49*, 484–485.

Kapur, N., & Butters, N. Visuoperspective deficits in long-term alcoholics and alcoholics with Korsakoff's psychosis. *Journal of Studies on Alcohol*, 1977, *38*, 2025–2035.

Kariks, J. Extensive damage to substantia nigra in chronic alcoholics. *Medical Journal of Australia*, 1978, *2*, 628–629.

Kariks, J. Personal communication, July 9, 1980.

Karp, S. A., & Knostadt, N. L. Alcoholism and psychological differentiation: Long-range effect of heavy drinking on field dependence. *Journal of Nervous and Mental Disease*, 1965, *140*, 412–416.

Kay, D. W. K., Beamish, P. O., & Roth, M. Old age mental disorder in Newcastle upon Tyne. *British Journal of Psychiatry*, 1964, *110*, 146, 148.

Keane, T. M., & Lisman, S. A. *Multiple task disruption of alcohol statement retention.* Paper presented at the annual meeting of the Eastern Psychological Association, New York, 1976.

Kennedy, C. A ten-year experience with subacute sclerosing panencephalitis. *Neurology*, 1968, *18* (supplements), 58–59.

Keschner, M., Bender, M. B., & Strauss, I. Mental symptoms in cases of tumor of the temporal lobe. *Archives of Neurology and Psychiatry*, 1936, *35*, 572–596.

Keschner, M., Bender, M. B., & Strauss, I. Mental symptoms in cases of subtentorial tumor. *Archives of Neurology and Psychiatry*, 1937, *37*, 1–15.

Keschner, M., Bender, M. B., & Strauss, I. Mental symptoms associated with brain tumor: A study of 530 verified cases. *Journal of the American Medical Association*, 1938, *110*, 714–718.

Kety, S. S. Human cerebral blood flow and oxygen consumption as related to aging. In J. E. Moore, H. H. Merritt, & R. S. Masselink (Eds.), *Research publications of the Association for Research in Nervous and Mental Diseases*. Baltimore: Williams & Wilkins, 1956.

Kiloh, L. G., McComaas, A. J., & Osselton, J. W. *Clinical electroencephalography* (3rd ed.). New York: Appleton-Century-Crofts, 1972.

Kimura, D. Right temporal lobe damage: Perception of unfamiliar stimuli after damage. *Archives of Neurology*, 1963, *8*, 264–271.

Kimura, D. Functional asymmetry of the brain in dichotic listening. *Cortex*, 1967, *3*, 163–178.

Kinsbourne, M. Eye and head turning indicates cerebral lateralization. *Science*, 1972, *176*, 539–541.

Kinsbourne, M. The neuropsychological analysis of cognitive deficit. In R. G. Grenell & S. Bafay (Eds.), *Biological foundation of psychiatry*. New York: Raven Press, 1976.

Kinsbourne, M., & Wood, F. Short-term memory processes and the amnestic syndrome. In J. A. Deutsch & D. Deutsch (Eds.), *Short-term memory*. New York: Academic Press, 1975.

Kish, G. B., & Cheney, T. M. Impaired abilities in alcoholism: Measured by the General Aptitude Test Battery. *Quarterly Journal of Studies on Alcohol*, 1969, *30*, 384–388.

Kleinknecht, R. A., & Goldstein, S. G. Neuropsychological deficits associated with alcoholism: A review and discussion. *Quarterly Journal of Studies on Alcohol*, 1972, *33*, 999–1019.

Klisz, D. Neuropsychological evaluation in older persons. In M. Storandt, I. C.

Stiegler, & M. F. Elias (Eds.), *The clinical psychology of aging.* New York: Plenum Press, 1978.

Klisz, D. K., & Parsons, O. A. Hypothesis testing in younger and older alcoholics. *Journal of Abnormal Psychology,* 1977, *38,* 1718–1729.

Klisz, D. K., & Parsons, O. A. Cognitive functioning in alcoholics: The role of subject attrition. *Journal of Abnormal Psychology,* 1979, *88,* 268–276.

Klonoff, H., Fibiger, C. H., & Hutton, G. H. Neuropsychological patterns in chronic schizophrenia. *Journal of Nervous and Mental Disease,* 1970, *150,* 291–300.

Koenig, H. Dementia associated with the benign form of multiple sclerosis. *Transactions of the American Neurological Association,* 1968, *93,* 227–231.

Köhler, W. Kriterien verstandesmassigen leistungsverlusts chronisch alkoholkranker in HAWIE. *Zeitschrift fur Experimentelle und Angewandte Psychologie,* 1974,*21,*103–114.

Korboot, P. J., Naylor, G. F. K., & Soares, A. Patterns of cognitive dysfunction in alcoholics. *Australia Journal of Psychology,* 1977, *29,* 25–30.

Kral, V. A. Senescent forgetfulness: Benign and malignant. *Canadian Medical Association Journal,* 1962, *86,* 257–260.

Kremer, M. Discussion on disorders of personality after head injury. *Proceedings of the Royal Society of Medicine,* 1943, *37,* 564–566.

Kretschmer, E. Die Orbitalhirm—und Zwischenhirmsyndrome nach schadelbasisfrakturen. *Allegemeine Zeitschrift fur Psychiatrie* 1949, *124,* 358–360.

Kretschmer, E. Lokalistation und Beurteilung psychophysischer Syundrome bei Hirnverletszen. In E. Rehward (Ed.), *Das Hirntrauma.* Stuttgart: Thieme, 1956.

Kristensen, O., & Sindrup, E. Psychomotor epilepsy and psychosis I. Physical aspects. *Acta Neurologica Scandinavica,* 1978, *57,* 361–369.

Kronfol, Z., Hamsher, K., Digre, K., & Waziri, R. Depression and hemispheric functions: Changes associated with unilateral ECT. *British Journal of Psychiatry,* 1978, *132,* 560–567.

Kwentus, J., & Major, L. F. Disulfiram in the treatment of alcoholism. *Journal of Studies on Alcohol,* 1979, *40,* 428–446.

Lacks, P. B., Colbert, J., Harrow, M., & Levine, J. Further evidence concerning the diagnostic accuracy of the Halstead Organic Test Battery. *Journal of Clinical Psychology,* 1970, *26,* 480–481.

Langworthy, O. R., Kolb, L. C., & Androp, S. Disturbances of behavior in patients with disseminated sclerosis. *American Journal of Medicine,* 1941, *12,* 589–592.

Larsson, R., Sjogren, T., & Jacobson, G. Senile dementia: A clinical sociomedical and genetic study. *Acta Psychiatrica Scandinavica,* 1963, supplement 167, 1–259.

Lauter, H., & Meyer, J. E. Clinical and nosological aspects of senile dementia. In C. H. Muller, & L. Ciompi (Eds.), *Senile dementia: Clinical and therapeutic aspects.* Bern: Huber, 1968.

Lavy S., Melamed, M., Bentin, S., Cooper, G., & Rinot, Y. Bihemispheric decreases of regional cerebral blood flow in dementia: Correlation with age-matched normal controls. *Annals of Neurology,* 1978, *5,* 445–450.

Lemere, F. The nature and significance of brain damage from alcoholism. *American Journal of Psychiatry,* 1956, *113,* 361–362.

Levine, J., & Feirstein, A. Differences in test performance between brain-damaged, schizophrenic, and medical patients. *Journal of Consulting and Clinical Psychology,* 1972, *39,* 508–511.

Levine, J., & Zigler, E. Humor responses of high and low premorbid competence in alcoholic and nonalcoholic patients. *Addictive Behaviors*, 1976, *1*, 139–149.

Levy, R., Isaacs, A., & Hawks, G. Neurophysiological correlates of senile dementia: I. Motor and sensory nerve conduction velocity. *Psychological Medicine*, 1970, *1*, 40–47.

Lewin, W. The management of prolonged unconsciousness after head injury. *Proceedings of the Royal Society of Medicine*, 1959, *52*, 880–884.

Lewis, A. J. Discussion on differential diagnosis and treatment of post-contusional states. *Proceedings of the Royal Society of Medicine*, 1942, *35*, 607–614.

Lewis, E. G., Dustman, R. E., & Beck E. C. The effect of alcohol on sensory phenomena and cognitive and motor tasks. *Quarterly Journal of Studies on Alcohol*, 1969, *30*, 618–633.

Lewis, E. G., Dustman, R. E., & Beck E. C. The effects of alcohol on visual and somato-sensory evoked responses. *Electroencephalography and Clinical Neurophysiology*, 1970, *28*, 202–205.

Lewis, G., Golden, C. J., Purisch, A., & Hammeke, T. The effects of chronicity of disorder and length of hospitalization on the standardized version of Luria's Neuropsychological Battery in a schizophrenic population. *Clinical Neuropsychology*, 1979, *1*, 13–18.

Linnoila, M., Erwin, C. W., Cleveland, W. P., Logue, P. E., & Gentry, W. D. Effects of alcohol on psychomotor performance of men and women. *Journal of Studies on Alcohol*, 1978, *39*, 745–758.

Lishman, W. A. Brain damage in relation to psychiatric disability after head injury. *British Journal of Psychiatry*, 1968, *114*, 373–410.

Lishman, W. A. *Organic Psychiatry: The Psychological Consequences of Cerebral Disorder*. Oxford: Blackwell, 1978.

Lishman, W. A., & McMeekan, E. R. L. Hand preference patterns in psychiatric patients. *British Journal of Psychiatry*, 1976, *129*, 1589–1640.

Liske, E., & Forster, F. M. Pseudoseizures: A problem in the diagnosis and management of epileptic patients. *Neurology*, 1964, *14*, 41–49.

Lisman, S. A. Alcoholic "blackout": State dependent learning? *Archives of General Psychiatry*, 1974, *30*, 46–53.

Litman, G. K., Eiser, J. R., Rawson, N. S., & Oppenheim, A. N. Differences in relapse precipitants and coping behavior between alcohol relapsers and survivors. *Behaviour Research and Therapy*, 1979, *17*, 89–94.

Løberg, T. Alcohol misuse and neuropsychological deficits in men. *Journal of Studies on Alcohol*, 1980, *41*, 119–128.

Lohrenz, J. G., Levy, L., & Davis, J. F. Schizophrenia or epilepsy: A problem of differential diagnosis. *Comprehensive Psychiatry*, 1962, *3*, 54–62.

Long, J. A., & McLachian, J. F. C. Abstract reasoning and perceptual-motor efficiency in alcoholics: Impairment and reversibility. *Quarterly Journal of Studies on Alcohol*, 1974, *35*, 1220–1229.

Loranger, A. W., Goodell, H., McDowell, F. H., Lele, J. E., & Sweet, R. D. Intellectual impairment in Parkinson's syndrome. *Brain*, 1972, *95*, 405–412.

Luchins, D. J., Pollin, W., & Wyatt, R. J. Laterality in monozygotic schizophrenic twins: An alternative hypothesis. *Biological Psychiatry*, 1980, *15*, 87–93.

Luchins, D. J., Weinberger, D. R., & Wyatt, R. J. Schizophrenia: Evidence of a subgroup with reversed cerebral asymmetry. *Archives of General Psychiatry*, 1979, *39*, 1309–1311.

Luria, A. R. *Higher cortical functions in man*. New York: Basic Books, 1966.

Luria, A. R. *The working brain*. New York: Basic Books, 1973.

Lusins, J., Zimberg, S., Smokler, H., & Gurley, K. Alcoholism and cerebral atrophy. *Alcoholism: Clinical and Experimental Research*, 1980, *4*, 222. (Abstract)

Lynch, M. J. Brain lesions in chronic alcoholism. *Archives of Pathology*, 1960, *69*, 342–353.

Lyon, K., Wilson, J., Golden, C. J., Graber, B., Coffman, J. A., & Bloch, S. Effects of long-term neuroleptic use on brain density. *Psychiatry Research*, 1981, *5*, 33–37.

Lyon, R. L. Huntington's chorea in the Moray Firth area. *British Medical Journal*, 1962, *1*, 1301–1306.

Madill, M. *Alcohol induced dissociation in humans: A possible treatment technique for alcoholism*. Unpublished doctoral dissertation, Queens University (Kingston Ontario, Canada), 1967.

Malamund, N., & Skillicorn, S. A. Relationship between the Wernicke and the Korsakoff syndromes. *Archives of Neurology and Psychiatry*, 1956, *76*, 585–596.

Malec, J. Neuropsychological assessment of schizophrenia versus brain damage: A review. *Journal of Nervous and Mental Disease*, 1978, *166*, 507–516.

Malone, W. H. Psychosis with multiple sclerosis. *Medical Bulletin of the Veterans Administration*, 1937, *14*, 113–117.

Marlatt, G. A., Demming, B., & Reid, J. B. Loss of control in drinking in alcoholics: An experimental analogue. *Journal of Abnormal Psychology*, 1973, *81*, 23–24.

Marlatt, G. A., & Rohsenow, D. J. Cognitive processes in alcohol use: Expectancy and the balanced placebo design. In N. K. Mello (Ed.), *Advances in substance abuse: Behavioral and biological research* (Vol. 1). Greenwich, Conn.: JAI Press, 1980.

Marsden, C. D. Cerebral atrophy and cognitive impairment in schizophrenia. *Lancet*, 1976, *2*, 1079.

Marshall, J. F., & Berrios, B. Movement disorder of aged rats: Reversal by dopamine receptor stimulation. *Science*, 1979, *206*, 271–280.

Marshman, M. A psychometric study of 55 consecutive admissions to a unit for alcoholic addiction which employs no selective criteria. *British Journal of Addiction*, 1975, *70*, 15–22.

Martin, M. Memory span as a measure of individual differences in memory capacity. *Memory and Cognition*, 1978, *6*, 194–198.

Matthews, C. G., & Booker, H. E. Pneumoencephalographic measurements and neuropsychological test performance in human adults. *Cortex*, 1972, *8*, 69–92.

Matthews, C. G., Cleveland, C. J., & Hopper, C. L. Neuropsychological patterns in multiple sclerosis. *Disease of the Nervous System*, 1970, *31*, 160–170.

Matthews, C. G., & Klove, H. Differential psychological performances in major motor, psychomotor, and mixed classifications of known and unknown etiology. *Epilepsia*, 1967, *8*, 117–128.

May, A., Urquhart, A., & Watts, R. Memory for Designs Test: A follow-up study. *Perceptual and Motor Skills*, 1970, *30*, 753–754.

May, W. W. Creutzfeldt-Jakob disease. *Acta Neurologica Scandinavica*, 1968, *44*, 1–32.

McCord, J. Etiological factors in alcoholism: Family and personal charcteristics. *Quarterly Journal of Studies on Alcohol*, 1972, *33*, 1020–1027.

McCord, W., & McCord, J. A. Longitudinal study of the personality of alcoholics. In D. P. Pitman & C. R. Snyder (Eds.), *Society, culture, and drinking patterns*. New York: Wiley, 1962.

McDowell, J. Effects of encodingd instructions and retrieval cuing or recall in Korsakoff patients. *Memory and Cognition*, 1979, *7*, 232–239.

McLachlan, J. F. C., & Levenson, T. Improvement in WAIS Block Design performance as a function of recovery from alcoholism. *Journal of Clinical Psychology*, 1974, *30*, 65–66.

McLaughlin, E. J., Faillace, L. A., & Overall, J. E. Alcohol studies: Cognitive status and changes during 28-day hospitalization. In M. Galanter (Ed.), *Currents in alcoholism* (Vol. 5). New York: Grune & Stratton, 1979.

McNamee, H. B., Mello, N. K., & Mendelson, J. H. Experimental analysis of drinking patterns of alcoholics. Concurrent psychiatric observations. *American Journal of Psychiatry*, 1968, *124*, 1063–1069.

Medina, J. L., Chokroverty, S., & Rubino, F. A. Syndrome of agitated delirium and visual impairment: A manifestation of medial temporo-occipital infarction. *Journal of Neurology, Neurosurgery, and Psychiatry*, 1977, *40*, 861–864.

Meier, M. J., & French, L. A. Lateralized deficits in complex visual discrimination and bilateral transfer of reminiscence following unilateral temporal lobotomy. *Neuropsychologia*, 1965, *3*, 261–272.

Mello, N. K. Short-term memory function in alcohol addicts during intoxication. In M. M. Gross (Ed.), *Alcohol intoxication and withdrawal: Experimental studies*. New York: Plenum Press, 1973.

Mello, N. K., & Mendelson, J. H. Alcohol and human behavior. In L. L. Iverson, S. D. Iverson, & S. Snyder (Eds.), *Handbook of psychopharmacology* (Vol. 12). New York: Plenum Press, 1978.

Mendelson, J. H., LaDou, J., & Solomon, P. Experimentally induced chronic intoxication and withdrawal in alcoholics. III. Psychiatric findings. *Quarterly Journal of Studies on Alcohol*, 1964, *25*, supplement 2, 40–52.

Merlis, J. K. Proposal for an international classification. In M. Galanter (Ed.), *Currents in alcoholism* (Vol. 5). New York: Grune & Stratton, 1970.

Merskey, H., Baum, J., Blume, W. T., Fox, H., Hersch, E. L., Kral, V. A., & Palmer, R. B. Relationships between psychological measurements and cerebral organic changes in Alzheimer's disease. *The Canadian Journal of Neurological Science*, 1980, *7*, 45–49.

Metrakos, K., & Metrakos, J. D. Genetics of convulsive disorders. II. Genetic and encephalographic studies in centencephalic epilepsy. *Neurology*, 1961, *1*, 313–323.

Metzig E., Rosenberg, S., Ast, M., & Krashen, S. D. Bipolar manic-depressives and unipolar depressives distinguished by tests of lateral asymmetry. *Biological Psychiatry*, 1976, *11*, 313–323.

Meyer, J. S., Ishihara, N., Deshmukk, V. D., Naritomi, H., Sakai, F., Hsu, M., & Pollack, P. Improved method for noninvasive measurement of regional cerebral blood flow by 133 xenon inhalation. *Stroke*, 1978, *9*, 195–205.

Miglioli, M, Buchtel, H. A., Campanini, T., & De Risio, C. Cerebral hemispheric lateralization of cognitive deficits due to alcoholism. *Journal of Nervous and Mental Disease*, 1979, *167*, 212–217.

Miller, E. Cognitive assessment of the older adult. In J. E. Birren & R. B. Solane (Eds.), *Handbook of mental health and aging*. Englewood Cliffs, N.J.: Prentice-Hall, 1980.

Miller, H., & Stern, G. The long term prognosis of severe head injury. *Lancet*, 1965, *1*, 225–229.

Miller, E., Adesso, V. J., Fleming, J. P., Gino, A., & Lauerman, R. The effects of alcohol on the storage and retrieval processes of heavy social drinkers. *Journal of Experimental Psychology: Human Learning and Memory*, 1978, *4*, 246–255.

Miller, W. R., & Caddy, G. R. Abstinence and controlled drinking in the treatment of problem drinkers. *Journal of Studies on Alcohol*, 1977, *38*, 986–1003.

Miller, W. R., & Hester, R. K. Treating the problem drinker: Modern approaches. In W. R. Miller (Ed.), *The addictive behaviors: Treatment of alcoholism, drug abuse, smoking and obesity*. Oxford: Pergamon Press, 1980.

Miller, W. R., & Joyce, M. A. Prediction of abstinence, controlled drinking, and heavy drinking outcomes following behavioral self-control training. *Journal of Consulting and Clinical Psychology*, 1979, *47*, 773–775.

Miller, W. R., & Orr, J. Nature and sequence of neuropsychological deficits in alcoholics. *Journal of Studies on Alcohol*, 1980, *41*, 325–337.

Milner, B. Effects of different brain lesions on card sorting. *Archives of Neurology*, 1963, *9*, 90.

Milner, B. Interhemispheric differences in the localization of psychological processes in man. *British Medical Bulletin*, 1971, *27*, 272.

Mindham, R. H. S. Psychiatric symptoms in parkinsonism. *Journal of Neurology, Neurosurgery, and Psychiatry*, 1970, *33*, 188–191.

Mindham, R. H. S. Psychiatric aspects of Parkinson's disease. *British Journal of Hospital Medicine*, 1974, *11*, 411–414.

Minski, L. The mental symptoms associated with 58 cases of cerebral tumor. *Journal of Neurology and Psychopathology*, 1933, *13*, 330–343.

Mocher, L. R., Pollin, W., & Stabenau, J. R. Identical twins discordant for schizophrenia: Neurological findings. *Archives of General Psychiatry*, 1971, *24*, 422–430.

Mohr, J. P., Leicester, J., Stoddard, L. T., & Sidman, M. Right hemianopia with memory and color deficits in circumscribed left posterior artery territory infarction. *Neurology*, 1971, *21*, 1104.

Mohs, R. C., Tinklenberg, J. R., Roth, W. T., & Kopell, B. S. Slowing of short-term memory scanning in alcoholics. *Journal of Studies on Alcohol*, 1978, *39*, 1908–1915.

Morrison, J. R. Diagnosis of adult psychiatric patients with childhood hyperactivity. *American Journal of Psychiatry*, 1979, *136*, 955–958.

Moses, J., & Golden, C. J. Cross validation of the standardized Luria Neuropsychological Battery. *International Journal of Neuroscience*, 1979, *9*, 149–155.

Moses, J., & Golden, C. J. Discrimination between schizophrenia and brain-damaged patients with the Luria–Nebraska Neuropsychological Battery. *International Journal of Neuroscience*, 1980, *10*, 121–128.

Moses, J. A., Jr., Golden, C. J., Berger, P. A., & Wisniewski, A. M. Neuropsychological deficits in early, middle, and late stage Huntington's disease as measured by the Luria—Nebraska Neuropsychological Battery. *International Journal of Neuro-science*, 1981, *14*, 95—100.

Moskowitz, H., & Murray, J. T. Decrease of iconic memory after alcohol. *Journal of Studies on Alcohol*, 1976, *37*, 278—283.

Murphy, M. M. Social class differences in intellectual characteristics of alcoholics. *Quarterly Journal of Studies on Alcohol*, 1953, *14*, 192—196.

Myers, R. D. Alcohol preference in the rat: Reduction following depletion of brain serotonin. *Science*, 1968, *160*, 1469.

Meyers, R. D., & Melchior, C. L. Alcohol drinking: Abnormal intake caused by tetrahydropapaveroline in the brain. *Science*, 1977, *196*, 554—555.

Myslobodsky, M. S., & Horesh, N. Bilateral electrodermal activity in depressive patients. *Biological Psychology*, 1978, *6*, 111—120.

Myslobodsky, M. S., & Rattok, J. Asymmetry of electrodermal activity in man. *Bulletin of the Psychonomic Society*, 1975, *6*, 501—502.

Myslobodsky, M. S., & Rattock, J. Bilateral electrodermal activity in waking man. *Acta Psychologica*, 1977, *41*, 273—282.

Naeser, M. A., Gebhardt, C., & Levine, H. L. Decreased computerized tomography numbers in patients with presenile dementia: Detection in patients with otherwise normal scans. *Archives of Neurology*, 1980, *37*, 401—409.

National Institutes of Health: *The dementias: Hope through research*. NIH Publication No. 81-2252. Bethesda, Md.: Author, 1981.

Naritomi, H., Meyer, J. S., Sakai, F., Yamaguchi, F., & Shaw, T. Effects of advancing age on regional cerebral blood flow in studies on normal subjects and subjects with risk factors for atherothrombotic stroke. *Archives of Neurology*, 1979, *36*, 410—416.

Nathan, P. E. Etiology and process in the addictive behaviours. In W. R. Miller (Ed.), *The addictive behaviors: Treatment of alcoholism, drug abuse, smoking and obesity*. Oxford: Pergamon Press, 1980.

Nathan, P. E., Goldmlan, M. S., Lisman, S. A., & Taylor, H. A. Alcohol and alcoholics: A behavioral approach. *Transactions of the New York Academy of Sciences*, 1972, *34*, 602—627.

Naus, M. J., Cermak, L. S., & De Luca, D. Retrieval processes in alcoholic Korsakoff patients. *Neuropsychologia*, 1977, *15*, 737—742.

Neuberger, K. T. The changing neuropathologic picture of chronic alcoholism: Revealing involvement of the cerebellar granular layer. *Archives of Pathology*, 1957, *63*, 1—6.

Newlin, D., Carpenter, B., & Golden, C. J. Hemispheric asymmetries in schizophrenia. *Biological Psychiatry*, 1981, *16*, 561—581.

Newlin, D., & Golden, C. J. Hemispheric asymmetries in manic-depressive patients: Relationship to hemispheric processing of affect. *Clinical Neuropsychology*, 1980, *2*, 163—169.

Newman, S. E. The EEG manifestation of chronic ethanol abuse: Relation to cerebral cortical atrophy. *Annals of Neurology*, 1978, *3*, 299—304.

Nielson, J. Geronto-psychiatric period-prevalent investigation in a geographically delimited population. *Acta Psychiatrica Scandanavica*, 1962, *38*, 307—330.

Normann, B., & Savahn, K. A follow-up study of severe brain injuries. *Acta Psychiatrica Scandinavica*, 1961, *37*, 236—264.

Norton, J. C. Patterns of neuropsychological test performance in Huntington's disease. *Journal of Nervous and Mental Disease*, 1975, *161*, 276–279.

Obrist, W. D. Cerebral blood flow and EEG changes associated with aging and dementia. In E. W. Busse & D. G. Blazer (Eds.), *Handbook of geriatric psychiatry*. New York: Van Nostrand Reinhold, 1980.

Obrist, W. D., Thompson, H. K., Wang, H. S., & Wilkinson, W. E. Regional cerebral blood flow estimated by [133]Xexon inhalation. *Stroke*, 1975, *6*, 245–256.

O'Leary, M. R., & Donovan, D. M. Male alcoholics: Treatment outcome as a function of length of treatment and level of current adaptive abilities.*Evaluation and the Health Profession*, 1979, *2*, 373–384.

O'Leary, M. R., Donovan, D. M., & Chaney, E. F. The relationship of perceptual field orientation to measures of cognitive functioning and current adaptive abilities in alcoholics and nonalcoholics. *Journal of Nervous and Mental Disease*, 1977, *165*, 275–282. (a)

O'Leary, M. R., Donovan, D. M., Chaney, E. F., & Walker, R. D. Cognitive impairment and treatment outcome with alcoholics: Preliminary findings. *Journal of Clinical Psychiatry*, 1979, *40*, 397–398. (a)

O'Leary, M. R., Donovan, D. M., Chaney, E. F., Walker, R. D., & Schau, E. J. Applications of discriminant analysis of level of performance of alcoholics and nonalcoholics on Wechsler–Bellevue and Halstead–Reitan subtests. *Journal of Clinical Psychology*, 1979, *35*, 204–208. (b)

O'Leary, M. R., Radford, L. M., Chaney, E. F., & Schau, E. J. Assessment of cognitive recovery in alcoholics by use of the Trail-Making Test. *Journal of Clinical Psychology*, 1977, *33*, 579–582. (b)

Ombredane, A. Sur les troubles mentaux de la sclerose en plagues. (An investgation into some psychiatric aspects of multiple sclerosis.) These de Paris, 1929. Quoted by D. Surridge, *British Journal of Psychiatry*, 1969, *115*, 749–764.

Orme, J. E., Lee, D., & Smith, M. R. Psychological assessments of brain damage and intellectual impairment in psychiatric patients. *British Journal of Social and Clinical Psychology*, 1964, *3*, 161–167.

Ornstein, P. Cognitive deficits in chronic alcoholics. *Psychological Reports*, 1977, *40*, 719–724.

Oscar-Berman, M. Hypothesis testing and focusing behavior during concept formation by amnesic Korsakoff patients. *Neuropsychologia*, 1973, *11*, 191–198.

Ota, Y. Psychiatric studies on civilian head injuries. In A. E. Walker, W. F. Caveness, & M. Critchley (Eds.), *The late effects of head injury*. Springfield, Ill.: Charles C. Thomas, 1969.

Overall, J. E., & Gorham, D. R. Organicity versus old age in objective and projective test performance. *Journal of Consulting and Clinical Psychology*, 39, 1972, 98–105.

Overall, J. E., Hoffman, N. G., & Levin, H. Effects of aging, organicity, alcoholism, and functional psychopathology on WAIS subtest profiles. *Journal of Consulting and Clinical Psychology*, 1978, *46*, 1315–1322.

Overton, D. A. State-dependent learning produced by alcohol and its relevance to alcoholism. In B. Kissin & H. Begleiter (Eds.), *The biology of alcoholism* (Vol. 2). New York: Plenum Press, 1972.

Overton, D. A. Major theories of state-dependent learning. In B. T. Ho, D. Richards, & D. Chute (Eds.), *Drug discrimination and state dependent learning*. New York: Academic Press, 1978.

Page, R. D., & Linden, J. D. "Reversible" organic brain syndrome in alcoholics: A psychometric evaluation. *Quarterly Journal of Studies on Alcohol*, 1974, *35*, 98–107.

Page, R. D., & Schaub, L. H. Intellectual functioning in alcoholics during six months' abstinence. *Journal of Studies on Alcohol*, 1977, *38*, 120–125.

Parker, E. S., Alkana, R. L., Birnbaum, I. M., & Noble, E. P. Alcohol and the disruption of cognitive processes. *Archives of General Psychiatry*, 1974, *31* 824–828.

Parker, E. S., Birnbaum, I. M., Boyd, R. A., & Noble, E. P. Neuropsychiatric decrements as a function of alcohol intake in male students. *Alcholism: Clinical and Experimental Research*, 1980, *4*, 330–334.

Parker, E. S., Birnbaum, I. M., & Noble, E. P. Alcohol and memory: Storage and state dependency. *Journal of Verbal Learning and Verbal Behavior*, 1976, *15*, 691–702.

Parker, E. S., & Noble, E. P. Alcohol consumption and cognitive functioning in social drinkers. *Journal of Studies on Alcohol*, 1977, *38*, 1224–1232.

Parker, E. S., & Noble, E. P. Alcohol and the aging process in social drinkers. *Journal of Studies on Alcohol*, 1980, *41*, 170–178.

Parkes, J. D., & Marsden, C. D. The treatment of Parkinson's disease. *British Journal of Hospital Medicine*, 1973, *10*, 284–294.

Parry, J. Contribution a l'etude des manifestations des lesions expansives observees dans un hospital psychiatrique. Thesis, Faculti de Medi cine de Paris, 1968.

Parsons, O. A. Neuropsychological deficits in alcoholics: Fact and fancies.*Alcoholism: Clinical and Experimental Research*, 1977, *1*, 51–56.

Parsons, O. A., & Prigitano, G. P. Memory functioning in alcoholics. In I. M. Birnbaum & E. S. Parker (Eds.), *Alcohol and Human Memory*. Hillsdale, N.J.: Lawrence Erlbaum, 1977.

Parsons, O. A., Tarter, R. E., & Edelberg, R. E. Altered motor control in chronic alcoholics. *Journal of Abnormal Psychology*, 1972, *80* 308–314.

Pearce, J., & Miller, E. *Clinical aspects of dementia*. London: Bailliere Tindall, 1973.

Pearlson, G. D., & Veroff, A. E. Computerized tomographic scan changes in manic–depressive illness. *Lancet*, 1981, *1*, 470.

Perret, E. The left frontal lobe of man and the suppression of habitual responses in verbal categorical behavior. *Neuropsychologia*, 1974, *12*, 323–330.

Perry, T. L., Hansen, S., & Kloster, M. Huntington's chorea: Deficiency and Y-aminobutyric acid in brain. *New England Journal of Medicine*, 1973, *288*, 337–342.

Peters, G. A., Jr. Emotional and intellectual concomitants of advanced chronic alcoholism. *Journal of Consulting Psychology*, 1956, *20*, 390.

Petersen, R. C. Evidence for alcohol state-dependent learning in man. *Federation Proceedings*, 1977, *33*, 500.

Peterson, L. R. & Peterson, M. J. Short-term retention of individual verbal items. *Journal of Experimental Psychology*. 1959, *58*, 193–198.

Petrie, A. *Individuality in pain and suffering*. Chicago: University of Chicago Press, 1967.

Phelps, C. *Traumatic injuries of the brain and its membranes*. London: Kimpton, 1898.

Phillipopoulos, G. S., Wittkower, E. D., & Cousineau, A. The etiologic significance of emotional factors in onset and exacerbations of multiple sclerosis. *Psychosomatic Medicine*, 1958, *20*, 458–474.

Pincus, J. H., & Tucker, G. J. *Behavioral neurology*. New York: Oxford University Press, 1978.

Pisani, V. D., Jacobsdon, G. R., & Berenbaum, H. L. Field dependence and organic brain deficit in chronic alcoholics. *International Journal of the Addictions*, 1973, *8*, 559–564.

Plumeau, F., Machover, S., & Puzzo, F. Wechsler–Bellevue performances of remitted and unremitted alcoholics and their normal controls. *Journal of Consulting Psychology*, 1960, *24*, 240–242.

Polich, J. M., Armor, D. J., & Braiker, H. B. *The course of alcoholism: Four years after treatment.* New York; Wiley, 1982.

Pollin, W., & Stabenau, J. R. Biological, psychological, and historical differences in a series of monozygotic twins discordant for schizophrenia. In D. Rosenthal, & S. S. Kety (Eds.), *The transmission of schizophrenia.* London: Pergamon Press, 1968.

Pollock, M., & Hornabrook, R. W. The prevalence, natural history and dementia of Parkinson's disease. *Brain*, 1966, *89*, 429–448.

Pond, D. A. Epilepsy and personality disorders. In P. J. Vinken & G. W. Bruyn (Eds.), *Handbook of clinical neurology* (Vol. 15). Amsterdam: North Holland, 1974.

Poser, C. M. Demyelination in the central nervous system in chronic alcoholism: Central pontine myelinolysis and Marchiafava-Bignami's disease. *Annals of the New York Academy of Science*, 1973, *215*, 373–381.

Post, F. Dementia, depression, and pseudodementia. In D. F. Benson & D. Blumer (Eds.), *Psychiatric aspects of neurologic disease.* New York: Grune & Stratton, 1975.

Powell, B. J., Goodwin, D. W., Janes, C. L., & Hoine, H. State-dependent effects of alcohol on automatic orienting responses. *Psychonomic Science*, 1971, *25*, 305–306.

Pratt, R. T. C. An investigation of the psychiatric aspects of disseminated sclerosis. *Journal of Neurology, Neurosurgery, and Psychiatry*, 1951, *14*, 326–335.

Price, L. J., Fein, G., & Feinberg, I. Neuropsychological assessment of cognitive function in the elderly. In L. W. Poon (Ed.), *Aging in the 1980's*, Washington, D.C.: American Psychological Association, 1980.

Prigitano, G. P. Neuropyschological functioning in recidivist alcoholics treated with disulfiram. *Alcoholism: Clinical and Experimental Research*, 1977, *1*, 81–86.

Prigitano, G. P. Neuropsychological functioning in recidivist alcoholics treated with disulfiram: A follow-up study. *International Journal of the Addictions*, 1980, *15*, 287–294.

Purisch, A. Golden, C. J., & Hammeke, T. Discrimination of schizophrenic and brain-injured patients by a standardized version of Luria's neuropsychological tests. *Journal of Consulting and Clinical Psychology*, 1978, *46*, 1266–1273.

Quitkin, F., Rifkin, A., & Klein, D. F. Neurologic soft signs in schizophrenia and character disorders. *Archives of General Psychiatry*, 1976, *33*, 845–853.

Rada, R. T., Porch, B. E., Dillingham, C., Kellner, R., & Porec, J. B. Alcoholism and language function. *Alcoholism: Clinical and Experimental Research*, 1977, *1*, 199–205.

Radford, L. M., Chaney, E. F., O'Leary, M. R., & O'Leary, D. E. Screening for cognitive impairment among inpatients. *Journal of Clinical Psychiatry*, 1978, *39*, 712–715.

Read, A. E., Gough, K. R., Pardoe, J. L., & Nicholas, A. Nutritional studies on the entrants to an old people's home, with particular reference to folic acid deficiency. *British Medical Journal*, 1965, *2*, 843–848.

Reed, H. B. C., Jr., & Reitan, R. M. The significance of age in the performance of a complex psychomotor task by brain-damaged subjects. *Journal of Gerontology*, 1962, *17*, 193–196.

Reed, H. B. C., Jr., & Reitan, R. M. A comparison of the effects of the normal aging process with the effects of organic brain damage in adaptive abilities. *Journal of Gerontology*, 1963, *18*, 177–179. (a)

Reed, H. B. C. Jr., & Reitan, R. M. Changes in psychological test performance associated with the normal aging process. *Journal of Gerontology*, 1963, *18*, 271–274. (b)

Reider, R. O., Donnelly, E. F., Herdt, J. R., & Waldeman, I. N. Sulcal prominence in young chronic schizophrenic patients: CT scan findings associated with impairment on neuropsychological tests. *Psychiatry Research*, 1979, *1*, 1–8.

Reisner, T., & Maida, E. Computerized tomography in multiple sclerosis. *Archives of Neurology*, 1980, *37*, 475–477.

Reitan, R. M. Investigation of the validity of Halstead's measures of biological intelligence. *Archives of Neurology and Psychiatry*, 1955, *71*, 28–35.

Reitan, R. M. Psychological deficits resulting from cerebral lesions in man. In J. M. Warren & K. A. Akert (Eds.), *The frontal granular cortex and behavior*. New York: McGraw-Hill, 1964.

Reitan, R. M. Assessment of brain–behavior relationships. In P. McReynolds (Ed.), *Advances in psychological assessment*. San Francisco: Jossey-Bass, 1975.

Reitan, R. M., & Boll, T. J. Intellectual and cognitive functions in Parkinson's disease. *Journal of Consulting and Clinical Psychology*, 1971, *37*, 364–369.

Reitan, R. M., & Davison, L. A. (Eds.). *Clinical neuropsychology: Current status and applications*. Washington: Winston, 1974.

Reitan, R. M., Reed, J. C., & Dykan, M. Cognitive, psychomotor, and motor correlates of multiple sclerosis. *Journal of Nervous and Mental Disorders*, 1971, *153*, 218–224.

Reyes, E., & Miller, W. R. Serum gamma-glutamyl transpedidase as a diagnostic aid in problem drinkers. *Addictive Behaviors*, 1980, *5*, 59–65.

Reynolds, E. H. Effects of folic acid on the mental state and fit frequency of drug-treated epileptic patients. *Lancet*, 1967, *1*, 1086–1088.

Reynolds, E. H., Preece, J., Bailey, J., & Coppen, A. Folate deficiency in depressive illness. *British Journal of Psychiatry*, 1970, *117*, 287–292.

Reynolds, E. H., Preece, J., & Chanarin, I. Folic acid and anticonvulsants. *Lancet*, 1969, *1*, 1264–1265.

Reynolds, E. H., Preece, J., & Johnson, A. L. Folate metabolism in epileptic and psychiatric patients. *Journal of Neurology, Neurosurgery, and Psychiatry*, 1971, *34*, 726–732.

Rieder, R. D., Donnelly, E. F., Herodt, J. R., & Waldman, I. N. Sulcal prominence in young chronic schizophrenic patients: CT scan findings associated with impairment on neuropsychological tests. *Psychiatric Research*, 1979, *1*, 1–8.

Riege, W. H., Miklusak, C., & Buchhalter, J. Material-specific memory impairments in chronic alcoholics. *Biological Psychiatry*, 1976, *11*, 109–113.

Rimalovski, A. B., & Aronson, S. M. Pathogenic observations in Wernicke–Korsakoff encephalopathy. *Transactions of the American Neurological Association*, 1966, *91*, 29–31.

Robbins, F. C. The clinical and laboratory diagnosis of viral infections of the central nervous system. In W. C. Fields & R. J. Blattner (Eds.), *Viral encephalitis.* Springfield, Ill.: Charles C. Thomas, 1958.

Robbins, S. L. *Pathologic basis of disease.* Philadelphia: Saunders, 1974.

Roberts, M. A., & Caird, F. I. Computerized tomography and intellectual impairment in the elderly. *Journal of Neurology, Neurosurgery, and Psychiatry*, 1976, *39*, 986–989.

Roberts, M. A., Caiard, F. I., Grossart, K. W., & Steven, J. L. Computerized tomography in the diagnosis of cerebral atrophy. *Journal of Neurology, Neurosurgery, and Psychiatry*, 1976, *39*, 909–915.

Robertson, E. A., Arenberg, D., & Vestal, R. E. *Age differences in memory performance following ethanol infusion.* Paper presented to the 10th International Congress of Gerontology, Jerusalem, 1975.

Rochford, J. M., Detre, T., Tucker, G. T., & Harrow, M. Neuropsychological impairments in functional psychiatric diseases. *Archives of General Psychiatry*, 1970, *22*, 114–119.

Rochford, J. M., Swartzburg, M., Chowdhrey, S. M., & Goldstein, L. *Research Communications in Psychology, Psychiatry, and Behavior*, 1976, *1*, 211–226.

Rodin, E. A. Psychosocial management of patients with seizure disorders. *McLean Hospital Journal*, Special Issue, June 1977, 74.

Roemer, R. A., Shagass, C., Straumanis, J. J., & Amadeo, M. Pattern evoked measurements suggesting lateralized hemispheric dysfunction in chronic schizophrenia. *Biological Psychiatry*, 1978, *13*, 185–202.

Roemer, R. A., Shagass, C., Straumanis, J. J., & Amadeo, M. Somatosensory and auditory evoked potential studies of functional differences between the hemispheres in psychosis. *Biological Psychiatry*, 1979, *14*, 357–373.

Roland, P. E. Astereognosis. *Archives of Neurology*, 1976, *33*, 543–550.

Ron, M. A. Brain damage in chronic alcoholism: A neuropathological, neuroradiological and psychological review. *Psychological Medicine*, 1977, *7*, 103–122.

Rosen, L. J., & Lee, C. L. Acute and chronic effects of alcohol use on organizational processes in memory. *Journal of Abnormal Psychology*, 1976, *85*, 309–317.

Rosenthal, R., & Bigelow, L. B. Quantitative brain measurements in schizophrenia. *British Journal of Psychiatry*, 1972, *121*, 259–264.

Ross, A. T., & Reitan, R. M. Intellectual and affective functions in multiple sclerosis. *Archives of Neurology and Psychiatry*, 1955, *73*, 663–667.

Roth, M. Classification and aetiology in mental disorders of old age: Some recent developments. In D. W. Kay & A. Walk (Eds.), *Recent development in Psychogeriatics.* Ashford, Kent: Headley Brothers 1971.

Roth, M. Epidemiological studies. In R. Katzman, R. D. Terry, & K. L. Bick (Eds.), *Alzheimer's disease: Senile dementia and related disorders.* New York: Raven Press, 1978.

Roth, M. The diagnosis of dementia in late and middle life. In J. A. Mortimer & L. M. Schuman (Eds.), *The epidemiology of dementia.* New York: Oxford University Press 1981.

Roth, W. T., Tinklenberg, J. R., & Kopell, B. S. Ethanol and marijuana effects on event-related potentials in a memory retrieval paradigm. *Electroencephalography and Clinical Neuropsychology*, 1977, *42*, 381–388.

Rothschild, D. The clinical differentiation of senile and arteriosclerotic psychoses. *American Journal of Psychiatry*, 1941, 98, 324–333.

Ruesch, J., & Bowman, K. M. Prolonged post-traumatic syndrome following head injury. *American Journal of Psychiatry*, 1945, 102, 145–163.

Runge, W. Psychiasche Storungen bei Multiler Skerose. In O. Bunke (Ed.), *Handbuch der Geisterkrankheiren* (Vol. 7, Special Part 3). Berlin: Springer, 1928.

Russell, E. W., Neuringer, C., & Goldstein, G. *Assessment of brain damage*. New York: Wiley, 1970.

Russell, R. W. R., & Pennybacker, J. B. Craniopharyngioma in the elderly. *Journal of Neurology, Neurosurgery, and Psychiatry*, 1961, 24 1–13.

Russell, W. R. Cerebral involvement in head injury. *Brain*, 1932, 55, 549–603.

Russell, W. R., & Smith, A. Post-traumatic amnesia in closed head injury. *Archives of Neurology*, 1961, 5, 4–17.

Ryan, C. M., Brandt, J., Bayog, R., & Butters, N. The persistence of neuropsychological impairment in male alcoholics despite five years of sobriety. *Alcoholism: Clinical and Experimental Research*, 1980, 4, 227. (Abstract)

Ryan, C., & Butters, N. Further evidence for a continuum-of-impairment encompassing male alcoholic Korsakoff patients and chronic alcoholic men. *Alcoholism: Clinical and Experimental Research*, 1980, 4, 190–198. (a)

Ryan, C., & Butters, N. Learning and memory impairments in young and old alcoholics: Evidence for the premature-aging hypothesis. *Alcoholism: Clinical and Experimental Research*, 1980, 4, 288–293. (b)

Ryback, R. S. Alcohol amnesia: Observations in seven inpatient drinking alcoholics. *Quarterly Journal of Studies on Alcohol*, 1970, 31, 616–632.

Ryback, R. S. The continuum and specificity of the effects of alcohol on memory: A review. *Quarterly Journal of Studies on Alcohol*, 1971, 32, 995–1016.

Sanchez-Craig, M. Random assignment to abstience or controlled drinking in a cognitive–behavioral program: Short-term effects on drinking behavior. *Addictive Behaviors*, 1980, 5, 35–39.

Sanchez-Craig, M. Drinking pattern as a determinant of alcoholics' performance on the Trail-Making Test. *Journal of Studies on Alcohol*, 1980, 137, 932–936.

Sandel, A., & Alcorn, J. D. Individual hemisphericity and maladaptive behavior. *Journal of Abnormal Psychology*, 1980, 89, 514–517.

Saucedo, C. *The effects of alcohol state-dependent learning on an encoding variability task: Clinical and neuropsychological implications*. Unpublished doctoral dissertation, University of New Mexico, 1980.

Schaie, K. W., & Schaie, J. P. Clinical assessment and aging. In J. E. Birren & K. W. Schaie (Eds.), *Handbook of the Psychology of Aging*. New York: Van Nostrand Reinhold, 1977.

Schau, E. J., & O'Leary, M. R. Adaptive abilities of hospitalized alcoholics and matched controls: The brain-age quotient. *Journal of Studies on Alcohol* 1977, 38, 403–409.

Scheinberg, P. Cerebral blood flow and metabolism in pernicious anemia. *Blood*, 1951, 6, 213–277.

Scheinberg, P., Blackburn, I., Rich, M., & Saslaw, M. Effects of aging on cerebral circulation and metabolism. *Archives of Neurological Psychiatry*, 1953, 70, 77–85.

Schenkenberg, T., Dustman, R. E., & Beck, E. C. Cortical evoked responses of hospitalized geriatrics in three diagnostic categories. *Proceedings of the American Psychological Association*, 1972, 7, 671–672.

Schlesinger, B. Mental changes in intracranial tumors, and related problems. *Confina Neurologia*, 1950, 10, 225–263.

Schneck, M. K., Reisberg, B., & Ferris, S. H. An overview of current concepts of Alzheimer's disease. *American Journal of Psychiatry*, 1982, 139, 165–173.

Schweitzer, L. Differences in cerebral laterality among schizophrenic and depressed patients. *Biological Psychiatry*, 1979, 14, 721–733.

Schweitzer, L., Becker, E., & Welsh, H. Abnormalities of cerebral lateralization in schizophrenic patients. *Archives of General Psychiatry*, 1978, 35, 982–985.

Scott, M. L., Golden, C. J., Ruedrich, S. L., & Bishop, R. J. *Ventricular enlargement in major depression*. Psychiatry Research (in press).

Scoville, W. B., & Milner, B. Loss of recent memory after bilateral hippocampal lesions. *Journal of Neurology, Neurosurgery, and Psychiatry*, 1957, 20, 11–21.

Selecki, B. R. Cerebral mid-line tumours involving the corpus callosum among mental hospital patients. *Medical Journal of Australia*, 1964, 2, 954–960.

Serafinitides, E. A. Laterality and voltage in the EEG of psychiatric patients. *Diseases of the Nervous System*, 1972, 33, 622–623.

Serafinitides, E. A. Voltage laterality in the EEG of psychiatric patients. *Diseases of the Nervous System*, 1973, 34, 190–191.

Shagass, C. EEG and evoked potentials in psychoses. In D. X. Freedman (Ed.), *The biology of the major psychoses: A comparative analysis*. New York: Raven Press, 1975.

Shagass, C., Roemer, R. A., Straumanis, J. J., & Amadeo, M. Evoked potential correlates of psychosis. *Biological Psychiatry*, 1978, 13, 163–184.

Sharp, J. R., Rosenbaum, G., Goldman, M. S., & Whitman, R. D. Recoverability of psychological function following alcohol abuse: Acquisition of meaningful synonyms. *Journal of Consulting and Clinical Psychology*, 1977, 5, 1023–1028.

Shelly, C. H., & Goldstein, G. An empirically derived typology of hospitalized alcoholics. In G. Goldstein & C. Neuringer (Eds.), *Empirical studies of alcoholism*. Cambridge, Mass.: Ballinger, 1976.

Shenkin, H. A., Novak, P., Goluboff, B., Soffe, A. M., & Bortin, L. The effects of aging, arteriosclerosis and hypertension upon the cerebral circulation. *Journal of Clinical Investigations*, 1953, 32, 459–465.

Shulman, R. Psychiatric aspects of pernicious anemia: A prospective controlled investigation. *British Medical Journal*, 1967, 3, 266–270. (a)

Shulman, R. A survey of vitamin B^{12} deficiency in an elderly psychiatric population. *British Journal of Psychiatry*, 1967, 113, 241–251. (b)

Silber, M., Hirschenfang, S., & Benton, J. G. Psychological factors and prognosis in peripheral neuropathy. *Diseases of the Nervous System*, 1968, 29, 688–692.

Silberstein, J. A., & Parsons, O. A. Neuropsychological impairment in female alcoholics. *Alcoholism: Clinical and Experimental Research*, 1979, 3, 195. (Abstract)

Sim, M., Turner, E., & Smith, W. T. Cerebral biopsy in the investigation of presenile dementia: I. Clinical aspects. *British Journal of Psychiatry*, 1966, 112, 119–125.

Sjogren, T., Sjogren, H., & Lingren, A. G. H. Morbus Alzheimer and morbus Pick. A genetic, clinical and patho-anatomical study. *Acta Psychiatrica et Neurologica Scandinavica*, 1952, supplement 82, 1–152.

Slater, E. The neurotic constitution: A statistical study of 2000 neurotic soldiers.

Journal of Neurology and Psychiatry, 1943, 6, 6−16.

Slater, E., Beard, A. W., & Glithero, E. The schizophrenic-like psychoses of epilepsy. *British Journal of Psychiatry*, 1963, 10, 95.

Smart, R. The relationship between intellectual deterioration, extroversion and neuroticism among chronic alcoholics. *Journal of Clinical Psychology*, 1965, 21, 27−29.

Smith, A. Duration of impaired consciousness as an index of severity in closed head injuries: A review. *Diseases of the Nervous System*, 1961, 22, 69−74.

Smith, H. H., Jr., & Smith, L. S. WAIS functioning of cirrhotic and non-cirrhotic alcoholics. *Journal of Clinical Psychology*, 1977, 33, 309−313.

Smith, J. W., Burt, D. W., & Chapman, R. F. Intelligence and brain damage in alcoholics: A study in patients of middle and upper social classes. *Quarterly Journal of Studies on Alcohol*, 1973, 34, 414−422.

Smith, J. W., Johnson, L. C., & Burdick, J. A. Sleep, psychological and clinical changes during alcohol withdrawal in NAD-treated alcoholics. *Quarterly Journal of Studies on Alcohol*, 1971, 32, 982−993.

Smith, J. W., & Layden, T. A. Changes in psychological performance and blood chemistry in alcoholics during and after hospital treatment. *Quarterly Journal of Studies on Alcohol*, 1972, 33, 379−394.

Smyth, G. E., & Stern, K. Tumours of the thalamus—a clinicopathological study. *Brain*, 1938, 61, 339−374.

Sneath, P., Chanarin, I., Hodkinson, H. M., McPherson, A. & Reynolds, E. H. Folate status in a geriatric population and its reaction to dementia. *Age and Aging*, 1973, 2, 177−182.

Sourander, P., & Sjogren, H. The concept of Alzheimer's disease and its clinical implications. In G. E. Wolstemholme & M. O'Connor (Eds.), *Alzheimer's disease. Ciba Foundation Symposium*. London: Churchill, 1970.

Sperry, R. W. Some general aspects of interhemispheric integrations. In V. B. Mountcastle (Ed.), *Interhemispheric relations and cerebral dominance*. Baltimore: Johns Hopkins University Press, 1962.

Sperry, R. W. Split-brain approach to learning problems. In G. C. Quarton, T. Melnechunuk, & F. O. Schmitt (Eds.), *The neurosciences*. New York: Rockefeller University Press, 1967.

Spies, T. D., Aring, C. D., Gelperin, J., & Bean W. B. The mental symptoms of pellagra: Their relief with nicotinic acid. *American Journal of the Medical Sciences*, 1938, 196, 461−475.

Spillane, J. D. *Nutritional disorders of the nervous system*. Edinburgh: Livingston, 1947.

Steadman, J. H., & Graham, J. G. Head injuries: An analysis and follow-up study. *Proceedings of the Royal Society of Medicine*, 1970, 633, 23−28.

Steffen, J. J., Nathan, P. E., & Taylor, H. A. Tension-reducing effects of alcohol: Further evidence and some methodological considerations. *Journal of Abnormal Psychology*, 1974, 83, 542−547.

Sternberg, S. High speed scanning in human memory. *Science*, 1966, 153, 652−654.

Storm, T., & Caird, W. K. The effects of alcohol on serial verbal learning in chronic alcoholics. *Psychonomic Science*, 1967, 9, 43−44.

Storm, T., Caird, W. K., & Korbin, E. *The effects of alcohol on rote verbal learning and retention*. Paper presented at the annual meeting of the Canadian Psychological Association, Vancouver, 1965.

Storm, T., & Smart, R. G. Dissociation: A possible explanation of some features of alcoholism, and implications for treatment. *Quarterly Journal of Studies on Alcohol*, 1965, *26*, 1111–1115.

Storm-Mathiesen, A. General paresis. A follow-up of 203 patients. *Acta Psychiatrica Scandinavica*, 1969, *45*, 118–132.

Strauss, H. Intracranial neoplasms masked as depressions and diagnosed with the aid of electroencephalography. *Journal of Nervous and Mental Disorders*, 1955, *122*, 185–189.

Strauss, I., & Keschner, M. Mental symptoms in cases of the frontal lobe. *Archives of Neurology and Psychiatry*, 1935, *33*, 986–1005.

Streissguth, A. P., Landesman-Dwyer, S., Martin, J. C., & Smith, D. W. Teratogenic effects of alcohol in humans and laboratory animals. *Science*, 1980, *203*, 353–361.

Strich, S. J. The pathology of brain damage due to blunt head injuries. In *The late effects of head injury*. A. E. Walker, W. F. Caveness, & M. Critchley (Eds.), Springfield, Ill.: Charles C. Thomas, 1969.

Strobos, R. R. J. Tumours of the temporal lobe. *Neurology*, 1953, *3*, 752–760.

Surridge, D. An investigation into some psychiatric aspects of multiple sclerosis. *British Journal of Psychiatry*, 1969, *115*, 749–764.

Swanson, J. M., & Kinsbourne, M. State-dependent learning and retrieval: Methodological cautions and theoretical considerations. In J. F. Kinsbourne & F. J. Evans (Eds.), *Functional disorders of memory*. Hillsdale, N.J.: Lawrence Erlbaum, 1979.

Talland, G. A. Cognitive functions in Parkinson's disease. *Journal of Nervous and Mental Disease*, 1962, *135*, 196–205.

Tamerin, J. S., & Mendelson, J. H. The psychodynamics of chronic inebriation: Observations of alcoholics during the process of drinking in an experimental group setting. *American Journal of Psychiatry*, 1969, *125*, 886–899.

Tamerin, J. S., Weiner, S., Poppen, R., Steinglass, P., & Mendelson, J. H. Alcohol and memory: Amnesia and short-term memory function during experimentally induced intoxication. *American Journal of Psychiatry*, 1971, *127*, 1659–1664.

Tarter, R. E. Dissociate effects of ethyl alcohol. *Psychonomic Science*, 1970, *20*, 342–343.

Tarter, R. E. An analysis of cognitive deficits in chronic alcoholics. *Journal of Nervous and Mental Disease*, 1973, *157*, 138–147.

Tarter, R. E. Brain damage associated with chronic alcoholism. *Diseases of the Nervous System*, 1975, *36*, 185–187. (a)

Tarter, R. E. Psychological deficit in chronic alcoholics: A review. *International Journal of the Addictions*, 1975, *10*, 327–368. (b)

Tarter, R. E. Empirical investigations of psychological deficit. In R. E. Tarter & A. A. Sugarman (Eds.), *Alcoholism, Interdisciplinary approaches to an enduring problem*. Reading, Mass.: Addison-Wesley, 1976 (a)

Tarter, R. E. Neuropsychological investigations of alcoholism. In C. Goldstein & C. Neuringer (Eds.), *Empirical studies of alcoholism*. Cambridge, Mass.: Ballinger/Lippincott, 1976. (b)

Tarter, R. E., Buonpane, N., & Wyant, C. Intellectual competence of alcoholics. *Journal of Studies on Alcohol*, 1975, *36*, 381–386.

Tarter, R. E., & Jones, B. M. Absence of intellectual deterioration in chronic alcoholics. *Journal of Clinical Psychology*, 1971, *27*, 453–454. (a)

Tarter, R. E., & Jones, B. M. Motor impairment in chronic alcoholics. *Diseases of the Nervous System*, 1971, *32*, 632—636. (b)

Tarter, R. E., McBride, H., Buonpane, N., & Schneider, D. U. Differentiation of alcoholics: Childhood history of minimal brain dysfunction, family history, and drinking pattern. *Archives of General Psychiatry*, 1977, *34*, 761—768.

Tarter, R. E., & Parsons, O. A. Conceptual shifting in chronic alcoholics. *Journal of Abnormal Psychology*, 1971, *77*, 71—75.

Taylor, D. C. Epileptic experience, schizophrenia and the temporal lobe. *McLean Hospital Journal*, Special Issue, June 1977, 22.

Taylor, M. A., Abrams, R., & Gaztanaga, P. Manic-depressive illness and schizophrenia: A partial validation of Research Diagnostic Criteria utilizing neuropsychological testing. *Comprehensive Psychiatry*, 1975, *16*, 91—96.

Taylor, M. A., Greenspan, B., & Abrams, R. Lateralized neuropsychological dysfunction in affective disorder and schizophrenia. *American Journal of Psychiatry*, 1979, *136*, 1031—1034.

Taylor, P. A., Dalton, R., & Fleminger, J. J. Handedness in schizophrenia. *British Journal of Psychiatry*, 1980, *136*, 375—383.

Teicher, M. I., & Singer, E. A. A report on the use of the Wechsler—Bellevue scales in an overseas general hospital. *American Journal of Psychiatry*, 1946, *103*, 91—93.

Templer, D. I., Ruff, C. F., & Simpson, K. Trail-Making test performance of alcoholics abstinent at least a year. *International Journal of the Addictions*, 1975, *10*, 609—612.

Terry, R. D. Senile dementia. *Federation Proceedings*, 1978, *37*, 2837—2840.

Terry, R. D., & Wisniewski, H. The ultrastructure of the neurofibrillary tangle and the senile plaque. In G. E. W. Wolstenholme & M. O'Connor (Eds.), *Alzheimer's disease and related conditions. Ciba Foundation Symposium*. London: Churchill, 1970.

Terry, R. D., & Wisniewski, H. Ultrastructure of senile dementia and of experimental analogs. In C. M. Gaitz (Ed.), *Aging and the brain*. New York: Plenum Press, 1972.

Terry, R. D. & Wisniewski, H. M. Structural aspects of aging of the brain. In C. Eisdorfer & R. O. Friedel (Eds.), *Cognitive and Emotional Disturbance in the Elderly*. Chicago: Year Book Medical Press, 1977.

Teuber, H. L. The riddle of frontal lobe function in man. In J. M. Warren & K. Akert (Eds.), *The frontal granular cortex and behaviour*. New York: McGraw-Hill, 1964.

Tharp, V. K., Rundell, O. H., Jr., Lester, B. K., & Williams, H. L. Alcohol and information processing. *Psychopharmacologia*, 1974, *40*, 33—42.

Thompson, G. N. Cerebral lesions simulating schizophrenia: Three case reports. *Biological Psychiatry*, 1970, *2*, 59—64.

Thompson, L. W. Cerebral blood flow, EEG, and behavior in aging. In R. D. Terry & S. Gershon (Eds.), *Neurobiology of Aging*. New York: Raven Press, 1976, 103—119.

Tomlinson, B. E. The pathology of dementia. In C. E. Wells (Ed.), *Dementia* (2nd ed.). Philadelphia: F. A. Davis, 1977.

Tomlinson, B. E., Blessed, G., & Roth M. Observations on the brains of nondemented old people. *Journal of Neurological Science*, 1968, *7*, 331—356.

Tomlinson, B. E., Blessed, G., & Roth, M. Observations on the brains of demented old people. *Journal of Neurological Science*, 1970, *11*, 205–242.

Tomsovic, M. Hospitalized alcoholic patients. I. A two-year study of medical, social, and psychological characteristics. *Hospital and Community Psychiatry*, 1968, *19*, 197–203.

Torrey, E. F. Neurological abnormalities in schizophrenic patients. *Biological Psychiatry*, 1980, *15*, 381–388.

Tress, K. H., & Kugler, B. T. Intraocular transfer of movement aftereffects in schizophrenia. *British Journal of Psychology*, 1979, *70*, 389–392.

Trimble, M., & Kingsley, D. Cerebral ventricular size in chronic schizophrenia. *Lancet*, 1978, *2*, 423.

Tsushima, W. T., & Wedding, D. A comparison of the Halstead–Reitan Neuropsychological Battery and computerized tomography in the identification of brain disorder. *Journal of Nervous and Mental Disease*, 1979, *167*, 704–707.

Tulving, E. Episodic and semantic memory. In E. Tulving & W. Donaldson (Eds.), *Organization of memory*. New York: Academic Press, 1972.

Tulving, E., & Thomson, D. M. Encoding specificity and retrieval processes in episodic memory. *Psychological Review*, 1973, *80*, 352–373.

Tumarkin, B., Wilson, J., & Snyder, G. Cerebral atrophy due to alcoholism in young adults. *U.S. Armed Forces Medical Journal*, 1955, *6*, 67–74.

Uherik, M. Interpretation of bilateral asymmetry of bioelectrical skin reactivity in schizophrenia. *Studio Psychologi*, 1975, *17*, 51–60.

Van Thiel, D. H., Gavaler, J. S., Paul, G. M., & Smith, W. I. Disulfiram-induced disturbances in hypothalamic–pituitary function. *Alcoholism: Clinical and Experimental Research*, 1979, *3*, 230–234.

Victor, M., Adams, R. D., & Collins, G. H. *The Wernicke–Korsakoff syndrome*. Oxford: Blackwell, 1971. (a)

Victor, M., Adams, R. D., & Collins, G. H. *The Wernicke–Korsakoff syndrome: A clinical and pathological study of 245 patients, 82 with post-mortem examinations*. Philadelphia: F. A. Davis, 1971. (b)

Vogt, M. Drug-induced changes in brain dopamine and their reactions to parkinsonism. In *The Scientific Basis of Medicine, Annual Review, 1970*. London: Althone Press, 1970.

Von Gall, M., Becker, H., Lerch, G., & Nemeth, N. Results of computer tomography on chronic alcoholics. *Neuroradiology*, 1978, *16*, 329–331.

Von Knorring, L. Visual average evoked responses in patients suffering from alcoholism. *Neuropsychologia*, 1976, *2*, 233–238.

Vuchinich, R. E., & Sobell, M. B. Empirical separation of physiologic and expected effects of alcohol on complex perceptual motor performance. *Psychopharmacology*, 1978, *60*, 81–85.

Walker, A. E., & Erculei, F. *Head injured men fifteen years later*. Springfield, Ill.: Charles C. Thomas, 1969.

Walker, D. W., & Hunter, B. E. Short-term memory impairment following chronic alcohol consumption in rats. *Neuropsychologia*, 1978, *16*, 545–553.

Walker, H. A., & Birch, H. G. Lateral preference and right–left awareness in schizophrenic children. *Journal of Nervous and Mental Disease*, 1970, *151*, 341–351.

Walton, J. N., Kiloh, L. G., Osselton, J. W., & Farral, J. The electroencephalogram in pernicious anemia and subacute combined degeneration of the cord. *Electroencephalography and Clinical Neurophysiology*, 1954, 6, 45–64.

Wang, H. S., & Busse, E. W. Correlates of regional cerebral blood flow in elderly community residents. In A. M. Harper, W. B. Jennet, J. D. Miller, & J. O. Rowan (Eds.). *Blood Flow and Metabolism in the Brain*. London: Churchill Livingstone, 1975, 817–818.

Warrington, E. K. The nature and significance of neuropsychological deficits associated with alcoholism. In J. G. Ranmkin (Ed.), *Alcohol, drugs, and brain damage*. Toronto: Alcoholism and Drug Addiction Research Foundation, 1975.

Warrington, E. K., & Weiskrantz, L. Amnesic syndrome: Consolidation or retrieval? *Nature*, 1970, 228, 628–630.

Watson, C. G. Cross-validation of the WAIS sign developed to separate brain-damaged from schizophrenic patients. *Journal of Clinical Psychology*, 1972, 28, 66–67.

Watson, C. G. Chronicity and the Halstead battery in psychiatric hospitals: A reply to Levine and Feirstein. *Journal of Consulting and Clinical Psychology*, 1974, 47, 136–138.

Watson, C. G., Davis, W. E., & Gasser, B. The separation of organics from depressives with ability- and personality-based tests. *Journal of Clinical Psychology*, 1978, 34, 393–397.

Watson, C. G., Thomas, R. W., Andersen, D., & Felling, J. Differentiation of organics from schizophrenics at two chronicity levels by use of the Reitan–Halstead organic test battery. *Journal of Consulting and Clinical Psychology*, 1968, 32, 679–684.

Watson, C. G., Thomas, R. W., Felling, J., & Andersen, D. Differentiation of organics from schizophrenics with Reitan's sensory–perceptual disturbances test. *Perceptual and Motor Skills*, 1968, 26, 1191–1198.

Watson, C. G., Thomas, R. W., Felling, J., & Andersen, D. Differentiation of organics from schizophrenics with the Trail-Making, Dynamometer, Critical Flicker Fusion and Light-Intensity Matching tests. *Journal of Clinical Psychology*, 1969, 25, 130–133.

Wechsler, D. The effect of alcohol on mental activity. *Quarterly Journal of Studies on Alcohol*, 1941, 2, 479–485.

Wechsler, D. *Manual for the Wechsler Adult Intelligence Scale*. New York: The Psychological Corporation, 1955.

Weckowicz, T. E., Tam, C. I., Mason, J., & Bay, K. S. Speed in test performance in depressed patients. *Journal of Abnormal Psychology*, 1978, 87, 578–582.

Weinberger, D. R. Ventricular size in schizophrenia. Paper presented at the NIMH conference on schizophrenia and CT, Washington, D.C. April, 1982.

Weinberger, D. R., Bigelow, L. B., Kleinman, J. E., Klein, S. T., Rosenblatt, J. E., & Wyatt, R. J. Cerebral ventricular enlargement in chronic schizophrenia: An association with poor response to treatment. *Archives of General Psychiatry*, 1980, 37, 11–13.

Weinberger, D. R., Torrey, E. F., Neophytides, A. N., & Wyatt, R. J. Lateral cerebral ventricular enlargement in chronic schizophrenia. *Archives of General Psychiatry*, 1979, 36, 735–739. (a)

Weinberger, D. R., Torrey, E. F., Neophytidfes, A. N., & Wyatt, R. J. Structural abnormalities in the cerebral cortex of chronic schizophrenic patients. *Archives of General Psychiatry*, 1979, *36*, 935–939. (b)

Weingartner, H. Human state-dependent learning. In B. R. Ho, D. Richards, & D. L. Chute (Eds.), *Drug discrimination and state-dependent learning*. New York: Academic Press, 1978.

Weingartner, H., Adefris, W., Eich, J. E., & Murphy, D. L. Encoding-imagery specificity in alcohol state-dependent learning. *Journal of Experimental Psychology*, 1976, *2*, 83–87.

Weingartner, H., & Faillace, L. A. Alcohol state-dependent learning in man. *Journal of Nervous and Mental Disease*, 1971, *153*, 395–406.

Weingartner, H., Faillace, L. A., & Markley, H. G. Verbal information retention in alcoholics. *Quarterly Journal of Studies on Alcohol*, 1971, *32*, 293–303.

Weiskrantz, L., & Warrington, E. K. A study of forgetting in amnesic patients. *Neuropsychologia*, 1970, *8*, 281–288.

Weissman, M. M., & Myers, J. K. Clinical depression alcoholism. *American Journal of Psychiatry*, 1980, *137*, 372–373.

Wells, C. E. The clinical neurology of macrocytic anemia. *Proceedings of the Royal Society of Medicine*, 1965, *58*, 721–724.

Wells, C. E. Transient ictal psychosis. *Archives of General Psychiatry*, 1975, *31*, 1201–1203.

Wells, C. E. Role of stroke in dementia. *Stroke*, 1978, *9*, 1–3.

Wells, C. E., & Duncan, G. W. *Neurology of psychiatrists*. Philadelphia: F. A. Davis, 1980.

Wexler, B. E. Cerebral laterality and psychiatry: A review of the literature. *American Journal of Psychiatry*, 1980, *137*, 279–291.

Wickelgren, W. A. Alcoholic intoxication and memory storage dynamics. *Memory and Cognition*, 1975, *3*, 385–389.

Wilkinson, D. A., & Carlen, P. L. Neuropsychological assessment of alcoholism: Discrimination between groups of alcoholics. *Journal of Studies on Alcohol*, 1980, *41*, 129–139.

Williams, J. D., Ray, C. G., & Overall, J. E. Mental aging and organicity in an alcoholic population. *Journal of Consulting and Clinical Psychology*, 1973, *41*, 392–396.

Williams, R. M., Goldman, M. S., & Williams D. L. *Alcohol due and expectancy effects on cognitive and motor performance* Paper presented at the annual meeting of the American Psychological Association, Toronto, 1978.

Wilson, S. A. K. *Neurology*. London: Edward Arnold, 1940.

Winocur, G., & Kinsbourne, M. Contextual cueing as an aid to Korsakoff amnesics. *Neuropsychologia*, 1978, *16*, 671–682.

Wood, F., & Kinsbourne, M. *Symposium on pathological forgetting*. Paper presented at the annual meeting of the International Neuropsychology Society, Boston, 1974.

Wood, W. G. The elderly alcoholic: Some diagnostic problems and considerations. In M. Storandt, I. C. Siegler, & M. F. Elias (Eds.), *The clinical psychology of aging*. New York: Plenum Press, 1978.

World Health Organization, Expert Committee on Mental Health, Alcoholism Subcommittee. Second report. *W.H.O. Tecnical Report Series*, No. 48, August 1952.

Yamaguchi, F., Meyer, J. S., Yamamoto, M., Sakai, F., & Shaw, R. Non-invasive regional cerebral blood flow measurements in dementia. *Archives of Neurology*, 1980, *37*, 410–418.

Young, I. J., & Crampton, A. R. Cerebrospinal fluid uric acid levels in cerebral atrophy occurring in psychiatric and neurologic patients. *Biological Psychiatry*, 1974, *8*, 281–292.

Young, L. D. Alcohol state dependent effects in humans: A review and study of different task responses. *British Journal of Alcohol and Alcoholism*, 1979, *14*, 100–105.

Yozawitz, A., Bruder, G., Sutton, S., Sharpe, L., Gurland, B., Fleiss, J., & Costa, L. Dichotic perception: Evidence for right hemisphere dysfunction in affective psychosis. *British Journal of Psychiatry*, 1979, *135*, 224–237.

Zelazowski, R., Golden, C. J., Graber, B., Blose, I. L., Bloch, S., Moses, J. A., Zatz, L. M., Stahl, S. M., Osmon, D. C., & Pfefferbaum, A. Relationship of cerebral ventricular size to alcoholics' performance on the Luria–Nebraska Neuropsychological Battery. *Journal of Studies on Alcohol*, 1981, *42*, 749–756.

Author Index

Subject Index

Abdominal reflex,
  absent, 112
  impaired, 116
Abscess, 38, 59, 64, 66, 68, 78
  extradural, 63
  subdural, 63
  symptoms, 64
Abstinence, 149, 154, 165, 173, 190,
  193, 194
Abstinence syndrome, 131
Abstraction deficit, 168
Acalculia, 87
Acetaldehyde, 177
Acetylcholine, 105, 128
Achievement tests, 64
Acquisition deficits, 130
Adolescence, 67, 83
Adhesions, 36
Affective disorder, 203, 221–230
Affective disturbance, 34, 46, 87, 113,
  177, 223, 225. See also Mood
  blunting, 44, 46
  psychosis, 46
  symptoms, 222, 223
Age–alcohol interaction, 149
Age–related norms, 98
Aggression, 75
Agitation, 87, 132
Agnosia, 45, 87, 91

visuospatial, 45
  finger, 62
Air encephalography, 174
Akinesia, 11
Alcohol, 135, 137
  ethyl, 143
  expectancy of receiving, 150
Alcohol blackout, 143, 145, 150–152,
  155, 179, 181, 190
  en bloc, 152
  induced storage deficit, 149, 154, 155
  partial, 151
  threshold, 152
Alcohol withdrawal syndrome, 141, 192
  and parkinsonism, 177
  and tumor, 179
Alcoholism, 90, 127, 130, 131, 134,
  141–195, 199
  chronic, 137
  duration of, 179
  gamma, 142
  and verbal therapy, 193
Alcohol dependence diagnosis, 141, 142
Aldehyde dehydrogenase, 177
Alexia without agraphia, 28
Alzheimer's disease, 63, 82, 84–87, 89–
  92, 137
  and genetics, 86
  aluminum involvement, 89